What Jesus Learned from Women

What Jesus Learned from Women

James F. McGrath

CASCADE *Books* • Eugene, Oregon

WHAT JESUS LEARNED FROM WOMEN

Copyright © 2021 James F. McGrath. All rights reserved. Except for brief quotations in critical publications or reviews, no part of this book may be reproduced in any manner without prior written permission from the publisher. Write: Permissions, Wipf and Stock Publishers, 199 W. 8th Ave., Suite 3, Eugene, OR 97401.

Cascade Books
An Imprint of Wipf and Stock Publishers
199 W. 8th Ave., Suite 3
Eugene, OR 97401

www.wipfandstock.com

PAPERBACK ISBN: 978-1-5326-8060-1
HARDCOVER ISBN: 978-1-5326-8061-8
EBOOK ISBN: 978-1-5326-8062-5

Cataloguing-in-Publication data:

Names: McGrath, James F., author.

Title: What Jesus learned from women / James F. McGrath.

Description: Eugene, OR: Cascade Books, 2021 | Includes bibliographical references and index.

Identifiers: ISBN 978-1-5326-8060-1 (paperback) | ISBN 978-1-5326-8061-8 (hardcover) | ISBN 978-1-5326-8062-5 (ebook)

Subjects: LCSH: Jesus Christ. | Women in the Bible.

Classification: BT590.W6 M34 2021 (print) | BT590.W6 (ebook)

Manufactured in the U.S.A.   FEBRUARY 16, 2021

For my wife Elena

Contents

Preface ix

1. Introduction 1
2. Mary: What Jesus Learned from His Mother 17
3. At Grandma's House:
   What Jesus Learned Visiting the Big City on a Hill 46
4. The Samaritan Woman:
   What Jesus Learned from an Israelite at Jacob's Well 67
5. The Syrophoenician Woman:
   What Jesus Learned from a Doggedly Insistent Mother 87
6. Suffering Daughters:
   What Jesus Learned from Two Women with 12-Year-Old Issues 108
7. Mary & Martha of Bethany:
   What Jesus Learned from Two Very Different Sisters 132
8. Every Last Penny: What Jesus Learned
   from a Poor Widow Who Shared Her Two Cents 162
9. Presumed Guilty: What Jesus Learned
   from a Defenseless Young Woman Accused of Adultery 175
10. Mary Magdalene: What Jesus Learned
    about the Power of Naming and Keeping Demons at Bay 205
11. Joanna: What Jesus Learned
    by Having a Friend in High Places 245
12. Conclusion 274

Bibliography 285

Preface

ONCE A BOOK IS completed, it can be difficult to trace what first prompted it to be written. I know that a number of factors influenced it, and enough people have asked me how I came to write this book that I feel I should offer some brief account. The key spark was having a student approach me about working on an honor's thesis and independent research that would allow her to explore two things that she had previously felt were in tension, namely her Christian faith and her feminism. As an academic whose work focuses on the historical Jesus, I immediately began to seek ways that the student in question might do something original and valuable in that area, perhaps something that might eventually lead to one or both of us writing an article or even a book on the subject. Since so many have written about Jesus' views of women and his openness to their learning from him, I began to consider the same subject in reverse, namely Jesus learning from women. The rest unfolded rather quickly as I began with the classic example (the Syrophoenician woman who changed Jesus' mind) and soon noticed other instances when women appear to have taken initiative and influenced him. The reactions of his disciples and others around him made clear that what we were witnessing on the pages of the Gospels was not Jesus illustrating things he regularly taught, but Jesus doing something for the first time. The rest, as they say, is history. Or better, I will let readers and my academic peers judge whether I've accurately reconstructed history. Either way, the rest is the book that you have begun reading.

My thanks are due to many individuals. First let me mention my wife Elena McGrath for being the woman from whom I have learned the most, as well as for reading and providing feedback on multiple drafts of the book's chapters throughout the writing process. Next I wish to thank Rachel Koehler for the conversations about her honors thesis research at Butler University which first gave me the idea for this book. I am grateful to Chris Spinks, editor at Cascade, who immediately responded with enthusiasm to my idea for this book and turned it from idea into contracted project. I have immense appreciation for the participants in my Sunday school class at Crooked Creek Baptist Church (Rev. Joy and Rev. John Amick, Marcia and Rev. Don Scott, Judy Spencer, Nicole and John Arnold, Ann and Jim Hickey, the Peacock family, and others who have at times joined us) for providing many opportunities for conversations that allowed me to explore and garner feedback on the ideas in this book, as well as in some cases reading actual drafts of parts of the manuscript and providing suggestions and observations that influenced the book in concrete ways. I owe thanks to many other conversation partners and readers of drafts such as Amy-Jill Levine, Sara Parks, Soozi Whitten Ford, Talita Adam, Dana Făgădar, Rose LaVista, Lydia Bringerud, Chuck Robertson, and my Butler University colleagues Deb Saxon, Claudia Johnson, and Mindy Welch. There are many other academics with whom I had helpful conversations, even if only briefly, about the concept or specific details, including April DeConick, Elizabeth Raine, and Ben Chenoweth. I am grateful as well to countless other scholars and academic works which are included in the bibliography but are too numerous to mention individually here, who served as conversation partners through the things you have written. I also wish to thank Patheos for hosting my blog, where I explored and received feedback on the concept for the book as well as specific ideas. Access to crucial resources was also provided by Butler University's Irwin Library (sometimes through Interlibrary Loan and PALShare), Christian Theological Seminary Library, Indianapolis Public Library, the Scarritt-Bennett Center and Vanderbilt Divinity School libraries in Nashville, and the State Library of Victoria in Melbourne, Australia.

I want to thank Macey Dickerson for the incredible artwork she created for the cover. The way she found inspiration in what I wrote led to a depiction of the Samaritan woman's encounter with Jesus that I feel captures the essence of the book perfectly, as well as being just beautiful. I wish to thank Mike Surber at Wipf and Stock for his work on the book cover. I wish to thank April DeConick and Adele Reinhartz for their endorsements. When I first saw the draft of the book cover with the artwork and endorsements, I was overwhelmed by emotion in a way that I never have been about any other book I've written before.

Introduction

THERE MAY BE SOME for whom the idea that Jesus learned *from women* will be controversial, and the pages that follow will hopefully make a persuasive argument to convince you that it is nonetheless the case. Before turning to that narrower topic, however, we should address the many Christians for whom the issue will not be who Jesus allegedly learned from, but that he learned at all. The fact that a significant number of people feel discomfort with the idea of Jesus learning really ought to surprise and shock us. It is an axiom of the historic Christian faith that Jesus was fully human—a complete human being, with a human soul (or what many today might prefer to call a human mind and personality). The classic definitions of Christian orthodoxy are quite clear about that point, as are the New Testament Gospels. The Gospel of Luke is emphatically clear about the matter, stating that Jesus "grew in wisdom" (Luke 2:52). Growing in wisdom is what learning is all about, and to be blunt, that statement in Luke is purely and simply incompatible with the idea that Jesus had no need to learn, no need to be taught. There appear to be widespread misconceptions about this nevertheless. The story that Luke tells immediately before that statement, about Jesus in the temple as a young man, is sometimes depicted in movies with Jesus *teaching* his elders. However, what Luke actually says is that Jesus was *listening to them and asking them questions* (Luke 2:47). Jesus is not depicted as something other than human, nor even as a supernaturally knowledgeable wonder child who has no need to learn. He is depicted in this story, rather, as an ideal student. It is his listening and asking questions that lead to his growth in wisdom, to his learning. Indeed, Luke mentions that he grew in both wisdom and stature. That second word can also mean "maturity," in which case the entire verse would be about Jesus's cognitive and emotional growth and development. But even if Luke had in mind the process of getting taller, that kind of growth is simply part of being human. No one who accepts that Jesus was a real human being envisages him being born or appearing in the world at his full adult size, much less as a giant. Yet when it comes to his knowledge and wisdom, the same does not hold true in the imagination of many. In fact, there are extracanonical sources that depict Jesus as speaking as an infant, or as schooling his would-be instructors. But that isn't the Jesus of history, or even the still altogether human Jesus of our earliest sources. At times, the depiction in the New Testament and the conclusions of historians are at odds. On this point, however, they largely converge. We should allow them to do so and accept what they tell us: Jesus learned.

If we ask the question, "Who taught Jesus?" we find that a number of names of women as well as men will immediately spring to mind. His mother was undoubtedly at least one of his teachers in his childhood. We do not know whether Jesus experienced any kind of formal education. There is debate about whether he was taught to read and write, and if so, to what degree of proficiency. Even if one treats the Gospel accounts of Jesus reading from the scroll of Isaiah in the synagogue and writing in the dust as straightforward historical descriptions, we know that many learn to sound out passages in the Hebrew Scriptures for their bar mitzvah without learning the Hebrew language to a high level of proficiency, and that many can scratch out some words but might not be able to write lengthy treatises. Whether Jesus had opportunity to go to school, and whether he was later one of John the Baptist's students or disciples, we can fortunately set aside in the present context. In the next chapter we will begin our exploration of this topic by considering his mother's possible role in teaching him, and in arranging other educational experiences. Jesus's first words were surely spoken under her tutelage. Some things we can surmise simply based on commonalities of human experience; others we can deduce from things we are told in our ancient sources. In the chapter after that, we will consider what he might have learned from his grandmother, in light of the few traditions about her preserved by the church, and once again drawing on common aspects of human experience. We will be on firmer ground, however, when we get into the stories in the Gospels about Jesus's encounters with women as an adult. We shall see that Luke's depiction of the young Jesus is not about characteristics he had only as a youth but indicates a trajectory that continued to characterize him into adulthood. Like all human beings, he eventually stopped growing in stature, at least in the biological sense. We will discover, on the other hand, significant evidence of Jesus as a lifelong learner throughout the Gospels.

Writing this as an educator, it surprises me that this aspect of the life of Jesus has received such scant attention in the past. Being an effective educator goes hand in hand with being a lifelong learner. Jesus encouraged his students not only to listen to his words and put them into practice, but to observe the world, including aspects of human behavior as well as non-human organisms and phenomena. Consider the lilies of the field, Jesus said, like the ancient teller of proverbs who directed students to look closely at the ant and learn a lesson. As Jesus taught, he continued to observe and to learn from what he saw, as well as from his interactions with other people, whether men or women. He taught his students to do likewise.

You may be wondering why the book's title speaks of what Jesus learned from women, as opposed to referring to what women taught Jesus, which would be less wordy. There is a reason for this choice. If we consider the story of the poor widow who throws her only coins into the temple treasury, for instance, Jesus's use of her as an example indicates things that Jesus learned from observing her action, which he then in turn taught others. We probably would not say that in this particular case the widow *taught* Jesus. Jesus learned from women not only when they were actively teaching him, but also when they may not have had the slightest inkling that he was learning as a result of things they said and did. We do not have any evidence that the poor widow we just mentioned even knew that Jesus was talking about her at that moment, much less that people would be hearing her story centuries later. We can learn from her because Jesus did so first and passed on to his disciples what he learned. We will talk more about what exactly that may have been in one of the chapters of this book.

History, Fiction, and Storytelling

For some readers of a book like this, it would seem sufficient to simply discuss the stories in the Gospels and leave it at that. If the Gospels say it, then Jesus did it. However, for those who have looked into the way historians investigate the life of Jesus or any other historical figure, an approach like that will simply not be adequate. It is the author's hope that readers will find the book relevant, interesting, and thought-provoking regardless of whether their focus is on the Jesus of history who lies behind the Gospels, or only the Jesus depicted in the Gospels with no further questions asked. For that to be the case, however, we cannot entirely sidestep historical questions, and indeed, the author is interested in all the possible aspects of this subject: the message of the Gospels as narratives, the traditions their authors drew upon, and the life of Jesus himself. These three are not nearly as far apart as they sometimes seem. One reason this is so is that ancient stories about the lives of famous people do not focus on their inner lives, their feelings, their psychological states, or their formative influences to the extent that modern biographies are expected to. In short, they do not focus on the details and processes of learning and education as we today conceive of them. That being so, it might seem that the historian and the student of literature will both equally experience frustration if they look to these ancient sources in search of a Jesus who learns. However, the fact that ancient biographers did not share our interests does not always preclude the possibility that they recorded information useful to us for our purposes. A close inspection, as we will show throughout this book, reveals a Jesus who learns. For those of us who are seeking to learn from Jesus, this should be an exciting prospect. Hearing the lectures of an educator is one thing. When we get to glimpse how they learn, and how what they learn informs their teaching that we find so impactful, our own educational experience can be shifted to a whole other level entirely, one that opens up new vistas for our own learning.

Some have expressed such skepticism and/or pessimism about the Gospels, even the very earliest of them, that they may despair of catching more than the faintest and blurriest glimpse of the historical Jesus. I do not share that pessimism, although I fully understand the concerns that motivate it. The Gospels regularly tell stories about Jesus that are laden with symbolism—so much symbolism at times that we cannot help but wonder whether they were concocted entirely for the purpose of offering a theological message about Jesus that has nothing to do with history. For earlier generations of historians, the quest for the historical Jesus was all about stripping away theology to find the bare facts. Jesus was not merely a student, however. He was a student of theology, and to find theological elements woven through the life and words of such an individual is to be expected. The fact that many find it uncomfortable to speak of "Jesus's theology" is directly connected to the discomfort many feel when mention is made of Jesus's education. If he learned as others learned, if he formulated a theological vision in a manner comparable to others who participate in that human endeavor, doesn't that undermine the purported divinity of who he was and what he said? Once again it must be emphasized that unless we are to deny the humanity of Jesus, we must understand him as one who participates in the experiences of growth and development not merely with respect to his biological shape but also his mental processes and cognition. Once we accept that, we will realize that Jesus was himself among the earliest interpreters of his own life and teaching, the first to offer a theological slant on what he said, did, and experienced. Having embraced that seemingly obvious point, it becomes possible to hope for, expect to find, and begin to seek out those threads in the teaching and traditions of the church that began with Jesus's own theology.

The broader issue, when it comes to the interpretation of Gospel stories, is how we can tell when we are dealing with history scripturalized, and when we are dealing with Scripture historicized.[1] By the former, "history scripturalized," I mean the recasting of a historical event in ways that echo texts from the Jewish Scriptures (what Christians call the Old Testament). An example of this can be found in the crucifixion account in the Gospel of Matthew. The scene of mockery echoes a well-known depiction of the suffering of the righteous at the hands of the wicked that is found in the Wisdom of Solomon, a text that was part of the Greek translation of the Jewish Bible (known as the Septuagint) and found in the Apocrypha in some but not all Bibles today. There is no doubt that Jesus was crucified, but Matthew presents the event in a way that echoes an earlier text that he felt could help readers interpret what they read. By the latter phrase, "scripture historicized," I mean stories such as Matthew's infancy narrative. We have no other evidence that Jesus was visited by astrologers or fled to Egypt, and the story most likely resulted from the author beginning with the story of Moses and then crafting a story about the experiences of Jesus's parents and their young son so as to compare and contrast the two individuals. This was done in order to present Jesus as a "new Moses" and yet at the same time as superior to Moses. The depiction of Jesus's temptation in the wilderness may be entirely crafted to present Jesus as obeying where Israel disobeyed in the wilderness, even though it may be the case that Jesus in fact spent time in the wilderness reflecting on his values and commitments. That the story is a symbolic

---

1. For this terminology see Goodacre, "Scripturalization," especially 39.

one doesn't mean that the historical Jesus did not confront alternative paths and decide to reject them, even if it didn't happen all at once. Some stories may be entirely or primarily one or the other, but many—perhaps the vast majority—involve a significant element of both these things. For example, the emphasis on Jesus facing temptation once again towards the end of his life, in a garden like Adam, does not mean that the incident in Gethsemane is not historical at its core.[2] In many instances it can be difficult to tell what category we are dealing with or whether the distinction is even meaningful. The effort to perceive the historical Jesus must begin with a close investigation of what was remembered and told about him afterwards. If what we find does not seem to get us beyond the level of the narrative, some will be thoroughly satisfied with that outcome. If we seem to catch glimpses of a figure behind and beyond the text, some will find that truly exciting. My hope is that readers with both sorts of interests will find value in the exploration in this book of Jesus's significant, life-changing interactions with women, and that studying these will lead readers into new insights into both the texts and the people in history that left their mark on them.

Some may fully appreciate the usefulness of a book on this topic and the appropriateness of its subject matter, and yet wonder who I think I am to dare to write about this subject as a man. I indeed do so with significant fear and trepidation. I have approached the project from the very beginning as one that requires me to seek significant input and feedback from women. Nonetheless, there are a great many reasons why it is not merely appropriate but important for men to engage in studies that focus on the exploration of women's perspectives and voices. First, there is the long history of marginalization of women's studies as an academic subject. Too often, one could find "regular" history courses galore that focus predominantly on men, and then a smaller number specifically on women's history which then tended to be taught by women to classes of mostly female students. That state of affairs is extremely problematic, just as it is when it has been almost exclusively women who pursued their right to vote, or equality of pay, or an end to sexual harassment in workplaces. Those who have historically been marginalized can certainly accomplish much on their own—that is not my point. The point is how disappointing it is that men do not at least rush to join in the marching,

---

2. See further McGrath, "Obedient Unto Death."

the petitioning, the protesting, and the studying alongside women who are turning attention to important yet neglected matters.

In the field of religious studies, it has long been recognized that one does not have to be a Muslim to study Islam or Jewish to study Judaism. In the same way, one does not have to be a woman to study women's stories any more than one has to be a man to study stories about and written by men. Doing any of these things I mentioned can provide a useful outsider's perspective. But more than that, it can foster empathy and understanding. If Hindus alone study Hinduism (problematic terminology, as I have come to learn through my studies!) there is likely to be an unhelpfully large gulf between how insiders experience that tradition and how it is perceived by outsiders. Study can challenge our preconceptions about others, but only if that study reaches those who are not already familiar with the object of study. This is true whether the different vantage points reflect differences of religion, ethnicity, gender, or anything else. Both insiders and outsiders to a tradition or identity stand to benefit from the conversation about how things look from their different perspectives.

Once one accepts that it is crucially important for men to study women's stories, the subject of this book becomes a natural one for me to write about, as appropriate as working on John the Baptist and what Jesus may have learned from him. It becomes simply another piece in the puzzle of the quest for the historical Jesus and the study of early Christian literature. Those fields are filled with numerous pitfalls that a study such as this one needs to take into account. One particularly large pitfall is the danger of anti-Semitism. In seeking to emphasize Jesus's positive treatment of women (or the distinctiveness of his teachings about any other subject for that matter) some have contrasted Jesus with his Jewish context and upbringing.[3] Denigrating Judaism to elevate Jesus simply will not do. Jesus was a Jewish man in a Jewish context, and it is thoroughly implausible to think in terms of Jesus vs. Judaism. If Jesus viewed and interacted with women in a manner that was not typical of his time, then we need to understand him as a first-century Jewish feminist.[4] We may then proceed to investigate how he learned and came to embrace values that went against what was dominant in his time not only in a Jewish context, but throughout the ancient Mediterranean world and beyond. It is important to get this right not only to avoid anti-Semitism, but simply

3. A classic treatment of this is Plaskow, "Christian Feminism and Anti-Judaism." See also Seibert-Cuadra, "La mujeren los evangelios sinópticos," 88–89.

4. See the discussion by Levine and Witherington, *Gospel of Luke*, 415–16.

for the sake of historical accuracy. Jesus was Jewish and was certainly not the only person who questioned and challenged traditional values and assumptions related to gender. But even if he were, it would have been as a Jewish man engaging in countercultural thinking and action.

I decided as I began work on this book that I didn't want to merely study the untold stories of women, but to try to imagine how they would express themselves either in those moments or recounting their own experiences from the perspective of hindsight. I knew that the things I got wrong, things that didn't ring true to female readers as I sought feedback on drafts of what I wrote, would teach me things that I probably could not learn any other way—things about myself as well as about the New Testament. In the process of seeking to flesh out the stories in this way, by writing historical fiction, I discovered that this can be more than a personal exercise, and more than a means of communicating history to a general audience, although it is definitely both of those things. Writing historical fiction deserves to be considered a scholarly tool in its own right.[5] Nothing exposes the implausibility of a historical reconstruction more quickly than the attempt to turn that reconstruction into a narrative. If we cannot find plausible motives for characters, or construct dialogue that doesn't sound stilted, or fill in the gaps around the pieces of historical data in ways that make sense, this tells us something crucial about either the historicity or otherwise of the event recounted in our sources, or our own reconstruction of what happened, and sometimes both.[6] I have found this to be a most rigorous form of testing of my own assumptions, views, and conclusions. It also has helped me to notice problems with assumptions that many of us make about these stories about Jesus.

Each of the chapters in the remainder of this book (except for the conclusion) thus begins with a bit of historical fiction that tells some part of the story that is the focus of the chapter in question. As you read those retellings, as well as my discussion and interpretation of the historical evidence that follows thereafter, you may feel there is a tension inherent in this project. If you have never read academic historical scholarship about the Bible before, I may seem to be unduly skeptical of things that are written in it. How, you might ask, can I not accept what is there on

---

5. On the importance of imagination in historical work on ancient women see Brooten, "Early Christian Women," 67–68.

6. See further Clark, "Lady Vanishes," 20–21, on this as well as some risks inherent in a narrative approach to history. See too the cautionary remarks in Perroni and Simonelli, *Mary of Magdala*, 21.

the pages of the Bible, and yet at the same time be willing to fill in details that are not in the text around or even in place of what it explicitly says? These are good questions, and a study of women in the New Testament is particularly well suited to providing an answer. To begin with, the fact that women's names are not included in the Gospels when men's names tend to be, the fact that these texts appear to all have been written by men, are unfortunately details that male readers often fail to notice or consider significant. Female readers, on the other hand, tend to notice them and find them significant. We do not have in the New Testament texts that were somehow miraculously protected from the biases human authors bring to any subject they write about. Gender, religion, culture, education, and many other things are factors that contribute to and influence an author's perspective. As a result of their assumptions and influences, these authors often left women in the shadows and on the sidelines without noticing they were doing so any more than most male readers of their writings tend to notice the omission. On the other hand, at least some of these authors can also be seen (when considered in comparison with one another as well as with other literature from their time) to at least sometimes have made a deliberate point of including women's stories. They do better than some and not as well as others.

It is not an insult to call the ancient New Testament authors *biased*. All human beings have biases. The double conclusion to the Gospel of John (20:30; 21:25) illustrates the more general point: not everything that could be included in a text will be, and an author's choices about what to include and how to tell the story have particular aims in view. Comparing the depictions of women and the way stories about them are told also illustrates another point about how historians must proceed when working with texts like these. If we consider the story of Jesus having perfume/ointment poured on him by a woman, there are significant variations in detail across the Gospels, and in the Gospel of Luke the setting, timing, and significance of the event are very different than in the other Gospels. Is this a case of multiple similar events? Did Luke adapt the story he found in Mark's Gospel, which he used as a source, for his own purposes? A historian *must* ask those questions, and all readers of the Gospels *should* ask those questions. The approach to the Bible that seeks to harmonize all difficulties and deny all differences and tensions silences these authors' distinctive voices, in a manner not unlike the way these ancient authors themselves often silenced women, not naming them or including speech by them as often as they do for men. Asking historical questions and recognizing that these texts do not give us "just the facts" is not undue skepticism but a response to listening to what the relevant ancient voices have to say with attention. The differences among them require us to make judgments about historicity. To deny the texts the opportunity to be heard individually because of one's doctrine about the collection they are now found in, or to deny ancient women the chance to be heard because ancient male authors did not provide us with the information we need to fully hear them, are both examples of us treating these ancient people with disrespect. I proceed in this book in the way that I do not only because I accept the usefulness of the methods of history, but because I believe these ancient perspectives—those of the authors and those of the women they wrote about—deserve better than they often get from the typical modern reader of the New Testament. As Elisabeth Schussler Fiorenza puts it,

> Androcentric texts and linguistic reality constructions must not be mistaken as trustworthy evidence of human history, culture, and religion . . . Rather than understand the text as an adequate reflection of the reality about which it speaks, we must search for clues and allusions that indicate the reality about which the text is silent. Rather than take androcentric texts as informative "data" and accurate "reports," we must read their "silences" as evidence and indication of that reality about which they do not speak.[7]

An older approach to historical investigation looked for individual details (words, phrases, actions) that could be judged historical. Only then could one try to weave those details into a big picture reconstruction of a person's life. More recent work has emphasized that this approach is wrongheaded. If we think of a forest, we can speak of its approximate location with confidence, and can describe its boundaries and extent with far more precision than we can say anything about an individual tree. In the same way, the gist of Jesus is what comes across in our earliest and best evidence on the whole. That is likely to be historically accurate even if expressed in some inauthentic or highly distorted stories and sayings. The famous cherry tree story tells us that George Washington was perceived to be honest and remembered that way. It does so despite not being a factual story about a historical event. (If you hadn't found this out before now, let me apologize that I failed to break the news to you more gently.)

---

7. Schussler Fiorenza, *In Memory of Her*, 29, 41.

Our discussion will at times seem like typical discussions of history, while at other times will resemble literary study, and at still others will seem either like a bit of both or perhaps not quite either. This partly reflects the conviction that the gist of our earliest Christian literature may convey an accurate impression of Jesus on the whole even if specific details cannot be shown to be factual, and partly reflects a genuine interest in the stories themselves. Very early stories that have been fabricated, distorted, and/or heavily overlaid with symbolism are nonetheless valuable to historians because they tell us what impression Jesus and his interactions with women made overall. When we add to these considerations the tendency of ancient male authors to marginalize or skip female perspectives and experiences, we have no choice but to try to triangulate as well as we can using as many different angles of approach as possible, and to fill in the gaps in our evidence as best we can. In some instances we may conclude that one, two, or three of the Gospel authors preserve material close to what actually happened, while one or more made significant alterations when retelling the story to apply it in new contexts. In other instances we may find that all the different versions are like ripples that allow us to detect at their center the impact of an event that none of them recounts in anything like a manner of straightforward reporting, and yet which we can nonetheless deduce from the evidence they provide.

Adopting a historical rather than a purely literary approach means that we are not focused exclusively on what Jesus is explicitly depicted as learning from women in written texts that we have. We are seeking to dig behind as well as fill in spaces around the texts in an effort to ask what Jesus as a historical figure may have learned from women. This historical enterprise involves a significant element of imagination; although, every effort has been made to reconstruct historical events in a way that is compatible with the historical evidence, it has been necessary to go beyond them. Trying to tell the reconstructed history as narrative from the perspective of a woman involves still more creative filling in of gaps.[8] These historical and literary challenges both stem from a common underlying problem, namely that ancient sources like the Gospels tell us so little about the activities of women, never mind offering us their perspective on matters. It is precisely the historical silencing of women that is a key motivation for writing this book, and it is a direct result of the fact that women's stories and perspectives were omitted that this book can

---

8. Cf. Schussler Fiorenza, *In Memory of Her*, 41; Bauckham, *Gospel Women*, 194–95.

only offer creative speculation about many details. Carla Ricci refers to this as an *"exegesis of the silence."*⁹ The effort to perceive the stories and perspectives of women in the time of Jesus in general, and who knew him in particular, involves seeking what ancient male authors sometimes ignored and sometimes deliberately downplayed or omitted. The enterprise is thus at once historical and imaginative. It seeks to take the evidence fully seriously and be compatible with it, and yet by definition is required to go beyond it, to explore silences and omissions and details around passing mentions. Sara Parks writes,

> So often . . . we lack the necessary information to uncover the lives and perspectives of ancient women; ancient data that could make women visible have been preserved only through thickly male-centered perspectives or have simply not been preserved at all. With Q, however, the evidence has been right before our eyes for a hundred years; it has been *our inattention to feminist questions* that have obscured what these data can tell us about early Jewish women in first-century Galilee and beyond . . . There is nothing that we as historians can do to change the fact that our source materials are male-centered. What is lost is lost forever. That said, there *is* a great deal we can do about our own readings of the material that is available to us.¹⁰

The Patriarchal Narratives

Understanding the patriarchal and other cultural values of Jesus's time is crucially important. Yet often we need to read our ancient sources against the grain in undertaking an investigation like this one. Those ancient texts were for the most part written by men to be read by other men. Is their judgment about women reliable? Did most men agree with various strictures that certain teachers and authors write about as ideal? Did most women follow the rules, and even if they did, was it because they felt they had no choice or because they embraced the values of their society despite them being to their detriment? We need the stories ancient sources provide us about Jesus and women in order to undertake a

---

9. Ricci, *Mary Magdalene*, 123 (emphasis hers). See also Taschl-Erber, "Mary of Magdala," 431–32; Moore, *Women in Christian Traditions*, 27; Rushing, *Magdalene Legacy*, 6.

10. Parks, *Gender in the Rhetoric of Jesus*, 151. See also Arnal, "Gendered Couplets," 75.

study such as this, but they don't tell us as much as we wish they would, and they rarely give more than a glimpse of the perspective of women. We need other ancient sources to fill in the cultural background, but at the same time we need to recognize that those sources offer particular perspectives on the norms of that time and place. When they insist that women ought to do something, is it more likely that they are articulating things that everyone did and took for granted, or that they are calling for this precisely because many do not do what they think ought to be done? That point is particularly important when it comes to the subject of women learning, teaching, and leading in a variety of capacities. Some male rabbis, philosophers, and pundits are adamant about what women should not do. That they felt it necessary to express themselves so strongly implies that not everyone agreed. Bernadette Brooten has done a particularly important service in publishing inscriptions that indicate the leadership roles women played in some ancient synagogues.[11] We must be careful not to make generalizations that simply aim to assert the superiority of one particular culture, religion, or period in history over against another.[12] Every human society, organization, and system has strengths and shortcomings, and we should be as honest about them as we can.

Patriarchy takes different forms, and gender expresses itself in different ways in different cultures. When we talk about the patriarchal values that were dominant in Jesus's time and place, we must not be understood to be offering a simple contrast between allegedly good modern values in the English-speaking world and elsewhere, and supposedly bad ancient or foreign assumptions and viewpoints. Even in our own time, the situation is much more nuanced and far from clear-cut. A country like the United States should not simply boast of not having dowries and bride burning without also addressing unequal pay and the fact that we have never (as of the writing of this book) had a female president. Even in modern times, in cultures that have embraced equal pay and job opportunities for women, one may still witness a tendency for women to talk with women and men with men in different halves of a living room

---

11. Brooten, *Women Leaders*. See also Thompson, *Mary of Magdala*, 94–105.

12. See for instance Boer, *Mary Magdalene*, 42; Ricci, *Mary Magdalene*, 189 on the lack of call accounts for women comparable for what we have for some male apostles. Parks's study (*Gender in the Rhetoric*) strikes a helpful balance in seeking to recognize the distinctiveness of Jesus in his time as indicated by the teaching attributed to him in the Gospels, without suggesting that this provides grounds for asserting the uniqueness or superiority of one religion or culture relative to another.

at a family gathering, or for men and women to end up sitting clustered at different ends of a table. No one will plan it, and quite possibly no one will notice that it occurs. Even if someone does notice, they may not feel that there is anything noteworthy about it. However, informal conversations often impact employment and advancement opportunities and perpetuate gender inequities. These dynamics are also relevant to our exploration of what Jesus is likely to have learned from women, as we also ask where and how that learning took place. Would informal opportunities to learn from women, to hear their perspectives and stories, have presented themselves naturally and frequently, or will they have required a concerted effort and perhaps even unconventional behavior on Jesus's part? Some stories in the Gospels hint at answers to these questions, answers that can help us think critically about our own time and context as well as about Jesus and his ancient setting.

There are countless books about Jesus's encounters with women and the women he met and knew. These fall into a variety of genres and sometimes span more than one: academic studies of Jesus as a historical figure, literary studies of the Gospels, historical fiction based closely or loosely on the ancient source material.[13] One thing that most of them have in common is that they make reference to the way these women's lives were transformed by their encounter with Jesus. Much rarer is any reference to ways in which Jesus himself was transformed by these encounters.[14] By fleshing out as fully as we can the lives and perspectives of the women Jesus met and knew, we not only get to know them better, but we also get to know Jesus better and understand his life in a richer way.

Further Reading

An extensive bibliography is provided at the end of this book, which includes all works that were consulted in the process of writing and not only those that are cited. These are included both for the benefit of those who wish to investigate the general topic or specific individuals or stories in greater detail, and to give credit to all those whose writings have shaped my impression of this subject matter and not only to those who provided specific information that was incorporated in my book. The bibliography

---

13. On the blurry line between history and fiction, especially when it comes to biography, see Bond, *First Biography*, 68–71.

14. A rare exception is Sebastiani, *Tra/Sfigurazione*, 17–18.

includes works that fall into a range of different genres. There are nonetheless so many older works, in particular devotional books and novels from the past, that touch on this topic in some way, that there was no way to be exhaustive. When an academic edited volume contained more than one chapter or entry that was relevant, the entire volume was listed in the bibliography, with reference then being made to the specific chapter and its author when it is referred to in a footnote. In addition to works whose primary focus is on women whom Jesus encountered, whenever a work on another topic is referred to in a footnote or was consulted in the writing of the book, that too has been included in the bibliography.

In certain respects it was quite wonderful to write this book and discover that there was no absolute need to cite the work of any male scholar. Although there are definitely some works written by men whose perspective and contribution added to the richness and detail of the final product, in no case would the omission thereof have prevented any of the main points of substance coming together much as they did. Yet upon further reflection, I think you will agree that there is also something troubling about this state of affairs, once it becomes clear what the root cause is. For the most part, female scholars have been the primary ones engaging in study of women in the New Testament, and their work is often ignored by male scholars.[15] I encountered this time and time again as I worked on the book. The same point also applies to the tendency of those writing in English to ignore publications in other languages. I am certain that there are things that I missed despite my efforts.

In this introduction I have hoped to explain and explore my motivations for writing this book, which I felt that a female author would be better poised to write, and would have written with a far greater depth of insight than I could ever hope to bring to bear on the subject.[16] I have also sought to clarify my approach for the benefit of those who are interested in those matters. I hope those who weren't interested in them skipped this introduction, but also express my deep admiration and profound appreciation for those who have impatiently been waiting for me to get to

---

15. Sara Parks refers to this as the "Brooten Phenomenon" in her 2019 article by that title, pointing out in that context the failure to ask "woman questions" of ancient sources, and the study of ancient women by men with patriarchal and kyriarchal assumptions, impoverishes the answers given to "malestream" questions as well. "The point, so simple and yet not to be underestimated, is that *closer interaction with gender dynamics in our texts can provide additional vantage points toward questions that do not have to do with gender*" (60).

16. Cf. Brooten, "Jewish Women's History," 27–28.

the substance of this topic, and yet have read this far even so. I hope that what is written here will be found persuasive, but also that the references and bibliographical information provided will lead you to seek out and listen directly to female perspectives both ancient and modern. The neglect of women's voices in the New Testament or in contemporary scholarship isn't a result of women not speaking. In the present volume I seek to listen to and learn from women even as I believe Jesus did, for reasons that I invite you to explore together with me in the chapters that follow.

Mary

What Jesus Learned from His Mother

Mary to Elizabeth,
Greetings, dear cousin. I am writing because we have just returned from visiting your son John at the Jordan, and I had sent word earlier that we hoped to stop and see you on our return journey, but circumstances prevented it. John looks well, and the number of people gathered to hear him and undergo immersion was remarkable.

I took the whole family to experience his immersion. It almost wasn't all of us. Jesus offered to stay behind to work and take care of things at home. When I pressed him, he said that he wasn't convinced that he needed to be baptized. We always raised our children to value what happens in the temple, not only because they have relatives who are priests, but because of what the Torah says. I am not surprised that they are confused by how we can now listen to someone who says that the water that flows down from heaven can purify as effectively as the blood of animals. Some of us have been present when John and Zechariah have argued about this, and my children respect their uncle and his years more than their cousin's perspective. We taught them to honor their elders, and so this too confused them. But the Torah itself shows us that those who are older are not always right, even if they are wiser in general than the young. Nor are brash and impetuous youth always wrong, though I fear what may happen now that John seems to have begun arguing with authorities other than just his father.

For all his initial hesitation, it was Jesus who found the experience of John's baptism most transformative. When he emerged from the water, one of the doves that are so common in the river valley landed right on him. Both he and John saw it as a sign. Jesus has gone from reluctance to deciding to stay and study with John as his disciple. As you know, that starts with a period of fasting. Jesus loves his food, but I could tell he was changed by the experience even more than the rest of us. Immersing in the water, with John speaking words about divine mercy and the river of life that flows from God's holy Jerusalem in the heavens, you feel forgiveness in a way that I have never experienced in all my years of visiting the temple. Surely this shows that John is right in his teaching, doesn't it?

Joseph always hoped that at least one of his sons would come to be called rabbi. He had enough sons to continue his family business even if several of them were to pursue other trades. I have long thought that Jesus would make an especially good teacher. He has a real gift for telling stories. He gets that from our side of the family. I am happy that, if he is to train as a teacher, it is at the feet of his dear cousin, learning about the kingdom of God; although, we both know how dangerous these times are for those who teach about such subjects. Joseph's father always believed that his family, being descended from David, would one day rise up again and rule over Israel. I think that when God's righteous arm is revealed, God will raise up all who have been downtrodden by the rich and powerful. I know that you believe this too, and that John has learned these things from you. If he had listened only to Zechariah, he would have supported those who now sit on lofty seats and occupy positions of power, including the priests and the system of costly sacrifices that burden the poor most of all. I am so proud of your son, as I know you must be too.

I will write more after I hear from you. I will make sure that when my son Jacob brings this letter to you and reads it for you, it is not when Zechariah is present. He is angry enough already at John, and at you for supporting him. I fear that if he thinks that you have converted your relatives as well, it will create a rift between you that may be impossible to heal. I certainly don't want to add to your strife.

I will be sending along some salted fish, bread, and olives. Please share these things with Imma and Rebekah as well if you can, unless you need them all for your own home. If you have date syrup that you can spare, I will be grateful if you can send some back with

Jacob on his return journey. He has business in Jerusalem and can pass your way both on his journey there and on his way back, if that is helpful.

God's blessing be upon you and your entire family.

In some ways, Mary ought to be the obvious place to start in an exploration of what, when, and how Jesus learned from women. There have been wonderfully imaginative portrayals of this, such as the movie *Mary, Mother of Jesus* in which Mary is presented as the author of the parables. They are stories she told Jesus as a child, which he then reused to good effect later in his life. The movie also portrays Joseph as sharing these dying words about Jesus with Mary: "Everything he is, you made him." For historians, however, Jesus's mother's influence on his values and words is more difficult to pin down. Nevertheless, Mary is a natural place to begin our exploration of what Jesus learned from women because a mother's influence on a child precedes that of any other human being. As we emphasized in the introduction, unless one wants to deny the humanity of Jesus (something that many in fact do in practice if not in theory), it can safely be assumed that Jesus learned from his mother without any need for controversy. Of course, that doesn't mean that there *won't* be controversy. When controversy results from affirming this seemingly straightforward point, that may helpfully highlight an area that deserves examination in certain theological systems. For anyone who accepts that Jesus was a historical human being, Mary's influence on him cannot seriously be doubted. However, that doesn't mean that we can figure out precisely how she influenced him and in what ways. Puzzling that out requires a close investigation of what we know about Mary, about Jesus, about Joseph, and about Jesus's siblings. It also requires a consideration of the evidence we have from ancient sources about the roles that mothers typically played in not just raising but *teaching* their children, seeking to do justice to the full range of diversity in this area. For those concerned about historical questions, there will still be a great deal of uncertainty. For those who are content to ask about the literary depiction of Mary in the New Testament and other early Christian literature, the picture quickly becomes fairly robust. In this chapter, we will try to plot a course between those two, focusing on what our earliest sources say about Mary and being historically cautious without allowing ourselves to be paralyzed by the fact that some tantalizing possibilities leave substantial room for doubt and unanswered questions.

Mary is not only a natural but a *necessary* place to begin in a book on this particular topic. For those who have difficulty accepting that Jesus learned, the role of a first-century Mediterranean Jewish mother brings the central issue into sharp focus. Apocryphal accounts abound in which Jesus begins speaking immediately after birth, or in which he goes to school only to begin instructing his instructors. However, to embrace those accounts as history—in essence if not in their specific details—is to utterly deny the humanity of Jesus. Before we wrestle with the question of what Jesus may have learned from men and/or women when he was older, therefore, we really do need to begin with the woman who may safely be presumed to have heard Jesus speak his first word, and who was responsible more than anyone else was for helping him to get there. This brings up a major question about what historians should do when they encounter silences in historical sources. If we do not have information, should we fill in the silence with what was typical, presuming that if something was left unmentioned, most likely it was deemed unnecessary to mention it because it was nothing out of the ordinary?[1] This matter comes up often in connection with the question of whether Jesus was married. If the New Testament doesn't say that he was, should we assume that it doesn't mention the fact because he was typical (and thus married), or that it doesn't mention the fact because there was no wife to mention (even though one might have expected his unmarried state to be noticed and commented on)? Both stances have their defenders.[2]

Beginning with Mary also provides the opportunity to highlight from the outset another important question: Can we learn about a figure's teaching by looking closely at those who learned from them? Can close attention to Jesus and his siblings tell us about Mary as mother and educator of her children?[3] We need to avoid two extremes. On the one hand, we should not posit that Mary was afforded a formal education that would have been exceptional in her time unless we have good evidence to support that conclusion. On the other hand, we could easily assume that Mary most likely conformed to our own stereotype of a woman's

---

1. Lee, *Black Madonna*, 28 discusses approaching Mary through historical generalizations given our paucity of specific information.

2. See on this, e.g., Sabar, *Veritas*, 73–74.

3. Whether the teaching of Jesus can provide insight into the teaching of John the Baptist is a similar question I have begun to explore in another book project.

and mother's role in a traditional society. Women were rarely given the opportunity to learn to read and write, but the same was true for men. The patriarchal character of the society meant that the tiny fraction of the population that could read and write were predominantly or exclusively men. It did not mean that most men were educated while women were not. Looking at the life of Jesus, we see an ability to express himself through stories, through word play, through evocative imagery. These skills were not the exclusive domain of men. If we sometimes get that impression it is because the majority of writing was done by men and they recorded their own words and those of their male peers far more frequently than the words of women. However, we have abundant evidence for women as effective storytellers in the ancient Mediterranean world. They were also an audience for literature, in most cases hearing it read aloud rather than reading it as words on a page, something that once again was also true in general of men. In some texts, when women's stories are recounted in a powerful and seemingly accurate way, we may have good reason to conclude that we are being given access to the words of eloquent women, even if they (like most people in that day and age irrespective of gender) may have had to rely on a male scribe to record their words in ink on papyrus.

Imagining the infancy and childhood of Jesus is the best test of whether someone takes the humanity of Jesus seriously or not, whatever else they may think about him beyond that. People can envision the adult Jesus as God dressed up as a human being, wearing human skin so as to interact with humankind, and persuade themselves that they are not denying his humanity. However, bring Jesus's infancy into the picture and things get awkward. If one asks whether God had a dirty diaper that needed to be changed, or was taught to say his first words, one will have to either rush headlong where some ancient apocryphal Gospels were happy to go, or will sense that something is not quite right about one's view of Jesus.

When it comes to concrete historical information about things that Jesus learned from his mother, we will regularly find ourselves wishing we had more information than we do. When we write a biography of a modern individual, we ask about their relationship with their parents, how they were brought up, and so on. We view a mother's influence, and a famous person's relationship with their mother, as crucial information if we are to understand them. Not so ancient biographies. Nevertheless, if we fully embrace Jesus's status as a human being, then we can be confident that Mary taught him all the things that a child learns from their mother, if not more.

Before we proceed further, one more thing needs to be said here: we ought not (if we are interested in the historical Jesus) to imagine Mary telling Jesus that he was virginally conceived and that his birth was heralded by angels. From a historian's perspective, it will be noted that such were the kinds of stories that ancient people created later, looking back with hindsight and imagining what the conception and birth of significant individuals must have been like. In what our earliest sources tell us about the adult life of Jesus, on the other hand, we are given the impression that Mary and Jesus's brothers wrestled with how to view his message and activity, at least at times. Mary is a consistent presence in Jesus's close proximity throughout nonetheless. Jesus spoke of families being divided on account of him, and there is a strong likelihood that his prediction about the families of his followers was based on his experience with his own family. If they were divided, we should probably view Mary as on the sympathetic side of the fence, given the evidence. This doesn't mean that she would not have worried about her son, questioned his judgment and decisions at times, and wished on occasion that he might have made different choices. She is there alongside him at key moments throughout his public activity.

Education (Mary's and Jesus's)

The New Testament does not depict Joseph as a character in stories about Jesus beyond his twelfth year of life. It is often assumed, quite plausibly, that Joseph died before Jesus reached adulthood. The depiction of Jesus on the cusp of adolescence in the Gospel of Luke already suggests a certain level of prior education. Luke tells us that Jesus listened to teachers and asked them good questions. That behavior suggests that this was not the first time that Jesus learned, and Luke explicitly indicates that it would not be the last. There is certainly an instinctive inquisitiveness that children around the world exhibit. We should reflect on this when we consider the tendency to interpret Jesus's teaching about children and childlike faith in terms of "unquestioning acceptance." Nothing could be less childlike! Children always insist on asking "Why?" and following up on any loose ends in the answer to that question with another "Why?" By age 12, however, such habits have often been lost. If Jesus was asking questions at that age, and asking *good, meaningful,* and *insightful* questions, then this is surely reflective of his own education and upbringing. A child's earliest asking of "why?" questions may have nothing to do with specific parenting. When inquisitiveness and a desire to learn from those with recognized expertise continues into adulthood, on the other hand, it shows that what may have been instinctive at one point in child development was encouraged, fostered, and refined by parents as well as any teachers they employed or sent the child to study with.

Even today, when the father in a traditional household dies, the children may be expected to put their education on hold in order to work and support the family. Yet in the Gospels we get the opposite impression, that Jesus pursued further educational opportunities as an adult by becoming a student of John the Baptist. In the New Testament, we might easily assume that this was a purely individual course that Jesus charted for himself, perhaps even in blatant disregard for what his family thought was appropriate. That most likely reflects the assumptions of modern readers about educational and vocational choices. An early Jewish Christian Gospel known as the Gospel of the Nazarenes, which was not included in the New Testament, depicts Mary as taking her children to be baptized by John, and asking Jesus whether he isn't coming too! Jerome quotes it as saying, "The mother of the Lord and his brothers said to him, 'John the Baptist is baptizing for the forgiveness of sins; let us go and be baptized by him.'" In that text, Jesus's family, led by the mother, pursues an association with John's movement and invites Jesus to join them. Whatever one thinks of the historical plausibility of this depiction, it raises crucial questions that modern readers of the Gospels may never think to ask. Where and how did Jesus hear about John the Baptist? There was no TV, no newspapers. If Jesus connected himself to John and his baptizing activity, there is good reason to think that the connection would have been mediated by his parents, or his one surviving parent, his mother, if Joseph was no longer around. Suddenly the movie's statement about Mary having been responsible for who Jesus became does not seem at all far-fetched. On the contrary, if we look even closer at the things we are told about Mary, we get the impression that she had a recognizable influence on him. We also get the impression that there were tensions at times, but we are not told that those tensions were because Jesus went to learn from John the Baptist and then began to proclaim the imminent arrival of the kingdom of God. According to the Gospels, John himself expressed doubts about Jesus's activity and whether he was the one they were all expecting to come. It might very well be because Jesus's mother and siblings were also followers of John that they had reservations about his direction, and that this caused tensions in the family.

Ancient Greek sources tend to depict mothers as nurturers and fathers as educators. Elizabeth Johnson writes, "In the absence of any formal institutionalized education, women socialized young children. They created the atmosphere breathed in by these young lives. They transmitted to them the culture, beliefs, and values of their Jewish heritage."[4] Even if Mary and Joseph played stereotypical parental roles, we should not conclude on that basis that what Jesus learned from Mary was minimal. Consideration of this topic often focuses on one particular formal category of education, i.e., in precisely those areas that distinguished male education from the opportunities typically given to women, as well as from the kind of education mothers and other women provided. Learning is a broader category than formal education, and so even if we were to limit Mary's role in Jesus's upbringing to the culturally-defined sphere of nurturing, we will surely still want to say that Jesus learned from her precisely as a result of what she did in this capacity.[5] However, given the disappearance of Joseph from the adult life of Jesus, it is a real possibility that Mary may have had to provide more than the prevailing culture expected mothers to under normal circumstances, because she found herself a widow. Susan Treggiari writes, "Mothers might, especially if widowed, have an important influence" on their son's education.[6] We see an example of this in a story about martyrdom that appears in 4 Maccabees (building on an earlier version in 2 Maccabees 7) featuring a woman, whose husband is no longer alive, and her seven sons. Tessa Rajak writes, "In the absence of the male, the woman takes it upon herself, after duly apologizing, to

---

4. Johnson, *Truly Our Sister*, 202.

5. On the depiction of Mary pondering the words of the angel Gabriel, and asking probing questions, as examples of learning activities that sages, seers, priests, and others engaged in, see Spencer, *Salty Wives*, 85–86, 93–94, 99–100.

6. Treggiari, "The Education of the Ciceros" in Bloomer, *Companion to Ancient Education*, 241. Christian Laes writes in "Masters and Apprentices" in the same volume, 476, "Free boys were usually sent by their fathers, and occasionally by their mothers, grandparents, or brothers. From a sample of 26 apprentice contracts, 42 percent (11 contracts) were made by someone other than fathers . . . Demographical calculations for Roman antiquity estimate that about 30 percent of children had lost their fathers by the age of thirteen. At age sixteen, this amounts to 40 percent . . . Being fatherless thus had a limited impact on the possibility of being apprenticed." See also Letters of Sidonius IV.XXI for an ancient viewpoint on owing a debt to one's mother as well as father.

exhort them in his place."[7] The woman is depicted as being well versed in the Jewish Scriptures and at least bilingual (4 Macc. 16:15).

What can we say about Mary's education, and thus the possibility that she herself may have taught Jesus, rather than merely arranging for him to study with a male teacher? For one thing, we should note the echoes of the Jewish Scriptures in the Magnificat (Luke 1:46–55).[8] One does not need to view it as an authentic historical transcript of a poem Mary spontaneously uttered for the point to remain valid. Luke depicts Mary as someone who knows the Jewish Scriptures well enough to be able to weave echoes and themes from them into her own poetry.[9] Luke also presents Jesus emphasizing similar themes in his own teaching to those in the Magnificat. It is clear from this that Luke wanted readers to understand that the perspective of Mary influenced Jesus. As Mary Foskett writes, Mary "introduced some of the key themes of her son's ministry. The deliverance of which Mary sings in the Magnificat . . . resonates with Jesus' inaugural sermon . . . Her voice echoes throughout the Lukan beatitudes, as well."[10] We should not miss, however, that Luke is also saying something about Mary's education in the Scriptures. She may or may not have been able to read them as words on a page.[11] Few people in her

---

7. Rajak, "Paideia," 63.

8. See Perry, *Mary for Evangelicals*, 77–78; Warner, *Alone*, 13; *Getty-Sullivan, Women*, 31–35; as well as the contributions by Donald Senior (105) and Richard Sklba (124) in Donnelly, *Mary, Woman of Nazareth*. Although Jeffrey Kloha, "Elizabeth's Magnificat," seeks to revive the case for this passage having originally been attributed to Elizabeth, within the context of Luke's Gospel it would seem to fit its context poorly if Elizabeth speaks it. While there is sometimes reason to prefer the more difficult reading, not all errors and changes to texts produce improvements in its sense or clarity.

9. There are some traditions created and/or passed on by the church that connect Jesus's mother with the Psalms. Sheingorn, "Wise Mother," 69 mentions traditions about Mary being taught the Law and singing of the Psalms. Albert the Great said she studied the seven liberal arts! Sheingorn also mentions traditions from the ninth century which asserted that Mary was studying the Psalms when Gabriel appeared to her (79n8). We will have more to say about Jesus and singing in the next chapter. Here we may note that, at the very least, the church recognized in Mary one who had not only studied Scripture but had given particular attention to poetic parts of it, fostering her own poetic ability.

10. Foskett, "Mary," 455. So also Spencer, *Salty Wives*, 80, who writes, "Mary's Magnificat functions as a paradigmatic agenda of Jesus' messianic ministry throughout Luke's Gospel."

11. On the tradition of depiction in art of Anne, Mary's mother, teaching her to read, see Hebblethwaite, *Six New Gospels*, 34–35n25. Hebblethwaite envisages Mary teaching Jesus to read, just as her mother taught her (35). See also our chapter in this

time could, as few were given the opportunity to learn this skill. However, a far greater number of people were given opportunities to study the Scriptures by hearing them read aloud and then engaging in discussion about them. Luke depicts Mary as someone who must have benefited from such opportunities. We see this as well in the very fact that Luke alone emphasizes that Jesus as a young man grew in wisdom. Luke could in theory have depicted the kinds of things that both his parents said and stood for, to illustrate their influence on him as he grew in wisdom, yet in his Gospel he only shows us the kind of influence Mary might have had on him. It would not be going too far to say, in including the wisdom of Mary in his Gospel, Luke invites us to learn important things from the one from whom Jesus himself learned them.[12] As Laurence Coutts writes of Luke's story about Jesus learning in the temple at age 12, "in his extensive and intimate acquaintance with Scripture, his deep love for it and hope for the Messiah, we may see a reflection of the heart of the one who gave us the *Magnificat*—Mary, the mother of Jesus."[13]

There are always things that some readers will think of but others will likely miss, depending on their experience. Courtney Lee suggests that Mary, like black mothers in the United States today, would have taught her child how to navigate interactions with authority so as to survive them.[14] She would also have known that he lived at constant risk. White readers miss this insight because we do not bring the experience of being on the receiving end of racism to the text. There is much Jesus learned from his mother and other women that we modern readers may fail to perceive because our own experiences are so radically different from that of first-century people. We need the perspectives of modern men and women of diverse cultural, ethnic, and socioeconomic backgrounds to challenge our assumptions and suggest other ways of understanding what we read if we hope to bridge that historical gap. In this particular case, we would not go so far as to suggest that Mary taught Jesus how to practice nonviolent resistance. (Indeed, there are debates about the extent to which that was something Jesus himself taught.) But to the extent that

---

book about Jesus's maternal grandmother. On Jewish women's education in general in this period see Ilan, *Jewish Women*, 190–204.

12. On Mary as teacher in the Magnificat see Gupta, "Teach Us Mary." Coutts, *Jesus' Encounters*, 72, writes, "Mary is not an ignorant, insensitive woman . . . Even though provincial, she is literate, informed, reflective and pious."

13. Coutts, *Jesus' Encounters*, 73.

14. Lee, *Black Madonna*, 88–89. See also Johnson, *Truly Our Sister*, 220–21.

Jesus recognized the dangers of interaction with authorities, and to the extent that patriarchal honor values made it likely he would encounter threats, it is reasonable to surmise that motherly concern played a role in conveying these realities to Jesus and warning him about them.[15]

Penelope Duckworth writes, "Jesus' treatment of women also tells us something about his mother. As his first teacher, she may well have challenged the prevailing view of women. Perhaps as a consequence of that, Jesus treated women as intelligent and capable people, regardless of their status."[16] Kenneth Bailey writes in a similar vein, "the reader is led to understand that Jesus was raised by an extraordinary mother who must have had enormous influence on his attitudes toward women."[17] In the Gospel of Luke, Mary is depicted as obeying the commandments in the Torah as well as submitting to divine revelation sent through an angel.[18] Mary provides Jesus with a multifaceted parental example of a woman who interacts directly with the divine and with Scripture and who takes responsibility for her own obedience. The emphasis in early Christian literature on Jesus as one who obeys and submits to God should not be separated from his mother's paradigmatic example as one who did the same.

Apocalyptic Imagery and Mary's Hometown

We now turn our attention to specific things that we can see in our sources or can surmise that Jesus learned from Mary. One is not particularly obvious, but it is a good place to begin because it connects with the topic of where Mary may have grown up and where her parents were from, which would have had an impact on her education and upbringing that in turn would have had an impact on Jesus. Jesus mentions pregnant women and nursing mothers in his prediction about the destruction of Jerusalem (Mark 13:17). Just as unfortunately remains true today, men

---

15. Watson, *Wisdom's Daughters*, 156 writes, "It was shocking to me at first to find that there is no record of a kind word spoken by Jesus to his mother in any of the four Gospels. Then I came to understand why ... Jesus must keep his mother at arm's length so that she cannot project her concern for his safety onto him."

16. Duckworth, *Mary*, 42. Duckworth also notes the tradition in the *Protoevangelium of James* that Mary served as a temple virgin, which would have meant that she "led a theologically active life" (51).

17. Bailey, *Jesus Through Middle Eastern Eyes*, 192.

18. Spencer, *Salty Wives*, 68–71, 89.

in the ancient world did not always notice or give due consideration to hardships that they themselves have never confronted and will never confront. What made Jesus pay particular attention to the difficulties for women in a city under siege who were pregnant or had young children? One possibility is that his mother had been nursing a child (whether Jesus or one of his siblings) when Varus attacked Sepphoris, the city that church tradition says Mary's parents lived in. Even if Mary did not live there at the time, the inhabitants of a town as close to Sepphoris as Nazareth would be frightfully aware of what was unfolding in their vicinity. A mere six kilometers or so separates the two, and the one is visible from the other. Mary also undoubtedly heard stories about what other women experienced a generation before her, perhaps including her own mother, in the events leading up to Herod capturing the city for the Romans. We will turn our attention to Mary's mother, Jesus's grandmother, in the chapter following this one. It is interesting that Herod took the city during a snowstorm, without a struggle since the city's would-be defenders fled, given that Jesus emphasizes the worse difficulties if Jerusalem is besieged in winter. Women would have told one another of these experiences if they lived through them and survived. Perhaps Mary's own mother had been pregnant or nursing a child at that time. Even if Jesus heard other women talk about it, Mary might have been the first to do so. Here, as often throughout this book, we may not be certain whether the specific woman that a particular chapter is about was the one from whom Jesus learned this or that. We may be able to conclude nevertheless that we are dealing with something Jesus learned from listening to the stories women told, even if we are not sure which woman or women did so. Focusing on women's distinctive hardships during a military siege of a city indicates attention to women's perspectives and experiences that is not typical of male authors. Mistreatment of women is sometimes used as a trope in stories about warfare, but typically it is but one detail in an extended male-focused narrative.[19] Jesus's concern for women is different.

In ancient times as today, it is much more common for people to move from the countryside to the city than vice versa. Indeed, the latter is extremely rare. Those who told the story of Mary's parents being from Sepphoris would have known this, and we should judge it more likely

---

19. On these details see further Reeder, *Gendering War and Peace*, 23, 199 and *passim*; Kern, *Ancient Siege Warfare*, esp. 80–85. That women were affected by sieges was well known, but it seems rare for a male author to focus exclusive attention on the impact on women in particular categories. See also Swidler, *Three Jesus Certitudes*, 93.

that they reflected real but less common events, than that they concocted a scenario that was neither typical, nor something fantastic that made the story more exciting. If he was a carpenter or mason working on the rebuilding of Sepphoris, Joseph was well poised to be an exception to the rule, potentially finding a wife in the city as he worked there. That scenario would place Mary in Sepphoris during the siege we mentioned. It would also make her a city girl living in Nazareth, which would make for her having had a highly distinctive kind of experience, one that would in turn have shaped how she taught and raised her children.

It may be that Jesus's apocalyptic discourse depicted in Mark 13 and parallels draws on still more of Jesus's mother's experience. Jesus recommends that those who see clues about unfolding events that will lead to Jerusalem's destruction, and who live in it or anywhere near it in Judea, *flee away from the city and its vicinity to the mountains.*[20] Did Mary have the experience of fleeing a city that could foresee a siege coming, whether with her parents, or being sent by them to stay with a relative, or with her husband and any children she may have had? Depending on the timing, perhaps Mary was sent to relatives in Nazareth and met Joseph on that occasion. Although there are discrepancies between Matthew and Luke that complicate any attempt to glean historical information from their stories of Jesus's birth and childhood, both place Jesus's birth during the time of Herod the Great. If this is correct, then Jesus himself was born perhaps a couple of years prior to Varus's attack on Sepphoris.[21] He would be too young to remember it, however, and so it would have been his mother and other relatives who told him stories about what had happened. Mary might have been pregnant with or nursing one of Jesus's siblings at the time it occurred, in which case Jesus's concern for future women attempting to flee before Jerusalem is besieged might have been

---

20. Mark 13:24; Matt 24:16; Luke 21:21. When it says they should flee to the mountains, this need not be interpreted in terms of hiding out in caves, something that could only be maintained for a short time. It suggests rather a flight from the area impacted by war and siege on a city to an area not directly affected, not least because it lay in a different jurisdiction in this particular case. According to one ancient strand of church tradition, Christians in Judea relocated to the city of Pella across the Jordan prior to the Roman assault on Jerusalem leading to its destruction in the year 70. While cities served the role of providing refuge and defense in times of war, there have been instances in which defense of a city has been felt to be impossible and so its inhabitants fled, rather than others fleeing to the city. See for instance the accounts of the Athenians deserting the city before the Persians attacked it recorded by Herodotus.

21. Josephus, *Ant* 17.10.9; *JW* 2.5.1.

directly shaped by his mother's experience as she recounted it to him. Even if one rejects the association of Mary's parents with Sepphoris and so does not think it likely that some or all of Mary's family moved from there to Nazareth, there would most certainly have been some movement of people from city to villages at that time, and awareness of what was happening in Sepphoris in nearby villages and towns. If Mary merely saw others flee the impending siege by moving to or through her village, the point remains that Jesus likely learned about these events from his mother as well as other female relatives, and what he learned from them is reflected in his advice for those who live during the time of the next major rebellion against Roman authority, which Jesus predicted would involve Jerusalem.

Historians doubt the historicity of the infancy stories for a variety of reasons, not least of which are the tensions between them as far as the timing of events and the geographical movements are concerned. However, we should be open to the possibility that the tradition of Jesus's family relocating to Bethlehem might be a garbled recollection of an actual historical relocation during Jesus's infancy. One does not have to accept the historicity of the miracle-filled infancy narratives in the Gospels to entertain the possibility that they might be built upon more mundane movements of the family that were known to the authors. Where precisely they fled from if anywhere, and where they moved to if anywhere, does not impact the overall point, however, which is that Jesus's prediction about Jerusalem reflects his mother's experience and/or perspective. Her recollection of Varus taking Sepphoris, and probably also a recollection via his grandparents of when Herod took the city in 39–38 BCE during a snowstorm, probably influenced how Jesus spoke of a siege in Jerusalem's future.[22] We are so very prone to forget that this kind of family storytelling was how information was passed on in those times. Jesus is unlikely to have read anything akin to a history book ever in his life, but on the slim chance that he did, it would not have been one that covered events his grandparents and parents lived through. If he knew about these events it was from oral storytelling, and the details related to women's experiences indicate that he listened to and learned from women. His older relatives were likely among these, if not necessarily the only ones who told him about such experiences. Perhaps not only Jesus's predictions of devastation, if the nation continued its present

---

22. Josephus, *Ant* 14.15.4; *JW* 1.16.2.

course in relation to Rome, but also his teaching about nonviolence and nonretaliation, reflect a deep, painful awareness of the history that his mother and grandmother lived through.

One other possible scenario related to the tradition of Mary's urban upbringing but rural marriage deserves to be considered. It is possible that Mary's parents were from Nazareth but had moved to Sepphoris, and the marriage was arranged between families who had a longstanding connection in the village. In such cases of first- and second-generation city residents, it was much more common for parents to seek a match for their child in the city. But in a period immediately following a military conflict, potential male spouses may have been fewer and further between. In addition, after a siege the possibility that women had been raped was significant, and according to some rabbis, all women inhabitants of besieged cities became ineligible to marry priests because of the mere possibility that they had been subjected to this kind of abusive molestation. If Mary was of priestly lineage (she is said to be related to Elizabeth who married the priest Zechariah) this might have been her family's expectation, with her fortunes changing in the aftermath of military conflict.[23] Alternatively, they may have sent her to relatives in nearby Nazareth in the hope of sparing her the fate that might befall women who remained in the city.[24]

In this section we have been addressing traumatic experiences to which women ancient and modern have been subjected more frequently than most men realize or pay attention to. Most women do not talk about such things with their sons, if they talk about them with anyone. We can only guess whether Mary talked about such matters with her son, whether it was an aspect of her own experience or only that of other women she knew. Men are the most frequent perpetrators of rape, whether in an ancient context or today, and more parents should be proactive in seeking to ensure their male children do not become rapists than is the case now or has been in the past. Even if Mary never spoke about these things to any of her children, children often overhear adults talking about things that they had no intention of the young overhearing. If Jesus overheard conversation, or even eavesdropped, and took what he heard to heart,

23. On this see further Schaberg, *Illegitimacy*; Sawicki, *Crossing Galilee*, 125.
24. See further Jarrell, *Fallen Angels*, 148. There are also some other cases in which a marriage between a city girl and a village boy might occur, such as if the latter came to the city to study and so had opportunity to be transformed by that urban (and urbane) experience.

that is to his credit. Perhaps he realized that he had more to learn from women than they explicitly told him.

Storytelling

The use of parables was not unique to Jesus—rabbinic literature is full of them. Nevertheless, not everyone who used parables did so in an effective and powerful fashion. There is evidence that in ancient times (as often since) mothers and other women played a key role in telling stories to children. It would be going too far to follow the movie *Mary, Mother of Jesus* in having Jesus simply recycle stories he heard from Mary growing up as part of his own teaching. Nonetheless, storytelling ability, the creativity to craft new stories, and the imagination and insight to see people and situations in a new way all owe at least something to upbringing. And in a traditional patriarchal society, that means that the men who played leading roles of any sort owed such abilities (rather ironically but delightfully subversively) to the formative influence of women in general, and their mothers in particular.

In our time, eloquence and the ability to read and write have become closely linked. In the time of Mary and of Jesus (as well as for centuries upon centuries prior to and subsequent to them) this was simply not the case. Mary may or may not have been given an opportunity for formal education, but that doesn't mean she was not as serious a thinker as most in her time whatever their gender. As Penelope Duckworth writes, "It may seem a leap to call Mary a theologian, especially if we think of a theologian as someone with an advanced degree. But we all do theology . . . Like us, Mary pondered and searched for meaning and understanding. She considered, weighed, contemplated, mused, studied, meditated, examined. In doing so she did theology."[25] In the same way, Mary may or may not have been able to read the stories of others or write down her own thoughts, but that has no bearing on whether she was able to articulate her own perspective and weave narratives with eloquence, and to teach her son to do the same.

---

25. Duckworth, *Mary*, 59. See also Johnson, *Mary Our Sister*, 67.

Prayer

Learning prayers from one's mother, perhaps at bedtime, has been a stereotypical part of traditional family life in Europe and North America (although one that I suspect has fallen to the wayside in many households in the present day). Would this or something like it have been true in ancient Galilee? It is hard to know for certain, but Mary Athans expresses the inherent probability of this well when she writes, "Since Jewish children often learned their first prayers and home rituals from their mothers, it is not unrealistic to presume that Mary would have taught Jesus his earliest prayers and instructed him in simple Jewish rituals."[26] We should not expect to have in our sources recorded details of Mary teaching her children to pray, whether kneeling at their bedside with them before sleep as per the custom in later times, or more likely doing so in a standing posture as was the custom then. There are many details we would love to have recorded about both Mary and Jesus that are simply not the kinds of things people wrote down in the ancient world. We do not need to have a record of precisely when, where, and how often she did so to have good reason to think the prayer life of Mary influenced Jesus. That is certainly the impression that the Gospel of Luke presents us with. Jesus's most famous prayer, "your will be done," whether we have in mind his own desperate utterance in the Garden of Gethsemane or his instructions to his disciples, is not that distant from Mary's "Let it be unto me" (Luke 1:38). Margaret Hebblethwaite envisages Mary teaching Jesus to pray specific things such as "Let your will be done" and "May your reign come."[27] Whether that actually happened we may never know, but one's instinctive reaction to find it inherently plausible or difficult to accept may tell us important things about how we view both Jesus and his mother. Considered historically, the fact that Luke, the earliest author to record Mary's ongoing involvement in the church, also depicts Mary's own poetry and prayer being echoed in those of Jesus, deserves to be taken very seriously.

---

26. Athans, *In Quest of the Jewish Mary*, ch. 5.
27. Hebblethwaite, *Six New Gospels*, 35,46.

Family Ties

The story is told (Mark 3:31–35 and parallels) of Jesus's mother and siblings wanting to see him when he was teaching. When the fact that they were waiting for him was pointed out, Jesus said that all who do God's will are his mother and siblings. Many assume that this was Jesus casting aspersions on his immediate family, denigrating and insulting them. That is certainly one possible interpretation of what was going on. But it rests on the assumption that Jesus's mother and brothers did not share in and support his effort to create a more broadly-defined family that transcends biological kinship. Some families are insular and build literal and/or figurative walls between themselves and outsiders. Other families are very different and are constantly welcoming unexpected guests, building bridges, and seeking to treat others as if they were their own flesh and blood. Why do interpreters tend to assume that Jesus's family fell into the former category? Perhaps it is because it makes Jesus seem more special. The desire to make Jesus alone the source of his perspective regularly drives a wedge between him and his mother that is historically implausible. Whether Jesus's family was supportive or not of his activity at this point in his public career, Jesus's words on this topic were certainly felt to be noteworthy. His words struck Jesus's disciples and made an impression on them, so much so that the disciples felt the words were worth remembering and recording. The question whether Jesus's family was also struck, shocked, and/or offended is a different one. Perhaps Mary nodded approvingly that Jesus was teaching others to think in the way that he had been brought up to. Either way, Jesus's family (including his female relatives) taught him something, whether through their support or their skepticism, or very possibly (in view of his statements about families being divided on his account) through both, depending on which member of his family happens to be in view.

One interesting question worth asking (alas, another one that we cannot hope to answer with certainty) relates to the family's reputation of being descended from David. They were by no means the only such family in that era. As far as we can tell, Joseph did not at any point claim to be the rightful heir to the royal throne. The family might have kept alive a memory of a royal connection in their ancestry nonetheless. Anyone who has done family history research, especially if they have heard rumors of noble ancestry, may have had the experience of finding surprising things in parish records. More often than not the evidence may show that one's family does not have the noble connections family lore claimed. Occasionally, however, connections with notable and influential figures turn up, sometimes even when there was no family tradition that kept the memory of that ancestral link alive. In the case of Jesus, we get a sense that his family was one of modest means although not destitute. At the same time, his opponents do not question his reputation as "son of David" as they might be expected to if this were a recent invention no one had heard before. How might it have influenced Jesus to be told as a child that he came from an illustrious royal line of ancestors? What might it have been like being told by one's mother growing up that one's family is descended from David? A what might it have been like to be told that and yet have neither wealth nor status that might be expected to go hand in hand with such a family identification, even if the dynasty no longer possessed a throne and crown? It seems appropriate to mention *Tess of the d'Urbervilles* (Thomas Hardy) as indicative of the way a supposed family line could potentially, for a relatively poor family, inspire hope that could lead to unanticipated and undesired consequences. But the setting of that novel does not correspond precisely to the time of Jesus and so it is probably best to not make too much of the comparison. What we can say is Jesus's family lived with a reputation that some admired and respected, and which may have led them to expect that one day they would eventually have an influence beyond their local trade and other roles in rural Galilean life. If nothing else, this may have awoken in the family as a whole, and in Jesus in particular, a sense of how the fortunes of royalty and thus perhaps also of ordinary people can change. The first can become last and the last first. That too may be a lesson that was at least in part shaped by his mother's teaching about their family history. It also may indicate that Mary mediated to Jesus not only knowledge of Scripture, but knowledge of other Jewish traditions and literature, in particular those connected with the figure of Enoch. 1 Enoch 46 not only envisages the coming messianic "Son of Man," but connects it with the bringing down of rulers and the powerful from their thrones, similar language to that used by Mary.[28]

---

28. Baynes, "Parables of Enoch and Luke's Parable," 144–45.

Social Justice, Prophecy, and Religious Vision

The New Testament gives the impression that Jesus's concern for social justice is something he got directly from his mother. Paula Trimble-Familetti writes, "Unlike most women in the Bible, Mary, the mother of Jesus, has a voice, although most of her story is told about her, rather than by her. We are given very few glimpses into the relationship between Jesus and his mother, even though she appears in all four gospels and in the Acts of the Apostles."[29] The Gospel of Luke attributes words to Mary, and what she says is noteworthy, especially when we consider them in relation to the words attributed to her son. The Magnificat (Luke 1:46–55) depicts Mary emphasizing that God would bring about a reversal of the situations of rich and poor. In Luke's version of the beatitudes (6:20–26), Jesus emphasizes the same thing. Together these texts convey the impression that Jesus learned these things from his mother. Cheryl Duggan writes, "Her strategy for confronting oppression unfolds within the Magnificat."[30] Expanding our survey to the rest of the New Testament, we find that Jesus is not the only member of this family who seems to have been influenced by teaching akin to what the Gospel of Luke attributes to Mary. James Darlack has said, "The Magnificat is right at home with the Epistle of James. I've often imagined Mary humming the Magnificat while bouncing James on her knee."[31] For our purpose, it doesn't matter whether that letter was in fact written by James the brother of Jesus, any more than it matters whether the Magnificat reflects an actual utterance of Mary. From a historical perspective it is sufficient that multiple early Christian authors indicate they had this impression of what Mary's teaching was and that she instilled these values in her children.

Duckworth notes how Mary's song takes up themes from the Hebrew prophets in distinctive ways, and then her son Jesus in turn takes them up and elaborates them. Three themes that she highlights in this regard are the mercy of God, God's alignment with the poor, and God

---

29. Trimble-Familetti, *Prostitutes, Virgins and Mothers*, 77.

30. Kirk-Duggan, "Proud Mary," 76.

31. Facebook comment from January 24, 2019. Darlack attributed the sentiment to McKnight, *Real Mary*, 102–5. See further Scot McKnight's blog post on this topic, in which he also mentions Alfred Plummer as one of the scholars who has also commented on the Letter of James and the Magnificat and connections between the two. https://www.patheos.com/blogs/jesuscreed/2006/09/12/woman-in-ministry/.

as the God of the humble.³² Readers of Luke's Gospel get the sense both that Mary had been educated in the Scriptures, and that she passed on her own education to her son who carried on in a manner faithful to his upbringing. We might add to this something else the prophets regularly did, namely talking back to those in authority. We noted earlier that Mary might have warned Jesus about the dangers of interacting with the powerful. We should not understand that to mean she cautioned him to avoid speaking and acting against injustice. Once again, perspectives from diverse experiences provide crucial insights. Black mothers in the United States can worry about their sons and prepare them with advice about how to survive encounters with police, and yet also infuse them with a strong spirit of activism for social justice. The two are not mutually exclusive.

Did Mary teach her son he would be the anointed one, the Messiah? Did she expect he might become a prophet, or a rabbi, or something else? How early did she foresee where Jesus might be headed, and what role did she play in influencing him in that direction? Commentators have often noticed the fact that Joseph and Mary gave their children solid biblical names, which may indicate something about their religious perspective. Sarah Hardman views the past tenses in the Magnificat as prophetic perfects, that is to say, statements about the future expressed as though they had already occurred, in the manner characteristic of Israel's prophets.³³ And of course, when Luke has her predict all generations will call her blessed, that too may be considered a prophecy. We cannot say whether Mary understood herself as a prophet, but Luke depicts her as one, and her son Jesus may have perceived her to be one in view of her manner of speaking about matters like social justice and future hope, and perhaps even right down to the poetic form and tenses she used.³⁴

Compassion

The story of the wedding at Cana is found only in John and includes a miracle of a sort that does not lend itself to natural explanation. This

---

32. Duckworth, *Mary*, 23–24. As we saw earlier, the deep awareness of major themes in the Jewish Scriptures also indicates something about Mary's own educational experience.

33. Gaventa, *Mary*, 58–59; Hardman, "My Soul Rejoices." See also Getty-Sullivan, *Women*, 35.

34. Foskett, "Mary," 455–56.

leads most historians to view the details and perhaps the entire thing as a story created for symbolic purposes, to depict Jesus as one who replaces water for observance of purity regulations with wine of rejoicing. However, once again one needn't accept the story as historical to accept the point we are making here about the impression of Mary, Jesus, and the relationship between the two that our earliest Christian authors had. They can be expected to have sought to create material that rang true to what people knew about the individuals in question, and to have had to argue strenuously if they were depicting them in a manner that was at odds with that shared knowledge. In the story about the wedding at Cana, Mary is portrayed as noticing the impending shame that loomed over the newly-married couple, and acting to seek a solution for them.[35] She then persuades Jesus to do something despite his reluctance.[36] Miraculous elements in stories are accentuated and increased over time, and sometimes miraculous details are added to stories that originally lacked them. Whether anything of that sort happened in this particular instance need not concern us here nor distract us from our main focus. Note what the author of the Gospel conveys about Jesus and his mother here. Mary comes across here as more compassionate than Jesus towards those liable to be shamed before their family and friends. She is persuaded that the need to act compassionately should take priority over all sorts of other things, perhaps even divinely-ordained timing. In his subsequent public activity, Jesus would be seen to act and tell stories that reflect this key emphasis. The Samaritan on the Jericho road prioritized compassion (Luke 10:25–37).[37] The need for healing and even simply being hungry

---

35. McKenna, *Mary*, 105; Nyirimana and Draper, "Peace-Making Mother," 6–7; Storkey, *Women in a Patriarchal World*, 89.

36. On the other hand, it has been suggested that Mary is simply noting the shortage of wine and suggesting that Jesus and his friends leave! See, e.g., Perry, *Mary for Evangelicals*, 99. There are many ways one might elaborate further on the story, perhaps imagining a whispered conversation taking place between John 2:4 and John 2:5. Storkey, *Women in a Patriarchal World*, suggests the reply of Jesus that his time had not yet come could be a joke: it isn't his wedding, so he isn't the bridegroom at this event, and so it isn't his place to ensure wine is provided.

37. Levine, *Short Stories*, 99–101 argues that the priest is not motivated by purity concerns as is often claimed. A priest might have appealed to Leviticus 21:1–4 to justify inaction in this circumstance. However, the Torah also required burial of corpses as well as compassion towards neighbors. Whatever one thinks the motives of the priest and Levite may have been, Jesus's point is not anti-Torah, but precisely that the Torah required the priest and Levite to act and they failed to. The Mishnah and Talmud provide evidence that the stance Jesus argues for here was widely accepted in Judaism and not original to him.

takes priority over the Sabbath (Mark 2:25–27). Jesus is famous for having emphasized these things when he taught others, so much so that we could easily fail to observe that in the story of the wedding at Cana, Jesus does not seem to have grasped the point as yet or to be putting it into practice.[38] Whatever the historicity of the incident, the story shows Mary teaching Jesus something that would later characterize his life and teaching.

Humility

Mary is depicted as responding to the angelic announcement of her conception with humility in the Lukan infancy story.[39] Yet Hebblethwaite writes of Mary's submissive "let it be": "The *fiat* has been damaging to women in their spirituality when it has been taken to imply an attitude of female submission rather than of human submission."[40] After discussing the problematic way that Luther and others have written about Mary, praising her humility and ordinariness, Hebblethwaite further observes, "It is difficult to imagine a man being praised so effusively for leading such humble, lowly life."[41] This makes a key point in the context of the present study. Mary did not merely provide an example of humility but taught her son to do likewise, following her example even when it meant behaving in ways that did not conform to expectations about masculinity in his cultural context.[42] If Jesus lived in a manner that didn't conform

---

38. Blue, *Consider the Women*, 141 writes, "She thinks he should make himself useful—he should help these people in this real moment in their real lives . . . Mary is thoughtful in this scene, but Jesus doesn't come across all that generous in this moment." See also Sergio, *Jesus and Woman*, 23–26. Perry (*Mary for Evangelicals*, 99–101) follows Brown et al. (*Mary in the New Testament*, 188) in seeing a literal level at which the wine has run out and Mary tells Jesus as a way of saying he should leave because the wine has run out, to avoid bringing shame on his own family. Mary's instructions to the servants, however, suggests that the author sees Mary as looking for Jesus to help remedy the situation in some way other than by merely departing before things get ugly.

39. Mackall, *Kindred Sisters*, 25–26.

40. Hebblethwaite, *Six New Gospels*, 24.

41. Hebblethwaite, *Six New Gospels*, p25–26.

42. On this topic see further Dreyer, "Jesus and the Full Personhood," 66–67, following Jacobs-Malina, *Beyond Patriarchy*. Conway, *Behold the Man*, highlights ways that New Testament authors emphasize the masculinity of Jesus in relation to cultural norms and values of their time. Also Wilson, *Unmanly Men*, esp. ch. 6; Myers, "Gender."

rigidly to gender expectations in his time and place, we can be certain he must have had mentors who were both men and women who provided important examples to him. If so, it may be that Paul's later theologizing, claiming that there is in Christ no male and female for all are one in Christ (Gal 3:28), may be at least loosely inspired by the impression that Jesus made on his followers.[43]

Self-Sacrifice and Hardship

Kathleen Gallagher Elkins has studied the paradigm of maternal self-sacrifice in ancient Jewish and Christian literature.[44] In the very process of bearing a child, mothers experience pain. They also regularly make sacrifices in the interest of their children throughout their lives. Jesus would have seen at least the latter in the case of his mother, and possibly the former if he had younger siblings. Ancient church traditions vary on whether Jesus was the oldest of many children that Mary and Joseph had together, or the first and only child of Mary who married Joseph when Joseph was an older widow who already had children from his prior marriage. Depending on which scenario is deemed more historically likely, Jesus might have been the oldest or the youngest child in his family. If the former, he may well have had the opportunity to witness and/or hear about his own mother's experience of childbearing. If the latter, he may have had older sisters who married and had children. Either way, we are told that Jesus made reference to labor pains in a manner that was an established part of Jewish tradition, the "birth pangs of the messiah" denoting the troubles that would come upon the world and upon God's people before the redeemer arrived (Mark 13:8). However, according to John 16:21 Jesus also chose to use the experience of labor and childbirth as a metaphor for enduring the hardship of separation as he prepared his disciples to cope with his death, promising that they would be reunited. If

---

43. We will revisit this point in our conclusion. Note as well that the idea of Mary as counterpart to Eve appears already in Justin Martyr and Irenaeus in the second century, and so was extremely early. Is it likely that Christians who had already come to view Jesus as the second Adam would turn his mother into the counterpart of Eve? Perhaps Jesus was not the first person in his immediate family to believe that he had a significant role to play in the fulfillment of God's plans for humanity. He may have inherited this, learned this, from his mother. See also Kateusz, *Mary*, on Mary as priest in later iconography. It would be interesting to explore how this too might potentially be relevant to how we think about the historical Mary.

44. Elkins, *Mary*.

Mary was present when he said this, it would have been particularly poignant. Jesus's choice to use this particular metaphor not only as a stock expression, but in other contexts and with greater attention to the detail of women's experience, shows he learned something from listening to women speak about the experience of giving birth.

Mothers continue to make sacrifices for their children long after the labor pains have ended. It is a challenge for feminist study of the Bible and of gender to find ways of affirming this as a choice women legitimately make while at the same time critiquing the *imposition* of self-sacrifice and motherhood on women as part of their gender role, irrespective of their own wills and to the exclusion of other possibilities of self-expression. There is reason to think that Jesus will have seen in his own mother both the pain of societal demands imposed and the beauty of self-sacrificing love freely offered. This in turn shaped his own attempt to walk a tightrope and to provide teaching to his followers that offered a vision of how that might be done not only individually but also communally, by men as well as women.

We will have opportunity to discuss Jesus learning from other widows in later chapters. But there is some evidence that Jesus's own mother may have been a widow by the time he was an adult.[45] Not only does Joseph not make an appearance in the Gospels other than in stories about Jesus's childhood, but there is a church tradition that Joseph was significantly older than Mary. That may or may not reflect accurate historical knowledge, but it was so common for women to die in childbirth and for men to remarry at least once that this is a possibility we should consider simply on its inherent probability, even apart from other evidence. When Jesus mentioned scribes devouring the property of widows, or made a widow seeking justice the focus of a parable, he had in mind primarily the widow without male children to serve as head of the household and provide income as well as defend the family's property and honor. These were among the most vulnerable people in this and many other ancient societies. But that doesn't mean that widows with male children had life easy. Moreover, if Mary was Joseph's second wife, the children of his first

45. On this see in particular Mbuvi, "Jesus and His Mother." Had Mary married an older man? Hebblewaithe (*Six New Gospels*, 41n35) claims it is unnecessary to think that Mary outlived Joseph as a widow, since women tend to live longer than men. However true this may be in the present day, it was not the case in the ancient world, in which women frequently died in childbirth. She also notes the possibility that John 6:42 could be taken to mean that Joseph is still alive but also notes the counter evidence in ch. 2 in which Mary alone of Jesus's parents appears to have gone to the wedding.

wife may have felt little obligation to assist and support her, and so there may have been times, in the years before Jesus was old enough to advocate effectively on her behalf, when Mary felt quite vulnerable.[46]

Jesus's compassion for society's most vulnerable in his adult life was built on the foundation of empathy formed in the crucible of loss of parent/spouse that he and his own mother appear to have suffered. The very need for a widow without adequate financial resources to rely on sons to advocate on behalf of the family made Jesus aware of how certain social dynamics worked in his time. Before he made reference to widows' hardships as an illustration in parables, he may first have caught a glimpse of their experience to at least some extent in his own mother's circumstances. He probably never saw her have to go to an unjust judge to plead her case (Luke 18:1–18). But he saw enough to later notice the hardships that some around him faced which were even greater than those of his own mother. What he learned from her about social justice and what he saw of relative vulnerability primed him to observe and learn still more. It prepared him to some small extent, as we'll see in other chapters, to have a change of heart when a Syrophoenician or Canaanite woman pled with him.[47]

Affirmation

We see Mary as an ongoing presence in Jesus's adult life and she is mentioned as a part of the continuing movement after his death (Acts 1:14). We have focused most of our attention in this chapter on Mary's influence on Jesus as a child, and that is appropriate, since one's upbringing shapes them in ways that nothing else does or can. But we should not neglect the fact that Jesus continued to learn from Mary in his adult

---

46. Blue, *Consider the Women*, 151 brings the Infancy Gospel of James and the History of Joseph the Carpenter into the picture, and imagines Mary taking care of Joseph's motherless sons who are not all that different in age from herself. On the other hand, the claim that he was the Davidic anointed one, with no competing suggestion that it might be one of his brothers, strongly supports the view that Jesus was the eldest.

47. On Mary's strength of character faced with a skeptical fiancée who tries to put her in her socially defined place, as depicted in first-person fictionalized accounts in the Syriac Christian tradition, see Harvey, "On Mary's Voice," 75–76. Hebblethwaite (*Six New Gospels*, 34n24) considers the possibility that Jesus's family fled from authorities as depicted in Matthew, and that the experience of exile and of reliance on hospitality was shared with him later, influencing his own teaching.

years. As we have already mentioned, it is sometimes thought that Jesus's family opposed his activity, but in view of what Jesus says about families being divided because of him, we ought to treat that as reflecting his own experience as well. Mary his mother and James his brother are depicted as involved in the early Christian movement without any sense that they have just recently reversed their viewpoint. Others in his family may have been less supportive, as John 7:5 suggests. The statement in Mark 3:21 does not refer explicitly to Jesus's family but only says, "those with him" or "those close to him" judged him to be "out of his mind." Most English translations assume this is a reference to his family, but there is actually a good reason not to draw that conclusion. The mention of the arrival of Jesus's mother and brothers in Mark 3:31 suggests they weren't the ones seeking to seize him just prior to that in v. 21. Jesus definitely called his disciples to leave family ties and responsibilities behind and dedicate themselves wholly to the kingdom of God. Some or all of his immediate family might have felt him to be shirking his responsibility to them. At the same time, Jesus is depicted as affirming the commandment to honor one's father and mother, even defending it against being undermined by a legal loophole (Mark 7:9–13). Even if there were sometimes tensions between Jesus and his family, including with his mother and sisters, we get a sense in the case of his mother that however much their relationship may have been strained, it was not broken. Far from viewing Mary as a critic of Jesus's activity, we ought to envision her defending him in the circle of his family connections, precisely because she saw her own teaching and influence reflected in what he said and did, and saw his openness to continuing to learn from his relationship with her even into adulthood. Perhaps the most important element in the relationship between adult son and mother would have been her indications that she was proud of him, of who he had turned out to be, and in particular, of the way he treated women and the things he taught about and to them.[48] Believing

---

48. Trimble-Familetti, *Prostitutes, Virgins and Mothers*, 89, imagines Mary the mother of Jesus speaking about Jesus and his female friends in this way: "One of his best friends was dear Mary Magdalene. She had been so ill before my son's healing presence in her life. There was fiery Salome and her sons. They were convinced that Jesus would establish the new government. Mary, Martha and Lazarus of Bethany were such good friends to my son. It was unusual for a man to have such close women friends, but my son saw the magnificence of everyone. Mary would sit and listen to Jesus teach, just like the boys who were allowed to go to school sat with their teachers." Swidler, *Three Jesus Certitudes*, 123–24 mentions the possibility of Mary's memoirs being an influence on Luke's Gospel.

in Jesus would become an important part of the movement around him and remains so down to the present day. The long history of focusing on belief in Jesus as a divine figure as a means to human salvation has made it nearly impossible for us to think of how other human beings responding to Jesus with belief, with trust and confidence, provided him with encouragement and support, facilitating belief in himself and self-confidence that made so much of what he accomplished possible. Christians may believe in Jesus in ways that are unique, but we should not allow that to negate the aspects of belief that were directed at him as a human being, who was affected by this as human beings continue to be in our ongoing experiences of human life. Parental confidence in us makes so much of what a child accomplishes throughout their life possible. In contexts such as the wedding at Cana, where Mary seems persuaded Jesus is ready when he believes he is not yet, we can imagine Mary as like a mother bird pushing her offspring out of the nest.[49] Jesus "flew" because of Mary, and in a motherly way can be said to be the first person who "believed in Jesus." Providing encouragement to one's child, showing confidence in them so that they gain confidence in themselves, is also a part of education, one that continues into adulthood.

Conclusion

Luke's Gospel emphasizes that Jesus learned (Luke 2:52). Luke is also the only Gospel author who gives us material that provides us with the opportunity to learn from the one from whom Jesus learned, by attributing words filled with rich content to his mother, content that would be echoed in Jesus's own teaching. In theory Luke could have provided examples of what Jesus might have learned from both his parents, giving Joseph a poetic utterance akin to the Magnificat. Whether he does not do so, but only offers us information about the theology and poetic ability of Jesus's mother, because that was all the information that reached him, or because it was what he judged most important and interesting out of a wider array of information at his disposal, we cannot say for certain. Perhaps it was because of her ongoing voice as active participant in the Christian movement. Whichever of these may be the case, it tells us something important. Luke more than any other Gospel author was

---

49. This image was suggested to me by Rev. Joy Amick in a conversation in my Sunday school class.

aware of and had information about the kind of person Mary was and what she had to say. In depicting continuity between mother and son in their words and emphases, Luke provides us with a natural place to begin exploring what Jesus learned from women, with the woman he learned from first.[50]

When others have adopted the view that Mary and Jesus were at loggerheads about his public activity, I suspect it is part of an effort to make Jesus "his own man" (or even a divine figure who needs no earthly tutors). Historical methods and inherent probability on the other hand converge on an affirmation that ought not to be controversial in the least: the human being Jesus was taught by and learned from his mother. Even if a few of the details in this chapter seem too speculative or uncertain, hopefully there is enough in the combination of what our early sources say and what we know about human family life in general to justify the conclusion that his mother Mary was the woman from whom Jesus learned first. She was by no means the only one, as the remaining chapters in this book will demonstrate. But by virtue of her role as parent, she was the natural place to begin. And in a sense, far from having speculated too much, there is a real sense in which we cannot possibly have gone far enough. Jesus must by definition have learned far more from his mother than the pages of this book could hold. We certainly may have gotten some things wrong. On the other hand, we have barely begun to scratch the surface of what Jesus undoubtedly learned from Mary, as that remarkable woman brought up this remarkable man in a way that clearly left her imprint on his way of living and thinking. His expectation that he would and should learn from women most likely began at home.

---

50. Hebblethwaite, *Six New Gospels*, 36 depicts Mary saying, "Joseph was the practical one of the family, and I was the one who introduced Jesus to theology, which became a burning passion in him. He could make a table too, and as he grew up he worked contentedly enough alongside Joseph to support the family. But it did not fulfill him: there was so much left over, so many dreams to live out, so many arguments to work through. He loved an intellectual challenge, and could defeat anyone he took on, and all the time he turned a chair leg his mind would be wrestling with what God was asking of his people in our day."

At Grandma's House
What Jesus Learned Visiting the Big City on a Hill

"Thank you, Jesus!"

My young grandson smiled as he delivered to me the basket of items I had sent him to the city market to fetch. It is hard to believe how fast he has grown. It seems like only yesterday that, when Joseph came into Sepphoris to work on a construction project, if Jesus accompanied him it was to stay here with me, as he was too little to be of help in building and would more than likely get in harm's way. Now, here he was running errands and making purchases for me. Soon he'll be able to help his father with construction work. Then I will see less of him. How time flies.

"What did you see in the city this time," I asked him. Nazareth was so close to the city, and yet life there was so different. Nothing that compares with the hustle and bustle here in Sepphoris. No theater, none of the beautiful mosaics, and nothing like the diversity of cultures we have here. That's the reason I encouraged Mary to send the children to visit me whenever she can, so that I can provide them with some of the experiences that she benefited from growing up. Not that I resent their living out there in Nazareth. Joseph was a good match for Mary, from an excellent family, with a good trade, and he treats her well. His work brings him and his children into the city often, and it is easy for Mary to visit, and for me to visit her, although the journey there and back seems to take longer these days. I am getting old.

"I saw soldiers!" Jesus said, excitedly. I felt the blood drain from my face. Even though Sepphoris had been rebuilt and was now prospering,

I cannot forget what happened after the rebellion, when I was younger. Roman soldiers came through burning, stealing, and doing unspeakable things to women and men alike. No families were left untouched.

"What did they look like?" I asked him. *My heart stopped beating so wildly as I heard his description. These were Herod's troops, Jews from around Galilee who served as peacekeepers and protected commerce. They were mostly trustworthy. Most of them. Most of the time.*

"What else?" *I prompted him to continue describing his experiences, as I returned to making lunch for when Joseph and his men took their break.*

"I heard loud voices coming from the theater," Jesus said. *I smiled. There had been no need for the boy to pass that way on the errands I had sent him on, and so he had clearly gone out of his way. I knew he found the theater in Sepphoris fascinating.* "Tell me, grandma, how do they make their voices so loud? I don't think I could shout that loud, to be heard by a large crowd, and even on the streets outside of a building. *I explained to him that they weren't shouting. Actors and singers learn to use their voices in a different way, to project the sound. My uncle who was a cantor had explained it to us when we were children. I sang a couple of songs with Jesus and explained it to him. He caught on quickly, and you could tell that he would develop a lovely voice if he kept working on it.*

"Did you understand what the voices in the theater were saying?" *I asked him.*

"Only a little. They use such different words than I hear in the marketplace." *Jesus had already picked up enough Greek to do shopping in our city, where there were sellers and buyers from many different places and peoples and so having at least a little Greek was essential to getting things done. Jesus would learn still more assisting Joseph in his work. The hired workers brought in to help on any really big construction project might include people from a variety of places. It might be worth getting him a tutor to learn more. It could certainly prove useful to Joseph's work, never mind if the child grows up to become a teacher or something else. I wonder whether his parents have thought of that. I'll have to ask. In the meantime, I can teach him a little more than he has already learned. It only takes living and shopping in Sepphoris to pick up quite a bit, although obviously it isn't the polished Greek of the actor or the philosopher.*

I was about to ask Jesus if he remembered any of the words that he heard but did not understand, when we were interrupted by shouting. Jesus's sister came running in shouting, "Grandma, grandma, come quick!" Jesus followed me as I set my food preparations aside and went with the girl. As we emerged from the house, James and Joses came into the courtyard, the former helping the latter, who had scraped his knee badly and was bleeding. I ran over to him to see how bad the wound was, and then went to work quickly, instinctively using skills that I had learned from my own grandmother. I poured some water on his knee, then rubbed some olive oil with thyme on it. Finally I spat on it and rubbed it again. I asked him how he felt and he told me that it seemed a little less painful already. Soon the two boys ran outside to play again, Joses definitely slower and more cautious on the one leg than the other, but already seeming better than when he came in. As I returned my attention to Jesus, I saw he had been watching me closely, as he often did when I applied what I knew of medicine to him or his brothers and sisters, and even sometimes Joseph or Mary. I remember once recently when Joseph had a headache, I suspected that someone might have afflicted him with the evil eye. I rubbed a mixture of oil and comfrey on his head, and then prepared some water with a few drops of the infused oil, saying a prayer before giving it to him to drink. He felt better quickly. Jesus had found the whole thing fascinating. Noticing his interest, I later asked him to fetch me some comfrey from the field, explaining to him what to look for and where to find it, and that the leaves and roots from that plant had been in the oil I had smeared on his father's temples. He watched with intense interest as I ground the leaves and roots of the plant he had brought me and then added oil to make more of the ointment I had applied to his father's head. Another time when his mother had pain in her eyes, I applied saliva to them seven times, as I had learned from the wife of a rabbi who lives in Tiberias. This too fascinated Jesus.

I know that remedies are mostly the province of women, passed on from generation to generation. But sometimes men become healers, and occasionally they show a real gift for it. I wonder whether Jesus will show an aptitude for that in the future. But as I turn to look at the grandson who was the focus of my thoughts, I find that he has already left me to join his brothers outside at play. I return to my food preparations, knowing that soon enough Joseph and his workmen would be here, famished from their day's labors. After that Jesus, James, Joses, and the others would come in to eat as well. It will only be a few more years until that will change, and one by one the sons of Joseph will change their roles and come to Sepphoris to work rather than to play . . .

Many might assume that, in the ancient world, relatively few people had the opportunity to know their grandparents. Lifespans, we are often told, were generally shorter than they are today in most parts of the world in which readers of this book are likely located. If a child knew a grandparent, it would more likely be the grandfather, because women's mortality rates were higher than those of men. However, this doesn't necessarily mean that knowing one's grandmother was something very rare in the ancient world, any more than we can generalize that everyone in a modern society today with lower infant mortality rates and increased lifespans, thanks to advances in medical care, has the opportunity to know their grandparents.[1] It is easy to misunderstand what the average lifespan in antiquity represents. When one factors out the increased likelihood of infant mortality and of death in childbirth in ancient times, lifespans of 50 to 60 years become the norm for those who survived childbirth, whether as the one being born or the one giving birth. We certainly know of individuals mentioned in ancient literature who were raised by a grandmother, and who interacted with her throughout their adult life. To the extent that one might attempt to generate a statistic or calculate odds based on the information available to us, it is as likely as not that Jesus would have known one or both of his grandparents at least while he was a child. Indeed, it was not all that infrequent for three generations of a family to reside in the same home at some point. We don't know for certain whether Jesus had the opportunity to meet one or both of his grandmothers, but it is a possibility that deserves to be explored.[2] There is certainly nothing implausible about those traditions depicting Mary's parents (named Anna and Joachim in sources outside the New Testament) as living at least long enough to see Jesus as a child, and perhaps even (as Anna is often portrayed as doing in paintings) to read to him.

---

1. 2 Tim 1:5 says that the recipient had learned from his grandmother as well as his mother.
2. For an exploration of statistics see Parkin, "Roman Life Course," 279, 284–85.

Some may wonder how we can hope to say anything worthwhile about this topic when neither Mary's nor Joseph's parents appear as characters in the New Testament. We have two genealogies that claim to trace Joseph's genealogy, found in the Gospels of Matthew and Luke, and they do not agree even on the name of Joseph's father, nor on the lineage that supposedly connected Joseph to David as a distant ancestor. Some have attempted to turn one of the genealogies into Mary's in an effort to avoid the contradiction, despite the fact that this maneuver contradicts what the Gospels explicitly state in the act of trying to avoid having them contradict one another! In ancient times, it was the father's genealogy that mattered, and despite the incompatible lists of names in Matthew and Luke, we have no reason to doubt that Joseph's family had the reputation of being descended from the illustrious king David. In the present day, when we have the assistance of DNA databases and online aids, many people who claim to have royal ancestors turn out not to, while others discover illustrious ancestors they had no idea they were related to. What a genetic test of Jesus might have revealed need not detain us. What we are interested in is what the church's stories suggest about female relatives in general, and grandmothers in particular, that might also indicate what Jesus learned from them. We can investigate the status and reputation of Jesus's family as evidenced in stories about him and them. How Jesus and his relatives were *perceived* in their time is all that a historian can hope to determine in this as in most cases throughout history.

As we have already noted, explicit stories about Jesus's grandparents are altogether absent from the New Testament Gospels. Once we look beyond the New Testament, however, we discover that the church told stories about Mary's parents, giving their names as Joachim and Anna, and also indicating where they lived, namely the city of Sepphoris (Zippori in Hebrew).[3] Many details in the stories told in works like the *Protoevangelium of James* (frequently depicted in Christian art down the ages) may not be factual. But the church often set the imagined stories it crafted against the backdrop of remembered historical details such as places, and did the same when it came to names of characters where such information was available. We have probably all read authors who failed to check basic facts, and thus made major blunders even when they could easily have avoided doing so. Historians must be cautious. Given the ongoing presence of members of Jesus's family in the church, however, we may

---

3. Ward, "Sepphoris," 396–97; Folda, "Church," 88.

realistically expect that information such as the name of his grandmother and the place where she lived could have been passed on and preserved. After all, a good author will prefer to make their story more realistic by using accurate names and descriptions, even if they are writing what we would call historical fiction. Interpreters of the Gospels and those seeking the historical Jesus have wondered why this major city, Sepphoris, does not get even a mention in the New Testament, and have speculated about whether Jesus might have visited it nevertheless. Nothing in the Gospels would have naturally led the author of a later work to place Mary's parents there. We may thus suggest that this detail is likely to reflect a tidbit of historically accurate information.[4] When we combine the likelihood of Joseph's work taking him to Sepphoris at some point, with the inherent plausibility of his in-laws living there, it becomes all the more likely that Jesus visited at some point.

Galilean Judaism

Today's readers of the Bible are often unfamiliar with the geography of the region in which Jesus lived as well as its history, political realities, and divisions. It is thus rare for anyone to ask how it came to be that so much of the population of Galilee were *Jewish*. It is possible to miss in English that the terms "Jews" and "Judaism" derive from the religious and ethnic identity of the tribe and territory of Judah. The historic kingdom of Judah was located far to the south of Galilee and had its political and religious center in Jerusalem. To the north of that was Samaria, where the majority of the tribes of Israel historically lived and where the northern kingdom of Israel had been. Galilee is to the north of that, and historically had been the place where Israel's northernmost tribes resided. Why then, in Jesus's time, did the inhabitants think of themselves as connected to Judah rather than to Samaria or as a separate entity from both? The historical background is the Hasmonean kings in Jerusalem extending their rule into the region, mainly in the second century BC. In the process, they

---

4. Massey, *Women and the New Testament*, 7, says that Mary's birthplace is variously assigned to Sepphoris, Jerusalem, and Bethany down the ages, although without providing specifics about which sources are being referred to. Nevertheless, Sepphoris still stands out as historically preferable, since of these three locations it is the only one not mentioned in the New Testament and thus unlikely to be a name simply chosen from there.

also made efforts to settle Galilee with Judeans.[5] Yet we should not assume the territory was devoid of Israelite population prior to that point. The archaeological record suggests both continuities and discontinuities, which is probably the reason one finds such divergent conclusions being drawn.[6] We may suggest in light of this that it is out of the confluence of Judean and northern Israelite traditions in the region of Galilee that a number of important streams of thought and movements were born, including that represented by Jesus.[7]

The names of Mary's parents preserved in church tradition are interesting in light of this. We don't have record of the name of the king of Judah, Jehoiakim, of which Joachim is a variant form, having been popular in this era.[8] This is perhaps not surprising, given the way Jehoiakim is denigrated by Jeremiah (Jer 26; 36) and the fact that this name was apparently given to him by the Egyptian Pharaoh (so 2 Kgs 23:35).[9] This

---

5. See further on this Sawicki, *Crossing Galilee*, 133, 140; also Turnage, "Linguistic Ethos," for evidence suggesting there was felt to be a historic connection between Judea and Galilee and that this was not simply a result of Hasmonean colonization efforts.

6. Root, *First Century Galilee*, 147–49 rightly emphasizes some problems with depicting these traditions as predominating in Galilee to such an extent that they were left with a radically distinct identity. Here we are envisaging the persistence of older Israelite traditions, not arguing that these were preserved among the majority of the region's inhabitants at any particular point.

7. For instance, 1 Enoch contains references that suggest it originated in Upper Galilee. See further Nickelsburg, "Enoch, Levi, and Peter."

8. The name of Mary's father in Greek as it appears in the second-century Protoevangelium or Infancy Gospel of James might more precisely be transliterated Yōakeim, which shows its derivation even more clearly. The same name, spelled in the same manner, is found in the story in Daniel 13 in the Apocrypha. Among possibilities that need to be considered are the author of the Infancy Gospel having borrowed the name from there, and perhaps even having transformed his wife Susanna's name into Anna, although there is such a thematic difference between the two stories that it is unclear why that might have been done. More likely is the possibility of Mary's great-grandfather having known that story and taken the name from there. It need not have been known in Greek in Galilee—the Greek story in the Septuagint may represent the recording of a widely-told folktale that circulated also in Aramaic. Whatever the precise date, it was included in the Greek version of Daniel prior to any likely date we might assign to the naming of Mary's grandfather, and so was presumably popular then as well as significantly earlier.

9. This is a fascinating detail that we cannot explore here. That king's name was previously Eliakim. It is unclear what interest an Egyptian ruler would have in changing the name of a king of Judah to one with the same meaning but containing a different divine name (Yahweh rather than El), nor what the significance of the change was understood to have been.

raises interesting questions about Mary's upbringing and its relationship to what became the dominant perspective in biblical tradition. Did some in the northern regions maintain a different view of Judah's history? Anna or Anne, the name of Mary's mother in church tradition, represents the Hebrew name Hannah. That was the name of Samuel's mother, who was from Ephraim, one of the northern tribes.[10] Of course, in ancient times as today, people sometimes named their children just because they liked them, or because of family tradition. If we presume a knowledge of history and/or Scripture on the part of Joachim's and Anna's parents, however, the choice of names in both cases is at least suggestive. Why that particular king of Judah? Why the mother of a prophet who embodied Israel's distinctive northern prophetic tradition even while also being the one who anointed David king?

Galilee was a place where newly-arrived Judeans would doubtless have encountered local Israelites who had their own distinctive traditions and perspective, related to yet not always identical to those of Jews or Samaritans. Jesus's father Joseph or his parents may perhaps have been one of those newer arrivals from Judah, given his reputation of Davidic ancestry. Marriage between newcomers and locals is one means by which these separate Israelite traditions would have combined. It is intriguing, to say the least, that we see hints of this in the names given to Mary's parents in Christian sources. And it is worth noting in the present context that the heritage of that northern tradition is most naturally connected with his grandmother's and mother's branch of his family tree. Did Jesus's vision for a united Israel including all the tribes, and his vocation that incorporated elements both prophetic and royal, owe something to his parents' different family backgrounds? Was this something that he learned from women, from traditions and identity passed along his matriarchal ancestral line?

Although Sepphoris was built into a major city that would become one of the most important in Galilee, it was in many respects a newly-established one. The site had a much older history of occupation, but in terms of the city as it existed in Jesus's time, it and Nazareth appear to have been built up and settled at around the same time, during the era of the Hasmonean king Alexander Jannaeus, when he made efforts to bring this northern territory under their control and settle it with Judeans. These events occurred during the lifetime of Anna's parents and/

---

10. Hannah is preserved as the form of the name of the mother of Mary (Maryam in Arabic) in Islamic sources.

or grandparents and likely shaped the family's identity and self-understanding in important ways. The family was not part of the ruling elite, but was not without status and education, if their depiction in ancient sources is anything to go by.

Sepphoris would become much more a place of confluence of cultures in later eras. In the time of Jesus, we should not imagine it as having equal numbers of Jews and non-Jews, or of Israelites and non-Israelites.[11] It was a predominantly Jewish city that nonetheless was influenced by northern Israelite traditions as well, with some non-Israelite diversity as part of the mix but not predominant. It was not yet the wealthy and lavish city that it would later become, but it was being developed towards that future, which meant the living conditions and way of life for its inhabitants during this time period were improving.

Understanding Sepphoris and the connection of Jesus's family with it on his mother's side is crucially important to understanding Jesus. Yet we must branch out further still to get an accurate sense of their situation. Because Sepphoris became the major hub in Galilee for a while, and was quite close to Nazareth, we might fail to notice the fact that a fortified village, one of the largest in Galilee, lay even closer to Nazareth towards the southwest, namely Yafia (sometimes spelled or referred to as Japha or Joffa). It apparently had a wall or fortifications in this time period. This means that Jesus's village was on the route from one important location to another. It was not a backwater. We mention all of this here because we learn some things simply as a result of where our ancestors were born and lived. The same is true of Jesus. Our education is shaped by the locations and ways of life that shaped our ancestors whether we had the opportunity to get to know them or not, because one way or another, directly or indirectly, they influence us. What Jesus learned from women in his own family and what he continued to learn from other women in his adult life reflects not only the experience of poor agriculturalists in rural areas, as we sometimes assume, but life within and in close proximity to urban centers and to networks between cities as well as between each city and the villages and towns surrounding it. Jesus's mother's family seems to

---

11. The synagogue in later times would feature a mosaic with a zodiac, with God represented as the sun in the center. This does not date from the time of Jesus, but also probably reflects the kinds of expressions that seemed appropriate to Jews/Israelites in this area, which a certain kind of developing orthodoxy elsewhere would have frowned upon if not indeed adamantly opposed. On these see further Hachlili, "Zodiac"; also Magness, "Heaven on Earth."

Access to Education

have played a key role in giving Jesus the opportunity to experience more of life beyond his hometown than he would have otherwise.

Some historians have asked whether Jesus worked with Joseph in Sepphoris. Few ask whether, before he was old enough to help Joseph, he might have been dropped off at his grandmother's home. If her parents had a different social standing and way of life simply by virtue of living in the city, what might Jesus have learned there that went beyond what even Mary, a product of their upbringing, might have found herself able to offer Jesus in Nazareth? What Jesus learned from (and through his connection with) his grandmother can sometimes be separated from the question of where she lived and whether Jesus visited her there, while at other times it depends on whether we think she was living in Sepphoris or somewhere else. He likely learned some things simply as a result of visiting her, as we've explored in the previous section. But he also learned from her, and because of her, in more formal ways.

Grandmothers sometimes played a direct role in the life of a grandchild. For instance, in Tobit 1:8, Tobit credits his grandmother Deborah with educating him. Pliny mentions an example of a grandmother making a recommendation about her grandson's education. St. Basil emphasized his grandmother's role in his own education and Christian upbringing: "And what indeed could be a clearer proof of our faith than that we were brought up by our grandmother, a blessed woman who came from amongst you? I mean the illustrious Macrina, by whom we were taught the sayings of the most blessed Gregory (as many as she herself retained, preserved to her time in unbroken memory), and who moulded and formed us while still young in the doctrines of piety."[12] In another letter he writes, "I never held erroneous opinions about God, or, being otherwise minded, unlearned them later. Nay, the conception of God which I received in childhood from my blessed mother and my grandmother Macrina, this, developed, have I held within me; for I did not change from one opinion to another with the maturity of reason, but I perfected the principles handed down to me by them."[13] Grandmothers became directly involved in cases when one or both parents died

---

12. Basil, Letter CCIV.
13. Basil, Letter CCXXIII.

prematurely, but not only in such circumstances.[14] Pamela Sheingorn has explored the later widespread artistic tradition of depicting St. Anne as teaching Mary, holding a book, sometimes with the young Jesus benefiting from the experience, whether depicted in Anne's arms or Mary's. Both Joachim and Anne hold books in art on occasion, but Anne does so more frequently, and she is the one who seems to read to and with Mary and teach her.[15] Might this reflect some recollection about the family and Anne's education?

Identity and Diversity

Archaeological evidence shows there were significant differences between life in a village or smaller town and life in a major city in Jesus's time, much as is true today. Cities are relatively cosmopolitan. One encounters people of other languages, religions, and cultures, most often as visitors but also among long-term residents. Sepphoris didn't only provide a more diverse experience than Nazareth was likely to afford. Jesus's visits to his grandmother would also have provided an example of a lived approach to being Jewish/Israelite/Galilean in relation to others who were different. Sepphoris was predominantly Jewish, and this kind of setting provides for a different experience of diversity than when one is part of a minority group within a diverse context that is predominantly something else. We don't know what the outlook of Anna and her husband may have been towards this cosmopolitan life, other than inasmuch as we may presume to catch a glimpse of it in the lives and words of those they influenced such as Mary, Jesus, and James. We should keep in mind that James the brother of Jesus was remembered as leader of the conservative Jewish stream of Christianity, which was originally the mainstream thereof, and a critic of the liberal inclusion of uncircumcised gentiles that Paul the apostle advocated. Whether Jesus's teaching and legacy were continued more faithfully by one or the other, or whether both moved things in directions that significantly departed from anything he taught or envisaged, is not a debate we can enter here. While we might be able to assume that two children of the same parent or two students of the same teacher provide a window into the influence of that mentor upon them if they

---

14. "When I was torn too soon from my cradle and my mother's breast, kindly was her early training though hid beneath stern rule" (Ausonius, *Parentalia* V).

15. Sheingorn, "Wise Mother."

agree, we cannot do the same when it is unclear whether and to what extent they did. Either way, however, visits to Sepphoris provided Jesus with opportunities to encounter multiple forms of coexistence as well as the inevitable tensions. The experience itself, mediated by Anna and her husband, would have taught him much. Jesus and his siblings might even have picked up some Greek in that context, whether formally or informally, whether in the home or in the marketplace.

A Sense of History

One thing we often get from grandparents is a connection with the past, as they share stories about their lives and memories. While we cannot actually listen in on the stories Anna might have told in Jesus's presence, there are historical sources that let us know what events Jesus's grandparents lived through. Sepphoris, as already mentioned, was a city that had changed hands, been captured for the Romans by Herod the Great, been seized by locals after his death, been destroyed by the Romans, seen the rebels sold into slavery, been rebuilt and turned into the capital of Galilee, and all this within the probable lifetime of Jesus's grandparents. Living there, they would either have experienced these things, or have moved there when it was rebuilt with a strong sense of awareness of the place's history (and with some particular motivation for doing so that we could probably never hope to surmise). Living there or moving there both indicate the likelihood that these were individuals with some means and status. The assumption that Jesus was a rural peasant doesn't fit with this. Of course, it could be that the traditions about his grandparents are wrong. But the impression given in our earliest sources, including the way others interact with him, suggests that we should allow the connection of Anna with Sepphoris to add to and reinforce the impression that Jesus was, while certainly not part of the upper echelons, not from a family of no reputation living in abject poverty either.[16] Such a family would tend to have a strong sense of identity (whether conceived primarily in relation to city, people, religion, region, or all of the above) and of the history that brought them where they were and made them who they were. Again, this is true whether that was a longstanding connection with Galilee or a sense of connection with Judea, from which they or their ancestors had come, recently or more distantly. Those with status, however modest,

---

16. See further McGrath, "Was Jesus Illegitimate?"

were also inevitably community leaders of some description, and so Jesus would have received not only information about the past, but a sense of the need for present-day action and involvement. The sense of connection with history brought with it a sense of what we today might call community and/or political activism, and a vision for the future—whether that was seeking a return to the "good old days" or an improvement beyond the terrible way things have been and are, and whether the hope was that it would come about through human action, divine intervention, or some combination of the two. While men in a society with an honor-shame system of values are the ones who are expected to go out and engage in an active way, women were far from passive or without influence, even in the case of those who accepted traditional gender roles.

Treating Illness

In the ancient Mediterranean world as in many traditional societies today, women were the repositories of wisdom and information related to illness and cures.[17] Many readers of the Bible may already know that before modern technology provided a fuller understanding of the causes of illness, the assumption was that malevolent spirits caused most maladies. This did not mean that they could not be treated with physical remedies, however. On the contrary, that separation between material and spiritual realms was not part of their worldview. The treatments were all things that today would be considered "natural" medicine. At that time, however, they were not "alternative medicine." They were the only thing available. Before the development of modern methods using double blind trials to discern genuine effectiveness from random chance or the placebo effect, all people had in their efforts to cure diseases was a multigenerational process of trial and error, coupled with the transmission across the centuries of anecdotal evidence about what had seemed to work on at least one occasion. This involved a form of experimentation, even if not in the modern sense. Sometimes the treatment worked because there is a substance in a particular plant that has a genuine effect. Sometimes the recovery of an individual was coincidental and had nothing to do with

---

17. Yamaguchi (*Mary and Martha*, 72) writes, "In the extant literature, the product of elite males, while women are visible as patients, they are almost invisible as healers." She goes on to note how archaeological discoveries show that "male literature of the time tended to trivialize women and make them less visible, even as patients." Contrast Parker, "Women Doctors," 131–38.

what grandma gave them to treat their ailment. Even in our time, when more reliable methods are available to test and study medicines to determine what genuinely works, many people still accept the efficacy of a supposed alternative treatment based on anecdotal evidence. Looking back on Jesus's time with an air of superiority is inappropriate.

Our sources indicate Jesus was known in his time as an effective healer and exorcist. While sometimes the Gospels depict him as healing with simply a word, we also have references to him providing other treatments in the form of saliva (Mark 7:33; 8:23; John 9:6, in the latter instance mixed with dirt to make a mud paste). Ancient humans had opportunities to see dogs and other animals licking their wounds to encourage healing, and drew the conclusion that saliva had a healing property. One of the key features of ancient wisdom was observation of the natural world in an effort to learn from what could be seen there. This approach to curing ailments did not originate with Jesus or in his time. His grandmother was undoubtedly one of the first places Jesus saw care for those who were ill that incorporated such features. He may have continued to learn from others, but ancient medicine, such as it was, began in the home. For an ancient healer like Jesus who provided assistance to those whose attempts at home remedies had been ineffective, the process of learning about healing and how to approach it started in the context of family and relatives, in particular grandmothers.

The Importance of Hospitality and Meals

It is not uncommon for historians to imagine that Joseph and Jesus would have traveled to Sepphoris to work there. The city was being rebuilt and expanded in precisely that period, and carpentry, stone masonry, and other such skills would have been in demand. They would have eaten at Joseph's in-laws' home when working in Sepphoris. That was simply what people did. Hospitality was a crucial facet of ancient life and the values of Mediterranean societies. Plutarch says, "[Lucius] recalled hearing from his grandmother that the table is sacred and that nothing sacred should be empty."[18] The idea that meals are sacred was widely held in ancient times, but the implications of this principle were a point of dispute among different individuals and groups. When he was older, Jesus would find himself at loggerheads with the Pharisees over precisely this point.

18. Plutarch, *Table Talk* VII.7.

Their approach was to bring the purity of the temple into everyday life and meals in particular. Jesus's approach was not concerned with purity in this way. Moreover, his inclusive table fellowship got him labeled as a glutton and drunkard, one who eats with all kinds of riff raff and sinners (Luke 7:34). The very act of complaining about Jesus doing this indicates that his opponents expected him to behave differently, and that tells us something about his status and upbringing.[19] Once again, we can only speculate about whether Anna's practices of hospitality, perhaps inviting to meals some whose presence others did not appreciate, helped shape Jesus's own approach to the symbolic significance of eating together and the transgressing of boundaries of both purity and status. But we can safely say that Jesus's grandmother and other female relatives played a role in conveying the importance of meals to him.

A Sense of the Theatrical

I'm not sure whether most readers will even have considered the possibility that Jesus might have gone to the theater growing up, or indeed at any point during his life for that matter. It is almost certain that he would have seen one in Sepphoris. While the impressive structure that can be visited in the remains of that city today reflects expansion and improvement happening after Jesus's lifetime, the evidence points at least to there having been a smaller theater at that location in the time of Jesus. The most interesting question for us is not whether Jesus passed the theater when he visited the city. We'd like to know whether he went in, whether he attended performances, and if so, what that experience may have been like and what impact it had on him. One piece of evidence that speaks to this is something that readers in English could easily miss. "Hypocrite" is a widely-used English word, and so we can miss entirely that the word comes to us from Greek, from a word that had a different meaning in Jesus's time. It didn't refer then exclusively or even primarily to someone whose words and actions are at odds with one another. It meant someone who was an actor. From there, by way of the idea of playing a role different from one's real identity and thus engaging in deception, it eventually came to have the meaning in English that it has for us today.[20] Jesus's way

---

19. See further McGrath, "Was Jesus Illegitimate?"

20. On this subject see in particular Batey, *Jesus and the Forgotten City*, ch. 3. Note as well how the English word "acting" illustrates the way that a word can have a general

of referring to "hypocrites" and the specific things he said about them influenced the subsequent history of the term. Before Jesus's time, one occasionally encounters references to acting (we might want to say "play acting" in this context) as a way of referring to "deceit." In Jewish literature, this usage occurs mostly in the Septuagint, the Greek translation of the Jewish Scriptures, and then only rarely. Could Jesus have picked up the term from there? Even if Jesus knew Greek, he lived in a context in which Aramaic predominated, and so he is unlikely to have read or heard these Jewish writings in Greek. But even if he knew the word from there, if he uses it as a Greek loan word when speaking Aramaic, expecting that his hearers would be likely to understand, that too would be significant.[21] Whatever the exact word or words used, he chose to speak of acting as a metaphor far more frequently than can be explained simply through literary influences. Compared to the occasional negative references to "play acting" and "theatrics" in the Greek literature prior to his time, Jesus used this terminology much more frequently, and with a connotation much more specific and akin to the way we use it today. Why did he do so? Why might he have found this metaphor particularly meaningful? What did he experience in Sepphoris (in the care primarily of his grandmother) that may have influenced his choice later in his life to talk about his opponents as "actors" in the way that he did?

A number of sayings across the Synoptic Gospels use the term. In at least a couple of instances, the reason the term is used is unclear, while in others the emphasis could simply be on performance and desire to be in the spotlight. In some of the sayings, the negative connotation is what we get in other Greek literature, focusing on deceit. However, in some instances in the teaching of Jesus, including the only one found in the Gospel of Mark (7:5–7), the focus appears to be in keeping with the meaning the term has come to have in our time, namely a disconnect between the real life of the performer and the role they play, the (literal and/or metaphorical) mask they wear.[22] It may be that we are wrong to lump these all together using the modern English word "hypocrite," since Jesus

---

meaning but also more specific connotations depending on context and usage.

21. In later Syriac, terms related to acting and theater tend to be borrowed from Greek. Hypocrites is not used in this way, which might suggest that it never was, but might also suggest that the term had negative connotations by then.

22. It is worth noting that in ancient times, the view of many seems to have been that the playing of a role involved actual transformation of the performer. See further Webb, *Demons and Dancers*, 151–63; also Schnusenberg, *Relationship*, 11, 34.

may have been using the word "actors" to make more than one analogy between stage performers and his opponents. Be that as it may, hypocrisy in the modern sense does indeed appear to be at least one of the points Jesus was making when he used the term.

If we dig further into this, we will find that there are fascinating implications to how Jesus used the term. We may usefully draw analogies with our own experience today. Our initial instinct when an actor portrays a role in film, on TV, or on stage is to assume that there is a match between their character and themselves at the level of traits and personality. The actor who consistently plays kind souls we assume to be kind, and the one who depicts malicious nasty individuals all the time we typically have no desire to meet in real life. It is only from seeing multiple performances with the same individual playing very different roles, or watching interviews with an actor, that enable us to recognize that there is no necessary correspondence between nice person in real life and nice person on television. Jesus obviously did not see television interviews with actors. So where might he have learned this? One possible source for Jesus's distinctive use of acting imagery is that he had the opportunity to see the same actors in very different roles. This would have been possible even in a single performance, given the likelihood that pantomime was performed there, since pantomime involved a single actor playing all the various roles using different masks to represent the different characters.[23] Whether he saw the same person in multiple performances or playing multiple characters in a single performance, a family connection to theater begins to seem likely, whether through regular attendance at performances, patronage of the arts, friendships with performers, or some combination thereof. The disconnect between the different roles the actor played, and/or between what he had seen in the theater and the persona of the performer off stage, made an impression on Jesus. Jesus's grandparents would have been the mediators of these learning experiences. Women as well as men were in the audience at performances in ancient Greek theater, and so there is no reason to exclude Anna, and she may have quite possibly been the one who was the biggest aficionado. That we can never hope to determine. What we can say, however, is that not only one of Jesus's favorite analogies, but our modern usage of the term "hypocrite" in English, owes something to what Jesus learned

23. Nagy, *Sepphoris*, 76 says pantomime and farce were all that was likely to be available in Sepphoris during Jesus's era, if any sort of theatrical performance was. See also Weiss, "Theaters," 628–29.

through his grandparents, at least including if not necessarily primarily his grandmother.

Having mentioned earlier the question of whether Jesus knew Greek and connected that topic to one we are currently discussing, it must be noted that the Syriac Gospels do not seem to have had a term ready to hand to express Jesus's meaning in texts like Matthew 23. They use terms like "takers of faces" that seem to be aware they are translating a technical term related to acting as practiced in the Greco-Roman world using masks. The fact that Jesus is described in the New Testament Gospels as using the term "hypocrites" primarily in reference to scribes and other interpreters of the Law, when the root meaning of the Greek word had to do with interpretation, seems unlikely to be a coincidence. Note that even today we talk of actors *interpreting* a role. We thus have an interesting situation in which the Greek Bible uses the Greek word for "actor" to denote a wicked person, without any focus on the profession of acting being evident, while Jesus appears to have used the term in ways that may well have simply used "actor" as a suitable metaphor for playing a role in public that differs from your own character. Either Jesus had studied the Greek version of the Jewish Scriptures and had an education that few historians attribute to him, or he had the opportunity to get to know not only the theater but actors in a way that enabled him to use whatever Aramaic term denoted that profession as a metaphor. Or perhaps he simply used the Greek term as a loanword and his hearers either understood or asked what he meant, probably a common situation in Aramaic-speaking regions in the Greco-Roman era.[24] Whichever of these was the case, Jesus ends up looking rather different in his upbringing and educational experience than most historians (and preachers, and Bible readers, and people in general) have assumed. There is something deeply significant here, and his grandmother in Sepphoris is likely to have been involved in what he learned and how he learned it.[25] If not, then the most likely alternative is that he was exposed to theatrical performances at the homes and/or in the company of the elite women who supported him, about whom we'll have more to say in a later chapter. Ultimately we can

---

24. On the terminology of "hypocrite" in Greek and Aramaic as well as Arabic, see Pennacchietti, "Dirsi 'ipocrita.'" I am grateful to Alessandro Mengozzi for directing my attention to this important article on the topic.

25. There is more we could explore here, including Jesus's reference to hypocrites sounding the trumpet to draw attention to their performance of charity. The trumpet appears to have featured regularly in Roman theater.

only say with confidence that Jesus spoke in a way that left his followers with the impression that he made more frequent metaphorical references to theatrics than was typical in his time.

Jesus may have gained more than just a useful metaphor from his experience of theatrical and perhaps also other kinds of performances in the theater in Sepphoris, in homes, and even on the city's streets. Jesus's model of itinerant proclamation of the kingdom of God is often viewed as distinctive. A prototype exists, however, in the way troupes of musicians and actors relied on a combination of sponsorship by wealthy patrons of the arts and hospitality from local communities, moving from place to place and then returning from time to time to some central base of operation. Before you say it, no, I am not suggesting that Jesus and his "troupe" sold tickets to their "performances." In that era, quite often neither did actors. It was common for rich patrons to subsidize the cost of performances so that the audience could attend for free, much as wealthy women supported Jesus.

Irrespective of whether the economic model for supporting his activity was drawn from theater, there was definitely something performative about Jesus's tales and one-liners, even as there is also an element of performance and even a necessity for a certain amount of theatrics on the part of preachers. This was also true of ancient healers and exorcists, regardless of where their income came from. Theatrics are not about charging people money for tickets, but the effective use of dramatic elements to make storytelling and other things more effective. How might it change our perception if we imagine Jesus not merely reciting a verbal parable about a man with a speck in his eye, but performing it as a skit, perhaps with assistance from his apprentices? Imagine Laurel and Hardy or Abbot and Costello acting out a scene in which one of them has a tiny speck of something in his eye and calls for help, and help comes in the form of his friend who has a problem of his own, a lengthy board sticking out of his own eye. Slapstick hilarity ensues. Not only is it possible to teach through entertainment, but genuinely comical (or otherwise engaging) performance can be particularly effective, as it lures the audience in and then challenges us after we've lowered our defenses. Most religious people know this from our experience of effective sermons and holiday pageants. Why do we tend to think that these tried and true teaching techniques were unknown to Jesus or somehow beneath him?

There are a variety of skills that come with involvement in theater. Those who have never sung nor acted may see little connection between the two. Those who have pursued either profession know them to be inseparable, and while this was not true in the same way in ancient times as it is today, the basic principle remains broadly applicable. If Jesus was able to effectively address large crowds, he must have learned to project his voice and use it effectively, including recognizing geographical settings that would facilitate his being heard. We are told that Jesus sang with his disciples in both canonical and extracanonical texts (Mark 14:26; Acts of John 94), and certain types of singing were simply part of life for people in general in ancient times.[26] Jesus may have gone beyond the level that was typical, however, as he had the opportunity to explore theater, music, and other aspects of the cultural life of Sepphoris. One of those was undoubtedly the marketplace, where children could be observed singing songs that were part of play, including emulating the kinds of singing associated with occasions of celebration or mourning. Adults did not have time to join in such frivolities. Whether from childhood memory, observation of such scenes as an adult, or both, Jesus found a useful analogy in this feature observable in the marketplace of this and other cities and towns (Luke 7:32 = Matt 11:17).

The Vulnerability and Value of the Elderly

Jesus, like most children throughout history, may have been cared for by a grandmother, only to later have played a role in reciprocating and caring for them. Jesus and his siblings likely delivered items from home to his grandmother to make her life easier when she became too old to go to the market. The elderly are repositories of wisdom who start out providing for their children and later grandchildren, but eventually experience a reversal of the roles. In the ancient world there were no retirement homes. It was the duty of children to care for their parents in their old age. Sometimes they even moved in together. However, even if extended across a distance of several kilometers rather than in a shared home, Jesus would have seen care provided first by and later to his grandparents. Since we do not know the order in which various relatives of Jesus died, we don't have any way to know whether Anna might have become a widow and been the first to make Jesus aware of the vulnerability that came with that status. It may be that Joseph died before either of Mary's parents. In either case, Jesus would have seen both need and care provided in both

---

26. On dancing as also part of this see Unnik, "Note on the Dance."

directions sooner or later, and would have participated himself in bringing goods between town and city, running errands, as well as providing care in other ways.

Across the Generations

Although we do not always reflect on it, generations prior to parents always have an influence on us, whether directly or indirectly. Much that Jesus learned from Mary, he learned indirectly from his grandmother—and her mother before her, and so on and so on. We began to explore the possibility of a connection between Jesus's family on his mother's side and the city of Sepphoris in the preceding chapter about Jesus's mother Mary and what he learned from her. Here we have seen that Jesus may have learned from other women precisely because in his family he had more than one example of a female relative from whom he learned, and recognized that he could learn and needed to learn, even in childhood. That fact, in and of itself, plays an important, if often unconscious role, in adult behavior later in life. That there is overlap between the things Jesus may have learned from his mother and those he may have learned from his grandmother should not be viewed as reflecting a mere historical uncertainty, but as precisely what we all experience as true about the influences in each of our lives that spans generations in a variety of ways. Jesus learned from his mother's side of the family, and some of their influence may have shaped his adult public ministry in very important ways.

The Samaritan Woman
What Jesus Learned from an Israelite at Jacob's Well

The walk to the well offers a welcome break from the tedium of the daily routine, but it always brings sadness too, no matter what time of day it is. Sometimes I go in the morning, when it is cooler, like most others in the town. When I do that I'll be passed on the way by countless young women. They greet me respectfully as they pass me by at the greater speed at which their youth allows them to move. If I had been blessed by God with children, or even just one, I would have sent them to make this trip instead of me. They would have walked at that same faster pace together with their friends. They would have had to wait at those busier times of the day, as so many of the town's young women gathered and drew water from the well. But they would have enjoyed it, talking about the kinds of things youth are interested in. I remember how much I enjoyed the trips to the well when I was a girl. Now, when I find myself at the well surrounded by young people, they are always polite—but I am never included in their conversations. Why should I be? When I was a girl, I would have done the same, whispering to my friends, giggling, leaving the older women to whatever it was that they were concerned with.

If I find myself instead among other older women, they never know what to say to me. These days I am never better, and never worse, and so even asking me how I am must seem like a chore to them. That is the lot of a childless widow. Their news about themselves involves their sons, their daughters, their husbands. I have *nothing of the sort to share. I see the concern on their faces if they talk about such things when I am around. I am sure they wish I wasn't there, so that they could talk about their joys without guilt.*

So I often go to draw water at a less busy time, when I can. Sometimes I even try to measure out the water use in the house, so that it is natural to fetch more around the middle of the day. It is quiet now, and I can think about God and matters of importance, provided of course this very act of walking alone, with no child to send on this mission, doesn't bring my mind back to focus on myself, my own tragic life story. That is what it seems to be doing today. Why is it the lot of a woman like me to be defined by the husbands she has lost and the children she never had?

Becoming lost in one's thoughts is dangerous. I didn't notice the stranger sitting at the well until I was very close—not that I could outrun him if he wished to do me harm. His clothing made clear that he was a Jew. With so many Jews living in Galilee, it was increasingly common for them to pass through Samaria. They couldn't help but stop for water on their way. Perhaps he came here at precisely this time to avoid encountering people like me. Such is their disdain for us! We have preserved the Torah of Moses and the covenant with God more faithfully than they have, yet they insist it is the other way around. They claim Jacob, whose well this was, as their ancestor, just as we do. They probably think this well is as much theirs as it is ours, even though we live here, striving to preserve the land of Jacob and to worship the God of Israel in as much unity and with as much fidelity as possible. The southern tribes always pulled in their own direction and tore at the unity of God's chosen people from the very beginning. Yet they are not content with that harm done in the distant past. It's not even enough for them that they demolished our temple! Today, when they pass through our land, they often harass us (and of course, we pay them back in kind and do the same to them). This man could be dangerous. Any strange man can be, but a man from among our enemies all the more so.

Getting closer, I see he has no vessel with which to draw water. Is he a fool who set out unprepared? A lunatic? Or was he unfortunate enough to have his things stolen or broken on his journey? Perhaps that's what he's hoping for—that other Jewish pilgrims like himself will pass by at a time when they can avoid us, and he can get water with their assistance, and make his way northward (or southward, if that's where he's headed) in their company? I should be grateful that Jews refuse to use vessels and utensils of Samaritans. He surely won't steal mine.

As I reach the well, I get a better look at the man's face. He doesn't look sinister, although you never can tell. He just looks tired, and possibly lost in thought. It is a face that I would have considered kind if he were a Samaritan. I will try to ignore him and go about my business.

"Give me a drink."

I turn around, wondering whether, in my attention to the man, I had missed that someone else had been coming along the road behind me from town. But no, it was the Jewish stranger who had said it.

"How can you, being a Jew, ask me, a Samaritan, for a drink?" I asked him. The different ways the Jews understood the Torah, the requirements of the covenant, and worship—it had always fascinated me. Maybe this man had studied the Torah and had realized that we, the northern tribes, the majority of Israel, had gotten it right all along?

"If you knew what God gives, and if you knew who you're talking to, you would have asked me, and I would have offered you flowing water."

Maybe I was dealing with a dangerous lunatic after all. Who does he think he is, and what on earth is he talking about? I pointed out to him that he doesn't even have a vessel with which to draw water from the well. He replied by speaking of water that eliminates thirst permanently. Is he a magician? A miracle-worker? A storyteller and poet? I should have thought first and foremost that he was probably mocking me, offering me something that doesn't exist, thinking Samaritans are stupid, and a woman all the more so. Or maybe I ought to have worried that he would try to give me poison, hoping to kill a Samaritan on his way through our land, thinking he could trick some foolish people among us into trusting him, and then laughing at us after getting us to inflict harm on ourselves? Yet something about the way he spoke made me think that wasn't where this was going with these words. What a strange man.

"Sure, I will happily have some of your water, if that will mean that I don't need to keep coming back to this well," I said, playing along.

"Go call your husband and come back," he said.

> *I sighed. No matter what I do, where I go, whom I speak with, things always come back to this topic. I can't escape it. "I have no husband," I told him—truthfully. No need to get into my long and painful story with a stranger.*
>
> *Then he said something that simply amazed me. I still find it hard to believe . . .*

Meeting at a Well

The author of the Gospel of John does not tell us her name. Perhaps he had heard it but did not care to pass it on. Perhaps it was others who passed the story on to him who were negligent in this regard. It is quite typical for ancient texts to fail to even mention the presence of women, and to omit their names when they do get a mention.[1] Despite her anonymity, the woman who features so centrally in chapter 4 of John's Gospel plays a significant role in the life and activity of Jesus. She has frequently been depicted as an immoral woman, a woman with a past. Yet we will find there is no hint of that in the story, once we read it against the backdrop of its historical context. As with the turning of Mary Magdalene into a prostitute (a topic we will address later in this book), the distortion of the Samaritan woman's story probably results from the desire of male interpreters of the Bible to downgrade and marginalize her status.

John tells us Jesus and his disciples were traveling from Jerusalem back to Galilee by way of Samaria. Jesus is tired and waits at Jacob's well while his disciples go into the city of Sychar to purchase food. While he is there, a Samaritan woman comes to the well to draw water. The story is told in such a way as to echo the story in Genesis 29 about Jacob meeting Rachel at a well. The fact that she went to the well at midday does not indicate that the woman was an outcast among her community, as is so often claimed.[2] When she later goes back into town to tell of her experience, the townspeople are receptive to what she says, and follow her to meet the man she has told them about. This is not the reaction she would have been met with, were she someone with a ruined reputation.

---

1. There is a church tradition that gives her the Greek name Photini. It might be best, when incorporating her into a more detailed retelling of her story that uses her name, to give her a Hebrew or Aramaic equivalent name that shares the connection to light that Photini has in Greek.

2. So rightly Asikainen, "Women out of Place," 187. Contrast Neyrey, "What's Wrong with This Picture?"

The location and timing are instead details that are supposed to make readers recall the meeting of Jacob and Rachel, which happened at a different well, but at the same time of day, around midday (Gen 29:7). This is the point of the timing of the story. The woman is not being flagged as a sinner or outcast when it tells us that she went to draw water at that time. The reader is being reminded of a famous story about Jacob and his future bride Rachel, and encouraged to view the meeting between this woman and Jesus through that lens.

Given the close match between details in John and in Genesis, some have suggested that the Gospel author simply made up the story. Perhaps it was invented in order to symbolize Christ taking the lost tribes back as his bride. The story also follows a pattern distinctive to the Gospel of John. This author loves to tell stories in which the dialogue begins with Jesus saying something that can be understood more than one way. Jesus's conversation partner inevitably understands it on a more everyday level. Jesus then provides a lengthy explanation of the meaning of his words on a deeper spiritual level. However, even if the story is told in this author's characteristic way, and has been embellished with symbolism, there is good reason to conclude that it has an actual historical event at its core. The Gospel of John regularly demonstrates accurate geographical knowledge and gets the details of places right, even when the words spoken against that backdrop reflect his distinctive style and vocabulary. The author of the Gospel would also have known that meetings at a well between a man and a woman consistently led to marriage in the Jewish Scriptures. The theme of Jesus as bridegroom notwithstanding, the author would probably not have simply invented an encounter that could be understood that way on a literal level. In view of these considerations, it is probably best to conclude that this story has a historical core rooted in an actual experience of Jesus, as well as a significant overlay of symbolism. We do not have to choose between those two possibilities. Both can be true simultaneously.

Eating and Drinking in Samaria

The Gospel provides an aside for the benefit of readers who may not be familiar with Jewish-Samaritan relations. According to John 4:9, Jews did not normally associate with Samaritans. Or, as some translations put it, Jews did not use the same dishes as Samaritans. Jesus himself was clearly not opposed on principle to eating the food of Samaritans. Had he been, it would have been out of the question for him to send his disciples into a Samaritan city to find food. In Jesus's time, people probably held different points of view on this subject. In later centuries, some rabbis considered food prepared by Samaritans to be appropriate for Jewish consumption, while others considered eating their bread equivalent to eating pork. Even those with only the vaguest familiarity with Judaism and its rules about kosher food will probably have heard that Jews are forbidden to eat pork. Some rabbis said Samaritans were to be treated the same as gentiles, while others insisted that they were to be treated as Israelites. It seems likely, in view of the conflicting evidence, that one could find acceptance, suspicion, qualms, and outright hostility towards the other in both of these communities, depending on whom one encountered. It is difficult to determine which attitudes were most widespread in Jesus's time. Communities can coexist peacefully for long periods and then violent conflict can break out when circumstances change. Communities can be wrapped up in war and yet within a matter of years find their way to peace. In the case of Jews and Samaritans there were longstanding tensions. A little over a century before Jesus was born, the Jewish king John Hyrcanus had destroyed the Samaritans' temple on Mount Gerizim (the place of worship the Samaritan woman mentions in her conversation with Jesus). During one Passover in the time of Jesus's youth, Samaritans had scattered human bones in the temple in Jerusalem, defiling it. It is entirely possible that Jesus would have been at the festival with his family when that happened. Even if they were not present, they would certainly have heard about it. Unless his family and upbringing were extremely atypical, he probably grew up hearing derogatory things said about Samaritans by those around him. He undoubtedly saw his parents and relatives behave differently when passing through Samaria, whether because of their own attitude towards Samaritans or concern about Samaritans' view of them, and perhaps both. In the story in the Gospel of John that is the focus of this chapter, Jesus expresses certain prejudices of his own, stating that "salvation is from/of the Jews" and that Samaritans worship in ignorance. Given the Gospel author's negative statements about "the Jews" throughout the Gospel, this positive statement stands out. Even when one is embroiled in conflict with others within one's own identity group, such matters can seem to lose their significance when a complete outsider enters the picture.

We do know that Jesus's attitude towards Samaritans will change over the course of this Gospel. When he is later accused of being demon possessed and a Samaritan (John 8:48), he will ignore the latter accusation and only rebut the former. If we ask why he might have done so, a likely answer presents itself. Think about the kinds of ways labels are used as insults, and how people respond when they are labeled in that way. If someone calls someone else a homosexual, a Communist, a liberal, a foreigner, or puts them in any other pigeonhole that presumes a negative view of the category, what does it convey if you respond by saying "No I'm not"? That way of answering makes it sound as though you may share your opponent's assumption that it is indeed bad to be in the category in question. Jesus's refusal to do so suggests that, by that stage, Jesus has not only rejected the stereotyping of Samaritans, but has had some practice in doing so, giving thought to how best to challenge prejudiced speech. It may be that it was his association with Samaritans that led to the charge that he himself must be one of them. That association began with his conversation with the woman at the well. Later still, of course, Jesus would make a Samaritan the hero of a parable (Luke 10:25–37). The path leading to that famous story begins here at the well, with what Jesus learns from this woman.

The Gender Gap

We can tell from the story that, prior to Jesus's encounter with this woman, it was not his custom to talk to women on his own in this way. The Gospel author makes a point of mentioning that none of his disciples questioned Jesus regarding his interactions with the woman (John 4:27). The assumption is clearly that they might have been expected to do so when they saw what he was doing.[3] The disciples are surprised, in a way that they would not have been if this had been something he did often. This clues the reader in that Jesus's teaching and actions prior to this point in time had not been such as to make what he was doing now seem unsurprising to those who knew him. Later, Jesus will treat women differently and teach his disciples to follow his example. He will also treat Samaritans differently and expect his disciples to do likewise. That is why we argue in this chapter that the encounter described in John 4 had a transformative impact on Jesus.

---

3. Peirano, "Una mujer que silenció a los discípulos," 988, 999.

The conversation between Jesus and the woman begins with a request for water. This makes Jesus less like Jacob, with whom the story compares and contrasts him at several points. In Gen 29:10, Jacob is the one who takes care of the provision of water for Rachel and her flocks. The Gospel story will go on to emphasize that Jesus can provide an even greater water. When the woman asks for that water, Jesus suggests that she go get her husband and come back. This may reflect a simple sense of propriety on Jesus's part, that he took for granted cultural gender norms in that time and place. The conversation can continue—but it should take place between men, or at least not continue without the woman's husband being aware of it and authorizing it.[4] When the woman responds that she has no husband, it leads to some interesting revelations about her background and life experience. But it also represents an assertion that there is no need for a man to come and represent her or speak on her behalf. She is an independent agent. And as we will see later, she is perfectly capable of carrying on a conversation about theological differences between Jews and Samaritans.[5]

Serial Widow

Jesus's statement that the woman has had several husbands, and is now connected to someone who is not her husband, may be one of the most badly misconstrued texts in all of Scripture.[6] Some readers seem to imagine the woman as a sort of first-century movie star who has married, divorced, and remarried many times.[7] There were no such pop-culture

---

4. Love, *Jesus and Marginal Women*, 38 notes evidence from Plutarch that women were expected not to speak in public unless their husbands were with them (*Comparison of Lycurgus and Numa* 3:5).

5. So rightly Tamez, *Jesus and Courageous Women*, 85; Asikainen, "Women Out Of Place," 187–88; Ghosn, *Encounters*, 36. Hebblethwaite, *Six New Gospels*, 66–67n18, mentions a sermon by John Chrysostom (*Commentary on St. John*, Homily 32) that expresses admiration for her interest in doctrine, which he contrasts with the lack of interest on the part of those in his congregation. Getty-Sullivan writes in *Women in the New Testament*, 96, "The woman proves herself to be a worthy student. She knows both her own traditions and those of the Jews." See also Mackall, *Kindred Sisters*, 58, who writes, "The Samaritan woman's personality comes across from the moment she enters the scene. She's spunky, quick, possibly flirtatious . . . She held up her end of the conversation with intelligence and wit."

6. Storkey, *Women in a Patriarchal World*, 91–92.

7. See for instance Lutzer and Lutzer, *Jesus: Lover of a Woman's Soul*, 25, where the

icons in Jesus's time, and if there had been, they would not be found drawing their own water from a well. Some who are familiar with Jesus's teaching about divorce may need to be reminded that the people of Samaria had not heard that yet. Divorce was not considered immoral at this time by those who followed the Torah, which permits it. That law was something Jews and Samaritans held in common. Even if the woman had divorced husband after husband, that would not have led to her being viewed as immoral in that time and place. That is unlikely to be what happened in the case of this woman, however. In the first century, not everyone agreed the Torah gave women the right to initiate divorces. Even if the woman had been in multiple marriages each of which had been terminated through divorce, we should not assume that she was the initiator. Nevertheless, it is extremely unlikely that a woman would be divorced and remarried so many times in this cultural context. Once a couple of husbands had found the same woman an unacceptable wife, it becomes implausible in the extreme to imagine other men in this era in history marrying her in spite of that fact. And so what are we to make of the fact that she has had five husbands? There is a ready explanation, one that is often ignored by modern readers. The woman had probably been widowed multiple times.[8] In our era of better sanitation and health care, for someone to have so many spouses die may seem unlikely. It may have been rare even in the ancient world for one person to experience this. The woman may have been an extreme case in terms of the sheer number of husbands who had died. However, if we had the kinds of marriage and death records for her time that societies keep today, we would probably find that she was not unique, or at the very least is ranked at the top of a category of misfortune in which there were a lot of contenders and close runners-up.

Ancient readers of the Gospel of John would have found their minds turning to the story of Tobit. The Book of Tobit is found in the Greek translation of the Jewish Scriptures, and is included in the Apocrypha

---

authors at least acknowledge the possibility of husbands having died or frivolously divorced her, yet still speak of "failed marriages" and her trying to "find the right man" in a manner that reflects modern American rather than ancient Mediterranean realities. Contrast Hollies, *Jesus and Those Bodacious Women*, 87–88, which conveys the woman's ancient circumstances to a modern audience. On this story see also Knust, *Unprotected Texts*, 237–40.

8. This understanding of the woman's situation is simply assumed by Nonnus of Nisibis in his *Commentary* (80) written in the ninth century. Previous generations and other cultures have brought different assumptions to the text than we do.

in Catholic and Orthodox Bibles today. In that story, a woman named Sarah has a series of husbands, each of whom is killed by a demon on their wedding night. The Samaritan woman's story would have been understood along similar lines, as a tragic one, not one that involved some immorality on her part. The most recent man in her life (assuming the man who is not her husband is not simply a relative that she now resides with) may have decided not to risk early death by marrying a woman whose previous husbands had all died, in case she was cursed in some way. Concubinage (what we today call common law marriage) was not considered either illegal or immoral in this time any more than divorce was. It is extremely irresponsible as well as profoundly unkind to take a woman's tragic life experiences and recast them as instead hinting at immoral actions on her part.

Indeed, if anything, it would have been the woman who worried about possible immoral actions by Jesus, rather than vice versa. Was this Jewish man here to do her harm? Should she flee? When there have been conflicts between peoples, sexual assault has always been a weapon of choice in the human arsenal. A lone woman going to draw water, finding a man waiting there on his own, would undoubtedly approach with hesitation, caution, and suspicion, aware that the man was a potential danger to her. That would be true regardless of where he was from, but especially true if he belonged to an enemy people. This would not have been the first time Jesus had seen a look of apprehension on the face of a woman who crossed his path. However, this may well have been the first time he saw that same look he had seen on the faces of Jewish women in the past on the face of one from Samaria. Few men would have learned the lessons that Jesus seems to have learned from such encounters, noticing worry and trauma that is inflicted specifically on women by ongoing cycles and habits of violence. Fewer still would have learned what Jesus appears to have learned on this occasion. In the shared expression of fear at potential danger in response to his presence, Jesus recognized a shared humanity between Jews and Samaritans. Soon, he would see in this woman a distant relative among the wider people of Israel, rather than a foreigner and enemy. A sensitive man would wish to figure out how not to be a cause of terror and panic merely through his presence. It would take a truly insightful one to recognize that there was nothing that he could do alone, as a solitary individual, to make such a change. It would require a radical reorientation of an entire culture and its shared values, asking those who are first to put themselves last, and to put themselves in the shoes of the last, to refrain from violence, actively lift up the downtrodden, and protect weaker and marginalized members of society. We find such things emphasized in Jesus's teaching later on. The moment we witness here is an important part of the journey that leads him there.

The Personality of a Prophet

Was Jesus an intuitive individual of the sort that might have picked up on these things? Would he have found his thoughts moving in such directions? I once asked my Sunday school class what they thought Jesus's Myers-Briggs personality type might have been. The usefulness of these kinds of personality tests has been questioned even when they are taken by or applied to people alive today. Trying to apply one of them across a great distance in time and culture, on the basis of scant literary evidence, to an ancient individual is even more problematic. I knew this, and yet proceeded to ask the question nonetheless. Why? Because in a context in which Jesus's humanity is often not recognized, or at least downplayed, the exercise might still be useful. The same factors that make it hard for some to think of Jesus learning make it hard for them to imagine him having a genuine human personality.

In our discussion of this topic, we noted things like Jesus's need to recharge by getting away from crowds. His quiet processing followed by remarkably insightful comments is often a characteristic of introversion. We recognized his close observation of nature, utilized to such good effect in his parables. He also noticed and paid attention to aspects of the lives of others that most around him overlooked. We acknowledged his empathy and his willingness to defer judgment. In the end, the class concluded that he was probably an ISFP. You can look that up if you want lots more details about what that means. This personality type is often labeled as "the artist." Painters and other kinds of artists must be sensitive to and perceive the world in ways that others do not. They then use their pictures and/or words to help others see the world as they see it. Modern personality tests aside, Jesus's parables provide evidence of his artistry. Good storytellers are artists every bit as much as painters and musicians. Jesus's interaction with the Samaritan woman here also provides evidence that Jesus had some of the attributes we associate with artists. He perceives her in a way that most men in his time, Jewish or Samaritan, would not have. He then finds ways of guiding his followers into that new perspective, and of telling stories and painting pictures with words that challenge others further afield to go and do likewise.

Artists are also often prophets. The line between a prophet and a poet is a blurry one. Such people, whatever label they wear, depict an alternative vision of reality and challenge others with it. They need to be deeply insightful into what is happening in the world around them and perceptive about where things are likely to be heading in the future. When Jesus tells the women that she has no husband now, but has had multiple husbands in the past, she opines that he is a prophet. What does that mean, from our perspective? One may attribute Jesus's insight entirely to supernatural knowledge if one is so inclined. But that isn't the only option, nor a necessary one. It might not even be the most miraculous possibility, depending on how one defines that term. For someone to have something revealed to them supernaturally would be astounding. When a person develops sufficient sensitivity to pick up on things even without needing an angel to whisper it in their ear, that might be considered equally impressive if not more so, albeit in a different sort of way. Whatever one's viewpoint, Jesus shows insight and perception about a woman he has only just met, and that would surely have made an impression on her.

Having been widowed multiple times, and not being married now, we can imagine the facial expressions of the woman and how they must have changed over the course of the conversation. Once she ceased to be worried that this man might assault her, she presumably relaxed. Jesus may have been the first person she had had a conversation with in many years who did not know her sad history. The first person who did not ask how she was with a pitying look already in their eyes. While we have already shown the problems with the view that the woman went to the well at noon when few others did because she was some kind of notorious sinner, she may have chosen that time in order to avoid people. Being known in a community only by one's grief and tragedy can be exhausting. And to be frank, some might not have wanted her around them, not because of a bad reputation, but because they viewed her misfortune as a sign that she was cursed by God, haunted by a demon, or both. Being around such people is often felt to place one's own well-being in danger. At the very least, it is an uncomfortable reminder of just how precarious that well-being is. Here, however, was an individual who didn't know that story. Even if fraught with potential danger because of gender and ethnic tension, the conversation may quickly have turned into a refreshing experience.

But then he asked her to get her husband. Her face may well have fallen, and the tiredness may have returned to her expression and been audible in her voice. "I have no husband," she sighed. It would not have taken a special revelation to intuit what this likely meant. Certainly, if Jesus immediately knew precisely how many times the woman had been widowed, that would entail something beyond normal human capability. But just as the Gospel of Mark depicts Jesus healing a blind man in multiple attempts and stages (Mark 8:22–25), it may be that Jesus perceived the gist of her situation and felt his way to the rest: "You've had three, four ... no, five husbands—and are now with someone who is not a husband to you." Her eyes probably grew wide at such intuited insight.[9] When someone sees us, understands us on a deeper level than we are used to, it can indeed be a miraculous and healing experience. Jesus may well have perceived the power that issued from him on this occasion, as he would on others.

From Sarah to Tamar

Jesus may or may not have read or heard the story about Sarah found in the Book of Tobit. It is hard to know how widely the story circulated in places where the Jewish Scriptures were not experienced through their Greek translation, of which Tobit became a part. (Fragments of the work in Aramaic and Hebrew were found among the Dead Sea Scrolls.) But Jesus surely knew the story of Tamar from Genesis 38. Tamar was another woman whose life may have mirrored that of the Samaritan woman in certain details. For if we ask why so many men had married her despite the deaths of her previous husbands, one possible answer is *obligation*. The Torah prescribes that if a man dies without children, his brother must marry his widow and have children with her that will be considered the elder brother's (Deut 25:5–10). In a patriarchal agrarian society typified by subsistence farming, this would have seemed to make good sense. Widows were protected from destitution by this way of doing things. The line of inheritance of farmland and other property remained unambiguous. It was a time of arranged marriages. Not everyone, male or female, would have been happy with their life partner. If a woman's husband died,

---

9. On Jesus's intuition see Watson, *Wisdom's Daughters*, 31.

marrying his brother might be viewed as just another arranged marriage. For some, it might mean being married to someone they already knew they disliked, while for others it may at least have seemed preferable to being married off to another stranger. These were different times, with different ways of doing things than most readers of this book will be used to.

In the story of Tamar, it is Judah her father-in-law who delays arranging the marriage to the next brother in line after two have died. Tamar viewed marriage to the third brother as a better option than remaining a widow in perpetuity without offspring. This custom of a woman becoming the wife of her late husband's brother is known as Levirate marriage. It seems quite likely that this provides the background to the story of the Samaritan woman. If so, then by the time Jesus met her, either she had ended up with a brother who refused to marry her or was too young to do so, or she had passed through a series of five brothers, all of whom died without children, and was now in the hands of some other man.[10] That individual may have been a man who was willing to take her as a concubine but not as a husband, perhaps thinking that misfortune befell anyone who married her. However, another possibility is that the reference to a man who is not her husband means that she was being cared for by a male relative in her family, whether a parent or uncle, and so was considered to belong to a man who was not her husband.

The woman asks Jesus whether he is greater than their father Jacob. According to the story in Genesis, Tamar is said to have been greater (or at least more righteous) than Jacob's son Judah, the ancestor of Jesus's own tribe. Being part of a family that traced its lineage back to David, Tamar was in Jesus's own family tree. She is one of several foreign women who get mentioned in the genealogy of Jesus provided at the beginning of Matthew's Gospel (1:3). The Gospel of John is concerned to emphasize that Jesus is indeed greater than Jacob. But Jesus himself may have found himself thinking in that moment about the fact that Tamar was greater than Judah. If she could be, then this Samaritan woman could be as well. Meanwhile, Jacob was their common ancestor, before Judah and Tamar. As Jesus's thoughts turned to such things, it may have helped him to see

---

10. This possibility is explored beautifully in Evans's book *Inspired*, 141–42. See also O'Day and Hylen, *John*, 53; Bird, *Permission Granted*, 38; Brant, *John*, 85; Sim, "Samaritan Woman," 15–19. Tamar and the Book of Tobit were also brought into the picture by Efrem the Syrian in his treatment of the Samaritan Woman, and following him, by Isho'dad of Merv (see McVey, "Efrem the Syrian," 248).

his connection with this woman who engaged in religious discussion on substantive matters. Jesus allowed the conversation to remain focused on such things. Where others might have seen a poor unfortunate woman, Jesus saw a worthy conversation partner.

Turning a Tragedy into a Test

Later in his public ministry, some Sadducees would use a scenario similar to that in the Book of Tobit as a puzzle to try to stump Jesus. They asked him about a woman who married a man and then each of his six brothers in turn, having children with none of them (Mark 12:20–24; Matt 22:25–32; Luke 20:27–38). Whose husband would she be in the resurrection, if there were indeed to be a resurrection? The reason Jesus was able to give a quick response may have been precisely because he had previously had occasion to think through a scenario of that kind. He had talked with a woman who had lived something like it—a fellow descendant of Jacob's whom he had met at Jacob's well. For the Sadducees this was a mere puzzle, a trap to try to snare him with. For Jesus, perhaps what was most troubling about these Sadducees was not their denial of the resurrection, but their use of the scenario they described as though it were a mere thought experiment and not a story of deep tragedy and loss.[11] His answer—that in the resurrection there is no marriage because people become more like angels—was not merely a solution to an abstract theological problem. Jesus had surely thought about this as a result of his conversation with the Samaritan woman. What did resurrection mean, and what did the kingdom of God offer, to a woman who had been passed around as property from one husband to another? From actually talking with at least one woman who had lived through this experience, Jesus learned that the kingdom of God, the resurrection life of the age to come, had to offer something better, something beyond what the Law did for the purpose of life in the present age. The Law offered a remedy that sought to lessen the damage caused by mortality and childlessness. It should not be denigrated for having done so. But it was a less than perfect solution. It was from this woman, and perhaps also others like her, that Jesus learned to view the Law in a manner that he explicitly articulates later. The Law makes allowances for the hardness of human hearts and addresses the hardships of human life (Mark 10:5). It is not at all a recipe

---

11. On the story in Mark see further Izquierdo, *La Donna*, 71–75.

for a perfect world of the sort he had come to hope for, and then to invite people to seek to enter in the expectation that it was drawing near.

First Jesus showed insight into her experience. Then he viewed her as a person in her own right, a worthy dialogue partner about the serious subject of worship. He did not view her as merely a representative of a category, whether "Samaritan" or "tragedy-stricken serial widow." Jesus may have caught a glimpse of his prophetic and/or messianic vocation, and his ability to be a healer, in this encounter. His insights and interaction with her brought healing into her life. Perhaps in light of this experience he caught a glimpse of a Kingdom that would be not merely for Judah, but would bring the northern tribes back as well as part of a united Israel. On this occasion he saw, perhaps for the first time, that the kingdom of God could not be set up in such a way as to be liable to be rent asunder once more by divisions over temples, tribes, or geography. It could not be focused on Jerusalem any more than on Mount Gerizim. Jesus's appointment of the Twelve symbolized his vision of bringing the tribes back together forever. That aspect of Jesus's ministry ultimately owes something to his conversation on this day as well.

As their dialogue progresses, the woman does not dwell on what Jesus had perceived about her life story. Presumably that was because Jesus himself did not dwell on it. Deep recognition of pain suffered, combined at the same time with seeing someone as more than their painful experiences, would be profoundly therapeutic and liberating. The woman would later single out Jesus's insight into her life as the thing that was so remarkable about him when she went back into town and spoke to her fellow townspeople. For them, it was probably her enthusiasm that seemed most striking. This was probably the first time they had seen her this excited, this filled with hope and positive emotion, in many years. No wonder they were eager to meet the prophet who had had this impact on her.

Worship in Ignorance

In speaking with the woman about theological matters, Jesus is said to have accused not just her individually, but her entire people, of ignorance, of worshiping what they do not know. The woman responds with an affirmation of knowledge, that she and her people know the most crucial thing: that God will not leave his people to languish in ignorance, but will send someone to clarify what they are mistaken about, reveal things that they do not know, and correct their errors. Being open to correction is one of the most crucial elements of learning, and resistance to that was something that the Gospels say frustrated Jesus about his audience time and again. It was not only teachers who encountered this, but also in particular prophets, who sought to challenge what peoples and kings were thinking and doing. The woman is already persuaded that Jesus is a prophet. Now she moves in the direction of viewing him as possibly *the* prophet, the anointed one, the figure that they hoped God would send in the future.

Many Samaritans hoped for such a figure, as did many Jews. But just as Jewish expectations differed dramatically from one another, so too Samaritan expectations were presumably diverse, as well as being different from those that predominated in Judaism. Samaritans were not expecting a Davidic anointed one, a king to impose rule from Judea over the northern tribes. While Jews looked back at the short period in history when that was the case as a golden age, the descendants of the northern kingdom of Israel remembered it very differently. Yet according to this story, the woman refers to the one that she and her people were expecting as the Messiah, the anointed one. While it could just be that the author of the Gospel is translating the Samaritan terminology for the benefit of readers, we could also understand the woman to be translating her own concept for the purpose of the conversation. She would then be saying that she knows that both Jews and Samaritans recognize things are not as they should be, and expect God to send someone to restore, to call to repentance, and to instruct God's people. She knows enough about her own tradition and those of Judaism to recognize that this is a point of commonality between them across the significant differences, and to translate her own people's expectations into Jewish language.

Jesus had already said that a time was coming that would break down geographical divides over sacred space. But in the process, he had reaffirmed the dominance of Jewish thought and practice in what he envisaged. Now at the end of this conversation, however, he is said to affirm that he is the fulfillment not just of Jewish expectations, but of Samaritan ones. Jesus had asserted their profound ignorance about God. The woman had responded with an affirmation that highlighted the character of God as one who would not leave the people of Israel to languish in ignorance forever. By the end of the conversation, Jesus recognized that hope for the future and openness to learning can be found among the Samaritans, and that was what mattered most, more than what they already knew or thought they knew, and what their differences over God, Scripture, and worship were that separated them from their neighbors, their relatives, in Judea and Galilee.

The story also highlights the woman's role as proclaimer of the good news about Jesus to others, illustrating to Jesus himself the important role that women could play in his mission. When Jesus said that others labored and the disciples will now reap the fruit of what others have sown, he was indicating that he had learned from the woman that the Samaritans were not as ignorant or as far from the truth as he had supposed. Indeed, they seemed better prepared to respond positively to him and his message than some of his fellow Jews had shown themselves to be thus far. But he may also have been referring more specifically to this woman and her proclamation.[12] Either way, Jesus went from seeing Samaritans as worshipers of what they do not know, to seeing them as ripe for the kingdom because others had spoken the truth among them beforehand. They were open to taking the next step in response to his teaching, more receptive than some of his own people. Within the Gospel of John, we have a noticeable contrast with Nicodemus, who appears in the preceding chapter. He had offered a confident "we know" much as the Samaritan woman did. The subsequent conversation had left Jesus disappointed with Nicodemus, it would seem, in ways that the conversation with the woman at the well did not disappoint him. On some level, Jesus might have already begun questioning the confident "we know" that Jews might be inclined to offer over against Samaritans, to say nothing of gentiles. Nicodemus was confident that he knew and yet there were things he did not. Here Jesus is similarly confident that Samaritans know not, and yet here comes this woman demonstrating what she and presumably others know. He may have judged it to be imperfect knowledge in need of completion through his teaching, but her openness to that teaching indicated there was a good foundation, or fertile ground for the planting of good seed, to use a metaphor that appears here in John as well as elsewhere in the Gospels on the lips of Jesus.

---

12. Tetlow (*Women and Ministry*, 111) suggests (following Brown) that the Samaritan woman is the one to whom Jesus referred he said that others have labored there before the male disciples who were with him. Hebblethwaite (*Six New Gospels*, 75–76n31) notes that Origen begrudgingly calls the woman an apostle, comparing her to the women who proclaim the resurrection on Easter morning. See also Schüssler-Fiorenza, *In Memory of Her*, 138; Swidler, *Three Jesus Certitudes*, 52–53.

From Enemy to Long-Lost Distant Cousin

To sum up, Jesus met a Samaritan woman, whose name the patriarchal transmitters of the story did not bother to record. They met at a well in a similar manner to Jacob and Rachel, and at the same time of day. Yet they met under the cloud of all that lay behind the parenthetical remark in the Gospel of John, "Jews/Judeans do not have dealings with Samaritans." In other words, representatives of two different Israelite tribes, separated now by a sense of religious and ethnic difference, met at a well like the one where their own ancestors met, two ancestors that both of them probably shared in common. From Jacob, renamed Israel, the children of Israel branch off in a variety of interconnected and intertwined directions. The tribe of Benjamin folded into the kingdom of Judah, and Simeon was also there in the south. The northern tribes were, like the southern, descended from Jacob and not only Rachel, but also her sister Leah. But whether the point is considered through both Jacob and Rachel, or only in terms of the role of Jacob as patriarch of Israel, the point remains the same. The geographical location where this Galilean man of Jewish extraction and this Samaritan woman bumped into one another was not only useful because it provided fresh water. It was a symbol of love. A well was a place where their shared ancestor had first encountered the woman that he would marry. They would both have assumed that this ancestor they shared in common had stood on that very ground where they stood, a very long time before they did. The well was a place that showed their separate stories to be part of one larger story that included them both.

Shechem, where the well is located, is mentioned in Genesis 33 soon after Jacob is reconciled to his brother Esau. It was a perfect place for the boundaries that had grown up between Jacob's own descendants, children of Israel, to be challenged, transcended, and overcome. This heroic act of reconciliation was not carried out unilaterally by Jesus, but bilaterally by him and his unnamed conversation partner. She deserves to be remembered for this, even if we still do not know her name. They both learned things on this occasion. Rediscovering a shared connection, even after more than a millennium has passed, can have a powerful transformative impact. It happened in the Gospel of John. It happens when white supremacists get their DNA test results back and see "African" in the mix. It happens when Protestants discover that significant things happened in church history between the New Testament and the Reformation. We should envisage this encounter as helping Jesus to formulate his own vision for the whole of Israel rather than just Judah. Those of us who follow him should be open to learning the same kinds of lessons that Jesus learned from the Samaritan woman on this occasion.

The Syrophoenician Woman
What Jesus Learned from a Doggedly Insistent Mother

I don't think I've ever been as angry at anyone as I was at Jesus. But then again, I had never been subjected to such humiliating treatment before in my life.

But let me start my story at the beginning. My friend Deborah told me of how she had heard from a relative in Galilee about a man named Jesus who was a healer and teacher. Deborah's eyesight had been failing and she feared that if she didn't find someone who could cure her soon she might end up blind. It was a full day of travel to get to Galilee from here where we live in the vicinity of Tyre, but she could stay with her relatives for a few days before returning. She would need them to make the introduction between her and Jesus.

I wished the best for her, I really did. She had tried all kinds of ointments and nothing seemed to help. But I have seen other cases like hers, and what typically happens when they seek out renowned healers. Such stories rarely have a happy ending. Meanwhile, some were already starting to say that there was not just something wrong with her eyes, but this was the work of a demon. It was the same kind of thing they said about my daughter, whose eyesight has gotten so bad that she can no longer even safely leave her bed anymore. Deborah knew what people were saying but insisted it didn't matter. Jesus was not just a powerful healer but an exorcist who had a reputation for being able to free people from malevolent spirits. As I said, I've known people who've gone to healers before. Sometimes they help a little, and sometimes they don't. It is best not to get one's hopes up.

But when Deborah came back, she said her eyesight was better than she remembered it being in years. I saw the difference in her and it was indeed remarkable.

I thought about seeking out this Jesus then, to help my daughter. But would he help the daughter of the friend of the relative of someone who knew him? And a foreigner at that? It seemed unlikely, even if he were an unusually kind individual. Plus I know something about Jewish scruples from my friendship with Deborah. My daughter's name is Astraia, and mine is Eurydice. Both make reference to the Greek gods. Deborah has a very negative view of my devotion to the gods, a much stronger sentiment than my own bewilderment at her worship of only one. I know that there are many Jews who are not like Deborah and would be friends with a woman who worships the gods the way people have since time immemorial. What was this Jesus like? It would be too disappointing to bear if we traveled all that way only to have Jesus refuse to heal Astraia. It is getting harder and harder to travel with her anyway, since it requires bringing along a servant to care for and guide her, as well as one to attend to me and my needs. So I put the matter out of my mind, although I was reminded of these thoughts from time to time. In the meantime, Deborah traveled back to Galilee to visit her relatives there with increasing frequency after her eyesight was restored, and not only because her healing made it easier for her to travel. She went to listen to Jesus, who was apparently a gifted teacher as well as healer. Deborah told me some of the things he said, and some of them were indeed interesting. Others made little sense to me. They probably required Jewish assumptions I didn't have to figure out what they were supposed to mean. Deborah sometimes brought gifts for Jesus and his followers when she traveled there, to support what he was doing. I could see that her life was impacted by the connection in more than just the practical way of benefiting from healing. She mentioned things Jesus said with increasing frequency.

Then one day she said that Jesus would be coming to stay with her and her family here near Tyre. He didn't usually come to Phoenicia, even though he had others besides Deborah who had links to Galilee and who traveled from here on occasion to see and hear him as she did. There were quite a few Galileans living here, but not so many that it made sense for him to focus his attention here. When I asked what the occasion of his visit was, Deborah said that Jesus was feeling exhausted and that Herod Antipas, ruler over Galilee, was starting to become nervous about Jesus's activities. She emphasized this was to be a visit of rest and recuperation for Jesus and that I shouldn't say anything about him coming here to anyone. With his increasing popularity, if word got out crowds might gather. They would tire him out, and that was what he needed to get away from. Recovering from exhaustion was the point of his visit. Here his personal and family connections were few enough that he could keep a low profile.

I said nothing to anyone. But the more I thought about the prospect of Jesus coming here, the more I thought that it was meant to be. I had contemplated going to seek him out myself, for my daughter's sake, and now he was coming here! The gods must surely be bringing him here for a reason, I thought. And it was never a problem for me to stop by at Deborah's unannounced. I would go to him, beseech him to help my daughter. Perhaps he would come and put his hands on Astraia's eyes and make her well, or perhaps his wisdom was such that he would recommend some treatment I could go home and try. I couldn't bring her there and risk having him refuse to see us or say or do something that would add insult to her injury.

It turned out I was right to be worried about this.

When I got to Deborah's home, Jesus was there in the main courtyard and so I saw him before he had a chance to avoid meeting this surprise guest. He didn't look majestic or noble, powerful or spiritual, as his reputation would lead you to expect. He looked exhausted. What Deborah had said about how the increasingly large crowds of people with illnesses pleading for his help were taking their toll on him ought to have prepared me, but when someone has an impressive reputation, seeing them tired is always going to be a disappointment compared with one's expectations. But I wasn't going to be deterred if there was any chance my daughter might be made well. Seizing the opportunity, I did what I had only seen my maidservants do when they had ruined my clothing or made some other blunder that meant they deserved a beating. I threw myself on the ground before him and began to wail and plead for him to show mercy towards my daughter. Surely just as I usually gave in to such pleading, so this Jesus would as well.

I was wrong.

He looked at me and sighed. At first I thought he might not say anything at all. But when he spoke, I wished in that moment that he had indeed chosen to remain silent. What he said pierced my soul with a cold shiver. He said, as if not even speaking to me but mainly to Deborah and anyone else who might be listening, that it wasn't appropriate to take the bread from children and give it to dogs.

Deborah gasped. Jesus looked at her with surprise, then back at me. I was furious, and turned to leave. Deborah's face was filled with apology and sorrow as I turned in her direction. But after a couple of steps I stopped and turned around. I wasn't going to let that man have the last word. I looked him in the eye and said that where I come from, even dogs get a chance to eat the scraps that fall from the table when children are eating. I know how Jews feel about our love for dogs here in Phoenicia. He had been making fun of my people and insulting me personally all at once. I had heard about his clever way with words, and was glad I repaid him in equal measure, even though I would still have to go home bitterly disappointed, not only with Jesus but also with Deborah for associating with him. I was also angry with myself for getting my hopes up as I had. I was glad I hadn't told Astraia why I was paying a visit to Deborah today, so that perhaps she might never hear about this incident. At least when I left, I could know that I turned his air of superiority towards Phoenicians back on him. They think they are superior for not wasting food on dogs. Our dogs eat what is left after we have been satisfied, and to deliberately starve a dog when the children have been filled and are satisfied wasn't merely wasteful, it was cruel.

I walked towards the doorway, but before I reached the exit from the courtyard I heard a sound. I slowed, then stopped even as everything in me wanted to leave there as quickly as possible. It sounded like laughter. I spun around, thinking that Jesus was mocking me as I departed, like the dog he considered me to be, leaving with my tail between my legs. I thought I was already furious, but in that moment I became angrier still, angrier than I ever remember being. But when I spun around and looked at him, something stopped me from saying the many things that had begun rushing through my mind. He didn't look as though he were mocking or spiteful. He didn't look angry. It took a moment until I could figure out what the way he was laughing and looking at me conveyed. But then it hit me: he looked like he was impressed, and that disarmed me. Before I could *find some other words to say, he spoke and said, "For that answer, go knowing your daughter is healed."*

I didn't know what to say. Deborah had told me that this man sometimes healed with just a word, but I didn't honestly believe it. Was that to be it? He'd just tell me to go, she's healed, and I'd go home and find her well? I hesitated, then gave an acknowledging nod and left. I couldn't smile or thank him after what he had said to me. I wasn't even sure I believed what he'd said at the end. I'd find out soon enough . . .

A Natural Starting Place

Were it not for the logic of starting with the earliest female influences on Jesus and proceeding from there chronologically, this story would be the natural one with which to begin this book. While there is always resistance and pushback from certain quarters whenever it is brought up, this instance is nevertheless the example par excellence of Jesus learning in the Gospels, period. It is the clearest example, and his teacher is a woman. In this case there is the least ambiguity, perhaps precisely because Jesus does not seem to be the willing student, eager to learn and to change his mind when necessary, that we might see him as in other examples. We should tackle some preliminary matters right away about where the story is set, what Jesus was doing there, and who the woman was. But even before that, for the sake of those who may not be inclined to accept that Jesus viewed this woman and her entire people in a negative way, let me pose three questions that it might be good to reflect on before proceeding:

1. Why might some of us be inclined to assume that Jesus was not deeply influenced by the negative statements about Canaanites in the Jewish Scriptures that he was brought up hearing throughout his life?
2. If Jesus ultimately accepted Canaanites and all peoples as potential participants in the kingdom of God, why do some assume that he *always* held this view, rather than having to learn it?
3. Some will accept without hesitation that Jesus might have needed to learn something, to discover something new, in order to include the Canaanites as part of his vision for the kingdom of God. After

all, the Scriptures called for their extermination in the territories where the Israelites established themselves. If one can accept that, why might they nonetheless resist the idea that this woman was the one who helped him learn this, who influenced him to change his mind and embrace a different perspective on himself, on her and her people, on the kingdom of God, and of the Jewish Scriptures?

Being Syrophoenician

There are a great many things we would like to know by way of background to this story. Why did Jesus go to the vicinity of Tyre and Sidon at all, when his focus was on Israel? Phoenicia was to the north of the historic location of the kingdom of Israel. Centered in the vibrant and important coastal cities like Tyre and Sidon, Phoenicia was the most influential representative of the collection of cultures we can group together under the heading of "Canaanite." This is not the place to go into the history in detail. But the terms that appear in the Gospels, with the woman being categorized as Syrophoenician, Greek, and Canaanite, can be confusing unless one digs at least a little into the history of the region. As it stands, all of them can be true. If they all reflect genuine knowledge about the woman (rather than being changes made for editorial purposes) they suggest that she was ethnically Phoenician and a person of status whose family participated in civic life as citizens.[1] This refers to a specific way of defining citizenship and the roles of citizens that had been developed by the Greeks. In Greek democracy, leadership of the *polis* (city) was in the hands of citizens. Not all residents in a city or region were citizens, as many readers of the New Testament may have learned in connection with discussion of Paul the apostle's status as a Roman citizen.

Why did Jesus go there to the vicinity of Tyre? Was it because it was not Herod's territory and he had heard that he was being sought? Or did he go with a view to carrying out certain activities, perhaps among Jews in that region. How many Jews lived there? How far was this from places he normally went? Mark 3:8 (and Luke 6:17) says Jesus attracted Jewish audiences from that region, and so we might and perhaps ought to assume that Jesus was following up with those people.[2] Yet another striking aspect of the version in the Gospel of Mark is that there is no

---

1. See further Andrade, *Syrian Identity*, 109–10.
2. Sankamo, *Jesus and the Gentiles*, 116; Aletti, "Analyse," 364.

mention of Jesus's disciples.³ The possibility that this trip involved leaving not only crowds but his immediate circle of followers behind is intriguing, although it may also be reading too much into this silence. Later versions of the story make a point of adding them in. While some of these questions may just be historical curiosity, it is natural to wonder whether ancient readers and hearers would have known things, and brought presuppositions to the story that are now lost to us, which filled in gaps and provided a framework for understanding the narrative different than our own.

One cultural assumption that most modern readers lack when reading ancient literature relates to travel. Jesus would not have journeyed to a place where he knew literally no one and checked himself into a hotel. Travel in the ancient world followed a network of relationships of family, ethnicity, shared trade, friendship, and acquaintanceship. Jesus undoubtedly either knew someone in the vicinity of Tyre, or knew someone who knew someone, and that was how arrangements would be made for him to have a place to stay. When we envisage the woman coming to Jesus in a house, it should occur to us to wonder whose house it is. It is obviously not a question we can answer in a very specific way, but even a more general answer can lead us to recognize that there was someone that knew Jesus who also knew this woman and revealed to her (whether intentionally or inadvertently) that this healer was staying with them.⁴ This entire chapter in the Gospel of Mark is about Jesus learning that his efforts to keep a low profile, or at the very least reduce the amount of attention he gathered, were doomed to fail. He would not cease to try. But even withdrawing to places like Phoenicia or the Decapolis simply increased his sphere of influence and renown. Telling people not to speak about him did not work. It is of course possible that Jesus knew this and that his travels and demands about secrecy were part of a strategy intended not to suppress but to enhance his reputation. To me, it seems more likely that Jesus genuinely wanted to delay what he had come to see as inevitable. Jesus could foresee that the attention he garnered would lead to his arrest and at least potentially to his execution. Increasing awareness of this impending end would in turn have increased the extent of Jesus's exhaustion

---

3. Tyson, "Jesus and Herod," 243–44.

4. For those who have seen *Downton Abbey* or similar shows, it may well be that the information reached the Syrophoenician woman by the network of servants that allowed gossip and news to flow between households even when families sought to keep secrets.

from his healing and teaching activities. Each one brought him closer to death, not because of power that drained from him, but because of what rulers and others in authority always did to anyone who assembled crowds and led a movement.

Another detail we are likely to miss is that the woman is not poor.[5] We are told that her daughter is lying on a bed, not merely a mattress. A bed does not seem like a luxury item to us, but in ancient times many people made do with a mat or something else more rudimentary than what this woman's daughter is said to lie on.[6] Alternative translations one encounters such as "couch" also conjure up a very different image today than what ancient people had and used. This small detail on its own would probably not be enough evidence to indicate her social status. Together with the description of her as of Syrophoenician ethnicity and yet at the same time Greek, however, we get an overall impression of her as part of a family with the status of citizens, which not everyone in ancient societies was. She may not have been part of the upper echelon, but she still had some status that elevated her above the majority. The mutual acquaintance who provided Jesus with hospitality would most likely have been someone with the means to do so, and the friendship that allowed information to reach one by way of the other likewise confirms their social standing. A woman of this status would not be accustomed to having to throw herself at someone's feet, although if she had become a widow this may not have been the first time the realities of her ancient patriarchal context had placed her in a situation that demanded she humiliate herself in this way.[7] Doing so would still have been felt demeaning rather than merely a matter of course, as it might seem to someone who grew up and lived their entire life as a slave or simply in the poorer levels of society, in which one inevitably had to plead with the powerful and wealthy

---

5. See the treatment of the story in Kinukawa, "De-colonizing," 142–43; also Ruiz, *Readings from the Edges*. Some recent studies consider the economic background of the story to be important to how we understand it. Tyre benefited from Galilee's agriculture yet maintained economic and religious independence and advantage. Was this relationship felt to be unequal? Did it lead Jesus to deliberately verbalize an inversion of the relationship between the woman and him as she herself may have perceived it? On the story's possible economic context see further Chinen, "Crumbs"; Nelavala, "Smart Syrophoenician Woman"; Hicks, "Moral Agency," 82.

6. Ransom, *Studies*, 109.

7. Rüggemeier, *Poetik*, 276. Even having to go herself rather than merely send a servant might have involved some humiliation for a woman of status.

for something. Having abased herself in this way, to be treated as rudely as Jesus treated her must have added insult to injury.

Schooling Jesus

Whatever unanswered questions we may be left with regarding the background of place and people mentioned, the connection of this story to the theme of this book is clear. Of all the characters that are the focus of chapters in this book, the Syrophoenician woman is the one about whom there is the most agreement that Jesus learned something from her. It thus seems appropriate to offer a range of quotations illustrating these perspectives and past work on this subject. For example, Martha Driscoll writes,

> Commentators say Jesus was at a moment of discernment of his vocation. He really did believe he was sent only to Israel. He did not intend to preach and work miracles among the Gentiles. He may have been up against a real moral problem. Helping the woman might have far-reaching consequences . . . And he worked out the discernment openly with the woman. She was clever and humble enough to bring him to the conclusion she needed.[8]

Sharon Ringe writes that "Her gift was not the submission or obedience seen as appropriate for women in her society, but rather the gift of sharp insight."[9] Rachel Wahlberg writes, "She used the debater's technique of latching onto what the person has said and turning it to her own advantage. A smart woman. A person so quick of mind she would have made a good lawyer . . . Further, as I read the story, it seems that *this woman influenced Jesus* . . . Scripture says 'Jesus grew in wisdom.' How? Perhaps he grew in his self-understanding because of people like this woman. He matured in his concept of messiahship as she challenged him to recognize her need."[10]

---

8. Driscoll, *Reading Between The Lines*, 41. See also Duckworth, *Mary*, 62; Connor, *Fierce*, 137; and for a poetic retelling see Hanrahan, "Syrophoenician Woman," especially 296. Buckhanon Crowder, "When Mommy Goes to Work," 84 notes that this is the first woman after Herodias to speak in the Gospel of Matthew, and the first to address Jesus. Cf. Roberts, "Speaking Out," 46.

9. Ringe, "Gentile Woman's Story," 71–72.

10. Wahlberg, *Jesus According to a Woman*, 17. See too Tucker and Liefeld, *Daughters*, 37; Kassel, *Das Evangelium*, 10.

Jean-Noel Aletti points out that there was a contradiction in what Jesus said as recorded in Mark, between the children being given first opportunity, and the seeming blanket refusal for any of the bread to be thrown to dogs.[11] The woman latches on to that and uses it in an effort to outwit Jesus. Janet and John Gaden write, "The syro-phoenician woman is not only an example of persistence and nimble wit. She shows that men have to accept correction at the hands of women whose experience of God is different and wider than theirs."[12] Claudia Setzer writes, "This is the only occasion in the gospels where Jesus is bested in an argument by anyone."[13] Gail O'Day writes, "in the story the Gentile woman gets the better of Jesus in an argument and he changes his mind . . . This portrait of Jesus's intransigence and the impingement of the Gentile woman has been a stumbling block to many interpreters. There is a hesitancy to recognize either the mutability of Jesus or the powerful presence of the woman. Both, however, are central to the text."[14] Susanna Asikainen says, "The encounter with the Syrophoenician woman is the only instance in the Gospels where Jesus loses a dispute—and to a gentile woman, no less . . . Jesus acknowledges that the woman's words persuaded him to change his mind."[15] Stuart Love writes, "She is a capable, worthy, and wise person who teaches Jesus."[16] Many others have argued similarly, that the

---

11. Aletti, "Analyse," 367, who nonetheless resists the interpretation that the woman "forces" Jesus's hand in getting him to unwillingly grant her request for a miracle.

12. Gaden and Gaden, "Women and Discipleship," 118.

13. Setzer, "Three Odd Couples," 77. See too Setzer, "Mark," 99. So likewise Asikainen, "Women out of Place," 183, who writes, "The Syrophoenician woman is an exceptional figure, because she is the only person in the Synoptic Gospels to best Jesus in a dispute." See also Schüssler Fiorenza, *In Memory of Her*, 137. Wainwright, *Towards a Feminist Critical Reading*, 105, 107 notes that the Canaanite woman is the first female character to speak in Matthew's Gospel.

14. O'Day, "Surprised by Faith," 114. See also 117 where O'Day proposes that the reason the story has been impossible to pigeonhole in form critical categories is because the woman rather than Jesus is the protagonist of the story.

15. Asikainen, "Women out of Place," 184. Also Seibert-Cuadra, "La mujeren los evangelios sinópticos," 94; Swidler, *Jesus Was a Feminist*, 64; Moore, *Women in Christian Traditions*, 32; Perkinson, "Canaanitic," 76; Roberts, "Speaking Out," 208. Sankamo, *Jesus and the Gentiles*, 154 writes, "In Mark 7:29 Jesus pays attention to the woman's reasoning and he is prepared to learn from her intervention. Precisely due to her *words* Jesus heals her daughter."

16. Love, *Jesus and Marginal Women*, 162.

Canaanite woman challenged Jesus's assumptions and prompted Jesus to rethink the limits of his ministry.[17]

How Insulting Was Jesus?

Asikainen writes, "the offensive nature of the passage should not be overlooked. Calling someone a dog was a common insult in Jewish writings and Greco-Roman literature from Homer onwards. In ancient Israel, dogs were not household pets, but street animals that scavenged for food."[18] Sharon Ringe says, "Jesus' flippant, even cruel, response to the woman defies justification."[19] There is of course a longstanding attempt to turn Jesus's insulting reference into one about cute, cuddly household pets. Unfortunately, the cultural and historical context makes such attempts look anachronistic, attempts to make Jesus come off better than he otherwise would. Keep in mind that Jesus probably spoke Aramaic with the woman, and so the Greek diminutive may already represent a toning down of what Jesus said that was lacking in the actual conversation. The setting is probably a domestic one, and so the dogs may well be household dogs, but I see nothing in the likely original form of Jesus's words to indicate that that was specified. It is striking that the Syriac (Aramaic) Gospels don't use a diminutive form of the word "dog" even though such a form existed. The Greek Gospels also use a non-standard form which may indicate that Mark quickly came up with an attempt to tone down Jesus's language in an effort to soften his words and tone. Asikainen points out, "the Syrophoenician woman talking about dogs under the table does not mean that Jesus is talking about household pets. It is the Syrophoenician woman who introduces the notion of the table and changes the meaning of the parable."[20] It seems to be the woman who, in answering Jesus, el-

---

17. Guijarro, "La Cananea," 54; Agosto, *Servant Leadership*, 37; Wainwright, *Towards a Feminist Critical Reading*, 112; Hartman, *Letting the Other Speak*, 97–98.

18. Asikainen, "Women out of Place," 183. Focant, *Gospel according to Mark*, 296 notes the string of diminutives the woman uses. Is "little dogs" used because the woman's young daughter is primarily in mind? On the insulting connotations of Jesus's words see further Cadwaller, "When a Woman is a Dog," 35.2.

19. Ringe, "Gentile Woman's Story," 69.

20. Asikainen, "Women out of Place," 188. For more on the range of views of dogs in ancient Israel and early Judaism, see Schottroff, "Behold, These Are My Sisters," 64–66; Miller, "Attitudes towards Dogs"; Schwartz, "Dogs in Jewish Society." See also Kinukawa, *Women and Jesus*, 58–60; Wahlberg, *Jesus According to a Woman*, 17.

evates the status of the dogs being discussed in their conversation. Either way the manner in which Jesus referred to her remains insulting. Saying that others are children while you're merely a pet is problematic, isn't it? Is it not insulting merely because pets are ranked above stray dogs and scavengers? Hopefully in our time we are becoming much more attuned to the problem of dehumanization. But that leaves Christian readers of the story with the problem with what to do with it and with behavior on the part of Jesus that we view as at best problematic. We should thus also not make too much of whether dogs were especially reviled by Jews in this time (or any other). As Geoffrey Miller writes, "Even in modern cultures where dogs are kept as pets, to call someone a dog is offensive ... To call a person a dog or a cow or any animal is an insult not because that animal is vile but because human beings are more dignified than animals."[21]

This isn't to say that it is not worth investigating whether "dog" had particular connotations either for Jews or for the people of Phoenicia. Rebekah Liu and Margaret Roberts have pointed out the relevance to our understanding of this story of the fact that a dog graveyard has been unearthed by archaeologists in Ashkelon, a Phoenician city.[22] Dogs may have had some sacred significance for the inhabitants of the region, although it is not clear what that significance was. This does not eliminate the problem, allowing us to imagine Jesus using Phoenician reverence for dogs as an endearing metaphor. Rather, we may envisage him choosing the insult precisely because the keeping of dogs as pets was something that was more typical of Phoenicians and Greeks than Galilean Jews. In other words, the Phoenicians might have been viewed negatively precisely because they not only took food and other resources from Galilean cities (much to the chagrin of the inhabitants) but shared it with dogs. That would give Jesus's words to her particular force. In effect, he may have been saying "Unlike you Greeks/Phoenicians, we Jews won't take food that should go to our children and give it to dogs." Her response would then be a rejoinder that perhaps conveys the meaning that, "Even among Jews there are dogs, domestic or even wild, which manage to get scraps that fall from the table while the children are being fed." In other words,

---

21. Miller, "Attitudes toward Dogs," 496.

22. Liu, "Dog Under the Table," 254; Roberts, "Speaking Out," 135–36. For different interpretations of the significance of the dog burial site see Stager, "Why Were Hundreds of Dogs"; Wapnish and Hesse, "Pampered Pooches"; Edrey, "Dog Burials"; Smith, "Ashkelon Dog Cemetery."

even within a Jewish frame of reference, if she and her daughter are to be denigrated as dogs and not children, it should be possible for them to indirectly benefit from the food that Jesus has brought to the children (of Israel). To deliberately withhold even crumbs from animals is to be deliberately cruel. It was a clever insult, characteristic of Jesus's adeptness in painting images with words, and it is a clever retort that is offered as a comeback. This woman is not the only person Jesus is depicted as insulting in the Gospels, although her case disturbs many readers more than the others do. There are multiple examples of Jesus engaging in thoughtful parabolic insult and polemic. Jesus's unkind rebuff of the Syrophoenician woman is not entirely out of keeping with that, although neither is it quite the same. Her response, on the other hand, stands out as the cleverest comeback anyone makes to Jesus (although, to be fair, male recipients of insults tend not to make much of a retort if any). That Jesus might have been impressed in the short term, and changed more profoundly in the longer term, is also in keeping with his character as we see it depicted in the Gospels, and as it has come into focus in the present study. It might even be that the developing Gospel tradition reflects not so much a desire to improve how Jesus comes across in stories like this one, but an increasing willingness on the part of later authors to incorporate perspectives that Jesus was known to have held later in his public activity. Things that we see only looking back on our earlier actions and experiences are not necessarily wrong or inauthentic as a result. Sometimes we see the past more clearly from a distance, with the benefit of hindsight. Just as Jesus seems to have been willing to change his mind on this occasion in the short term, deciding to heal the daughter when initially he refused, he may also have changed his mind about gentiles in more profound ways as he looked back on this encounter and others and took them to heart. One experience can change us profoundly, but in most cases changes in our thinking result from multiple experiences, however crucially important one of them might be that may make it stand out from among the others.

Ultimately the question should not be whether Jesus used an especially bad insult in speaking to this woman, but whether he insulted her, period. He did. Comparing someone to a household pet may not be as bad as comparing someone to a wild scavenger, but both are dehumanizing. We sometimes find ourselves inclined to pretend otherwise because of an instinct many of us have to defend Jesus's reputation if not indeed his perfection and infallibility. Rachel Wahlberg gets at this issue nicely when she writes, "We say glibly that Jesus was *human*, but whenever he displays a *humanly-conditioned prejudice*, we feel we must deny it."[23] On the other hand, Elizabeth Watson cuts Jesus some slack, noting that healing involved power going out from the healer, and that Jesus was thoroughly exhausted and seeking to rest and recharge.[24] We all sometimes fail to respond with courtesy when exhausted. She nonetheless feels that "The greatness of Jesus shines through this story." Jesus demonstrates humility in the sense in which twelve-step programs define what it means to be humble, namely a "willingness to become teachable." Too often Christians will say Jesus was humble, but do not really mean it, because this human trait is incompatible with their theology. Here Jesus is a paradigm for what he calls his followers to be and do, namely being humble in the practical way of being open to correction and learning. Jesus's later emphasis on those who humble themselves being exalted, as well as his skill at turning his opponents' would-be traps into counter-traps, are points at which Jesus mirrored things that he at least could have learned from this woman. She put him in his place, and he benefited and became greater as a result of the humbling moment. In that respect, as Jim Perkinson suggests, we may view this woman as a mentor or teacher to Jesus at least on this point.[25]

A Defenseless Widow?

Many assume the woman in this story was a widow, perhaps understandably. Indeed, even if she was not a widow, Jesus may have assumed she was, given the facts that she came to him without a husband and no male from her household came to Jesus instead, which would have been deemed more appropriate in that cultural setting.[26] Her assertiveness also

23. Wahlberg, *Jesus According to a Woman*, 15. See also Korpman, *Saying No To God*, 58–62.

24. Watson, *Wisdom's Daughters*, 62.

25. Perkinson, "Canaanitic," 77–78, referring to what we see in the story on the literary level.

26. Roberts, "Speaking Out," 45. Love, *Jesus and Marginal Women*, 152–54 argues that the woman, having no man to represent her, is most likely a prostitute. She may have been in one of the other categories of women without a male to represent her in social interactions, such as an orphan, unmarried, or a widow. But women in such circumstances were often reduced to prostitution as a means of making ends meet. It should also be noted that, if tax collectors and prostitutes were as important a part of Jesus's following as is claimed, then we should expect there to be at least one story about a prostitute's encounter with Jesus.

represented in that cultural context the adoption of the role of a male in advocating for family needs. The woman advocating as she does on behalf of her daughter would normally have implied something about her lack of male head of household. As Jesus thought more about the woman, he may have learned things that influenced his thinking not only about widows or about women, but also about God. Ought we not to view Jesus's parable of the persistent widow (Luke 18:1–8) as reflecting his experience of seeing or knowing one or more such people? Should we hear a hint of repentant self-deprecation when Jesus depicts God as greater than the judge who only granted the request because of weariness at the supplicant's persistence? Could he have been telling a story that reflected his own experience with this woman, emphasizing God's greatness because God doesn't require the insistent persuasion that human beings do—that he himself had? Might it be appropriate to combine several of the sayings attributed to Jesus in the Gospels, a couple of particularly controversial ones, and paraphrase them as follows? "No one is good but God alone. The Father, who is greater than I, has no need to be bested in an argument as I was" (Mark 10:18 = Luke 18:19; John 14:28). It is interesting that Luke places his version of that statement soon after the parable of the persistent widow, and that he omits the story of the Syrophoenician woman. There are undoubtedly instances in which a story in a source gets turned into a parable in the Gospel of a later writer (and also sometimes the reverse, that a parable gets turned into a narrative). That may be what happened here, in which case the parable could give us one early ancient interpreter's understanding of the story we have been exploring in this chapter. It is also possible that parable is substituted for story not because the author turned the one into the other, but rather because within the larger framework of tradition and memory in the early church, Jesus's followers were aware of instances in which a parable was a result of an experience in the life of Jesus, and they substituted the one for the other.

Expanding Jesus's Vision and Mission

Stuart Love suggests that this woman brought Jesus's emphasis on mercy and compassion, and the purity boundary of Israel that he was still taking for granted, into tension/conflict, forcing him to recognize that sometimes one must choose between them.[27] Human beings rarely see

---

27. Love, *Jesus and Marginal Women*, 13–14.

tensions in their thinking unless an encounter with another person challenges them. Once again we get a chance to see Jesus as human, and we can say it is humanity at its best. While some might say the ideal is to be entirely free from prejudice from infancy to death, that is not humanity as it exists in reality. If we do not discriminate in particular ways, we inevitably do in others. If we do not judge people based on skin color, we may do so based on their accent, educational background, or place or origin. What is truly remarkable is that human beings are capable of learning throughout life and setting aside prejudices both instinctive and taught. For there to be a human being that was inherently incapable of prejudice would indeed be remarkable. But it would not be a biological human being of the kind we are, and it would not be one who was (as the author of the Letter to the Hebrews puts it) "tempted in every way like we are." There is no way to be susceptible to prejudice and immune to it at the same time. In overcoming prejudice, having it part of his cultural and biological heritage and yet to managing to set it aside, is the best a human being can achieve and truly praiseworthy, including when the human being in question is Jesus.

Several authors see poignant symbolism in the stories that the Gospels of Mark and Matthew tell in close proximity to this story. For example, Schüssler Fiorenza notes that the Greek word for being satisfied appears only in this story and in those about the feeding of the crowds.[28] Santiago Guijarro makes an interesting connection between the collecting of every fragment of the bread Jesus provided in the feedings of the 5,000 and the 4,000 in Matthew and the discussion of crumbs going to the dogs.[29] F. Scott Spencer notes that the subsequent feeding Matthew narrates takes place in a gentile region and features the number 7 rather than 12 (denoting the tribes of Israel). He writes, "The dogs are getting much more than crumbs now from Jesus. He has learned his lesson well."[30] Kara Lyons-Pardue notes how Jesus is depicted as rejecting the disciples' words about scarcity of bread and sees it as a direct result of his encounter with the woman.[31] We may decide that Jesus's encounter with a Roman centurion seems to have been the more direct impetus for Jesus's

28. Schüssler Fiorenza, *In Memory of Her*, 138. Mark 6:42; 8:4, 8.

29. Guijarro, "La Cananea," 43–51. Matt 14:20; 15:37.

30. Spencer, *Dancing Girls*, 65. See also Roberts, "Speaking Out," 176–77, 213. Jesus being in the Decapolis in Mark and providing food presumably while still there can be understood in a similar way.

31. Lyons-Pardue, "Syrophoenician Becomes a Canaanite," 246. Mark 8:15–20.

statement that "many will come from the east and the west" to dine with the patriarchs (Matt 8:11 = Luke 13:29). But Jesus only got there because of what he had already learned from a woman who pushed him to consider who eats at the messianic banquet. By the time he encountered the centurion he was no longer refusing to help gentiles, nor even offering them merely crumbs.[32] Posing the matter in this way assumes of course that the centurion was a non-Jew. The rendering of the Greek term used in the story in English with the familiar Latin technical term "centurion" conveys this impression more strongly than the story itself does in the original language. Especially in the parallel version in John 4, the possibility must be considered that this was a high-ranking soldier in Herod Antipas' forces, and thus Jewish. This possibility is further reinforced by the fact that there was no Roman troop presence in Galilee at this time, which was not under direct Roman rule the way Judea was.[33] It is also important to distinguish between any originating historical incident and the literary depictions in the Gospels. Whether or not Luke and/or Matthew present the story as involving a Roman soldier in order to present Jesus's openness to gentiles, it is unlikely that a Roman centurion was regularly present or stationed in Galilee so as to help locals build their synagogue, as Luke depicts.[34] It should also be emphasized that the position of the story in Matthew and Luke, where it is inserted prior to Jesus's encounter with the Syrophoenician woman, does not in any way provide counterevidence to the historical relationship between the two encounters that we have proposed in this chapter.[35] For the Gospel authors, the point was

---

32. Guijarro, "La Cananea," 59–60. Note, however, that Jesus may still have expressed hesitation at the idea of going to a gentile's ritually impure home. Boer (*Mary Magdalene: Beyond the Myth*, 35) notes the possibility that Jesus's words to the man in Matt 8:7 ought to be translated, "Must I come to help him?"

33. See further Bond, "What Can We Know"; Zeichmann, "Beyond the Gay Centurion," 49–50.

34. On the question of this character's nationality in Q as well as in Matthew and Luke see Catchpole, *Quest for Q*, 238, 296–308. On the centurion story's positioning in Q to serve as a frame for Jesus's teaching see Fleddermann, *Q: A Reconstruction and Commentary*, 353. If the story is from Q it is the only narrative of its kind in that source, and so even those who accept the likelihood that Matthew and Luke used this no longer extant source should nonetheless consider the possibility that this story reached them both by some other means.

35. Stuart Love explores how the Gospel of Matthew treats the story. There the woman is said to be Canaanite and so represents a further extension of inclusivity beyond merely being a gentile, to a category explicitly censured in the Jewish Scriptures (*Jesus and Marginal Women*, 162–64). It is therefore not surprising that Matthew (and

a progression from Israel to gentiles and among gentiles from Romans to the most despised of all in the biblical tradition, the Canaanites. In the life of Jesus, however, the order of events was not always that depicted in the Gospels, as we see clearly from the Gospel authors' willingness to rearrange material in order to make their points.

We may explore this point about the changes Gospel authors made to stories by returning to a point we touched on earlier. Andrzej Kowalczyk notes that in Mark unlike in Matthew, Jesus does not praise the woman's faith, but simply says that because of what she said she should go and her daughter will be healed.[36] Jesus's words to her are terse rather than expressing a reaction of being impressed. Did Matthew enhance Jesus's positive reaction to the woman, or did Mark downplay it in relation to the story as he had normally heard it before he wrote, which Matthew may also have been familiar with? Or could both Gospels preserve an element of truth and be correct, in the sense that Jesus's immediate reaction was not as lavish with praise for the woman as he would be about her subsequently, as a result of the longer-term impact she had on his view of non-Jews in general or Canaanites/Syrophoenicians in particular? That we see things differently with the benefit of greater hindsight does not make that perspective incorrect. It may be that some of the divergences in the Gospels provide more of a glimpse of Jesus's human development than has traditionally been considered by those studying them.

There is another question worth asking about the order of material in the written Gospels and whether it corresponds to the order in which events transpired in the life of Jesus. In pronouncing woes on the Galilean towns Chorazin and Bethsaida (Matt 11:21–22 = Luke 10:13–15), Jesus compares them with Tyre and Sidon. When does Jesus utter these words? Matthew says it was before Jesus went there and healed the woman. We could treat the statement as indicating his plan to travel there. However, if our understanding of the story is correct, Jesus learned from the Syrophoenician woman that a Canaanite may respond more positively than an Israelite, and that generalizations about any people group, whether positive or negative, have exceptions, which should not be used to stigmatize a nation or culture in its entirety. It therefore seems more likely that Jesus had that transformative encounter with her first, and then was

---

Luke) insert the story about the centurion, not found in Mark and thus presumably in Q, where they do in relation to Jesus's encounter with the woman Mark labels Greek and Syrophoenician.

36. Kowalczyk, *Origin*, 232.

motivated on that basis to say that if he had spent more time there and done more in that location, the response would have been better than in his native territory.

It is possible that we see a direct impact of the woman's words to Jesus reflected in the stories that Jesus himself later told.[37] His parable about giving the children's bread to dogs had spectacularly backfired, but he learned from the experience. In the parable of the rich man and Lazarus (Luke 16:19-31), the poor man longs to eat from the rich man's table, and dogs show compassion to him that the rich man is seen to be lacking. Should we not see in this both Jesus's humble self-criticism, and his acknowledgment of what he learned from the Syrophoenician woman? Withholding the crumbs from one's table—not necessarily by not distributing them, but simply by keeping the hungry outside and excluded—can lead one to be excluded from the messianic banquet with Abraham, at which Jesus comes to explicitly include gentiles (Matt 8:11; Luke 13:29).

Continuing Her Story

Elisabeth Tetlow notes that Luke adds an element of proclamation to the Syrophoenician woman's story, and that this stands out both in the tradition of telling this story, and in contrast with what Luke says about women's roles elsewhere.[38] That too may reflect awareness beyond the historical moment of what this woman had done. If I had told more of this woman's story further in my fictional retelling, beyond that first encounter with Jesus, that is one of the things that I probably would have explored. Here are some others. The Syrophoenician woman may have been impressed by how she heard from Deborah that, in light of the encounter that day, something had changed in his teaching when she went to hear him. Not immediately, but over time. He had told parables about gentiles coming from the far reaches of the earth and becoming part of

---

37. I am indebted to Storkey, *Women in a Patriarchal World*, 119 for drawing attention to the connection between the Syrophoenician woman's words and those attributed to Jesus in Lukan parables. She also notes the possibility of a connection with the story of the prodigal son (Luke 15:11-32) in which the son longs to eat what is left from the pigs' table, an ironic reversal of the image of animals longing for humans' leftovers. Storkey suggests, however, that the woman might have been familiar with Jesus's teaching, whereas her distance from his usual location and lack of prior connection to him makes the reverse (i.e., that her teaching influenced his later words) seem more likely.

38. Tetlow, *Women and Ministry*, 104.

the kingdom, even while some of the children of the kingdom had to give up their seats to them. Foreigners came to him for healing and he didn't refuse them, often expressing how impressed he was with their faith. He had changed his mind. *She* had changed his mind. Not everyone was willing to do that. Some thought it was a sign of strength to never waver, but those who themselves are strong recognize the strength and courage required to examine one's assumptions and even abandon longstanding convictions in light of new evidence. There is reason to think that Jesus's willingness to change his mind would have made an impression on the Syrophoenician woman and perhaps may have changed her mind in due course as well. In Acts 21:3–7, Paul stops in Tyre and seeks out the disciples there. It is not impossible that he was welcomed by a church that met either in the home of the woman who is the focus of this story, or in the home in which Jesus stayed when there and in which the action takes place. It is all but certain the two women we have focused on in this chapter—host and/or hostess who welcomed Jesus and the Syrophoenician woman—were among those who welcomed Paul, prayed with him, and bid him farewell when he departed.[39]

The Pseudo-Clementine literature gives the woman a name, Justa. Since she is said to have been a Greek, in our retelling we gave her a Greek name with a similar meaning to that Latin one. According to that source the woman became a disciple of Jesus and was divorced by her husband because of her conversion. She is depicted as a woman of some means—she gives her daughter in marriage to a man who shares her faith even though he was poor (indicating that she herself was not), and she purchases two male slaves and raises them as sons. Perhaps most interestingly, because the Pseudo-Clementine literature represents a conservative Jewish-Christian outlook, the author expressly agrees with Jesus's initial stance. Perhaps deliberately trying to counter the impression conveyed by the story as we find it in the Gospels, that author says that it is wrong to provide healing to gentiles, and therefore Justa must have been a proselyte and already begun to live in accordance with the Law.[40] That seems more like an attempt to reason around what we see in this story about

---

39. Acts 21:5 makes a point of saying that women and children were there for the sendoff. The Greek word for "women" is frequently translated in this passage so as to limit the reference to wives. The Greek word can indeed denote wives, but its range of meaning is broader and may not be so narrow here.

40. Ps.-Clem. *Homilies* 19. See also Wainwright, "Not Without my Daughter," 126–37; Zetterholm, "Jewish Teachings," 85n56.

Jesus rather than a historical reminiscence about Justa. The history of avoiding the implications of this challenging story is truly ancient, and it is not over yet.

Meeting someone from another culture, religion, or ethnicity who impresses you is what most often expands someone's thinking to view the members of that group more favorably. As I sought to highlight in the brief fictional retelling with which we began the chapter, it is possible that Jesus learned what he did on this occasion with help not only from the Syrophoenician woman but also from her friend, the lady of the house where Jesus was staying. The reaction of one of his followers to how he treated her friend may have influenced him. She grew up surrounded by and interacting with a more diverse range of cultures and people than Jesus had, and so in that sense she had an advantage, an important insight to offer. As we shall see confirmed in later chapters, Jesus was willing not only to teach but to learn from his students, his disciples, something that is one of the hallmarks of a truly great teacher.

Suffering Daughters
What Jesus Learned from Two Women with 12-Year-Old Issues

"*I mostly blame myself for what my daughter went through,*" Salome said. She looked uncomfortably at her daughter, who had brought me with her to her childhood home to introduce me to her mother and get her to tell me the story of their first encounter with Jesus, the famous healer. Salome was not that old, but she seemed to have a frailty and weariness about her that added years to her apparent age. The daughter was now older than her mother Salome had been when these events had transpired. As her daughter's third child, her oldest granddaughter, had reached the age of twelve, it had made Salome want to tell this story and talk with her daughter about what had happened all those years ago from her perspective, as she remembered them.

"When I was her age, it was my older sisters who explained to me what was happening," Salome told me, referring to the experience of beginning to menstruate. "Our mother may have talked to my oldest sister about it, but by the time I had my first period, it was all in the hands of my sisters to deal with. They told me I wasn't dying—that always seems to be a girl's first thought—and that soon father would start talking with the parents of boys in the town about arranging my marriage.

"It is always a stressful experience, but I don't think I understood what it would be like for my daughter as an only child. She

108

must have felt so isolated, not only at that time of the month, but as her father engaged in whispered conversations with parents of boys, and as everyone around her behaved differently and treated her differently. With no siblings to support her and advise her. It is no wonder she became ill."

Salome glanced briefly at her daughter before returning her gaze to her hands in her lap. Her daughter moved from where she had stood behind me and approached her mother. Placing one of her hands on her mother's shoulder, she crouched down and took one of her mother's hands in her own. Salome began to sob and struggled to continue telling the story. When she managed to resume speaking, she was no longer telling it to me, but was now addressing her daughter directly. Perhaps she found it easier to do so both because of how her daughter had drawn near to her. Or perhaps it was mainly because where she was now positioned alongside her, she did not have to meet her gaze as she spoke.

She seemed to go off in a different direction into unrelated events at this point, but the connections soon became clear. "I have—had—a close friend, Berenice, whom Jairus made me sever all connections with, because she had developed an ailment that caused her bleeding to continue throughout the month, leaving her perpetually impure. For Jairus, purity became crucially important. Not because he personally adhered to the teachings of the Pharisees or anything like that. Heavens, no! In fact, the reason he became leader of our synagogue was precisely because he was acceptable to both them and people who had serious reservations about their teachings. Jairus was known to be pious, observant of the Law, trustworthy. Normally that wouldn't mean great concern for purity except when one was preparing to travel to Jerusalem. In Galilee, so far from the holy place, the Law does not require us to be as stringent. At least, that is how almost all of us have always understood things, from generation to generation. But as the years have passed and so many troubles have befallen God's people, many groups have appeared offering their 'solution' to our plight. The Pharisees say that if we would all live as though we were a nation of priests, and our entire land and homes the dwelling place of God, then God would visit us to save and redeem us. They are not so numerous as to make everyone do things their way, yet they are influential enough that alienating them would cause a rift in our community that would divide the synagogue. Jairus was proposed as *leader of the synagogue precisely because he was fair and balanced. He wasn't a Pharisee himself and so the majority trusted him not to impose their will on the whole community, while on the other hand, the Pharisees saw him as upright and at least sympathetic to their perspective. He didn't need to be personally as rigid as they were in matters that went beyond what the Law strictly required. But if his wife were in constant contact with menstrual impurity while they were trying to live their lives in avoidance of all that was unclean? They would have opposed his appointment and things would have gotten ugly. Jairus and I talked about it a lot, and I accepted that he was the man our community needed. I was proud of him. But it cost me a dear friend, and it cost my friend more than I realized it would as others followed my example. Soon she could barely show her face in community gatherings where she has previously been an honored guest. Her family is quite wealthy and influential. She spent a great deal seeking a cure for her ailment, but to no avail."*

Salome hesitated, as though ashamed. *"Berenice and I actually were pregnant at the same time. That created a bond between us. We shared stories, compared experiences, commiserated one another on the foods we could no longer eat or even stand to be around the smell of. We went into labor less than a week apart. I gave birth to a healthy daughter. Berenice would have had a son . . . but he was stillborn. And after that, her bleeding just wouldn't stop. I comforted her and remained her friend when others assumed she must be cursed. But then Jairus got appointed to his position and said I had to cease contact with her. I was ashamed to treat a good friend so poorly. But I had to stand by my husband, and he insisted that we had no choice in the matter. But it still didn't sit right with me. It still doesn't.*

"When our daughter came of age, we made sure that she was secluded away during the time of the month that the Pharisees' interpretation of Torah required her to be, and every time her bleeding stopped, I would think of Berenice and her perpetual exclusion. I have Roman acquaintances who are astonished by many of our Jewish laws and customs. They too regard a woman's menstrual flow as powerful and dangerous, maybe more so than we do. They are so similar in some ways, and yet at the same time so very different from us. There is avoidance of contact, much more like our own traditional way of life than what the Pharisees advocate. Taboos about

menstruating women are something that Jews, Greeks, and Romans share in common."

She could just as easily have been telling this to me as to her daughter, but suddenly Salome stopped generalizing and looked directly at her daughter as she addressed her. "You know how much your father doted on you when you were a little girl," she continued. "You're his only child, and while some pitied him, pitied us, for not having a son, he wanted to give you everything he could. He taught you things he would have taught a son if he had had one, and took you with him with pride where others brought only their male children. That must have only made it worse when suddenly you had to be kept at home so often, not just for the sake of purity but because of the leering gaze of men in the town who knew you were of age. We treat women so differently when they reach puberty, and I didn't do enough to help you understand what you were going through."

Salome returned to addressing me at this point. "The first time she became ill after that, it was minor. But her father suddenly was at her bedside, kissing her forehead, doting on her the way he used to. Regardless what time in the month it was, if she was ill, he would lavish attention on her when no one was present apart from us. When she recovered, things changed again, back to the way they had been, the new normal. I think this experience kept making her sick, making her worse." There was another long pause, after which Salome looked up at her daughter and resumed telling the story to her directly once again. "When you stopped periodically getting better, your father became increasingly distraught. He stopped focusing on trying to arrange your marriage, and spent his time trying to find a healer."

Salome looked at me again. "A good parent will do anything for their child. There are lots of people ready to take advantage of that. Charlatans! For months and months, it seemed that we had a constant stream of people, some rabbis, some old women from a nearby village, each of whom had a reputation for treating illnesses. None of them were worth the food I set before them, never mind the money my husband paid some of them. Most of them wouldn't touch her. They just muttered their incantation from a distance or lit a lamp and made a terrible smell with some concoction that they said would drive away the spirit that was causing it. I wouldn't be surprised if these people made her worse. They certainly sickened me!"

As her mother began weeping again and seemed unable to continue, the daughter took up the role of storyteller. It seemed that she too had things she needed to share with her mother. "I remember how I felt, when father would suddenly shift from holding me close and taking me with him, to isolation and being avoided, then back again to closeness, then separation again, month after month. But I don't think I was as traumatized by that experience as much as I was by other things, by what other people said and by how father reacted to their words. Did you know that when Jacob's father came to the house to discuss with father the possibility of us marrying, he told my father that Jacob would be to him the son he never had. When I was there and could hear it! I know father's expressions well enough to understand, now that I am older, that he was being polite and holding back something he felt like saying. But at the time it seemed to me as though father agreed with him—that deep down he wished he had had a son instead of me. That was when I first became really ill. I couldn't bring myself to eat or drink anything. That was probably the main problem."

"I think you already know some of the other details about what happened that day," Salome said as she took over the role of storyteller and began addressing me once again. "Things that I didn't learn until later. But you asked me earlier when I started to believe that things were going to get better. I think it was when Jairus got over the obsession with purity that his leadership role had imposed on us enough to go ask that odd holy man Jesus, whom we'd heard had caused a stir by eating with all kinds of unclean people, to come to our home and place his hand on our daughter. If he was willing to prioritize our daughter's healing in that way, I was sure there was still hope for us yet. I later learned about how Berenice had dared to insert herself into the crowd around Jesus when he was on his way here. She too had heard about his reputation as a healer and that he was visiting our town. I heard how she carefully tried to avoid having Jairus or anyone else spot her, hoping that she could simply touch the hem of Jesus's cloak and then sneak away. But then suddenly Jesus had stopped them all and asked who touched him! People told me Jairus had become white as a sheet when he saw Berenice and heard what had happened. Jairus later told me what he felt when the news reached him that his own daughter had died, right after healing power had flowed from Jesus to make well the woman he had insisted we *must shun. He felt that God had punished him fairly. Jesus had seen his reaction and seemed to understand, and had spoken comforting words to him. Jesus said something at the time that didn't make sense right away. He had seemed to recognize from all he had seen and been told that the trouble was something other than a plague or evil spirit, that it was a kind of sleep that had come over her and not in fact death at all. I still remember the moment he restored her like it was yesterday. After we had put so much pressure on our daughter as she went through this phase of growing up and becoming a woman, Jesus said . . . he said . . . "*

Salome was sobbing uncontrollably and couldn't continue. Up until now I had waited patiently in such moments, but I forgot myself and my manners in that moment, so eager was I to hear the rest. "What did he say?" I asked.

It was the daughter who replied. "He called me 'little girl,'" she said . . .

Blood Issues

If some Christians struggle with the idea that Jesus *learned*, presumably talking about the fact that Jesus *experienced puberty* will risk sending them completely off the deep end. If anyone traumatized by that very notion has kept reading into this next sentence, they will now be relieved to learn that this book will not be exploring Jesus's experience of puberty. We don't have any information that would allow us to say more than we could about any male human being in general. We can and should assume that Jesus's experience was most likely pretty typical. However, returning to the focus of this book, the experiences of men and women are very different when passing through puberty. Ancient cultures with strict purity rules about menstruation are very different from anything experienced by most modern people, whether male or female. To understand the experiences of the two women who are the focus of this chapter, whose stories are already intertwined in the Gospels, we need historical information, but also the imagination to perceive the impact of ancient cultural rules and norms about menstruation on at least some of the women who lived in and had their experiences impacted and shaped by them.

This chapter focuses on the story of two women.[1] The chapter about Mary and Martha also features two women, but there the connection between them is different: they are sisters who appear together in stories about their household.[2] This chapter, on the other hand, focuses on two women who were not (as far as we know) related. One was a young girl, the other a woman whose age we are not told but who had lived long enough to have struggled for a significant length of time with the ailment that afflicted her.[3] The reason for bringing them together in this chapter is that the earliest account of their stories, found in the Gospel of Mark, also connects them. The author of that Gospel more than once sandwiches one story within another. Sometimes multiple things happen at the same time, so that events overlap and become inseparable even if distinct. In this case, the connection between the stories appears to be both historical and literary. The author encourages us to perceive more than just one event that transpires to interrupt another. Instead we are meant to reflect on what connects the two events. Far too often, precisely because these two women are so different, we tend either to simply treat the two incidents as separate, to treat one as a mere frame for the other, or to treat one as an interruption of the other. In this chapter we will ask what happens if we take seriously the possibility that the author of our earliest account saw them as linked because they were indeed similar and related in important respects that go deeper than mere timing, such that it was natural to connect them, to tell them together as a single narrative.

Very few commentators offer much in the way of explanation of the significance of the fact that the woman's hemorrhaging began around the same time that Jairus's daughter was born.[4] Not that it isn't mentioned, but the discussion, such as there is, typically revolves around the

---

1. I have actually brought a third woman whose role in the Gospel is downplayed (Mark 5:40) into center stage in my fictionalized retelling, namely Jairus's wife, the mother of the sick girl. Her story is also explored in Coffey, *Hidden Women*, 61–64.

2. See Schrader, "Martha of Bethany," on manuscript evidence that raises the possibility that Martha was inserted into the Gospel of John after it was completed.

3. See Gosbell, *Poor*, 259–63 on a variety of ways the women are explicitly and implicitly connected and parallel in their situations to one another.

4. Mary Hanrahan ("At the Wedding of Jairus's Daughter" in Burgess, *Bare Feet*, 93–95) depicts the woman who had been hemorrhaging attending the wedding of Jairus's daughter, and reflecting on the fact that her own daughter who had been stillborn would have been the same age. Selvidge (*Woman, Cult, and Miracle Recital*, 20) provides evidence that the woman healed of hemorrhaging, and the story of what had happened to her, may have become renowned.

symbolism of the number twelve. To be sure, this number had significant resonances for the people of Israel, representing the number of tribes. For example, Jesus's choice of twelve apostles conveyed the idea that Jesus was doing what he was doing for and in relation to Israel. Whether Mark inserted the number or adjusted the time frame in order to introduce this biblically significant number, or whether he recalled it and found it significant because of that symbolism, we should still ask what he as author and we as readers are supposed to think the significance is. Presumably the answer is that these very women whose stories highlight the danger of ritual impurity associated with women in that ancient society are nevertheless part of the people of Israel, and thus worthy of healing and restoration into the community.[5] Women in ancient society bore the brunt of the risks involved with marriage and childbirth, including not only the risk of early mortality but also the risk of ostracization if things went wrong which caused ongoing bleeding, by which we don't necessarily envisage *constant* bleeding, but unpredictable bleeding rather than with monthly regularity. Women were the ones who made the ongoing existence of the tribes of Israel possible generation to generation through their reproductive role and power, even as they faced potential stigmatization for anomalies.

This is at the level of the telling of the story in the Gospel. However, Jesus's actions on this occasion, if they are depicted accurately here, show that this recognition of the hardships and challenges women experienced, imposed on them by a society that feared rather than honored the very aspects of their lives that made it possible for families and societies to persist, goes back to Jesus himself. Mark felt that the words Jesus spoke were noteworthy, including a quote in Aramaic, but also other significant details. A man comes asking that his little daughter be healed, if Jesus would only touch her. Religious people are sometimes willing to set aside rules they rigorously insist that others follow when it is a matter of urgency or expediency for themselves or their own families. We are not told all of the details we might have liked to know that would have allowed us to situate Jairus in relation to purity concerns. Was he aligned with the majority of Pharisees? Did he agree more with Jesus and if so to what extent? The hints that we are given point in a particular direction. Jairus

---

5. Gosbell, *Poor*, 271, 277. Love, *Jesus and Marginal Women*, 110 notes the avoidance of menstruating women in rural Greece, because of fear they can bring harm on people, crops, etc. See too Schottroff, *Let the Oppressed*, 97; Evans, *Year of Biblical Womanhood*, 150–56.

was the leader of a synagogue, in a time when groups concerned with observance of ritual purity (such as the Pharisees) were increasingly influential.[6] We know this not only from literature from the time (including but not limited to the Gospels), but also from the archaeological record, with immersion pools for purification having become more widely used in the generation immediately prior to this. This is why, in retelling the story, we have suggested that, whatever Jairus's own views, his role as synagogue leader would have entailed him at least keeping the more observant appeased, if not indeed holding their viewpoint himself.

Jairus came seeking healing for his daughter. Jesus allows himself to be interrupted in the process of responding to that request by another woman whose story, it is hinted, is somehow connected with that of Jairus and his daughter. We are not told explicitly how in the written Gospels, and so we are left to fill in the gaps and connect the dots.[7] What we are told, however, is significant and gives us much to go on. Jesus calls the woman who touched the hem of his garment "daughter." We tend to assume that someone who had been suffering as she had for 12 years must be an older woman, but that is not necessarily the case. Women were married early and began having children right away. Whether her medical condition appeared as soon as she hit puberty or was due to complications with a pregnancy as we suggested in our retelling, she could still be in her mid to late twenties.[8] The story depicts the woman as having had to fend for herself, and having largely succeeded in doing so, in the sense that she had financial resources she could spend on medical treatment, albeit without results. Where was the woman's father? Was he still alive and providing for her? Had he died and left her with some property and/or other wealth? Ancient laws regarding women and inheritance limit the

---

6. On what we know about the role of the "head/leader/ruler of the synagogue" see Brooten, *Women Leaders*, 27–30.

7. It is easy for modern readers to forget that the Gospels were written in cultures where oral communication was still primary. The written texts of the Gospels may well have served primarily as memory aids for those who retold stories about Jesus in the setting of Christian communities, where they would elaborate further based on what they knew and add details in response to questions from their audience.

8. There are a variety of medical conditions that could be behind the sparse information we are provided in the Gospels. Postpartum acquired hemophilia is one that would fit well with the details that we included in our retelling. Uterine fibroids is a far more common one. The woman's story suggests that her condition and the resulting situation were particularly bad, but we should not neglect the possibility that her story was something that was not uncommon, rather than a rarity.

number of scenarios in which a woman might have been in a position to have personal resources that would enable her to fend for herself. Perhaps her father was alive and gave her an allowance and arranged for her to live somewhere in seclusion, as he and other family members sought or at least hoped for a solution to the woman's contaminating impurity. Perhaps her father had died and in the absence of other male relatives with a claim, she had inherited what her father left behind. The latter is more likely in view of the way Mark 5:26 is worded: "she had spent all *she* had." Either way, however, the woman would feel the lack of parental support in her chronic suffering. It is hard to imagine her surviving without spouse, children, or parent to care for her, and so her story raises questions that we cannot answer about how she managed to do so, but the wording makes clear that whether she was literally without family to support her, or was at a distance imposed so that they might avoid constant exposure to her impurity, she was fending for herself. Constant unpredictable impurity excluded the woman from the Temple, which makes the number 12 in the story symbolic of how her healing allowed her reentry into the worshiping community of Israel. Elsewhere Jesus's teaching highlights the prioritization of care and hospitality over purity. He undoubtedly learned this lesson at least in part from observing the treatment of women in situations like this one, when purity was made paramount. He would subsequently enshrine this emphasis in his famous parable of the Samaritan.[9]

In the Hands of Doctors

When we are told that the woman suffered much at hands of doctors, this in itself should convey something important to the reader to whom this information is being imparted. Jesus and his male followers listened to her story of what her life had been like when she was still suffering from her ailment. Even the best doctors in the pre-modern world were liable to recommend things that we today would find appalling, and not merely unlikely to help address either symptoms or underlying causes. Ancient sources mention treatments for vaginal hemorrhaging among those for other ailments.[10] These included ingredients such as manure

---

9. Perroni and Simonelli, *Mary of Magdala*, 32 view this encounter as leading Jesus to overcome the taboo against women's blood.

10. Haber, *They Shall Purify*, 132–33 says the woman likely suffered from vaginal

or urine from animals, sometimes to be applied externally, in other cases ingested.[11] Such background information clarifies some of the ways this woman may have "suffered much at the hands of doctors" without improvement.[12]

Jesus clearly paid attention to the stories of women in general, and we should assume that when he visited a particular place, he was told stories more specifically about local people and their situations. We should envisage Jesus choosing his words carefully in light of what he knows, since he knew that being an effective healer (as well as an effective teacher) depended on using the right words in the right way at the right moment. Calling the woman daughter was not an example of Jesus using language that he characteristically did.[13] He felt it apt for this particular circumstance, and perhaps necessary for this woman to come to experience wellness. Many readers of the Bible in English are used to living in cities in which people can remain somewhat anonymous. In most of the places that Jesus went, he may have arrived as a stranger, but the locals knew one another.[14] When the woman tells her story, it is for Jesus's benefit and that of his entourage, not for the local community. They would have known all too well what her story was. She would not know whether Jesus might have heard something about her when he arrived and perhaps even prior to his visit, as a healer seeking to learn about the illnesses and sufferings of people there. It is not justified to assume that Jesus didn't know at least something of her story already even before meeting her. Of course, he would not have been able to recognize her from what he had been told. However, based on what he had heard he would have been able to surmise who she was from her behavior in relation to him

---

bleeding even though this is not stated explicitly, and she claims purity was the reason for how the woman approached Jesus (133–34, 140; contra Levine, "Discharging Responsibility," 75). See as well Wassen, "Jesus and the Hemorrhaging Woman," 644–645.

11. Barker, *Women and the Liberator*, 56 provides examples from Pliny and the Talmud.

12. See also Izquierdo, *La Donna*, 27n1. B.' Abodah Zarah 29a has remedies for an ailment some translate as referring to hemorrhage in childbirth, although that may be incorrect given that the remedies are said to be applied to male rabbis!

13. Lutzer and Lutzer (*Jesus Lover of a Woman's Soul*, 89) note that this is the sole instance of Jesus addressing someone as "daughter," although he does make reference in the third person to another woman as "daughter of Abraham," on which see the conclusion of this book. See also Haber, *They Shall Purify*, 135.

14. In Matthew 4 Jesus relocates to Capernaum. Jonathan Reed (*Archaeology*, 149–52) estimates its population at this time as between 600 to 1,400.

and the crowd. Jesus probably perceived some additional details of her story even before she told him. We can imagine him glimpsing a woman in the crowd not daring to rise to her full height, fearful of being seen and recognized, reaching out to touch his clothing. Jesus would have known what this action meant for her. He would have known that the community gave her a wide berth due to her condition. He would have recognized that some religious people would try to protect him or stand up for him on behalf of their community, perhaps kicking the woman, perhaps merely jeering at her and insulting her. He would have compassionately recognized that a key part of her being made well required restoration to that community. It may have been for that reason that he made a point of drawing attention to her experience. Why else make a scene about having been touched in this way? The disciples recognized the oddity of what Jesus was doing. Perhaps we can make sense of it if we recognize that her telling of her story—including its ending with her being made well—was the point of it all. He made a scene to ensure her well-being and her reintegration into the local town community and into that of the nation and its religious life.

Jesus's Exact Words

Readers used to the way scholars write about Jesus may be surprised by my confidence about what Jesus said as related in this passage. Anyone who reads widely about the historical Jesus will be aware of the skepticism with which historians need to and tend to proceed. It is simply a matter of language, however, and not historical skepticism when scholars tell you that we do not, for the most part, have the exact words of Jesus. Jesus spoke Aramaic as his primary and native language, and yet almost all of the words attributed to him in the Gospels are in Greek. We thus read Jesus's words in translation when we read them in the original language of the Gospels, and most readers of this book will read them in translations of those translations in English. Occasionally there are sayings that can be translated back into Aramaic and, when we do so, we discover that there were word plays. We can probably offer a reasonable guess about words that Jesus used in those instances. But that isn't the same thing as having Jesus's words offered to us in their original form in a text. One major exception, of course, is Jesus's use of the Aramaic word *abba*. Hopefully readers have not been misinformed that this word meant something like "daddy." It didn't. It is simply the Aramaic word for "father." It pops up not only in the Gospel of Mark but in Paul's letter to the Galatians. Paul's use of the term is particularly striking, writing as he was to non-Jews in Asia Minor who didn't speak Aramaic. It is hard to explain Paul's decision to do this unless he could assume that his readers had already been introduced to the term when they learned about Jesus's words. That is why most historians are confident that Jesus used the word and was remembered to have done so.

When a voice comes to us across time as Jesus's does we often have to settle for such tiny snippets. In the story that is the focus of this chapter, we have two words together, *talitha qum* (sometimes spelled *talitha koum*), that are probably the very words of Jesus. Translated they mean "Little girl, get up." Some readers may be thinking that they remember reading those words in the New Testament with an "i" at the end of the second word. Your recollection is not letting you down: some English versions do indeed give the word in that form. Our manuscripts differ in the spelling, and that difference is one of the reasons that some historians feel particularly confident about there being a historical core to this story. As Maurice Casey explains, "The majority of manuscripts read the technically correct written feminine form *koumi*, but there is good reason to believe that the feminine ending '*i*' was not pronounced. It follows that *Talitha koum* is exactly what Jesus said."[15] Casey is here referring to something that appears to have been true in the way Aramaic was spoken in Galilee.[16] Here we hear the voice of the Galilean Jesus, *his exact words* and even his regional way of pronouncing them, making it through to us despite an instinct on the part of copyists to correct what seemed to be a misspelling, and despite the tendency of the Gospel authors to simply translate what he had said into Greek, a language that was more widely spoken in the eastern part of the Roman empire. Whether the author of Mark or a source he used, someone had written down what they had heard Jesus say, with these two words exactly as he had pronounced them. The presence of what seems like a precise recollection of Jesus's Galilean accent ought to give historians and other readers of the Gospels confidence that, even as the authors of these ancient texts were capable of taking liberties with their source material and transforming stories in

---

15. Maurice Casey, *Jesus of Nazareth*, 109 (see also 269 on the different ways the same Aramaic word is sometimes spelled in English).

16. This is akin to what happens when speakers of Cockney English drop the "h" from the beginnings of words, for those who may find the analogy useful.

creative ways, they were also capable of recalling essential details. They often preserve the essence and gist of what Jesus said and did. Occasionally they do more than that.

Was Jesus Lying?

Some readers of the New Testament will object to the idea that Jesus performed what we today would call psychosomatic cures. They may feel this diminishes his incomparable supernatural power. They should perhaps have another more pressing concern, however, if they insist that Jairus's daughter must really have been dead and brought back from literal death through a supernatural intervention. That is incompatible with what Jesus actually said. Whatever one's view of miracle stories, another issue that needs to be addressed is whether Jesus was telling the truth or not when he said that the girl was not dead but only sleeping. It is certainly true that sleep can serve as a euphemism for death. We see that in the New Testament, including on the lips of Jesus. In John 11:11, Jesus says Lazarus is sleeping, but soon thereafter he responds to further probing from the disciples and says bluntly that Lazarus is dead. In the story under discussion in the present chapter, however, we get something significantly different. Jesus does not merely say that Jairus's daughter is sleeping. He says that she "*is not dead* but sleeping." If Jesus had merely said that the girl was sleeping, we might indeed understand it to be a euphemism for death. But that isn't all that Jesus is depicted as saying. He explicitly says that she is not dead. There are perhaps ways that one could avoid the plain meaning of the text and find alternatives instead. But why consider that to be an appropriate response, when it pulls in a different direction than what the text actually says and says quite emphatically?[17] As Donald Capps points out, "if he did *not* mean what he said, it is the only statement or comment attributed to him in the Gospels where he affirmed something *that he did not hold to be true.*"[18] It seems reasonable to deduce that Jesus's confidence on this occasion reflects some prior experience of similar circumstances. Had Jesus not found other girls of

---

17. Given the possibility of an apologetic concern in the Lazarus story to address the claim that Jesus might not have been permanently dead, since he was in the tomb for less than 3 days, the blunt statement that Lazarus was dead, after he was said to be sleeping, might be concerned to address claims that Jesus raised people from sleep not from death.

18. Capps, *Jesus the Village Psychiatrist*, 122.

this age, with similar descriptions of their condition by a parent, to not be dead but sleeping, would he have made such a statement? Why would Jesus suggest that this was merely a case of remarkable insight or divinely-revealed knowledge if he believed it was to be one in which miraculous divine healing power would be displayed? Jesus's words suggest that he has dealt with other girls who become bedridden and may even be mistaken for dead when under the pressures of coming of age in that society. He may also have known some specific things about Jairus's family and their history with the woman who had just been healed by touching his garment. Some of that he may have been told, but some he undoubtedly deduced by witnessing their reactions to one another as well as their interactions with him. The restoration of the two women really would be intertwined and depend on one another. We will see that as we now consider their ailments and their healing together and their connection with concerns about ritual purity.

Contagious Purity and Wholeness

When considering the social status of the woman with the menstrual ailment, we need to balance the financial situation created by spending all of her money on doctors, with the fact that she apparently had had the means to spend a significant amount on doctors in the first place.[19] We are told that she had spent her money, not that a father or husband had done so. Whether she had a living parent or had ever been married, we cannot determine with certainty. Nevertheless, some possibilities are more likely than others, and even running through the options and their implications in her circumstances will give us a sense of the life this woman had been forced to lead. If she had been married, her condition would have been considered grounds for divorce, since intercourse during menstruation was prohibited, and her presence in the home would have rendered it and those who lived in or entered it unclean, spreading out with them to impact others.[20] Perhaps she lived somewhere in isolation, receiving money and food from family. Of course, it is possible that the majority of Galileans in general or of these townspeople in particular did not tend to worry about ritual purity except immediately prior to a trip to Jerusalem.

---

19. Driscoll, *Reading Between The Lines*, 30.

20. Schiffman, "Matthew," 16–18; Lutzer and Lutzer, *Jesus Lover of a Woman's Soul*, 85; Gosbell, *Poor*, 263.

Some of them presumably did, however, given the woman's reaction to becoming the center of attention for having touched someone.[21] And as we have already noted, Jairus would have felt a responsibility to the community for upholding the concerns of those who believed purity rules should be followed everywhere and at all times, a stance that could have a detrimental impact on the lives of women, even if that was not his own personal view of the matter. His role in the community as a religious leader suggests a status at least comparable to that of the woman who could afford to seek medical attention at least for a period of time. In suggesting that the two families knew each other in the fictional retelling with which we began, we were not engaging in mere speculation. Their implicit and explicit status, the realities of life in an ancient town or city large enough to have a synagogue, and the connections the Gospel makes between the two healings all point to there being an underlying connection between the two lives that are impacted and the two experiences of being made well.

To understand what would have been running through the woman's mind as Jesus asked who touched him, we need at least some understanding of ancient ideas about ritual purity. She may have presumed that this holy man had felt her uncleanness contaminate him and was looking for the perpetrator so as to reprimand them. But what Jesus experienced as a result of the woman's touch and the circumstances that led to it would teach him something radical, something that turned the whole system of purity thinking on its head as far as he was concerned. The assumption was that the impure contaminated the pure, which was the reason for avoiding physical contact with it. His experience on this occasion challenged that view of things. Instead of impurity flowing from her to him through that unclean touch, healing power had flowed from him to her.[22] This meant that purity and divine power were stronger than impurity.[23]

How far could the implications of this be extrapolated? Forgiveness was stronger than sin. God was more powerful than Satan. Healing was

21. See Haber, *They Shall Purify*, 136 on the fact that Jesus does not abrogate purity laws, and on Jesus's likely observance of purity laws when going to the temple.

22. Moss, "Man with the Flow of Power," 516–17.

23. Swidler, *Jesus Was a Feminist*, 24 and 95 notes this is the only time Jesus touched a corpse. In view of our considerations here, perhaps the fact that Jesus touched her confirms that he did not think she was dead. On the other hand, the parable of the Samaritan makes unambiguous that Jesus believed that helping someone was worth the risk of corpse impurity. But did he learn that by first taking the risk himself? Did Jesus consider that his assessment of the situation could be incorrect?

more powerful than illness. One approach to righteousness and health proceeds by isolating oneself from the constant threat of unrighteousness and disease that is all around threatening our well-being. This was the approach that the Pharisees and Essenes took, and Jesus may have admired that approach at some point. Eventually, however, he shifted direction in a way that may have placed him at odds with some of his family, as well as his former teacher John. At the very least he does not seem to have gotten this from them. Instead, we can and should imagine there being a slow accumulation of experiences and insights that paved the way to this insight. Often, however many experiences may have preceded that can be seen with the benefit of hindsight to have influenced a person, there is one critical moment that lets it all click into place, as the things one has seen and thought suddenly shift and reorganize themselves into a new stable arrangement. This woman gave Jesus that experience.[24]

Berenice's Story

Hopefully the chapter thus far has made it clear that these stories deserved to be told together, and perhaps had to be told together in order to be fully appreciated and understood. Our earliest source of information about these women's encounter with Jesus, the Gospel of Mark, liked to utilize the sandwiching technique used here. In this case, however, the stories are depicted as not merely being combined or set side by side in order to see what resonances result from the juxtaposition. They are instead a single story that diverged along two paths, which had nonetheless remained entangled for twelve or so years, awaiting a resolution.[25]

24. In doing so, she taught Jesus something that would influence not only him, but the entire history of Christianity, inasmuch as Christianity's lack of concern for ritual purity fostered any number of developments from the inclusion of gentiles to the esteeming of relics. Moltmann-Wendel (*Women around Jesus*, 104) notes that there is an account in which Jesus is accused of leading women and children astray into impurity. Swidler, *Jesus Was a Feminist*, 160 indicates the source or preserver of that tradition is Epiphanius. It is possible that the shift from assuming that Satan's kingdom would persist to believing that it was destined to be brought down through his activity was associated with this recognition about purity. If the presence of purity can render the impure pure, rather than vice versa, then the presence of God can overwhelm the presence of Satan and of evil. See further Myrick C. Shinall Jr., in *Miracles and the Kingdom of God: Christology and Social Identity in Mark and Q* (Lanham: Lexington/Fortress Academic, 2018), who detects a difference between Mark and Q on whether Jesus was defeating Satan or merely engaging in battle.

25. On twelve as connecting the two stories, as well as resonating with the number

The church historian Eusebius names the woman suffering from chronic vaginal bleeding Berenice or Veronica, identifying her as the same woman that (according to tradition) supposedly wiped Jesus's face of blood as he went to the cross and discovered a remarkable image left there as a result.[26] There would be an interesting poignancy if Jesus helped her when she was bleeding and she returned the favor later. However, given that Eusebius situates her in Caesarea Philippi and implies that she was a gentile, that does not fit well with the impression we are given in the Gospel of Mark either of the woman or of the location where events unfold. It may be that confusion resulted between two women with the same name, and so I have used the traditional name here, without implying that I believe her to have been present along the Via Dolorosa on the day that Jesus was crucified.

It would be unfortunate if the treatment of the story of these two women in a single chapter of this book silenced the voice of one of our two main female protagonists, however appropriate and indeed necessary that they be kept together. I am thus including here an additional short fictional retelling of the incident from the perspective of the woman with the hemorrhaging:

My child had died and my path to years of isolation had begun when Jairus's daughter had been born. Surely now that their little girl lay dying and I had exhausted my resources trying in vain to find a cure for my own illness, the same healer might bring not just one of our stories to a happy conclusion, but both. Had I not been able to persuade myself of this, I would not have been able to reach out and touch the hem of the garment of this healer that I had heard so much about, who was on his way to Jairus's house. I did not act out of malice. My thought was not to spread my impurity to the healer and interfere with the salvation of that little girl. I was jealous all these years, I will freely admit. Who would not have been, and who could blame me for envying a successful birth and a child who, until recently at least, had been healthy and vibrant, when I had lost my

---

of apostles and tribes of Israel, see Wray, *Good Girls*, 5, 67.

26. The early church historian Eusebius says that in his time there were statues depicting the healing located at the home in which the woman had lived in Caesarea Philippi, which the woman herself had erected (*History of the Church* 7.18).

child and in the process my status in our community? I had lost so much, but I never desired that Jairus and his wife should suffer loss as well. On the contrary, I wished them all that I wished for myself, and perhaps more. My expectations for myself had been lowered by tragedy. I merely longed that I too might experience some hint of the happiness that they had. I believed he would help the little girl, and that there was enough power in him to spare for me as well. So I reached out my hand to touch the hem of his garment with not the slightest hint of malice. I hope you believe me. I was of course taking a risk that my doing so might interfere with this healer. But if he could not heal the perpetually bleeding and unclean, how could he heal the sick unto death, someone who was now wasting away as she traveled on the same path of womanhood that had in my case led to such tragic consequences? Women bear the heaviest burdens when it comes to bringing a new generation into existence to support and eventually replace the previous one, yet whether we succeed or fail as mothers, we find ourselves confronted with unreasonable expectations. I believed God appreciated what women did for Israel even if most men did not. And I had heard that Jesus was not typical in this regard, but was more sympathetic. I would soon find out. Either this man had come from God to heal both of us, or he was a fraud like all the other healers I had been to. I was resigned to accept either possibility, but I was certain that if this man was the genuine article, he was here to heal us both and not just Jairus's daughter. I had pled to God with my whole heart, and I refused to believe that God despised one who sought him wholeheartedly. That girl and her family deserved happiness and a future. So did I.

My loss was not only made more unbearable by Jairus and Johanna's overwhelming joy at the birth of their daughter. Johanna had ostracized me, and so had the rest of the community, following their example. I did not fault her for not fighting them, for not standing up to them or standing out at the risk of her own acceptance by everyone else, and most of all her husband. She was not merely thinking of herself. She was thinking of her husband's new position, as well as of her daughter. This was her family. If my daughter had lived, I would surely have done the same if the situations had been reversed. I was angry with Jairus, though, for pandering to the Pharisees, and I was even more angry at the latter. I did not mind that they held different views from me on how to interpret the Scriptures. I was angry, and still am, that they took my friend away from me when I needed a friend most.

I was finally able to let my bitterness go as hope took hold of me, hope that I had not allowed myself to feel lately after so many years of disappointment. Jesus the renowned healer was coming to our town! It could not be a coincidence that now, when twelve years had passed, the girl had become sick even as she too had begun to issue blood and follow the path of women. It could not be a coincidence that a healer whose reputation was different from so many others had come here now, at this precise time, and that Jairus had sought his help. Twelve, like the tribes of Israel, the list of male ancestors that left us daughters on the sidelines. Twelve, like the months of the year. It could not be a coincidence. I had to believe, I really and truly did believe as I never had when I sought the help of any other healer, that in this moment now God was at work, that something was planned that would happen for the good of us daughters of Israel, to be included more fully in all that the number twelve symbolized for us.

I was not disappointed. I touched the fringe of the garment of the healer, hiding myself lest someone blame me for spreading my uncleanness to them. The healer might blame me, and perhaps my touch would render him unable to heal. But I did not believe it. I had been hearing stories about what he did in other towns and villages. Those who were bleeding, the dead, those with flaking skin, and those with ailments of every other sort had experienced restoration. We were the unclean, something that we shared in common even if our illnesses were different. Surely God meant now to touch us, meant for a true healer to touch us and make us well. I believed, as I had never believed before, and I reached out to touch the tassels that the Law required this man to wear. I did it, and I felt it. Immediately, something was different, and I prepared to sneak away. I could later go visit Johanna and Jairus, who would surely also be rejoicing, and tell them my good news. I believed, I hoped, and I reached out and felt it.

But then the healer did something that at first made me terrified, but in the end made me blessed. He asked who had touched him. He was the real thing. It was not just me who had felt it. He had felt it too. Or perhaps he had simply spotted me sneaking through the crowd. If that was it, then I am even more impressed. At first, for the briefest moment, I thought he had felt my uncleanness, had experienced my contamination and meant to blame me. But soon I realized *that wasn't it at all. He had brought healing to me, but he meant to do more than that. He let everyone know that I had touched him, that if they thought that my touch must be avoided and ruined the one I came in contact with, then this healer should be shunned now as well. He was challenging Jairus, challenging the community, to rethink their stance towards me and all others like me. If Jairus, the leader of the synagogue, welcomed this man into his home after this, he would be taking a stand different from the one he had adopted for more than twelve years now, during which time he united the community by placating the loudest and most adamant voices, even though most in the community did not accept their interpretations of the Law. For Jairus, this had seemed to be the way to avoid conflict, by appeasing those most prone to cause trouble and controversy. But this healer seemed to know what I needed and longed for more than just for my bleeding to stop. There had to be an acceptance of a new way of being holy, one that could touch an unclean woman like me and, instead of being rendered impure, render me and others like me pure. An experience of powerful and life-transforming holiness.*

My touching of the man's hem lasted only a moment. The time between his stopping and asking who touched him and my getting the courage to say it was me felt much longer. But the wait for Jairus's decision about what to do next seemed to last an eternity. I didn't move, but I couldn't avoid looking in his direction. I saw him grow pale as he saw me, recognized me, knew who I was and what had happened and what it meant for me as well as for him. As he ushered Jesus onwards, placing his daughter above the demands the Pharisees imposed on him, I knew that a new day was dawning for our community. Assuming, of course, that his daughter did indeed recover as I had . . .

Jesus may have deliberately placed Jairus in a situation that forced him to accept the presence not only of this ritually unclean woman, but a man whom he had invited to come to his home who was now rendered ritually impure.[27] Jairus had to decide whether to prioritize compassion or avoid-

27. Serio, *Jesus and Woman*, 67. Did Jesus have a reputation for touching leper's that preceded him and Jairus would have heard? Mark 1:40–42 precedes this story and may provide indication, but it is not clear whether that story depicts a regular practice on Jesus's part which would have created a reputation that might have followed him

ance of controversy, hospitality and potential healing for his daughter or placating the Pharisees. When duties conflict we gain insight. Longtime ostracization will not always vanish immediately just because the thing that led to it has been rectified. Once one has grown accustomed to shunning someone, it is hard to treat them as beloved members of society. Jesus's words and actions do what is possible to ensure the excluded woman will be welcomed back into her community as a full member who is beloved of God rather than an object of divine punishment.

While some may feel that we have negated the miraculous element in the story, the wording of the story strongly indicates otherwise. Moreover, ancient and modern specialists in healing and heath care agree that there is a close connection between psychological well-being and healing of the body. Ancient authors associate ailments with women at these particular times in their lives, i.e., the start of menstruation and menopause when it ceases. They regularly use unhelpful terms like "hysteria." When we listen more attentively to women who talk of their experience, we can find better words for the mental and physical anguish that often emerges at the intersection between the biological realities of their existence and the demands and impositions placed on them by patriarchal society. In the story we have been exploring in this chapter, we get the impression that both the daughter of Jairus and the woman have suffered from prolonged illness. Jesus's actions appear to be undertaken to achieve changes in behavior and understanding which can not only lead to healing, but to the acceptance of the healed back into the community. Jesus is depicted as healing the woman with the flow of blood publicly, while he urges those present to keep quiet about Jairus's daughter's healing. Jairus was thus forced to let the focus shift to the woman most wronged by his stance on purity, and away from him and his family. In doing so, Jesus may have healed rifts between family members with burdened consciences, creating an opportunity for long-term wellness not only there but in the community in which they had such influence.

---

or even preceded him to that locale. Wassen, "Jesus and the Hemorrhaging Woman," challenges the idea that a woman with this ailment who had washed her hands would have been viewed as transmitting uncleanness via touch, presenting in the process evidence of the diversity of Jewish views and perhaps also of practices.

Conclusion

Jesus calls the young woman experiencing puberty and traumatized by it "little girl." A woman of status who was at least old enough to be the little girl's mother he called "daughter."[28] He does so in the presence of someone who had presumably also spent much (time as well as money) to see his own daughter cured, and who now worried that they might reach her too late. The modes of address converging in this way cannot be a coincidence. Jesus saw their two situations as parallel and related, regardless of how much detail he knew at that time about the interconnectedness of their personal and family histories. An insightful healer does not always need to know the complete stories of people in order to have sufficient insight to bring relief. Both were women who suffered as a result of a patriarchal stance on purity that isolated and burdened them. Jesus paid enough attention to the experiences of women and learned from them sufficiently to be able to offer healing to them and others like them. In focusing all our attention of the wonder of recovery from illness, all of us—but male readers in particular—are liable to miss the extent to which these women's stories provide evidence of Jesus listening to women and learning from them, so that he as a practitioner of healing could provide a remedy for what ailed them and others like them.

Given how frequent it is for Christians to misunderstand the Gospels in terms of Jesus and his followers "rejecting Jewish purity laws," it is important to emphasize before ending this chapter that that is not what we see going on in this story. Jesus did not replace or oppose Jewish purity laws. He opposed one or more Jewish interpretations of purity with another one that was equally Jewish and which was not unique to him. He cured illnesses, including but not limited to ones connected with impurity, so as to restore people to the community of the pure who could worship in the Temple in Jerusalem. When Jesus argued with the Pharisees, he was not engaged in an argument *against* Judaism but an argument among Jews *about* Judaism. This misunderstanding has resulted in untold harm down the ages, and it is thus important to emphasize this point here. Even today, many Jews today hold views similar to those Jesus advocated—not, to be clear, because they have been influenced by Christianity, but because they like Jesus represent some of the many Jewish viewpoints on this and other topics. It is crucial to keep reiterating this point, lest our depiction of Jesus the ancient Jewish man who learned

---

28. See Capps, *Jesus the Village Psychiatrist*, on the possible effect of this (130).

from ancient Jewish women (among others) be misunderstood as contributing to and reinforcing an extremely problematic anti-Jewish reading of the Gospels that elevates Jesus at the expense of his own people, heritage, and culture. As this chapter hopefully illustrates clearly, Jesus was a participant in his own culture and heritage and as such also a participant in his people's and his era's vibrant debates about the scriptures, traditions, practices, and identity they shared in common.[29]

---

29. Amy-Jill Levine (*The Misunderstood Jew*, 121) writes, "The social-justice Jesus who promotes a healthy interpretation of the Torah, peaceful response to oppression, the healing of women's bodies, and the recognition that the God of Israel is the God of the Gentiles as well is enormously appealing, and enormously useful. The image may also be substantially true. The problem emerges, however, when these observations are enhanced by the depiction of Judaism as rejecting such concerns. Jesus was not the only Jew to care about these issues; his social-justice interests make him a Jew rather than distinguishing him from Judaism." See also Fredriksen, "Did Jesus Oppose the Purity Laws?" 23–24; Levine, "Discharging Responsibility," 71, on issues with Marcus Borg's characterization of purity. For more extreme views of purity and the exclusion of menstruating women than those some of the Pharisees held see the Temple Scroll found at Qumran.

Mary and Martha of Bethany
What Jesus Learned from Two Very Different Sisters

I know you may not believe me when I say this, but I honestly wasn't trying to cause a scene or make a point on either occasion. I know you've heard stories about what happened. I've heard them too. I'm often surprised by how different some of them are from each other, as well as from my own recollection of those days. Just ask my sister. Even she and I can't agree on everything.

Both times, Jesus was visiting Jerusalem, and as was his custom when he did so, he would stay in our home in Bethany. The city is an easy walk from here, and the view of the temple and of the city as a whole from the Mount of Olives is better than approaching it from any other direction. Our family is from Galilee and our families actually knew each other going way back, and have remained connected. Even if Jesus hadn't stayed in our home, I'm certain he would have spent time here. If he hadn't, we would have gone to wherever he was. We were friends.

His words enthralled us women as much as they did men. Jesus never minded that we hung around the edges of his group and listened, once we were done with food preparations and other such things. But this one time, Jesus was telling a story that I just couldn't pull away from. Martha had even come and tugged at my garment, whispering in my ear that she needed help. But I knew that if I left now, I would be left with half a story, and would be completely distracted until I found out what point Jesus had made, what the interesting twist was at the end that would have everyone amazed, *or laughing, or deeply challenged. This time, it would probably be all three of those things at once. That often was the case with Jesus's teaching. This felt like one of those stories. So I hung around the edges a little longer, and then decided to sit down. People were constantly arriving and seated themselves down around Jesus to listen if they arrived when he was in the middle of teaching. I thought I would remain unnoticed at least for a while, and then could sneak out once Jesus had finished this particular story.*

I was wrong.

Someone spotted me sitting among the men and gave me a disapproving look. Then several more shooed me with their hands. I even overheard Peter whisper to someone else, "Get Mary out from our midst. Who does she think she is? Doesn't she know that women aren't worthy of the life of the age to come that Jesus speaks to us about!" I saw Jesus turn his gaze—without interrupting his story—in the direction of Peter. He frowned, then spotted me sitting there among the men, and looked surprised only for a brief moment. Then he smiled and carried on telling his story with renewed vigor.

The men quieted down, and that might have been that. But Martha spotted me, and she isn't one for quiet disapproval any more than Peter is. She interjected right in the middle of what Jesus was saying! It wasn't mid-sentence, but she certainly didn't wait for him to reach a natural pause between stories or subjects. She told him—yes, my dear Martha made demands of Jesus!—to tell me to help her with the responsibilities in the kitchen. And she wasn't wrong. It was unfair of me to leave her to manage those things on her own. I hadn't figured out yet what Jesus expected from us, men and women, when it came to matters like this. The men left their fishing and their masonry and listened to Jesus's every word. By this stage, women were following him around too. Some of us even took care of the needs that he and his disciples had not just when they visited our homes, but on the road as well. We learned a lot from him. But we were always around the edges. Were we supposed to remain there? Was it never to be our time to sit down and listen as well, to leave our food preparations as the men had left the work of catching or growing the food that they then passed on to us to prepare? I found out when I sat down at Jesus's feet that time. Jesus said there were many things that one can feel need to be done. But when he is speaking, only one thing is strictly necessary: listening to him. He complimented me on having chosen to do that! I felt so bad for Martha. She glowered at me, and was mad at Jesus about the whole thing for a while, too.

Then there was the time that Jesus came to visit us, and he arrived while we had the servants out fetching water. I could see that he had sought to make fast time so that he could be here a full week before Passover. We hadn't expected him until later that evening. He was tired from the journey, indeed, he seemed more tired than I had ever seen him before. And we were out of water and could not even wash his feet and that of his disciples. The servants were gone and we were out of water. I felt so incredibly embarrassed. Jesus was kind and showed no irritation at all. But knowing how much of an honor it is that he always stays with us, and how much he is burdened by the possibility that the authorities will intervene to stop his activity, I felt overwhelmed by guilt.

As Jesus sat and gathered his students around him in the cool of our home to eat as well as to teach them, and as people who were expecting his arrival began to show up with the servants still not having returned from the well, I began to cry. I have always been prone to cry on such occasions. Martha has always been able to hide her grief—even when our brother died she kept her composure, while I was a complete mess. As I wept about our failure as hosts for Jesus and our guests—his guests—I saw one of my tears strike the dirt floor and it gave me an idea. I grabbed a basin and used my tears to begin cleaning Jesus'ss feet in the way that I knew he deserved. It is always the custom to have servants wash the feet of guests when they arrive in your home. I think you probably knew that, but people from so many different places have begun to follow the Way of Jesus, that I find myself wondering when I need to say more about our customs when telling our stories to a stranger. We had failed to show hospitality, and I wept, and my weeping gave me a way to try in some poor and inadequate way to do what we had not been able to: to wash Jesus's feet.

The water provided by my tears was not enough, even though this very fact caused me to weep more profusely. Then I remembered the perfume. Our father had given Martha and I each a small vial of spikenard before he died, so that we should have an adequate dowry when we married. I think he foresaw that due to his prolonged illness he would not be able to provide it when the time came. If the time came. Of course, neither Martha nor I had married. Martha had used most of her vial to anoint Lazarus's body when we buried him. I still had mine, unopened. I ran quickly to get it. When I stood before Jesus with it, however, a few drops on his feet seemed inadequate. Also, the entire atmosphere of expectation and hope at the approach of Passover, with Jesus not even getting the hospitality he deserved, never mind royal honor fit for the son of David, all struck me powerfully. I was holding an expensive oil and standing before the one that I believed God had ordained to one day be our king. My king. I barely hesitated before I broke the vial open and poured the entire contents over Jesus's head, rather than just sprinkling some on his feet as I had intended.

The comments had begun the moment I had stooped to try to wash his feet, but now with this new twist to what I had done, much louder and more outspoken criticism was not long in coming. Some of his disciples got a whiff of the perfume and knew it must be expensive, and said we would have been better off selling it and giving it to the poor than using it in this way, to wash feet. A Pharisee who had come to listen to Jesus and dine with him made remarks about me, especially my using my hair to wipe his feet. Using my clothes or some other cloth seemed inadequate, and to be honest when I had first started letting my tears fall on Jesus's feet, I simply hadn't thought about how I would wipe them. I used what I had available to me. The Pharisee (I think his name was Simon) asked what kind of loose woman I must be to touch Jesus in that way. I don't think he even knew that this was our home, and that he himself was our guest in it! Jesus immediately stood up for me. He asked Simon why he hadn't taken it upon himself to do what needed to be done. He had seen that Jesus had not been refreshed by having his feet washed. Why hadn't he offered? What kind of love did his lack of action display, and what kind of love did mine display?

I hadn't meant to put Jesus into the position of having to defend my odd actions once again. Really, I hadn't. But here he was again, sticking up for me.

And then he said something that changed the mood in the room entirely. He said that I had anointed him . . . for burial. In advance. At first I thought he was going to finally say something unambiguous about being the anointed one—the Messiah, the Christ. It is what we all think, and the things Jesus says about the kingdom of God and his role in it are clear enough. But he always tells us not to speak openly *in such terms. He says that it is God who installs the Messiah, not the Messiah or his followers. If he exalts himself, he will be humbled.* Few of those present outside my family knew that Jesus was echoing words that I had spoken with him at Lazarus's funeral. I had told him that Mary had used much of her perfume to anoint Lazarus's body for burial. The rest of that and some of mine would serve for her burial when the time came. The rest of mine could be kept for the day of my own burial. I was no longer anticipating any likelihood that it might still be used as a dowry. It shouldn't go to waste. I had said this to Jesus. Perhaps the smell had reminded him of Lazarus's burial, as it had also for me. Clearly my words from that earlier occasion were also in his mind when he connected what I did to him with his own burial. Lately he had been talking about how much he will need to suffer before he enters the glory of the Kingdom. He had been hinting at more than hardships and harassment, much more than having to put up with people not washing his feet when they should. He had been mentioning the Romans more often and he knew that if the high priest and ruling council felt they needed to hand him over in order to prevent bloodshed, they would do so. Now, however, he was talking about death and burial. He was sure that if he were to be executed, he wouldn't be given an honorable burial. He said that I took care of it ahead of time, so that we wouldn't need to worry when the time came. It was such a sweet gesture—at the time, I mostly thought that he was simply finding another way to defend my action.

Then they killed him, and that whole day took on a new meaning for me, and for many others.

Looking back now that we've seen him again, now that we believe that God rescued him even from the grave, I can laugh at some of the versions I've heard of my own story. In one of them, the house we are in belongs to the Pharisee, rather than being our own home, and I'm just some woman with a sinful past who has wandered in off the street! I'm glad I don't get mentioned by name in that version. Have you noticed the way that men, when they hear that a woman is "sinful," never think that she is engaging in trade using unequal weights? They always make everything about sex.

For me, both these instances are about the same thing. Jesus emphasized equality, but after I sat at his feet to learn, he went further. Martha of course asked what would happen if all the women were to simply join the men around the teacher. Who would cook?

What would we eat? Jesus saw the need to answer that and began teaching his disciples that if they want to be great in God's Kingdom, they will do "service"—what most people think of as "women's work"—here and now.

And not long after I washed Jesus's feet with my tears and perfume, at our last meal with him, he got up from dinner with his disciples, wrapped himself in a towel, and began to wash their feet . . .

The Lesson Mary Taught Jesus by Sitting to be Taught

It's perhaps understandable why Lazarus, the brother of Mary and Martha, sometimes gets more attention than his sisters. A story about a dead man returning to life is bound to draw attention. According to the Gospel of John, that's precisely the response there was to the story about Lazarus as it began circulating. The story was met with widespread interest: concern on the part of authorities as well as a more enthusiastic response in other circles. It is even more understandable that he grabs a certain amount of attention when we consider the tantalizing possibility that he might be the source behind the Fourth Gospel. Lazarus is singled out as "the one whom you love" when his sisters send word to Jesus about his illness, after which point we begin to get reference to "the disciple, the one whom Jesus loved" who is eventually said to be the one responsible for the writing down of the things found in the Gospel.[1] Be that as it may, many will know the story about Mary and Martha just as well if not better—and not only if they just happen to be more familiar with the Gospel

---

1. We cannot explore here the possibility that the Secret Gospel of Mark records an early tradition about the raising of Lazarus that we find in more developed form in John, and how the inclusion of that material might contribute to the interaction of Jesus with Lazarus's sisters. It is unfortunate that there has been a tendency to treat the text as definitely a modern forgery, when the evidence for this is not at all as decisive or even as impressive as some seem to find it. Elizabeth Schrader's work on the textual history of references to Martha in the Gospel of John may require adjustments to our understanding of who was explicitly mentioned in John's anointing scene (see her 2017 article "Martha of Bethany"). Whether that requires different historical conclusions about events that unfolded would need more detailed discussion than we can give the matter here. Schrader's proposal that Mary Magdalene and Mary of Bethany are the same person is a possibility. The family in Bethany seems to have had a Galilean connection. It is difficult, however, to imagine Lazarus being known as "Lazarus of Bethany" (John 11:1) and yet for his sister to have been nicknamed Mary Magdalene, assuming of course that moniker meant "Mary of Magdala." Unfortunately we cannot explore this topic in more detail here.

of Luke than the Gospel of John, where they also appear. Even in John, the sisters are also said to have been loved by Jesus, just like their brother. But let's turn to Luke first, where we see one of the sisters taking the initiative to learn from Jesus, and teaching him something in the process.

The scene depicted in Luke 10:38–42 is well known to most Christians. In this story, Martha takes care of "service" (the Greek word is the same one that the term "deacon" derives from), while her sister Mary sits and listens to Jesus, presumably inserting herself in the midst of a predominantly male cohort of disciples (or, if you prefer, students) of Jesus who are likewise listening to his teaching intently.[2] In this cultural context, there is no expectation that the men ought to help with household activities such as food preparation, serving guests with the food once it is prepared, or any other household chores for that matter. Controversy ensues when Martha asks Jesus to tell Mary to help her with what everyone simply took for granted were women's duties. When Jesus praises Mary, many readers assume that Jesus is using her to illustrate a point that he had made before. However, if this were the case, it would be hard to explain how it is that Martha had failed to grasp Jesus's teaching about the matter. Jesus would presumably have invited both of them to listen to him on this as on previous occasions. Even if this were the first time he was visiting their home, and if it were already Jesus's usual practice to encourage women to leave the responsibilities usually expected of them in that cultural context and instead take on the role of students, then presumably Jesus would have extended that invitation to both Mary and Martha when he arrived, or at least prior to beginning teaching.[3] They also undoubtedly would have heard stories about him doing so even before their first meeting, were it something he was known for.

We might be able to concoct a scenario in which Jesus might in fact have done what I described, yet without Martha being aware of it. Perhaps this was indeed his first visit to their home, and Martha had been out when Jesus arrived, and upon arriving home, she quickly dove into the role expected of the "woman of the house," missing an invitation to sit

---

2. On the relationship of following and serving and the terminology used see Perroni, *Le Donne di Galilea*, 20. See also 68–77 on the tradition and redaction history of this story and the teaching of Jesus embedded in it.

3. Ashcroft, *Spirited Women*, 58 notes how striking it is for this story, a domestic scene with no miraculous healing or something of that sort, to have been included in a Gospel at all. This is indicative of the significance of the incident for later understanding of Jesus's aims and teaching.

and learn. Perhaps it was only after some time passed that she even realized that her sister had failed to be a proper hostess to these guests, not because she too was out, but because she had the audacity to sit herself there among the men instead! However, we have no evidence for this scenario, and many details in the story tell against it. Even the name of their brother Lazarus (although not mentioned or associated with them in the Gospel of Luke) would lead us to draw a different conclusion. The name Lazarus seems to have been quite common in this time period. It derives from the traditional Jewish name Eleazar. The transformation of that name into "Lazar" (which then becomes Lazaros in Greek) was probably due to the distinctive way that Galileans tended to drop certain sounds in Aramaic—precisely those sounds represented by the letter "e" in the English spelling of the name "Eleazar." Leave those out, and you get "Lazar." Stick a Latin ending on that and you've got "Lazarus." In view of this, it is very likely that Lazarus and his sisters, or perhaps their parents, were from Galilee.[4] That Jesus connected with Galileans living in Bethany is not a coincidence. When people traveled in the ancient world, they did not check into hotels in the impersonal manner common in the English-speaking world today. Just read Paul's practice upon arriving in a new place throughout the book of Acts, as well as the stories about Jesus in the Gospels, and you'll find this reflected.[5] Even if they did not know anyone personally, people who traveled sought out local communities of the same regional, religious, linguistic, and/or ethnic background as themselves, sometimes arriving with a letter of introduction to help them to be accepted. Whenever possible, however, they stayed with someone they knew or with whom they shared a mutual acquaintance who could make the connection. For this reason, it is unlikely that, even if Jesus had arrived in this home of this family for the first time on the day of the incident described, he had arrived with no warning and no word about him having reached him first.

If it had been Jesus's custom prior to this to invite women to learn alongside the men gathered around him, even when that meant neglecting playing the expected cultural role of hostess, that is precisely the sort of thing that one would expect the members of this household to have heard about Jesus prior to his arrival even on his first visit to them.

---

4. Driscoll (*Reading Between The Lines*, 49) assumes Jesus and they were distant cousins. Watson (*Wisdom's Daughters*, 85) has them be family friends since childhood.

5. See Kenneth Bailey's famous treatment of the cultural background to Luke's infancy story for more on this.

Women connected with Jesus's movement are mentioned earlier (Luke 8:3) as having served and supported him and his followers. This in itself may have involved some stretching of what were considered traditional female roles. However, it does not suggest that Jesus had at that point adjusted their role into one of disciples who learned from him when he taught by sitting alongside the men. The evidence as a whole indicates that Jesus had up until this point been conducting himself in the more typical manner of a teacher in the ancient Mediterranean world, gathering around himself an audience of men, while women who supported the movement did so not as disciples but in other ways that, at least for the most part, upheld and worked within the framework of traditional cultural gender roles. Jesus's twelve apostles (emissaries or representatives) were men, and the choice of them may reflect a period in his life when he simply proceeded in a manner that was in keeping with the gender norms he had been brought up with. Irrespective of whether the twelve apostles were appointed before or after this point, the fact remains that if Jesus had been emphasizing that women ought to be given the opportunity to learn, rather than being forced to focus on other matters while the men did so, then Martha could be expected to know this. If she hadn't heard it from Jesus himself or by way of stories and rumors about Jesus, then surely his followers who were present could have been expected to relay this detail to Martha when they saw her busying herself with food preparation when they had been taught that everyone, male and female, to sit and learn together. Had the disciples been told this previously and yet failed to grasp it, we might expect Jesus to rebuke them for their failure to grasp his teaching. If Martha should already have known that Jesus expected her to sit and learn as well, we would expect him to remind her of that in his response. We are thus left with only one option that really fits precisely what is described as unfolding in this incident. Jesus was caught off guard by the decision of Mary to place herself there in the audience at his feet. To be sure, his teaching and attitude must have been such that she felt able to do this, that it would at the very least be tolerated. Martha's reaction to Mary's action remains inexplicable if Jesus had explicitly invited Mary to do what she did, or it were simply taken for granted that this was what he taught and expected. Mary took the initiative, and both Jesus's immediate response and longer-term changes to his teaching and practice reflect what Jesus learned from her choice.

Those who teach know that, however clear our thoughts and values may be with respect to a particular matter, the questions, observations, and actions of our students regularly help us to achieve still greater clarity, crystallize our thinking, and discover new implications and applications of our core values. That may be what happened when Jesus taught in the home of Martha and Mary. When Mary chose to sit and become a student, she was not doing something she had done previously.[6] The choice and the action surprised her sister, even as we see that it surprised Jesus and presumably everyone else in the room. Those present would have looked at Jesus to see what he had to say about this, or what his facial expression indicated. Had his face shown disapproval, others would have acted to minimize the disruption. However much it may have come as a surprise to him when Mary sat among his students, Jesus's expression must have quickly turned from any hint of astonishment to delight or at least nonchalance. And so there she remained, now as a student herself. Where she led, others would follow, inspired by her example. They would also presumably be invited to do so by Jesus himself as his words and actions increasingly reflected what he learned from Mary.

Only Luke tells the story we are considering here about Martha and Mary. This serves to confirm the impression that this marks a turning point in Jesus's activity and the inclusiveness of his group of students. We have already seen how earlier in that Gospel women support Jesus without becoming his students who sit at his feet. If we turn to the book of Acts, there we find that the term "deacon" (which had been used in reference to Martha and the activities of other women in serving Jesus) is

---

6. Haughton, *Re-Creation*, 30 says Jesus "affirmed her right and power to choose a thing of which women were socially and religiously deprived. She, like the men, had made a free choice, and that should not be taken from her." Cooper, *Band of Angels*, 42 writes, "Luke gives us a Jesus who wants to change the place of women in the spiritual landscape. His explicit statement has been invaluable to queens, abbesses, and younger sisters across two millennia. Luke sends a clear message that Jesus welcomed women to his circle of disciples." So also Bird, *Permission Granted*, xiii, 103 who likewise notices that Jesus affirms not only Mary sitting at his feet and learning, but her choice and her right to make it. Mackall (*Kindred Sisters*, 72) notes that Jesus made a pun related to food preparation and consumption. We might say that Mary had chosen the good *portion* or perhaps even the "larger slice." Given what we know about Jesus's penchant for puns, wordplay, and striking imagery, that adds to the case for this being an authentic saying of Jesus, connected with a well-remembered incident in Jesus's life. See further Reid, *Choosing the Better Part?*, 147. We could also make an additional wordplay in English that wasn't available in Aramaic or Greek, and say that Mary had helped herself to the best *serving*, playing on the fact that she was feasting on Jesus's teaching when the expectation was that she should be preparing and *serving* the food to others. Having a love for puns myself, I am tempted to say that on this occasion Mary stirred the pot while Martha simmered.

transformed into a term that is used with reference to what men as well as women who are part of the Christian movement do. In the epistles we can also read about deacons who could be either men or women (Rom 16:1–2; 1 Tim 3:11). By that stage Jesus's teaching and example were understood to challenge strict adherence to patriarchal gender norms and assumptions. The Gospel of Luke provides us with evidence that Jesus's own practice was influenced by something he learned from a woman named Mary, who dared to take it upon herself to adopt the role of student despite not having received an explicit invitation from him to do so. Jesus's teaching and attitude were themselves surely inviting enough to have encouraged her to think this would be met with acceptance rather than a rebuff. Mary detected a willingness on the part of Jesus to part with convention, even though when it came to this particular matter Jesus had not done so—at least, not yet. Jesus's practice and teaching from then on appear to change. Luke highlights this through the way that he refers to the other women who were connected with Jesus. Even at the end of the Gospel of Mark, the women are characterized as those who ministered to him previously (Mark 15:41). In Luke's version, the women are said to have followed him, but not to have ministered to or served him (Luke 23:49,55). This makes for a contrast between Luke and one of his sources with regard to the roles of women. Internally to that Gospel, a development is visible between the roles women play in Luke 8:3 and the roles they play later. Mary's action should be viewed as a key turning point in the development of Jesus's thinking on this topic.[7]

Some reading this may be tempted to conclude that things are depicted this way in Luke and Acts because it is an emphasis of Luke's rather than one that stems from Jesus. That is possible, but seems unlikely, because the impact of the change has left traces in other Gospels and early Christian sources, even if the story of what led to those teachings and actions is not included. For instance, when Jesus says that he himself "did not come to be served but to serve" (Mark 10:45), using related language, we ought to think of it in relation to this story. Mary saw something in Jesus that invited her to do more than serve food. Perhaps he had already said that the last would be first and the first would be last, but had not yet applied it to roles assigned according to gender. Perhaps he would

---

7. Boer (*Mary Magdalene Beyond the Myth*, 38) writes, "It is unimaginable that Jesus had women with him solely to meet his material needs." It may be unimaginable if one considers Jesus's entire public activity as a unified whole. It is imaginable, however, that the teaching of Jesus and the practices of the group around him evolved.

later utter those words after having the opportunity to reflect on Mary's action and its implications. Mary had prompted Jesus to notice and think further about the gender norms that were widely and uncritically accepted. Once he did so, it led him to take on a servant role himself, and expect his followers to do likewise. In Luke 12:37, Jesus says that when a master comes and finds his slaves faithfully waiting for him, he will serve them rather than vice versa. It may be a parable; it certainly isn't depicting an ordinary state of affairs. Indeed, later in the Gospel a more typical situation is depicted: in Luke 17:7–10, Jesus talks of a slave who comes in from outdoor work very tired, but is still expected to serve the needs of his master before being permitted to take care of his own. The relationship between those two passages deserves more attention than we can give here. Perhaps it represents Jesus seeking to counterbalance his earlier emphasis on role reversal, because some were seeking to take advantage of it for their own benefit or comfort, rather than applying it as an admonition to themselves to serve others. Be that as it may, the scenario of role reversal between the one who normally has power and the one who does not, the one who is served and the one who serves, the first and the last, becomes typical of Jesus's ethical teaching, and is reiterated still more strongly in Luke 22:26–27. Perhaps Jesus had already emphasized this: Mark 9:35 and 10:43 talk about the one who would be great taking on the role of a servant, using the same terminology yet again, highlighting thereby the fact that the role Martha assumed as appropriate to a woman in her culture was a subservient one (as though there were any doubt about this point). Whether or not Jesus had taught some of these things to his followers already, however, Mary of Bethany appears to have been the first to test whether Jesus's principles applied equally to women as well as men, including in their relative roles in relation to one another in that society. This is confirmed by the fact that Jesus neither commends Mary for doing what he taught, nor criticizes Martha for not doing what he taught. Rather, Jesus commends Mary for her choice, for her initiative. The action and its motivation come from her, even if Jesus's teaching and attitude up to this point provided a framework and an opening. If there were an invitation addressed specifically to women, it was at best an implicit one, which Mary perceived where others did not. When Mary made her choice and took that initiative, she discovered that Jesus was willing to affirm it, to back her up. It might not be inappropriate to say that Jesus himself made the same discovery as Mary did in that circumstance. He learned from Mary a new way to apply the things he was already teaching.

Martha's Lesson for Jesus: Shared Responsibilities and Serving the Servant of All

I have no idea whether Martha followed up immediately with a further question right after the scene that Luke reports, but well she might have. I expect she voiced it later, privately, as Martha seems to show more concern for propriety as defined then. Nevertheless, there was a question that needed to be asked if Jesus's new teaching were to be put into practice. Asking it would help Jesus further explore the implications of what he had done in that moment. Mary helped Jesus take one step, Martha the next. The question is this: If Mary is to be welcomed to sit and learn, will this mean that those women who take seriously their social responsibility to provide hospitality and other forms of service will henceforth do double duty, their own tasks they have always had as women, plus those of disciples?[8] It was a traditional division of responsibilities that allowed men to learn and be fed. Martha saw right away that this could not be changed in only one aspect, at least not without it burdening women even as it opened up a new opportunity. However many conversations with Martha and others may have played a role in the development of his thinking from that point on, it is clear that ultimately Jesus learned important things not only from Mary, but from Martha, as we see both

---

8. Schottroff, *Let The Oppressed*, 116–17 concludes that Jesus meant for women to do double duty in precisely this manner. If Hanson, *New Perspective*, is correct that Mary was a disciple, a "sitter at Jesus' feet" who was not present on this occasion precisely because as a disciple she was out proclaiming the good news, then our interpretation in this chapter would need to be adjusted. The point about what Jesus learned from Martha would remain, however. The issue coming up on this occasion suggests that Jesus had not yet addressed the need for men to participate in household chores and hospitality equally with women, to counterbalance their mutual involvement in proclaiming the kingdom. That he eventually did so could still be a takeaway from this occasion, albeit a longer-term one given his immediate response. Acts 22:3 provides a parallel to the use of "sat at the feet" in this non-literal sense, but that in itself does not demonstrate that the non-literal meaning is intended in Luke 10:39. Either way, however, it is clear that Mary of Bethany relates to Jesus in the story as Saul related to Gamaliel, as student to teacher (Schüssler Fiorenza, *But She Said*, 59; Hebblethwaite, *Six New Gospels*, 84–85; Boer, *Mary Magdalene*, 36; Tucker and Liefeld, *Daughters*, 26; Sebastiani, *Tra/Sfigurazione*, 17; D'Angelo, "Reconstructing 'Real Women,'" 107; Swidler, *Three Jesus Certitudes*, 67).

him and his disciples acting in ways that reflect the influence of both sisters on him.[9]

One particular example provides especially clear evidence that Jesus addressed Martha's concerns, that he learned things from both sisters' perspectives rather than merely affirming Mary's choice. At some point Jesus began to teach not only that women could learn in the manner that had previously been reserved almost exclusively to men, but that this would be accomplished fairly as men participated in work previously considered the purview of women. How do we know this? As Jesus sent his disciples to find the place where he would eat the Passover with them, they are told to look for a man carrying a water jar. Commentators often note that this man would have stood out in his time and place, since fetching water was considered a woman's or slave's task.[10] For some, this is a miraculous anomaly leading them to a place where the divine will would cloud the mind of the proprietor and allow Jesus and his entourage to eat there seemingly inexplicably, with no prior arrangement or warning. Others have suggested that the man was an Essene, part of a group that consisted only of men, and this was a way of finding members of this movement with which Jesus also had a connection. Still others have suggested that this was simply a pre-arranged sign, with a man carrying the jar while onlookers gaped, merely so that he could guide Jesus's friends to the place. When we think about these interpretations, it becomes clear that none of them seems to make much sense.

There is, however, an interpretation that *does* make sense, and it is one that offers itself to us as almost obvious once we have considered the teaching and experiences of Jesus we have explored in this chapter. The man in question was someone who had learned from Jesus previously, whether directly or indirectly. This could be seen in the fact that he did not treat the fetching of water as "women's work" and thus beneath him, or simply someone else's responsibility. Both women and men (as well as slave and free) could fetch water, and both women and men could sit at Jesus's feet and learn. Jesus may or may not have had in mind that a

---

9. Hebblethwaite, *Six New Gospels*, 83–85 nicely captures the injustice of some having to bear the burden of all the food preparations and cleaning and being deprived as a result of the opportunity to listen to Jesus which others enjoy unencumbered by such concerns.

10. Slaves could be asked to fetch water. Even then it tends to have primarily been female slaves that carried out this function, although slavery largely overrode otherwise prevailing distinctions between gender roles. See Blundell, *Women*, 74; Hezser, *Jewish Slavery*, 63, 84; Stewart, "Slave Labor in Plautus," 367.

student of his lived in this area and would at some point fetch water from the well that provided this essential lifegiving necessity to those living there. But it seems likely that he would have. In that circumstance, he could have sent his disciples to the well in question, to wait until they saw someone behaving in a manner that he would expect one of his disciples to behave. Most likely, Jesus would still have sent some advance word to the disciple in question, rather than descending with a crowd on him with no warning. Sometimes such circumstances could not be avoided in an era before telecommunications. But it still seems far more straightforward to envisage Jesus sending word, and perhaps even having the host for the event offer his fetching of water, acting in a distinctive manner that flagged him as someone who learned from Jesus, as the thing for Jesus's emissaries to watch out for when they were trying to find the place they were looking for. They were to look for a man who took on a stereotypically woman's role, as he had learned from his master to do. His master, in turn, had learned it as he had seen his close women friends torn between their desire to learn from his teaching, and the responsibilities they were required by culture and custom to shoulder. Immediately before this, there had been footwashing. But well before that, the same family had challenged Jesus with the desire of one of them to simply listen to what he had to say, in a manner that men were free to do without meeting criticism, and yet which it was still surprising if not shocking for a woman to do. What Jesus learned, he passed on to others, both men and women. Those teachings and his example were in turn taken to heart and put into practice, so that those who knew Jesus's teaching and knew what to look for could find one of them fairly easily, by looking for behaviors such as a man carrying water from a well. They could look for egalitarianism with regard to chores. Those who sought to learn from and practice Jesus's teaching grasped this core emphasis of his. How many knew that Jesus's teaching about sharing of work and equality of status were things that he himself learned from his interactions with and actions of women, we can only speculate. But we have enough information in stories like those about Mary of Bethany to be able to conclude that she played a role not merely in illustrating such teachings that he had previously formulated, but in actually helping Jesus to learn these things, become convinced of them, and make them part of his own emphases as he instructed still larger numbers of followers.

Many readers of the story of Mary and Martha understand it to be an affirmation of women learning, but rarely if ever see it as presenting women teaching, never mind teaching Jesus something. It is interpreted as Jesus praising Mary and criticizing Martha. However, it is not necessary to understand Jesus to be rebuking Martha, much less doing so harshly. Are we to understand him to be benefiting from her hospitality and yet at the same time criticizing her for offering it?[11] But if we are correct that Jesus learned something from Mary, then it is to be expected that the new insight would require some further exploration, and it would take some time to work through the full ramifications of it. Not only the example of the man carrying the water jar, but also the activities of those who cared for widows and "waited on tables" in the early church as depicted in Acts 6:1-6, shows that the practice of Jesus's followers came to be one of shared service, with men and women involved in tasks that previously had been divided along gender lines. Jesus not only affirmed Mary's choice to learn, but Martha's concern that women would either have to choose between learning and household chores and hospitality, or be unfairly burdened with the expectation that they and they alone do both. Jesus learned from both these sisters.[12] It is no wonder that he valued their friendship so highly.

---

11. See Cooper, *Band of Angels*, xiii, 44; Watson, *Wisdom's Daughters*, 90–91. Cooper emphasizes that Martha is probably the head of household, and that places a different spin on the dynamics of the roles and relationships in the story. Lutzer and Lutzer, *Jesus Lover of a Woman's Soul*, 121 note the significance of the wording of Luke 10:38, namely that this was Martha's home to offer hospitality in. The fact that Martha is sometimes mentioned before and/or independently of Lazarus is interesting. Perhaps he was frequently ill, and the women were thus the more prominent members of the household, with Martha the eldest as head (as suggested by Watson, *Wisdom's Daughters*, 90, and also hinted at byDriscoll, *Reading Between The Lines*, 50). Mercedes Lopes ("Martha" 92) suggests that this might simply reflect wider knowledge of them in the Gospel tradition, but even if that is the main reason for them sometimes being mentioned first or on their own, it still calls out for a sociological explanation of why that might be the case. Yamaguchi (*Mary and Martha*, 137–38) notes that the sending of word by the sisters also conveys the sense that one or both of them is the head of household.

12. Moloney, *Woman First Among the Faithful*, 71–72 suggests that the proximity of this story to the Good Samaritan, in which practical meeting of another's needs is praised, helps maintain a balance between the aims and attributes of Mary and Martha that can be lost when this story is read independently of that literary context.

Washing Feet

A particularly clear example of how Jesus, having learned from Mary, in turn taught his disciples to do likewise is found in the story in the Gospel of John (13:3-17) about Jesus washing the disciples' feet. What she had humbled herself to do for him, he did for his disciples, offering not only himself but Mary as an example for them to follow. The washing of feet is a ritual practiced in some churches. In the time and place in which Jesus lived, it was a common practice, much like we might invite someone to visit the bathroom of our home after they arrive after a long journey, providing an opportunity to freshen up. In an era of dusty roads and travel mostly by foot, this was a major aspect of courtesy. It was the task of a slave, as some readers of the New Testament may recall from background information they learned in connection with the statement of John the Baptist that he is not even worthy to untie the sandals of the one coming after him. Contact with sandals and feet was the responsibility for whoever had the lowest status. John insists that he is too low in relation to the one who was coming even for that. Mary was a respected woman of status, and humbled herself, providing an example that Jesus in turn followed, saying that his disciples also should as well.

In each of the four New Testament Gospels there is a story along these lines. But there are also major differences among them. Luke alone moves the incident away from the passion narrative and places it much earlier. Typically the woman is unnamed, but in John we are told that it was Mary of Bethany who had performed this action. In my retelling of the story, I have tried to imaginatively explore one possible explanation for the differences. Lots of people were surely gathered when Jesus arrived in town. Perhaps some didn't know whose house they were in, or who the woman was who did this to him. It is entirely possible that multiple versions of the story began to circulate from multiple contradictory perceptions of what transpired, right from the outset. However, we need to acknowledge that there are other possible explanations for what we find in the Gospels. It could be that Luke radically rewrote the story he inherited because of how it fit his aims and emphases. There could have been two events, one an anointing of Jesus's head and the other a washing of his feet, between the stories of which some people's memories jumbled details. Even though we are proceeding here under the assumption that there was one such incident with one woman involved, that is not the only possibility.[13] Given Luke's propensity for creative rearrangement of material, shifting sayings and stories to a new context so as to transform their meaning, it is reasonable to assume that is the case here as well.[14] If Luke changed the story, a possible motive for doing so comes readily to mind which would fit with the author's emphases in his Gospel. Luke may have been hesitant to depict disciples criticizing Jesus for any reason, but especially for not encouraging a disciple to sell expensive property to give to the poor. Of course, it may have been someone prior to Luke who deliberately transformed the story, or it may have slowly changed over the years before it reached him verbally in a different form than what he found written in the Gospel of Mark. Either way, however, precisely because we know that Luke used the Gospel of Mark, his omission of the anointing at Bethany a week before the Passover shows us that he considered his version to be an alternative version of the same story, rather than a separate but similar event.[15] For this reason we have tried to make sense of the diverse traditions as about a single event, while also doing justice to the mention of anointing of head and washing of feet across the different versions. In the story as we told it, both those things happened, and it was Mary of Bethany who did them to Jesus.

In our confusion over how to relate the different Gospel accounts of a woman anointing Jesus to one another, we are liable to miss another important detail. Soon after Mary of Bethany did this to Jesus, according to the Gospel of John, Jesus in turn did it to others.[16] The relevance of that to the theme of this book should immediately be obvious. Jesus saw

13. See Hanson, *New Perspective*, 108–17, for a consideration of various options. Hanson concludes that the confusion is caused by there having been two actions of this sort, both carried out by Mary of Bethany, but one early in Jesus's public activity and the other towards the end. See also Haughton, *Re-Creation*, 28.

14. Getty-Sullivan, *Women*, 106–7, 213. See for other examples what Luke does with Jesus's teaching about the unforgivable sin and his prediction of the temple's destruction. Luke also may borrow a phrase from another story in the words he attributes to Jesus in his version. "Your faith has saved you, go in peace" is the same language used of the woman with vaginal hemorrhaging. What might the significance of that be?

15. Hebblethwaite (*Six New Gospels*, 102n12) comments, "Sadly but perhaps predictably, it is Luke's theologically impoverished version, in which the anointing woman is not a prophet but a sinner, which most people remember, and which has been depicted in art, to the virtual exclusion of the other three accounts."

16. See in particular Moreno, "Un gesto de mujer," 182–88 and Yamaguchi, *Mary and Martha*, 115, 122–23, both of whom draw attention to the many ways the Gospel of John highlights parallels between Mary's footwashing and that of Jesus.

the importance of what a woman did to him, and imitated her in doing likewise to a group of his disciples. That Jesus did not imitate her action precisely by wiping their feet with his hair could be taken as evidence that Jesus's own hair was shorter than has often been depicted in art. He is also not said to have poured costly perfume on their feet, either. Of course, I am being somewhat facetious here. But the serious point remains: at least one woman if not two, most likely Mary of Bethany, washed Jesus's feet in a manner that Jesus subsequently imitated.[17] We can only speculate why she took on a responsibility as a member of the household that a servant ought to have undertaken. If the story of a "sinful woman" in Luke arose from this act of radical hospitality, we can speculate that it might have been the case that servants had been sent on other errands, and Mary felt so determined to provide appropriate hospitality that she took on the role of a servant in their absence.[18] Jesus was clearly moved, and not only does he do something similar according to John 13, but commentators have sometimes seen echoes of this incident in Phil 2:6–11, in which Paul says that Jesus took upon himself the very form of a servant.[19]

Near the beginning of Jesus's public ministry, John the Baptist is said to have spoken about one who would come after him, the thong of whose sandal he was unworthy to untie. In that context, we hear nothing of Jesus protesting such rhetoric, and the Gospel authors seem to be happy to embrace the Baptist's self-abasement in the interest of elevating Jesus above him. By the end of Jesus's public ministry, however, we see Jesus acting out a conviction that no one is beneath touching his feet, and indeed he will humble himself still further and wash the feet of his own students, a role as lowly or perhaps even lower than that of the slave who might merely untie the strap of a sandal. What had changed in the

---

17. Tetlow, *Women and Ministry*, 113 notes the structural importance of Mary's washing of Jesus's feet, drawing the Book of Signs to a close, and the next section opening with Jesus washing his disciples' feet. Swidler, *Jesus Was a Feminist*, 97 (and 101n68), notes echoes that resonate between the various stories about Mary of Bethany, even between those in Luke and in John. Mary sits at Jesus's feet to learn. Mary is sitting in mourning then falls at Jesus's feet. While Martha is taking care of food, Mary anoints Jesus's feet.

18. Yamaguchi (*Mary and Martha*, 123) attributes to Marianne Sawicki the suggestion that a story about oil being poured down was transformed into a story about hair being let down in the transmission process. The same verb that conveys the former can refer to the latter in the middle voice.

19. The connection is made by Cyprian of Carthage in his *Ad Quirinium* 12.3.11 (noted by Egasse, *Lavement*).

interim? Jesus had been shaping his own ethical teaching about humility and status, to be sure, throughout the intervening years. But something specific seems to have prompted a recognizable shift, and that was Mary of Bethany humbling herself in a manner that made an impression on Jesus. Jesus learned from her to such an extent that he emulated her example.[20]

Historians tend to be skeptical of information found only in one Gospel, especially if that Gospel is John. It includes a lot of unique material in a very distinctive style. Are John's stories unique because the author took creative license, or because he knew or chose to include things that others did not? Perhaps both are true. In the case of the story about Jesus washing his disciples' feet, however, it is easier to explain the other Gospels omitting the tradition, than to imagine John inventing it. Jesus was humiliating himself in a manner that would have been profoundly uncomfortable for those who esteemed him and sought to honor him. One can imagine that Jesus's disciples would sooner have debased themselves in a subservient role, than have seen Jesus do so. For those in the English-speaking world where honor-shame values may be unfamiliar, an analogy may help you to appreciate the point. If you are a male and found yourself bullied in the schoolyard, it may have been humiliating to be beaten up. But someone saying "I can beat you up" was not as severe an affront to our honor as someone saying "my dad can beat up your dad." For shame to befall someone we honor above ourselves, and yet to whose honor our own is inextricably tied, is somehow far worse than our own individual reputation. For Jesus to behave as a servant was shocking in the context of his time and its values, for anyone who witnessed it. But one imagines that it would have been his disciples more than anyone else who felt the full force of this, who squirmed with discomfort, even

20. Hebblethwaite, *Six New Gospels*, 106 recalls the words of John the Baptist in the context of Mary's action. Hanson, *New Perspective*, 125 writes, "In her anointing of his feet, Mary first sets the footwashing example(s) before Jesus, who then demonstrates the same servant-leadership at the following dinner of John 13. In a way, she may have led Jesus himself, by setting this example, which he followed a few days later." Hanson, *New Perspective*, 57 discusses a parallel to a woman washing a man's feet in Joseph and Aseneth, where it is an expression of the latter's great love and devotion to her husband. Hanson writes (83), "This action of Mary's could be a symbol of hospitality, honor, embalming for death, or consecration for kingship, each of which could be an appropriate interpretation." Mery Rodríguez Moreno notes connections with Joseph and Aseneth, 1 Sam 25:41, and Abot de Rabbi Nathan ("Un gesto de mujer," 170–73). See also Beattie, "Discipleship of Love"; Esler and Piper, *Lazarus, Mary and Martha*, 66.

as Peter insisted that this thing cannot and should not be. That detail is entirely plausible. Other Gospels may have omitted the story precisely because of this discomfort. Even so, the Gospel of Luke recounts that there was a discussion of who was greatest at the Last Supper, and that Jesus instructed his followers that whoever wished to be great in the kingdom he proclaimed must be servant of all. That Jesus illustrated such words with a lived example should not seem implausible to anyone. On the contrary, it seems thoroughly in keeping with the impression we are consistently given of Jesus by our earliest sources. Some could not bear to tell the story. Even for those who sought to follow his teaching, and who thought they understood it, it still seemed worse to have one's hero humiliated than to be humiliated oneself. Yet the fact that we have these stories in any of the Gospels at all is an indication that some men were paying attention to what Jesus did, if only because they recognized that what he said and did with respect to women had implication for them. In some instances it probably indicates that the Gospel authors were at least trying to emulate Jesus inasmuch as they too listened not only to the stories of men, but those of women as well.

Anointing for Burial and/or as King

There is debate about whether Mary of Bethany understood her anointing of Jesus as a messianic anointing, that is to say as the anointing of him as king. In the context of the Gospels which place the occurrence about a week prior to Jesus's death, it is interpreted as an anointing beforehand for burial. Some will view this as simply an attempt by Mark and others to have the disciples do in advance what they were prevented from doing in the moment. Despite the famous artistic depictions that readers are undoubtedly familiar with such as Michelangelo's *Pieta*, the family and disciples of Jesus were not given his body to bury in the manner they saw fit. And despite what the Gospel of John claims, Jesus was not given an honorable burial in an unused tomb with a quantity of spices fit for a king.[21] Both of those involve a significant rewriting of what we find in our earliest account in the Gospel of Mark. It would not be surprising if Jesus's followers reinterpreted an anointing that had different connotations in the moment as an advance anointing for burial. Yet on the other

---

21. On this see further James F. McGrath, *The Burial of Jesus: What Does History Have To Do With Faith?* (Denver, CO: Patheos, 2012).

hand, we must understand Jesus to have seen what happened to his mentor and other figures like himself, and to have known what was coming, perhaps even to have made arrangements and preparations. If his inner circle of disciples did not grasp what was coming, there were surely close friends with whom Jesus spoke more plainly, who did understand. Perhaps Mary did indeed intend to anoint him for burial in advance.[22] It would be a beautiful gesture in a world in which even today we too often only say things at funerals, after someone has died, that we wish we had said when the person was alive. More likely the action had one or more significances to those involved as it happened, and took on still other levels of significance and symbolism over time when viewed from the perspective of hindsight.

The action is not merely lavish, but excessively so. For common workers, the value of the perfume was close to a year's wages. We need to translate that into modern terms to fully grasp this. Take what you consider an appropriate entry-level annual salary in today's workplace and imagine spending that amount on perfume. (If it is easy for you to imagine this because you do it all the time, please send me an email, as I would love for you to support the work I do.) Clearly Mary and her family were not commoners. Those who did not have the means to afford such luxuries would naturally have asked why such an expensive perfume was not sold so that the poor could be fed with the money.[23] Think again about how much good can be done with the equivalent of a year's salary in terms of helping others with urgent needs. Doing that with the perfume would have been in keeping with Jesus's teaching about caring for the poor. Wasn't this wasteful, frivolous, an action that only a wealthy person could possible countenance, accustomed as they were to

---

22. Ring (*Women Who Knew Jesus*, 191) writes, "Only Mary of Bethany appears to be aware that Jesus' death is imminent." On the other hand, Bond, *First Biography* 212–14, highlights reasons for thinking that, even if Jesus saw a connection with burial or some other deeper significance, the woman anointing him did not necessarily view the action in the same way, at least as depicted in our earliest account in Mark. See the interesting suggestion of Wainwright, *Healing Women*, 155–58, that the action may have been intended to provide Jesus with healing at a time when his mind was deeply troubled.

23. See Love, *Jesus and Marginal Women*, 181 on the angry reaction of the disciples in connection with other texts in which disciples express anger, including how these all relate to the Roman patronage system and its values. Ashcroft, *Spirited Women*, 20 writes, "Maria stands as one who knows what she values and holds faithfully to it in defiance of societal pressures." Jesus surely learned something about doing likewise from women like her.

taking for granted that which lay completely beyond the means of most other people?

Some suggest that Mary was doing more than just pouring perfume in an act of ridiculously lavish generosity. She was anointing Jesus as Messiah, effectively proclaiming his kingship in the traditional manner.[24] This would be highly significant not only for what it tells us about Jesus and this turning point in his life, but also for Mary, as she would be taking on the role and authority of ancient prophetic leaders like Samuel. However, the fact that Mary anointed Jesus with perfume rather than olive oil makes it less likely that Mary had planned this in advance to be

---

24. Moltmann-Wendel (*Women around Jesus*, 98) says the woman who anoints Jesus is "a prophet who anoints the Messiah, consecrates him and equips him for his task." She notes, however, that both the act itself (unknown woman rather than recognized prophet anointing the king) and its connotations (the king will die rather than reign over a nation) are subversive and controversial (as does Watson, *Wisdom's Daughters*, 94; Yamaguchi, *Mary and Martha*, 115). As the one who grasps that Jesus is the Messiah who will die, "a woman knew of the messianic secret before all the disciples" (Moltmann-Wendel, *Women around Jesus*, 99). Driscoll, *Reading Between The Lines*, 53 notes that "Martha and Peter are the only two disciples whose declaration of faith in Jesus as the Messiah, the Christ, the Son of the living God has been recorded in the gospels. They are also the only two to be reprimanded sharply by Jesus." See also Yamaguchi, *Mary and Martha*, 120; Sebastiani, *Tra/Sfigurazione*, 35; Hebblethwaite, *Six New Gospels*, 90n18). Tetlow (*Women and Ministry*, 104) perceives Luke to allow women to learn but not to proclaim. She also suggests (112) that Martha's confession takes the place of Peter's in the Synoptics, making her the focus of apostolic authority for the Johannine community. Beirne, *Women and Men*, 132 says something similar, emphasizing that John thus depicts Martha as a comparable sort of leader. Watson treats this in a combined version drawing on multiple Gospels, in which the "sinful woman" is a fortune teller, and based on her reading of the stars and planets she deliberately buys anointing oil to anoint him (93–100). Ring, *Women*, 196 writes, "Because this woman is called a sinner, many interpreters have called her a prostitute, although the text does not explicitly make this connection. Given the male tendency to see women as sexually seductive and immoral, the prostitute label has persisted even though there is no textual foundation for it." Driscoll (*Reading Between The Lines*, 57) envisages Simon being one of her customers, and him not objecting to her presence lest she reveal his secret! However, if we ask what sort of woman could be known as a sinner throughout the city, and yet have the status that Simon would accept her in his house even if begrudgingly, then we must be dealing with a woman of status and not a prostitute or some random adulteress. Why not presuppose a connection between the two, that the status of the woman and the perception of her as a sinner was connected and that she was notorious for immoral business practices or something like that (Getty-Sullivan, *Women*, 109)? Indeed, why not identify the woman as Joanna the wife of Chuza and the immorality as having to do with the behavior and ruthlessness of the Herodian family?

a royal anointing.²⁵ It is of course theoretically possible that the Gospel tradition played down the direct messianic pronouncement by Jesus and his movement. Yet it is hard to imagine them deliberately substituting expensive perfume in place of olive oil, so as to turn a shocking political and religious act into a different shocking economic one. There remains another possibility: that Mary understood Jesus to be a radically different Messiah, one destined to die rather than rule, to such an extent that she anointed him with burial ointment rather than in the manner customary for kings.²⁶ That perspective seems more likely as a reinterpretation from the perspective of hindsight, than something those involved in the events as they happened would have understood, much less intended. It remains a possibility nonetheless, and an intriguing one, even if at the same time one that seems to us historically less probable than what we have depicted.

Trying to discern what actually happened, and puzzle out and disentangle the intentions of the one who did it, the interpretation given to it by Jesus when it was done to him, the interpretation of those present, and the additional meanings it took on to those who eventually wrote it down seems impossibly challenging. We must attempt to figure out as much as we can nonetheless. In the process, we must do justice to the fact that not only do events have different significances for different individuals involved, and change with time as we reflect on them, but they can also evolve quickly in the very moments they are unfolding. That Mary's action may have begun with one intention does not mean that it could not have quickly taken on another as she was doing it, in that very instant, as well as further still with the benefit of hindsight from a greater distance in time. The action of Mary may have led Jesus to see that moment in his life in a different light, in ways that neither of them intended or planned in advance. If so, this might also explain the diversity of ways the incident is depicted. As the interpretation quickly changed, the memories and revisions would have interacted to spur a number of trajectories that both ensured the ongoing preservation of stories about what transpired, it being recognized as an important occurrence, and at the same time made

---

25. When tears alone did not provide sufficient water for the task at hand, it may be that Mary considered using olive oil to finish. She may have thought about the symbolism of anointing the humble king, the honor it would bring her to be the one to do so, and yet also considered that oil would refresh Jesus less than perfume would.

26. Schüssler Fiorenza, *In Memory of Her*, xliv.

it more complicated for a historian to separate out what happened as it might have been intended and understood in that very moment.

If we believe that Jesus saw royal significance in what was done to him, and not just a connection with burial, then that tells us something important. Notice the different reactions of Jesus to Peter's declaration of him as the anointed one, and Mary anointing him. Is that difference due to the difference in timing, a difference in how Jesus assessed Peter's and Mary's perceptions of his aims, the expression of the recognition of his royal destiny through action as opposed to in words, or several or all of the above? Prophetic anointing of kings in the Jewish Scriptures was connected with a theological-political view of the institution of monarchy in which kings are subject to the authority of prophets as divine spokespersons.[27] This might have motivated a downplaying of there being any literal anointing of Jesus by another human being, since it potentially elevated the anointer's authority above that of the one anointed. The early church's emphasis on Jesus himself being a prophet and one with prophetic authority may also have played a role. Giving Mary prophetic authority to anoint Jesus may have been too much for some for reasons both christological and patriarchal. Yet even if Mary's role as prophetic anointer of the king is not highlighted for the reasons mentioned, by having her anoint Jesus in advance for burial, the woman's status as prophet, as one who foresees in advance where his path is leading him, is highlighted in the process nonetheless.[28] Being left with a high degree of ambiguity about whether it was intended as a royal anointing is on one level deeply appropriate, given the ambiguity about Jesus's messianic identity in his own teaching and his own frequent efforts to keep such ideas from circulating widely. We should also consider that, even if it was not a typical royal anointing with olive oil, the lavish amount poured on Jesus made it nonetheless the sort of anointing fit only for a king. Even in the act of signifying that Jesus is a different sort of messiah, one who will die rather than conquer through military might, Mary affirms his royal status.[29] As Mark looked back on the event, he may have seen in this preparation beforehand for Jesus to be laid without due honor in a grave for criminals,

27. Ghosn, *Encounters*, 70 notes the prophetic character of the woman who, according to Mark, appears to simply arrive and enter, select Jesus from among those present, and pour oil specifically on his head.

28. Cf. Love, *Jesus and Marginal Women*, 184; Guijarro and Rodriguez, "Messianic Anointing."

29. Seibert-Cuadra, "La mujeren los evangeliossinópticos," 95.

an act that ensured that he would nonetheless buried as a king.³⁰ Perhaps that explains the different reactions on the part of Jesus to Mary's action and to Peter's earlier declaration. Mary's brought together precisely what Peter's had tried to keep separate, namely that in Jesus's understanding of his own royal vocation, "the Son of Man must suffer."

Unused Dowry?

One sometimes reads in popular treatments of the story of Jesus's anointing that the ointment might have been part of Mary's dowry. Most of the time, no basis for this claim is provided in any ancient sources, and those sources that are cited often bear at best a very general relation to the subject of dowries, with few specific examples available of perfume or ointment being part of what a bride received from her father to accompany her in married life.³¹ Yet even if the suggestion that the ointment might have been intended for Mary's dowry is speculation, it is not an implausible one. In our retelling, we tried to take into account the fact that Martha appears to be the head of the household in which these siblings live together, suggesting the earlier death of their parents as well as the family having been one of above-average means.³² Ointment is precisely the kind of gift in kind that one can envisage a father giving to a daughter to provide a dowry for her when he senses that he might die before he is able to do so, something that would not get apportioned out to others or otherwise taken from her if there were some dispute over inheritance or division of his property after he was gone. The value of the spikenard seems about right for the purpose of provision of a dowry sum

---

30. The author of the Gospel of John felt the need to add even greater royal burial pomp and honor, and to have it take place when it ideally ought to, in conjunction with the burial itself, where the other Gospels only have it occur awkwardly earlier. The amount of spices Nicodemus is said to have brought would have been even more valuable than Mary's spikenard (see Kitzberger, *Interfigural Readings*, 99n45 and also 203–7; Haag, *Quest*, 90). We cannot fully explore John's motives for inserting a male character into the story who does something even more lavish than Mary. Note however that he is not criticized for doing so the way Mary was. Consider also Nicodemus is a far more ambiguous figure in the Gospel. Nonetheless, if his lavish act is appropriate, then Mary's was as well, if not indeed more so.

31. See, e.g., the sources cited by Julius Preuss, *Biblical and Talmudic Medicine*, 372–73.

32. Wyant, "Giving Martha Back Her House," discusses textual evidence for the house having been identified as belonging to Martha.

in kind in the case of a family that was above the level of poverty, yet not among the extremely wealthy at the opposite (and, then as now, sparsely-populated) end of the spectrum.

Given Mary's circumstances caring for a sickly brother, managing a household, and presumably also overseeing a family business in their patriarchal society, she might well have seen her prospects for marriage slipping away, especially if Martha had been following a similar trajectory ahead of her. Although the awkward phrasing about "keeping it for the day of my burial" in the Gospel of John is most likely the result of that author catching himself while retelling the familiar story, recalling his intention to give Jesus a proper burial that the Gospel of Mark tells us he had been denied, I wove it into the story as an echo of something that Mary might have shared with Jesus in a moment of melancholic reflection after her brother's funeral.[33] I imagine Martha, the older of the two sisters, using most of her similar dowry to anoint their brother's body for burial. Mary would have mused in such circumstances that what remained of the expensive perfume could be kept for the days of their burials, so that there would be something for others to hopefully use to provide the sisters with an honorable burial. Mary would have seen this lonely future, as she would likely be the last survivor of this family. Martha seems clearly to have been older and possibly the eldest.[34] Lazarus may have been any age but ill health and frailty meant that he had all along been unlikely to outlive Mary, and probably unable even to serve as head of household as the only surviving male. With none of them having children, there was no guarantee of a proper burial, especially for the last of them left alive. Leaving behind a vial of expensive ointment for the purpose might just possibly, if she was also held in some esteem by those in the employ of the family business and/or the wider community, increase her chances of being laid to rest honorably in their family tomb. For Mary to have said something along these lines, and for Jesus to have listened attentively and recalled her words, weaving them into something that he himself said later on, is in keeping with the recorded details as well as with the character of Jesus as we have seen it come into focus throughout this book.

33. Esler and Piper, *Jesus, Mary and Martha*, 73 suggest that Nicodemus anointed Jesus with ointment provided by Mary, thus making it the case that she did indeed "keep it for the day of my burial."

34. Tetlow mentions how unusual it is that Lazarus is mentioned last, after his sisters (*Women and Ministry*, 112).

If the ointment was part or all of what had been left to Mary to serve as a dowry, what would it mean for her to pour it all out? Was it merely being resigned to the fact that, at the age she was, the likelihood of anyone proposing marriage would be increasingly slim? Or did it indicate more than that, whether confidence that the kingdom of God would soon dawn and preclude the possibility of marriage, a choice to forego marriage to devote herself exclusively to the work of proclaiming the kingdom of God as a disciple, just a sacrificial gift whose cost lay not only in its monetary value but also the impact on future marriage prospects, something else, or perhaps some combination of these possibilities?

It seems likely that Martha would have been similarly provided for by her father just as Mary had been and thus would have had her own alabaster vial. As the eldest surviving sibling and a practical, sensible, and responsible head of household, she would have used some or all of her own ointment for Lazarus's burial, allowing Mary to keep hers since the possibility of her marrying in the future was greater, even if it diminished with every year that passed. That Martha had made a sacrifice of her own with a vial of spikenard that was hers seems likely, given everything we are told about her and her family combined with what we have reconstructed about their circumstances. The smell of the ointment might well have reminded both Mary and Jesus of death if it was used at Lazarus's burial.[35] That makes Jesus thinking of his own death and burial in response to Mary's anointing of him far more historically plausible than it might otherwise be felt to be.

Lazarus had been found alive when Jesus went to the tomb. From the sisters' perspective, Jesus not only undid their brother's death, but also prevented them sinking into the category of unmarried orphan women, a vulnerable situation in ancient patriarchal society.[36] Attributing this to Jesus and his power, they would have felt it appropriate to pour the perfume on Jesus. Jesus, in turn, had heard Mary say that she would now "keep it for the day of my burial" and echoed her words in expressing his appreciation for what she had done to him. This was not merely a luxury item given from out of an abundance of wealth. It was sacrificial in a variety of ways. Nor was it merely a symbolic act of no practical

35. Commentators do not discuss this possibility. Esler and Piper make a narrative connection between the anointing of Lazarus and Jesus, but without an olfactory one for the characters involved in this story (*Lazarus, Mary and Martha*, 59–60).

36. The depiction of Jesus going to a tomb and the young man crying out from inside offered in the Secret Gospel of Mark may be a precursor to the account in John.

use, an expression of competitive self-abasement that turns humility into new form of jostling for honor (although a woman participating in that male activity would have been subversive in her own way.) It did not merely express devotion through lavish excess, the wasteful pouring out of something valuable. As we have explored in this chapter, however hard it is to pin down all the ways it was costly for Mary and all the layers of symbolism she and others placed on it, this was a significant act, and in relation to the theme of this book, one that led Jesus to see that a climactic moment had arrived. Mary's act combined practicality, symbolism, compassion, friendship, care for the other person, and much else in a manner that was nearly perfect. This woman had understood what Jesus taught better than he dared hope any disciple could. Having been given a royal/burial anointing by a woman who so profoundly understood his teaching indicated to him that the time had come for him to suffer at the hands of authorities. As something valuable that could have been sold to support continuing teaching and healing activities of the same sort that Jesus had been engaging in, Mary's pouring it out may also have prompted Jesus to decide that this signified a change, that it was time to end that mission in the form it had taken until then and enter a new and final phase. It was literally a sweet-smelling sacrificial offering. It was also so much more than that in the eyes of Jesus. That Mary could have the confidence to take on the role of king-anointing prophet, and at the same time do so with such humility and so self-sacrificially, indicated that Jesus had made the impact he hoped for, that he had passed on what he had learned from women, as evidenced by this woman who had both learned from him and at the same time taught him so much.

Beyond the New Testament Gospels

We have already hinted that in Acts we see the ongoing impact of what Jesus learned from Mary and Martha, as men took up the role of serving that characterized female followers of Jesus in the Gospels.[37] Do we see that elsewhere? I believe we do, in the letters of Paul in the New Testament as well as other texts outside of the traditional canon. Gospel of Thomas 114 depicts Simon Peter saying that Mary (it isn't clear which

---

37. Barbara Reid writes, "In the Gospels only women characters are the subject of *diakonein*. In contrast, *diakonein* and *diakonia* are used only of men in Acts" (*Choosing the Better Part?* 47). Luke often uses the same or similar language about different people between his two volumes as a way of connecting them.

one) should depart from among them, because women are not worthy of life. Jesus is depicted as saying that he will make her male so that she too can be a living spirit like them. Saying 22 in that same work has Jesus talk of the two becoming one so that the male is no longer male and the female no longer female. Scholars disagree about the date of the Gospel of Thomas and how its contents relate to the New Testament Gospels. Irrespective of one's view on that matter, the Gospel of Thomas may still be influenced by and preserve traces of historical recollection of what Jesus said and did.[38] Together the sayings we referred to may reflect the shift in Jesus's thinking that we have traced in this chapter. Initially, he was open to women participating in male activities and becoming men or like men. But eventually he recognized that, for this to work, something more was required, with men becoming women or like women as well, reducing socially-imposed distinctions between their roles and their rights. Might it be the case that Paul's creed-like statement (Gal 3:28) that asserted that in Christ differences between male and female and slave and free were obliterated was actually based on a saying of Jesus?[39] Perhaps Paul elaborated it, placing at the front a statement about the further implication that he had drawn to apply the principle to the distinction between Jews and Greeks. But the pairing of male-female and slave-free would make perfect sense in light of what we have explored in this chapter. If not based on something Jesus said, it certainly enshrines something that Jesus taught about women—after, of course, women taught it to him.

The impact of Mary and Martha, among others, on the church beyond the lifetime of the historical Jesus cannot be surveyed here, but it deserves a mention. We see the ripples of their influence well beyond the Gospels. Jesus learned important things from them. In a variety of ways, but perhaps most powerfully in his washing of his disciples' feet, he not only offered himself as an example for his disciples to follow, but directed attention to the women that he learned from as well.

---

38. See further DeConick, "Memorial Mary," 273–78; Schussler Fiorenza, *In Memory of Her*, 51.

39. On what appears to be an early Christian creed that Paul is quoting see Patterson, *Forgotten Creed*.

Every Last Penny

*What Jesus Learned from a Poor Widow
Who Shared Her Two Cents*

When I heard that young teacher saying those things, I knew I wanted to invite him and his students into my home. I could not afford to show them hospitality the way I wanted to. I was starving, to be honest. But for that very reason, I wanted to encourage him. He seemed to understand and care about the situation of poor widows like myself. I was fortunate that my village was on the road he was taking as he made his way up to Jerusalem. I was also fortunate that he and his followers decided to stay in the village for several days, when Jerusalem was such a short journey from here that they really needn't have stopped at all.

When they came to my home, I gave them an embarrassingly small chunk of bread and some salt to share. None of them complained either in spoken words or through the expression on their faces about the inadequacy of what I set before them. When they left, the teacher told me that he and his group would return the following day and he would teach his students there. I did not know what to say. I wanted to plead with him not to, not because I didn't want them devouring my last loaf, and I was already ashamed by my poor hospitality today. I did not want to feel even more embarrassed as my meager food was shared among what would undoubtedly be an even larger group. But I said nothing.

The next morning he arrived early at my house with a few of his disciples, to prepare for the larger group of his disciples that would come there to be taught by him. Their arms were full of food. They made busy preparing it and setting it out. I pulled one of his female disciples aside and asked her if *the teacher didn't understand how this shamed me—not that a poor widow has any real honor left. I was grateful, but also felt humiliated to be unable to provide for the guests in my home myself. The woman explained to me that this was simply the way of Jesus's group. They shared their possessions and their means. The rich gave generously, but everyone contributed what they could, and no one had to suffer want. This was simply their practice and thus she need feel no shame.*

I began to weep and told her I felt like the widow of Zarephath. She said the teacher loved that story and referred to it often. Later that day, I told the teacher about myself and my history. My family had never been wealthy, and I had had the misfortune to outlive not only my husband but my two sons and my daughter, none of whom survived the cholera outbreak 4 years ago. We had little money saved, and even though I could not farm the tiny piece of land that had been ours, I knew that if the ownership of it passed to my husband's brother as was his right, my future was even more grim. He said I should be happy that he let me stay in this house which also now passed to his possession. But what is a home without even a tiny patch in which to grow some vegetables so that I might have just a tiny bit to eat? Spending what remained of my dowry, which wasn't much, I hired legal experts to see if there were some neglected law that might save me and allow me to retain that tiny parcel of land. It was only when my money ran out that they told me what I then realized they must have known all along: there was no exception or loophole. Property and inheritance passes to male relatives when there are any. There was nothing to be done, and no protection or salvation for a widow with no male relative to support and defend her. The teacher wept at my story, and I felt terrible for having saddened him after he and his group had been so incredibly kind to me.

When the time came for them to leave, I invited the teacher to return to my home as often as he wished. I could at least provide a roof, even if a crumbling one, to keep the sun off their heads. They did come back, and the food they shared with me kept me alive. I told all my friends about him and many of them came to listen to the teacher. It took a while until I realized that I genuinely felt no shame any longer, even though others knew that they were guests in my home and yet were eating food that I had not provided myself. His approach to life changed me in more ways than one, and I started to imagine a future in which everyone lived like this. The teacher called it the "kingdom of God."

One time the teacher's disciples gave me two copper coins before they left to continue their journey to Jerusalem, saying they had noticed a hole in my roof and since they didn't have time to repair it now, they wanted to leave me something to help with getting that fixed. I thanked them, sobbing as I did so. I am sure they had no way of knowing that this was all the money I had, that there was nothing else, and the coins could not be used to repair my crumbling home. If I spent them on food, it would only keep me alive for another few weeks or so.

They set out on their journey earlier than I did. I saw the teacher and his disciples one final time, when I was in the temple the following day. They were seated not far from the treasury's box for gifts, and he seemed to be commenting on the steady flow of wealthy people who made lavish gifts. I almost turned back, embarrassed once again by my poverty. But I pressed on anyway and placed the coins in the box. As I turned to leave and make my journey home, I looked at the teacher and said a prayer for him. I knew the coins could not have helped me much, and so I felt better giving thanks to God with them for this man and his group. The value of the coins was scarcely equivalent to a tithe on the food they had provided me with. But I gave the little I could, just as these kind souls had done for me . . .

Paying Attention

Jesus noticed the situation of widows, mentioning them often in his teaching.[1] In one sense, all we need in order to ascertain the relevance of this particular widow is her singling out for mention by Jesus. Jesus at some point had begun to learn that it was worth paying attention to women's experiences, and more generally that it was worth observing people. He noticed this woman, and pointed her out to his disciples, presumably from afar, in such a manner that she probably did not know he was doing so. Before one can single people out as an example of something that they should learn, one has to have learned it themselves. Jesus had done so. End of story?

If we ask more probing questions, we find there is more that may intrigue us and draw us in further to the intersection between this woman, Jesus, and her impact on him. How exactly did Jesus know she gave all that she had? Some will leap immediately to the suggestion that he had miraculous knowledge, while others will regard it as an assumption based on the way she was dressed (which may have indicated both bereavement and poverty). We should, however, consider another possibility,

---

1. Swidler, *Three Jesus Certitudes*, 49–51, 124–25.

especially in view of how specifically Jesus says that the woman gave not just proportionally more than the wealthy gave, but all she had. Jesus had opportunity to know people, or to hear about them from others who knew them, in many instances in which we are not told about this sort of transfer of information in the stories themselves. Why should that not be our first consideration when we read a story in which Jesus knows details about another person? Why do we prefer him to be someone supernaturally endowed rather than someone who listens and pays attention to people?

Missing the Point

In the history of Christian interpretation of this story, the point of it is usually said to be to encourage generosity, to applaud the generosity of the poor by comparison with that of the rich. The donations of the latter can seem impressive when one focuses on the total amount given. If we ask about what it cost someone to give as they did, however, the actions of the rich may impress us far less than truly sacrificial giving by the poor. Our comparison should focus on the ratio between total income or wealth and the amount given. There is certainly a genuine insight in this interpretation. More recently, however, a number of commentators have suggested that this interpretation is wrong at a fundamental level, inasmuch as its focus is most likely not on what Jesus would have been concerned to highlight. Jesus, it is suggested, may have been appreciative of the widow's generosity, but was more focused on drawing attention to an unjust system.[2]

The system of charitable giving and donations was unjust in a number of ways. To begin with, we may mention the placement of the donation boxes in a public place that allowed proportional kudos to be accorded by onlookers to those who gave large amounts. Jesus criticizes those who give, pray, or do anything else in a public setting which can be motivated by the acclaim from other people that it earns. There is, however, something even deeper than this. At a more fundamental level than the system set up for charitable giving was (and is) an approach to economics that allows some to give enormous amounts and be applauded for it, while others struggle to survive. The latter nonetheless feel

---

2. See Levine, "'This Poor Widow,'" on some of the strengths and weaknesses of these two interpretations.

obligated to give as well, because it is expected of them, even though they have so little. To make matters worse still, when the poor give proportionally more of their meager means, they are not appreciated for doing so in the way that the wealthy who already reap the financial benefits of this economic system are. Some get the cash and also the kudos for giving some of it away, while others get neither!

That so many of us fail to notice the economic underpinnings of the way charitable giving is handled and viewed in Jesus's teaching reflects the place of privilege from which most modern readers of the Bible in English interpret the text. Historically and globally speaking, however much almost any North American or European who might be reading this earns, and however much we might give away, we are nonetheless more like the wealthy person in the story than the widow. We might hear the story as a challenge to give even more than we do. But we don't hear it as a challenge to question the economic way of life that has allowed us to live in relative comfort compared to others, and compared to most of humanity down the ages as well as around the globe in our time. This is why so many of us have heard Jesus's words on this subject on multiple occasions, yet it hasn't occurred to us that he might be doing more than praising generosity in a way that makes the wealthy feel better about our wealth, while doing nothing to change the societal structures that we have put in place that keep us comfortable in this way. To do so would be to sacrifice privilege in the interest of a different vision of economic justice, one that considers fairness to involve everyone having enough, rather than fairness being a matter of those who achieve certain capitalist aspirations being rewarded with a disproportionate piece of the pie. Ancient people more than modern people tended to think of wealth as like a pie. Not literally, just to be clear (although the ancients did indeed have forerunners to our modern pies). But in the metaphorical sense, they believed that if some took larger slices, it meant less to go around for everyone else. For those who wish to look into this further, this view of economic realities is sometimes referred to as the concept of "limited good."

How do we know that Jesus cared about this? The Gospel of Luke depicts Jesus as starting out his public ministry in his hometown with a sermon from the Book of Isaiah, specifically a text that talked about good news for the poor, one which resonated in the minds of its ancient hearers with the laws in the Book of Leviticus about the sabbatical and Jubilee years, at which time debts were canceled and slaves set free. It is unclear whether Israel ever put the Jubilee law into practice on the national level, not only freeing slaves and canceling debts but also returning land to the families that previously owned it.[3] But if rabbinic discussion of the sabbatical and Jubilee years are any indication, there must have been some observance of the stipulations, otherwise the detailed exploration of the real practical impact of doing so is hard to explain. The rabbis, for instance, recognized the potential for the wealthy who have the means of giving a loan to the poor to ignore the biblical injunction not to withhold their generosity when the sabbatical or Jubilee year approached, lessening their likelihood of being repaid. A system was developed (attributed to Rabbi Hillel, Jesus's famous contemporary) whereby people could deposit their IOUs with the temple and retrieve them from there when the year of debt cancelation was over. This workaround known as the *prosbul* might, from one perspective, be judged to have effectively undermined the spirit of the Law with regard to the sabbatical and Jubilee years altogether. However, some rabbinic legal thinkers were much more concerned with the harsh realities of the real world than with such idealism. What good was the cancelation of debts if one died of starvation, unable to get a loan to purchase seed for planting precisely due to the imminent cancelation of all debts? The poor knew what the rich were like when there was no real chance of being repaid, no matter how much the Scriptures demanded that they be generous to the poor even so. While Jesus doesn't specifically mention the *prosbul*, he does mention another related legal matter, a decision concerning the law of korban which said that a vow to give something to God meant the parents of the one who made the vow could claim no entitlement to what was so dedicated. We actually have evidence that later rabbis were rather closer to Jesus's view on this subject, while Philo of Alexandria, another older contemporary of Jesus, adopted the view that Jesus criticized. Jesus was one of many Jews who was wrestling with what to do when various laws as well as practical day-to-day situations bumped up against and conflicted with one another. The Scriptures also say that the cause of widows and orphans

---

3. There is a lot that could be said about how this approach to and view of land ownership relates to questions of land, ethnicity, and nationhood in the present day. Exploring that subject here would take us far from the focus of the present study. Any who wish to explore it further should consider not only the visionary Israelite author who crafted the Jubilee law that returned land to its original Israelite possessor, but also the fact that (within the framework of the Pentateuch as it now stands at least) this law is embedded in a narrative that tells of the land being permanently stolen from prior inhabitants who are to be wiped out.

is to be defended by those in power. In practice this often didn't happen, and the laws which might have offered some relief to their hardship often failed to do so for one reason or another. Keep the sabbatical year law in effect and there would be debt relief at regular intervals, but the rich would refuse to loan money close to those years. Find a workaround, and the debts remained as an ongoing financial burden. There were multiple possibilities that could be pursued, but none of them worked in favor of the poor.

Jesus may have had the aha moment that many men and women have when they come to recognize how the oppressed embrace the very social values and practices that contribute to their oppression. This poor widow gave away the little she had. Why would she do that? Sure, it was lavish spending relative to her situation, and in that sense more generous than what the wealthy did. But it would do little to help anyone else, really, and it might make the difference between life and death for her. If we ask what motivated her to act in this way and give every last penny into the temple treasury, there is only one answer we can give in the end. She did it because she felt obligated to do so. When we say that she felt obligated, we do not mean that she felt an obligation to her peers or human authorities. Most likely she felt she had an obligation to God. Yet it was those human authorities, and ultimately her own thinking shaped by longstanding shared values, that in fact imposed this apparent obligation. She almost certainly did not see matters in this way. Few of us do. But her very failure to see it helped Jesus to see it, or at least to see it more clearly. The woman feeling she ought to make this sacrifice, rather than accepting help herself from the generosity of those who could afford to give, is an injustice.[4] Even more of an injustice is the economic system which allows or causes people to end up in these impoverished circumstances to begin with. The context of the story in the Gospels indicates that the point is indeed to highlight injustice rather than to praise generosity. Addison Wright has this to say,[5]

> Virtually every commentator notes the linkage of the two units by the catchword "widow," but it is more than a catchword—the previous unit is the immediate context of the story of the widow's mites in both Gospels. There is no need to reach back for context to the saying about the two great commandments of Mark 12:28–34//Luke 10:25–28, or elsewhere, as many do.

---

4. Binz, *Women*, 133.
5. Wright, "Widow's Mite," 261. See also Izquierdo, *La Donna*, 76–80.

The context is immediately at hand. In both Gospels, Jesus condemns those scribes who devour the houses of widows, and then follows immediately the story of a widow whose house has beyond doubt just been devoured. What other words would be more appropriate to describe it?

The same system that creates rich and poor, which Leviticus tries to address, underpins the reality of the wealthy lending to the poor. Indeed, it is the lending of money that is central to the loss of land that the Jubilee law seeks to address. What tended to happen in the ancient world was that most people were agriculturalists. Without modern farming technologies, including fertilizers, pesticides, irrigation, and the crops themselves, people were lucky if they could grow enough to feed their families and have a little left over to trade for other "products and services," including other crops they did not grow themselves as well as tools and utensils. One poor harvest could leave one spiraling into debt, and a serious drought or pestilence left you not only without food but also without seed to plant for the next year. There was no choice but to borrow money to buy seed. Doing so, one put up one's land as collateral that the loan would be paid back. Another year of crop failure, whether total or partial, could leave you unable to pay back the loan. In those circumstances you lost the land that you inherited from your father. In most cases you might get to remain on the land and work it, but now as a tenant, in exchange for paying the biggest part of your crop yield as rent. Fail to pay the rent, and the land's wealthy current owner would sell you and your family into slavery in an effort to recoup their losses. As in the story of Jesus observing what happened in the temple, one could look from a perspective of privilege, of financial comfort and stability, and see only how crucially important the generosity of the wealthy was to the survival of the poor. It takes deeper probing to see what sometimes even the poor do not see, a system that praises benefactors while it is set up to create inequality and amass wealth in their hands at the expense of others. Those who have wealth inevitably amass more and more land in this system, while more and more people become poor and eventually slaves. The Jubilee law sought to address this in a way that is neither capitalism nor socialism in any of its modern forms. It allowed families to both prosper and fall on hard times, and once in a generation the society essentially hit the reset button and gave everyone a fresh start, so that the channeling of wealth into the hands of fewer and fewer families did not become a perpetual state of affairs.

In the present context we simply cannot address the question of how the vision of the Jubilee year might be applied to our own time, as interesting as that would be. Our focus must remain on what Jesus thought about it, and how what he learned from women relates to it. Before digging into the details of what Jesus said related to this topic, it is important to address a question that some may have. Didn't Jesus learn to care about Jubilee ethics from Leviticus, from the Jubilee law and his exposure to the Jewish Scriptures that contained it, rather than from listening to women? He certainly will have encountered the law through hearing Leviticus read, and perhaps in other ways. But the "rather than" is problematic. This is not an either/or question. Often we can learn about the way a society functions and the hardships some face, and yet not fully grasp the implications nor embrace the need for change until we see how this plays out in the life of an individual whom we have an opportunity to get to know. That Scripture and present experience resonated with one another in the life and experience of Jesus is suggested by the story of the widow of Nain in Luke 7:1–17. The way the story is told recalls the story of Elijah and the widow of Zarephath in Sidon (1 Kgs 17:7–16).[6] Luke depicts Jesus as mentioning that story in his inaugural sermon, to convey the impression that Jesus knew from the very beginning that his ministry would bring together the Jubilee and God's care for the marginalized, including those excluded by the religious and political borders of Israel. However much he may or may not have had things like this in mind from the very beginning of his teaching activity, encounters with women in general and widows in particular continued to inform how he read Scripture and what he emphasized from and about it.

Specific things that Jesus mentions illustrate his viewpoint on subjects related to economic justice and what we would call charitable giving. If Luke 22:25 reflects how Jesus spoke on one occasion or the gist of what he said in general, then there is an ironic assessment of the way rulers are called (and may even think of themselves as) "benefactors."[7] The point is

---

6. Ghosn, *Encounters*, 53. On connections between the story of the widow of Zarephath and the Syrophoenician woman see Lyons-Pardue, "Syrophoenician Becomes a Canaanite," 248–50.

7. The parallel versions in Mark 10:42 and Matt 20:25 agree more with one another over against Luke. However, it is important to note that Jesus taught the same basic content more than once, and so while we should never assume that differences between Gospels reflect different oral traditions and/or memories from different occasions when Jesus spoke in slightly different ways, neither should we exclude that possibility outright.

that rulers benefit more from their subjects than the reverse. Those who rule generally truly believe that without them the common people would be defenseless and unprotected. But they only need protection because of those who embrace an understanding of lordship as dominance, and seek to extend their borders and enrich their empires. The world they create and contribute to then feels the need for protection, and they turn around and provide this service. They may be benefactors, but only because they have been beneficiaries, profiting from the system to which they now contribute back only a tiny fraction of what they have taken from it. In the life of the widow, Jesus saw one from whom the system had taken everything now giving into its hungry jaws the meager pittance that she still had.

What was the role of women in general, and widows in particular, of making Jesus more acutely aware of these social dynamics than he would otherwise have been? Very great, it would seem, given the close connection between his ardent passion for social justice and critique of the status quo, mentions of women in those stories in which it features, and his own mention of widows in talking about these as well as other matters. Some examples are obvious, in which widows explicitly appear. Others are less obvious, but still connect with the kinds of things Jesus mentions widows doing and experiencing. For instance, the Mishnah (Shekalim 6:1,5) talks about the thirteen collection chests in the temple. They are said in some places to have had a trumpet-like opening for money to be put into. Did this influence Jesus's language about "trumpeting" what one gives? Did this incident of observing the widow, or that use of the image in his teaching, come first? Only Matthew has the saying (6:2) while only Luke has this story about the widow giving her last two small coins. Perhaps we should view the one as a variation on the other. While it could be that one of the Gospel authors turned story into parable or vice versa, it is also possible that Jesus remained with the mental image of a poor widow he saw throwing a tiny amount into the treasury, making an embarrassing sound compared to the impressive clattering of donations from the wealthy, and having recognized the profound injustice of it all, incorporated the image into his teaching.

We could also mention the parable of the lost coin. Wahlberg suggests that most women did not receive an income, and so coins were more precious to them.[8] Levine, on the other hand, claims "the woman who has

---

8. Wahlberg, *Jesus According to a Woman*, 31.

ten drachmas, silver coins, is by no means marginal, outcast, or poor. She's not only relatively well-off; she has her own home and her own set of friends... women have access to their own funds, and Jewish women are hardly the poorest of the poor." Either could be true, since then as now the situations of both men and women varied greatly. These coins, about ten days' wages, could have been all she had or coins she prepared to pay workers that day from her more significant wealth.[9] Whatever her precise circumstances, there is still a theological point being made through this female image of God, which reflects an awareness of female perspectives. The kind of earnest seeking Jesus depicts is something that few of us today can fully appreciate. We may look frantically for misplaced car keys, but having ten coins and being unable to find one involves a different level of concern and urgency for an ancient person. Whether they represented their life savings or money they have set out in order to pay employees, few ancient people, men or women, could afford to lose the equivalent of a day's wage. Jesus's mention of the story of the widow of Zarephath also reminds us that, in addition to paying attention to his living contemporaries, Jesus learned from women's stories in Scripture.

Returning to the poor widow who has been our focus in this chapter, Jesus had learned through contact with her, if not sooner, that the entire temple system harmed or at least disadvantaged the poorest. I suspect that he learned that from John the Baptist as well in the time he spent in his entourage. John offered an alternative means of atonement that did not require the purchase of animals. This was undoubtedly motivated by a concern for the inequity of access to forgiveness when costly sacrifice of an animal was required. In essence this meant that the rich could afford to make mistakes in a way that the poor could not, and could have their consciences soothed even while exploiting the poor who lived with burdens of guilt they could not afford to alleviate. It is likely that Jesus had at least been primed to pay attention to the vulnerability of widows through his time spent with John. This is not irrelevant to our project in this book. John was a male teacher and role model who influenced Jesus in the direction he took, including with respect to how he included and considered the situations of women. It would in fact be extremely negligent if we did not touch on this important point. Seeing other men learn from women and honor their wisdom, or refuse to do so, shapes the behavior of each new generation of men. Jesus did not spontaneously begin

---

9. Levine, Short Stories, 46; see also Levine and Witherington, *Gospel of Luke*, 416–17.

to pay attention to women in a social context in which no other men did so. Jesus had male role models that helped shape his openness to learning from women, even as I hope that Jesus may serve in that capacity for men in the present day who might otherwise be lacking such a role model.

However much Jesus may or may not have been mentored by John specifically to pay attention to female perspectives, it was definitely a combination of John's concern for how the poor in general were impacted by the temple system, and input from women who were detrimentally impacted by its purity and financial demands in specific ways, that shaped Jesus's religious outlook. What he did is something that everyone can and ought to do, yet not everyone does. Every human institution negatively affects some while benefiting others. Every human system can be improved or replaced so as to lessen the harm it does and widen the range and reach of the benefit it provides to individuals (in particular the most vulnerable) as well as society as a whole. One of the things that sometimes keeps us from looking closely at this side of things is the conviction that those systems are divinely ordained and thus by definition perfect. As a woman who could not afford to do so nonetheless gave her last pennies out of a sense of obligation to a supposedly perfect system, its imperfections were revealed to him in a manner they had not been previously. Whether that woman from whom Jesus learned ever found out how important she was in bringing Jesus to this crucial insight that shaped so much of his teaching, unfortunately we will never know.

One of the last things that we are told that Jesus did before he was killed was to predict the destruction of the temple and/or drive the moneychangers and sellers of sacrificial animals from the temple's Court of the Gentiles. The Gospel of John has Jesus talking about it and carrying out that symbolic action early in his public activity, so early that he was still associated with John the Baptist's movement as John had not yet been put into prison. Rather than get into the debate here about whether John or the Synoptics is closer to the truth, I will just note here the likelihood that John the Baptist would have had a message of doom for the temple, given his offer of a different means of atonement and his passion for social justice. Mark 13, with parallels in Matthew and Luke, has Jesus talking at greater length about the destruction of the temple towards the end of his public life and activity. It isn't clear that he ever dropped this emphasis from his teaching. But his renewed focus on it towards the end was surely a result of the closer look at the impact of the temple and the way it functioned as an institution on the poorest and most vulnerable members of society. His vision of a different way was influenced and inspired, renewed and energized, by the poor widow we have made the focus of this chapter, and undoubtedly others like her. It is sad and ironic that, as the church has failed to pay attention to what Jesus learned from women, we have allowed ourselves to become an institution and to produce new structures that burden and disadvantage the poor and vulnerable in exactly the same way that Jesus learned to oppose. This is another instance of finding in what Jesus learned from women an invitation to join him in learning the same things as well.

Presumed Guilty
What Jesus Learned from a Defenseless Young Woman Accused of Adultery

Don't let anyone tell you that our forefathers abolished child sacrifice. We still sacrifice our children.

It is fitting that I saw an example of it in the temple. I sometimes wonder how sacred that place can be, when the walls didn't fall in to protest what was happening. Perhaps they will if we continue without heeding the warnings.

They brought in a young woman—a child really, a girl—the same age as I was at the time, about fifteen. Standing on the steps by the Nicanor Gate I could see it all. There had been a rabbi teaching on the steps, and for some reason they wanted him to provide a legal ruling on what should be done. I think everyone in the crowd knew what the girl's uncle had been doing to her. Their home was a large one and was shared by the families of several siblings of that generation of the household. Surely someone had noticed how she cringed and cowered every time he was around. But how could she say anything?

I hated the girl's parents then. Surely such things couldn't happen under their roof without them knowing, or without them caring enough to protect their daughter whom they say they love. Looking back now, I still cannot forgive them, but I understand them better. To confront the uncle, expose what he had been doing, would bring shame on the entire family. What family could survive without honor, if its reputation were so badly tarnished that their business dealings suffered, and they lost their influence in the community? Then not only the girl but the entire family would suffer. They felt their hands were tied.

I come to the temple often, to ask God how such things can be, whether it isn't better to be dead than to live like that, and whether God will one day set things right. I ask for forgiveness for my own sins, for those of my family, for those of my community, and for those of the nation. The high priest tells us each year on the Day of Atonement that the scapegoat must suffer so that the nation can be spared. On that day, the young girl was the goat. She had been found to be pregnant just before her wedding was to take place, and the quarrels between her family and that of the husband began. The husband refused to recognize the child as his. It was a scandal. Something had to be done. Of course, they could have confronted the problems that led to this. But they did what people usually choose to do in such circumstances. The girl could be made a spectacle of, and if necessary put to death. Then everything both beautiful and sickening in our community would be able to carry on as it always had. Once this matter was out in the open, they all felt they had no good options. Once you have made an accusation, if it is shown to be true, there must be consequences. The husband, the parents, even the uncle, none of them wished her to die. They just valued other things more than her life, and her life was the price of keeping those things.

I heard they brought the matter to the Pharisees. They were famous for finding ways of avoiding a death sentence. I bet they could have, too, if anyone had been willing to compromise, or to be completely honest. But the new husband, however much he cared for his bride, couldn't bear the thought of the girl's uncle's incestuous bastard perhaps becoming his heir. I've already told you about the girl's parents and family. No one was willing to budge enough to find a solution. No one was willing to lay the blame where it belonged.

I suppose that's why, on that day, they brought the matter to the rabbi from Galilee. He always taught there in the court of women where anyone from the people of Israel could come and listen to him. He was supposed to be compassionate, and a healer of divisions rather than a divider of people. Some of the Pharisees held him in high regard even though he wasn't one of them and disagreed with their views. Some detested him. No one gave him any information about the girl and her circumstances that might have been useful in finding a solution. None of that information had helped the Pharisees do so, and so it surely wouldn't help him to know more either. But some were certainly motivated by a desire to put him to the test and show him up. They too put their interests before the girl's well-being.

The rabbi looked at the girl they had brought here to the steps at the Nicanor Gate, then around at the crowd. He spent more time looking at some of the people in it than they were comfortable with. Then he bent down and began moving his finger across the dust on the mosaic floor. This continued for some time and for a brief while the crowd was patient. But eventually they began to insist that he say something. It was interesting to observe who was most eager for him to offer a ruling. It spoke volumes about their motives, their intentions, their role in this whole disgusting affair. It revealed things that they would have hidden if he had asked them directly, accusingly. He kept his eyes on the ground as they did so. Had he stood and looked them in the eyes, it would have been a confrontation and they would have offered attacks and defense of themselves in response to him and his words. I've never seen anything like it.

When their questions had told him enough that he seemed to grasp the nature of the situation despite being from outside the community, he stood up. He had a ruling to offer. I held my breath, wondering what he would say.

"Let whichever of you is without sin cast the first stone."

At first I was horrified. He was going to let them kill her after all. Indeed, he seemed to be encouraging them to proceed with the execution.

The crowd was strangely silent. Crowds are never silent at trials. This was something no one had seen before. Without any need for anyone to point fingers, eyes turned from throughout the crowd in directions that showed that people knew many of the facts of the case. This too was extremely revealing. But the rabbi kept his eyes on the ground and continued moving his finger through the dust. He would not be watching to see who left or where people turned their gazes with a view to seeking them out later. If they left, it would be over. It would take the entire group in the end, as they would all need to depart before it would be truly over. But someone would have to take the first step.

It wasn't really that long, but it felt like an eternity before anyone moved. The uncle was the first to leave. Then the husband. Then *the father.* And with that suddenly the crowd of men was dispersing, until every last one of them was gone.

I've heard people tell the story of what happened that day. There are lots of different versions. Some get most of the details right. Some get a great deal wrong. One thing that bothers me is the ending. They get right that he didn't ask the girl any questions until her molester and the entire crowd were gone. He understood how hard it would have been to say anything, never mind utter the truth, while they were there. But then they sometimes have him tell the girl to go and sin no more. That suggests that, in the end, he wasn't convinced that she was an unwilling victim. Of course, she didn't know it herself at that point. She felt guilty. She felt that she must have done something that led her uncle to do what he did. She felt that it was her fault. Perhaps the rabbi couldn't be sure and didn't want to fail to point her on the right way if it was needed. Perhaps he knew that the law held her culpable unless she cried out for help and wanted to encourage her to do so in the future. Maybe he really did think she shared in the blame, as men always seem to. Maybe he simply knew that, in a mere few moments, he couldn't hope to do anything meaningful to resolve her feelings of guilt, and so did what he could do, which was to tell her that she could leave these things behind her. I admit that I don't remember hearing him say those words, although I was so far away at that moment, and so troubled by what I had witnessed, that I may not have heard it. I might even be selectively forgetting. He is a man, and so however understanding and compassionate, he may still be unable to shake himself free of the view of us women that led to the events of that day, and expects us to shoulder all the blame. But from my perspective, the rabbi's words that dispersed the crowd and ended the girl's ordeal, at least for the moment, came like the ram in the thicket that saved Isaac from Abraham's knife. I'd forgive him for just about anything he may have said that was unkind.

To be honest, I am more disappointed with the tellers of the story who end it there and begin a new story. They never ask what happened to the little girl. They don't even mention the women of the community gathering around after the men had left, to comfort her and take her away. They don't ask whether the girl had to return to her home, whether the abuse continued if she did, or whether her new husband took her away and whether they could begin a meaningful life together after all this.

They simply don't ask . . .

Working on this book led to many discoveries. As I approached the text with the question of what Jesus learned from women in mind, time and again things came into focus that I had simply failed to notice before. One of the most thrilling involves a story that, as you probably already know, is included in some manuscripts of chapter 8 of the Gospel of John but omitted from the copies that are judged to be earliest and most reliable, the story of a woman accused of committing adultery. Approaching the story with the woman's experience as my central focus led me to find a new explanation to one of the story's most mysterious and puzzling details, the mention of Jesus writing on the ground. Initially it seemed like an exciting possibility merely because no one seemed to have proposed it before. On further examination it came to seem like even more than that, an interpretation that I believe to be genuinely compelling, one that not only fits with but at the same time helps make sense of the rest of the story. It is rare to find oneself able to offer anything new in response to a puzzle that has frustrated interpreters for almost two millennia. I am convinced that paying more attention to the stories about and perspectives of women in the New Testament will unlock other doors as well. Jesus paid attention to women's experiences and viewpoints, and unless we do likewise, some of the things he said and the things his early followers said about him will remain obscure.

Left Out or Added In?

I apologize for introducing the chapter in this way only to now keep the reader in suspense. Before proceeding, however, it is important to discuss the status of the story, for the reason I mentioned above. The story is missing from our earliest and best manuscripts of the Gospel of John. In most modern English translations it will be in brackets or in some other manner flagged as of doubtful status. It tends to be included just because of how long it has been part of the Gospel of John as most readers know it. But most scholars consider it a later addition. While it is not impossible that controversial implications of the story motivated its removal, we can accept the preponderance of evidence and the judgment of the majority of textual critics and other scholars that it was not originally part of the Gospel of John. What we must add immediately, however, is that its status as part of the Gospel of John is not the same question as the status of its historicity. The story was known to Papias, one of our earliest post-New Testament Christian authors. And it was so widely known in the early church that at some point someone, in all likelihood, being unable to believe it was not anywhere in the Gospels, took it upon themselves to add it in. The event described likely happened, even though it is not included in the earliest Greek manuscripts of the Gospel of John.[1] We know that not everything that the church remembered was written down in one of the four New Testament Gospels, just as we also deduce that some things written in the Gospels are unlikely to actually go back to Jesus. We can hopefully note and yet also set aside the textual question, and explore this story as one that appears to reflect genuinely early Christian memory and storytelling about an incident in the life of Jesus. However, we need to be cognizant that it is a story that circulated orally for a longer period of time than those recorded in the original versions of the New Testament Gospels. This makes changes and alterations to the sense more likely. We see evidence of the variations if we compare the version that gets incorporated into the Gospel of John with other authors who tell the story, such as Didymus the Blind and the writer of the Syriac work Didascalia Apostolorum. And so while as always we will try to stick closely to the evidence provided by our earliest sources, in this particular instance our written accounts of what transpired are late and multiple, such that more deduction is required to work back to an underlying historical event. When efforts at deduction fail, however, we will make sense as best we can of the version that found its way into the Gospel of John.

Caught in the Act?

The story unfolds like a mystery, and so the fact that we ourselves have questions that the story seems to resist providing answers to is actually an important clue to what kind of story this is and what is going on in it. We will find that Jesus has questions too, questions that resist his attempts to deduce answers. If you like detective mysteries, this story is for you, in more ways than are usually realized. It is not the only story in the Bible that can be placed into that genre. The story of Solomon's wise

---

1. Lutzer and Lutzer, *Jesus Lover of a Woman's Soul*, 102. They suggest that the woman's adultery was in response to some sort of abuse at home (100) and that the worse evildoers in the story are the men who bring her but not the other party before Jesus, making her a pawn in their effort to trap Jesus (101, 104).

ruling about whose child was the living one (1 Kgs 3:16-28) might be considered one, even if a very short one, in which the judge is also the detective. Two additional stories that are included in the book of Daniel in the apocrypha (Susanna and the Elders, Bel and the Dragon) are even closer to the genre. The story of Susanna is particularly interesting, since it involves an accusation that a woman was caught in the very act of adultery, which the wise Daniel exposes as a false accusation through his clever deductive and cross-examination skills.[2] Would readers of this story have thought of that one? Might that earlier story in the Greek version of the Jewish Scriptures have influenced the author of this one?

Interpreters of this story typically notice the same problem with the accusation that also appears in the story in Daniel. A woman is accused of being caught with a man who is not her husband, and yet she is brought alone before the community for judgment. No one commits adultery alone, so something is amiss. In the Daniel story, the men who falsely accuse Susanna claim that there was a young man with her who fled the scene, when in fact those accusers had themselves asked Susanna to sleep with them, and their accusation was retribution for her refusal to do so. In the case of the woman brought to Jesus, we are not provided with any such details, and notice their absence. Presumably we are to understand that Jesus was presented with the same situation as we are as readers: an accusation but a surprising and disturbing lack of details. The narrator tells us those who brought the woman to Jesus were testing him, and so it is perhaps not surprising that they do not assist him but leave him to ask questions and puzzle out what he can. We as readers, so far removed in time, will require additional information just to be poised to begin trying our hand at solving the mystery in the way that Jesus and then ancient readers of the story would have.

One important detail we may lack is the significance of the fact that they say the Law of Moses requires her to be stoned. The consensus was that an adulteress should be executed by strangulation, since no specific mode of execution is called for. In the case of a betrothed virgin, on the other hand, it specified explicitly that she was to be stoned together with the other guilty party at the gate of the town (Deut 22:22-24; m. Sanhedrin 7:9; t. Sanhedrin 10:10). Jesus would be expected to recognize that this was a betrothed virgin simply from the mode of execution that they said the Law required. While others might not make this distinction, we

---

2. Knust, "Can An Adulteress Save Jesus?" 411-13 and Ponessa and Manhardt, *Gospel of John*, 74 note the connection between the story of Susanna and that in John.

are told that it is a group of Pharisees, the precursors of the later rabbinic tradition, who state the matter in these terms. For them the statement that the Law requires stoning indicates an instance when that mode of execution is explicitly specified. Yet there are tensions between what they say, what the text demands, and the situation actually presented before Jesus's eyes. They say they have caught her red-handed, in the act, and yet come with only her and no other, and bring her to Jesus in the temple court rather than taking her straight to the city gate for execution. There must be something more to this case. We are not told what it is, because that was the point: they brought her to Jesus to see if he could figure it out. We the reader are along for the ride, and invited to try out our own deductive skills in the process.

We have already noted that she is said to be "caught in the act." The Greek word used indicates that her guilt was felt to be evident, not necessarily that she was apprehended in the very process of committing adultery. That leaves open another possibility: the woman was found to be pregnant and thus was felt to have been obviously unfaithful to her fiancé, who was considered for all intents and purposes to already have the status of husband with respect to her.[3] If she were found to not be a virgin on her wedding night inasmuch as she did not bleed from her hymen rupturing, she could also be accused. The custom was for the woman's family to keep the bloodstained sheets as evidence against such an accusation, and for the woman to be found guilty they would have to produce unstained sheets. When necessary people might spot sheets with blood by some other means in order to use this fabricated evidence to defend a girl's virginity and thus the family honor. For a family to produce unspotted sheets and sentence a girl to death in doing so would be unusual. Is that what happened in this case? It was unlikely, but Jesus would have had to consider the possibility before rendering a judgment. Later rabbinic discussion recognized that the absence of bleeding was not clear evidence of lack of virginity and that the production of bloodstained sheets was not clear evidence of virginity, and so demanded that additional witnesses be

---

3. Peter Gruber, "Pregnant Interpretation," is one of the few others to suggest this possibility. On the expectation of a bride being found a virgin on the wedding night see Ricci, *Mary Magdalene and Many Others*, 66–67. On rape, pregnancy, and blame of women for adultery in ancient societies see Moorehead, *Healed*, 28–29. On the possibility of a link between indeterminate fatherhood of a pregnancy and the *sotah* ritual we discuss below see Haberman, "Suspected Adulteress," 19, 25–28.

produced who actually saw the girl with a man.[4] At any rate, the narrator tells us she was caught, but it is only the accusers who claim it was "in the act." The difference in wording may or may not be significant. Her guilt was felt to be "manifest," but that could be due to pregnancy prior to the wedding if her fiancé did not acknowledge that he was the father, a man being seen leaving her house when she was there on her own, no bleeding on the wedding night, or any number of other scenarios. There are many possibilities. Does it matter to solving the case?

In any of the above scenarios we have mentioned there is a further aspect that we need to consider, at the intersection between the norms and laws of our own context and those of the original ancient context, centered on the possibility that the girl might have been raped. In fact, although I mentioned it as a possibility, in one sense I would like to present it as an absolute certainty given what we know of the circumstances. Girls were betrothed around when they hit puberty, around age twelve or so, and betrothal lasted for perhaps a year and maybe less. The woman at the center of this story, in contrast with the typical cinematic depictions, was a girl in her mid-teens.[5] Even if she did not resist or fight back against the man, we would still consider it rape, statutory rape at the very least. We today would not judge her culpable. She is a minor whom we would consider to be unable to meaningfully give consent. The ancient world did not think in those ways. When ancient authors say that a betrothed virgin is to be executed for "adultery," they know full well what age of girl they are referring to. We shall have to reflect on this further before we end the chapter, but we raise the matter here because it is important to how we think about the situation, the accused woman before Jesus, and how Jesus positions himself in relation to these ancient cultural values and laws. It is also important to view the scene fully aware that, in our terms, we are not dealing with someone our laws or morals would consider an adulteress, but a victim of rape in one sense or another of those words. If we ask who the man was that raped the girl, we are forced to confront the likelihood that it was a relative, with a family acquaintance also a possibility. Was that the oldest member of the assembled group who departed

---

4. Tigay, "Examination," 130.

5. Realizing this would (or at least should) rule out the possibility that is sometimes suggested, that the story of the sinful woman in Luke is a sequel to this story featuring the same woman. However differently the ancient world may have viewed the situation that is the focus in this chapter, it would not have labeled the young girl as a "notoriously sinful woman"—at least, not at this stage in her life and story.

first, when Jesus turned the attention onto the sin of those present? Did Jesus read the crowd and sense that the guilty party was present? Was the accuser a relative responsible for caring for the girl who instead raped her and, now that she was of childbearing age, had to try to hide the evidence for what he had done? Could he sense that others knew there was a child molester among them?

The story of Susanna that we have already mentioned provides a useful comparison as well as contrast to this one. According to the Law, the woman was considered guilty unless she cried out for help. That was what Susanna had done when assaulted by the two elders, and we see in her case that even when a woman follows the rules and expectations of her patriarchal context, it counts for little when men with power choose not to respect even the limited rights and protections the law provides to women. Be that as it may, a major difference between the story of Susanna and this one is the age of the main female protagonist. Susanna was an adult woman who was capable of advocating for herself, to the limited extent possible within the constraints of a patriarchal system and culture that would not trust her testimony. In that story, her protestation of innocence was ineffectual in that context without male assistance. If the girl in our story had not screamed and the rapist was a stranger, she may have been paralyzed with fear.[6] But we may presume that then as now in most instances the rapist was not a stranger to her, most likely a male relative. Could the girl give meaningful testimony under the threatening gazes of her rapist and the unsupportive community? I am struck by how Jesus clears all those people away before asking her questions. And when Jesus does ask her questions in John 8:10, there is nothing accusatory, nor even inquisitive about the details of what she went through. The focus is entirely on the community and their departure, indicating that they will not carry through with her execution. As much as the men who brought the case to Jesus focused attention on him and themselves, expecting him to speak, he remained quiet. He placed the onus on them to offer witnesses and evidence, rather than accepting that he must be the one to elicit the relevant details from individuals present. Women's testimony was often discounted in ancient courts. Yet the only witness there as far as we know was the woman herself and no one was listening to her. Jesus, through his silence, seems to have been trying to make room for her voice. He was also interacting with the men in the crowd in a non-confrontational

---

6. Even in a case of a stranger's unwanted sexual displays or advances, one may find oneself frozen. See Parker, "And the Word Became . . . Gossip?" 259–60.

manner that forced them to be the ones to speak and reveal things if there were to be any progress.[7]

There is a lot that is troubling about everything that is going on in the scene depicted, as well as a lot of unanswered questions. It is important that we do justice to it as a cruelly traumatic experience for a teenage girl to undergo, and not merely a puzzle to be figured out or a case to be solved. As Martha Driscoll writes,

> As Jesus slowly took in the chaotic scene before him with all the senses of his body and his spirit, he groaned inwardly with disgust and revulsion. He saw in an instant all that had happened that night. The woman's soul was laid bare before him, but the men's hearts were laid bare as well. Their viciousness made him close his eyes in horror at the human penchant for masking evil and violence under the guise of justice and law . . . They were just using this poor woman to attack him. They were not treating her as a person, not even as an animal, but as a thing—a plaything for their amusement and their political manipulations . . . The perversity of it all struck him like a spear.[8]

The Setting: A Crucial Yet Neglected Context

Whether one is approaching a story with questions of history in mind or simply as a piece of literature, paying attention to setting is important. In this story, we are told that the court of the temple in Jerusalem is the backdrop to the scene that unfolds. We can be more specific than that, when we consider key details in the story in connection with an important but neglected scriptural framework that I believe provides the key to unlocking some of its more puzzling details. But even just knowing this transpires within the temple precincts is important. In light of information that is presented unambiguously within the text, the depictions of

---

7. Bailey (*Jesus Through Middle Eastern Eyes*, 235) concludes that Jesus wrote his verdict, which was that execution was appropriate. He then stood to indicate the mode of execution—stoning, with the one who has not sinned going first. In doing so, he upheld the Law and perhaps gave them what they wanted in terms of ordering an execution that may have flouted Roman authority in reserving the right of execution for themselves. He thus creates a situation in which it cannot be the mob that does the act, but some individual must identifiably throw the first stone. In looking at the ground again, he spares them humiliation rather than gloating.

8. Driscoll, *Reading Between The Lines*, 101. See also Swidler, *Jesus Was a Feminist*, 67.

the crowd as standing there with stones in their hands becomes ludicrous. Sometimes the scene is even set against rocky terrain with the temple not even visible, never mind the actual setting. No one would carry out an execution within the temple unless they had no concern whatsoever for its sanctity. This was a hearing with a view to reaching a verdict related to the girl's alleged crime and the punishment that should ensue. Their words make it sound as though they could have taken her to a place of execution and stoned her. But they instead ask Jesus to weigh in on the case. This is yet another indication that there is something strange, something unusual, about this particular case. But it is still not a scene where an execution would be occurring. Paying attention to the setting, both in terms of the physical location and in terms of the cultural significance thereof, is important.

There is more that attention to the background can tell us as we move beyond the physical location to what we know about the Pharisees who are in some way directly involved in bringing the case to Jesus. Why would they do so? It is quite common to hear Christians give voice to antisemitic ideas, assuming the Pharisees were determined to rigidly apply a death penalty and would accuse Jesus of wrongdoing if he didn't sentence the woman to death. That is almost the exact opposite of what our ancient sources about Pharisaism would lead us to believe. Certainly the Pharisees were known for emphasizing observance of the commandments and could be quite rigid on certain matters. They were also famous for finding loopholes and creative solutions to problems. In particular, their interpretations of the Torah always sought to find a way to avoid the death penalty.[9] If the Pharisees wanted to test Jesus, it would have been in his ability to resolve the case and avoid the death penalty, not to see whether he would rigidly enforce it. Once one begins to envisage that latter scenario in detail in the way so many seem to imagine it, it becomes quite hard to do so plausibly in relation to any of the parties involved. Our question then becomes why the case proved a challenging one, especially when the language used to describe it might suggest it was clear cut, and what it was about the nature of the details that prevented them from finding a way to avoid the death penalty in this instance. In

---

9. See Josephus, *Antiquities* 13.294 as well as many discussions in rabbinic literature, helpfully discussed in Hakola, *Identity Matters*, 69–70. Alan Watson, "Jesus and the Adulteress," suggests that the Pharisees were testing Jesus's ethic at a point at which it differed from their own, and so they had brought him a remarried divorcee. While a very creative suggestion, nothing in the story clearly points in that direction.

contemplating that, we may ask who it most likely was that brought the case to the Pharisees seeking a loophole. The betrothed? The parents of the girl? Both together in the hope of finding an arbiter that could mediate and resolve their disagreement? We have no way of knowing, but the fact that we do not typically ask why this case is being debated at all shows a lack of attention to detail and an approach insufficiently informed by relevant background knowledge that all parties in the story would simply take for granted.

Jesus would have been aware of the fact that the Pharisees tended to seek to avoid the death penalty, and so if they were testing him, that was the outcome they were testing to see if he could achieve. Yet this group of Pharisees, in order to test him, also appear to be holding back information and thus potentially putting the survival of the woman at risk. They were compassionate, but not so compassionate that when it came to competition with a rival teacher for honor, they might not be willing for one life to be put at risk. They may of course have stood ready to provide that missing information after Jesus failed, but he couldn't be certain. The Pharisees were also a community engaged in vigorous debate, and so not everyone would agree if it came to the point that the woman's life might be forfeited just to make Jesus look bad. But should he rely on there being sufficient dissenting voices present in this particular crowd on this particular day? Jesus needed to find a solution that didn't depend on the woman being either acquitted or convicted, nor figuring out whether another guilty party were also present among them, whether fellow adulterer or false accuser. It does sound as though the physical location creates an element of irony: the accusers have brought a woman into the temple and yet the aim does not seem to be to seek forgiveness through sacrifice, correction through instruction, mercy through refuge, nor even the possibility of vindication through a trial either of word or of ritual, all of which are functions with which the temple is (or at least should be) associated. Nonetheless, we must remember that none of the Pharisees are at all likely to be approaching this with a desire for the girl to die. They are, however, perhaps feeling something similar to a detective who has been unable to solve a case and sees it passed on to a rival on the police force. You do not inherently want the case to go unsolved. But having failed yourself, you may hope deep down and perhaps even consciously that your rival fails.

The temple setting, and the specific location that appears to be implied in the court of women, has the potential to unlock some of the story's longstanding mysteries, as well as provide an explanation of why the case had proven unusually difficult to resolve. Numbers 5 describes the *sotah*, a ceremony often rendered into English as the ritual of the bitter waters. It was designed precisely for cases in which a husband was jealous and had suspicions about whether his wife was faithful and whether a child that she was carrying was his. If he lacked a basis for accusing her of adultery, he could subject her to this rite, in which she would be taken to the steps in court of women. That location was certainly, at the very least, within immediate view of the place where the story we are focused on in this chapter unfolded. There she would be given water to drink, to which dust from the temple floor and a scroll with writing on it had been added. She was threatened with curses if she drinks it and has been unfaithful to her husband. The language used suggests that God would not only cause her harm, but that this ritual would also terminate her pregnancy if it were the product of infidelity. It seems like precisely the sort of thing that might have been applied in the current circumstance. Tivka Frymer-Kensky points out that the *sotah* ritual was precisely for cases that could not be solved, in which there was suspicion but not decisive evidence.[10] It was an obvious choice to go there for this whodunnit. The ritual, in essence, allowed God to decide the case.[11] Even if the ritual was unfair in its gender bias, a way of handing suspicion over to God rather than letting it fester was needed. We will return to the question of why the *sotah* ritual might not have been implemented in this case in just a moment. But first, let us focus in on some of the connections between that ritual and what we know about it on the one hand, and this story on the other.

First, we have good evidence that the location where this ritual took place was the approximate location of the scene depicted in the Gospel of John. Rabbinic sources mention the woman who is being subjected to the trial of the bitter waters as being brought to the Nicanor Gate, which was the gate that led from the court of women deeper into the temple.[12] We are told in John 10:23 that Jesus was talking in Solomon's Porch which is a covered portico running along the court of women in the same vicinity.

10. Frymer-Kensky, "Strange Case," 11.

11. Frymer-Kensky, "Strange Case," 22–23; Greenfield, "Theater of Deviance," 117, 132; Haberman, "Suspected Adulteress," 34.

12. Destro, *Law of Jealousy*, 4–5, 18–20, 81. The Nicanor Gate symbolized division between genders and exclusion just as a wall further out symbolized exclusion of gentiles. Paul or someone writing in his name would later say Christ has broken down the wall of separation between both Jew and Greek and between male and female.

The previous location where Jesus was in John 7 for the Feast of Tabernacles (Sukkot) was likewise the court of women where the procession and major ritual actions of that festival were focused: the lamps, water bowls, as well as singing and dancing in celebration took place there. In the book of Acts the early church meets in Solomon's Porch (Acts 3:11; 5:12). That they were following Jesus's example in doing so may have been so well known that it didn't require explicit mention, emerging only in passing on occasion but assumed elsewhere, including in the story in John 8. More generally, however, the mere fact that Jesus was teaching in a location in the temple courts where a woman was brought to him makes it certain that he was within sight of this location, and the fact that he was teaching makes it reasonable that he might have placed himself on the steps that lead up to the Nicanor Gate, which is the location a woman accused of adultery ought to have been brought—not to seek a verdict for stoning, but to undergo the ritual of the bitter waters.

The connection of the scene with this ritual in the temple provides us with the key to make sense of what for many is the most intriguing question about this story: why did Jesus write in the dust, and what if anything was he writing? We have mentioned already the way the scene is misrepresented when it is relocated to a rocky wilderness landscape where stones could be picked up and held, ready to be thrown. That incorrect setting also provides ground into which one can make a deep enough groove to produce legible letters. Some parts of the temple floor were covered in multicolored tiles set in geometric patterns.[13] Areas without roof protection had larger stone tiles. In either sort of area, there could be enough dust on it that one could trace one's finger through it in order to make a pattern. But these were all well-trafficked areas which meant that any dust present bore signs of human walking. It is extremely unlikely that letters traced through the thin layer of dust on any sort of stone tiles under such circumstances would produce something legible to those present. If Jesus did this in one of the areas that had an ornate pattern, any words would be even less legible. This assumes, of course, that he wrote words. The term used to describe what Jesus did could equally denote that Jesus traced his finger across the tiles, whether following along their edges or making shapes or other patterns. Whether his finger traced letters or not, however, the effect would not be much different from the perspective of observers. The point of Jesus's action could

---

13. Snyder et al., "Temple Mount Floor."

not have been to write something for the benefit of those present around him and which could be understood by them. All these considerations give us good reason to conclude that the message in Jesus's action was not in words written but in the act itself.[14] Writing on the dust on the floor of the temple recalled the use of dust in the *sotah* ritual.[15] The ritual also involves writing an oath on a scroll, and that scroll is then erased so that the words become part of the bitter waters. Jesus was writing not on a scroll but directly on the dust, words that could easily be erased, and which perhaps he did erase in a further imitation of the ritual. I am persuaded that Jesus moved his finger through the dust on the mosaic tile floor not to write or draw something that was the focus of the action, but to draw attention to the dust itself and the act of writing which were the key and distinctive components in the *sotah* ritual. When we combine all these considerations and the direct connections between the scene and the *sotah* ritual, it explains why John draws attention to what Jesus did and yet does not tell us whether Jesus spelled out words, and if so what they were. That was not the point.

Some of the issues that have been noted by commentators on this story connect directly with the *sotah* ritual in interesting ways that would have made it natural for it to be brought up in this context. English translations of Num 5:13 sometimes put it in terms that sound a lot like what we find in English translations of John 8:3–4, but whereas the woman in our story is said to have been "caught in the act," Numbers says that the ritual of bitter waters is for cases where the woman was not "caught in the act." The same Greek word is not used in these two texts, but that isn't

---

14. Matthew Schneider ("Writing in the Dust") says, "writing in the dust presents a striking conjunction of gestural clarity with representational ambiguity." It is intriguing to imagine that, if the girl was placed on the steps and Jesus was with the crowd below, he wrote something in the dust that only she could read from her vantage point. However, even a very simple message might not be intelligible to a typical young girl, given what we know of ancient education of women with respect to reading. But perhaps it was a message intended for someone else who stood with her on the steps, whether part of the accusing crowd, the Sanhedrin, or the temple priesthood. I remain persuaded that it was the writing in the dust that was the point and not what was written. What John tells us is sufficient to highlight that Jesus was making a non-verbal connection to the sotah ritual. Whether someone on the steps could read something he wrote, and if so what it was, we could only guess.

15. On dust in the sotah ritual as explored in the Babylonian Talmud see Tal Ilan, *Massekhet Hullin*, 395–97. See also Josephus, *Antiquities*, 3.11. Philo, talking about the *sotah* ritual (in *De leg. spec.*, 10:59) refers to holy ground (the word John uses, which also means "earth") rather than to mere dust from the floor.

the main contrast. Despite the impression we are given by the woman's accusers, at least as their words are rendered into English, the case in the Gospel of John does not appear to be about a woman "caught in the act," at least not literally. The lack of any male who is accused alongside her, and the fact that no testimony is offered in John 8 about any second participant who might have been spotted but have managed to flee the scene without being apprehended, seems to leave room for doubt, and thus at least potentially make it an option for the *sotah* ritual to apply.[16]

Hadn't they thought of that? If they had, why do they seem to almost be avoiding that option by giving the impression that the woman was "caught in the act" even while the entire situation indicates otherwise? For the *sotah* ritual to be an option, the fiancé would have to at least be open to accepting the child as his. If he was aware that the woman had been raped by a close relative, the idea that a child of incest might become his own supposed firstborn and heir might have been unacceptable. Marriage in that era was above all else about the provision of legitimate heirs to inherit property, with love something that most people hoped would also end up a characteristic as well, but certainly not the starting point of the process. The *sotah* ritual was supposed to bring about an abortion if the child was not the husband's, but perhaps people had seen that the ritual was above all else a means of assuaging a husband's jealousy and had lost faith in its efficacy.[17] If that was the situation, it would be easy for us to view the man as cruel for allowing his bride-to-be to be executed instead of rescuing her from her appalling home situation. However, we must understand that the cruelty is not just on his part alone as an individual, but systemic in character. Did the fiancé know what was going on in the girl's home, what the girl was being subjected to? How many people in the crowd that day knew? We should not avoid thinking about the possibility that the men of this patriarchal society preferred to sacrifice a young woman's life rather than confront and punish the male rapist, which would require they reevaluate the broader culture that typically allows men to get away with such things. Once again we find ourselves looking at an ancient society that is at once so very different from our own, and yet in so many ways so similar and familiar. We recognize individuals in the story and see the resemblances there as well. According to later rabbinic tradition, the *sotah* ritual only worked if the jealous

---

16. Of course, women then as now are often assumed to be guilty and not believed in any case of suspicion.

17. Cf. Haberman, "Suspected Adulteress," 16.

husband was not himself guilty in the same way that he suspected that his wife was (b. Sotah 47b). Jesus's words about those who are without sin casting the first stone may have been alluding to the *sotah* ritual. In essence he would be suggesting that in precisely the same manner as was true of the efficacy of the *sotah* ritual, the ritual of stoning should be rendered ineffective when the accuser shares in the guilt. If the community knew what was happening to the young woman and did not prevent it and protect her, they too were guilty.

Another possibility is that the husband (or husband-to-be) would have liked to apply the *sotah* ritual but was prevented from doing so by a new circumstance that intervened. According to the Mishnah, the use of the ritual was discontinued by the famous rabbi, Yohanan ben Zakkai, an older contemporary of Jesus.[18] Had this option been removed from the table just as it was needed to save a woman's life from a situation in which everyone wanted a better outcome, but no one was willing to challenge the status quo in doing so? Jesus was drawing attention to the ritual by focusing everyone's attention on the dust of the ground and the act of writing there in the location where the ritual occurred. Was this act, like his much less subtle one of clearing of the temple of moneychangers and sellers of animals, another criticism of the religious powers that be, their decisions, and the way they were running things? The selling of sacrificial animals within the temple precincts was also a recent innovation in Jesus's time. It is intriguing to consider the possibility that the ploy to find something of which to accuse Jesus might have wished to pit him against his older and well-respected contemporary Yohanan ben Zakkai, and/or any priestly authorities involved in the discontinuation of the practice.[19] Might this be why he alluded to the ritual through writing in the dust but made no verbal mention of it? He might have been clearly pointing

18. Tosefta Sotah 14:2 simply says that they ceased by his time. The difference of wording may reflect acknowledgment that however influential the rabbis lacked the authority to decide such matters. See further Rosen-Zvi, *Mishnaic Sotah Ritual*, 176–80. It is interesting to consider this matter in connection with another famous detail about Yohanan ben Zakkai. At some point he spent a significant amount of time in Galilee (he settled in Arav, roughly a five-hour walk north from Nazareth), only to declare at the end of it that Galilee hates Torah. Was his (largely unsuccessful) endeavor to promote Pharisaic views in Galilee motivated by his encounter with a Galilean teacher whose views he found so troubling that he felt the need to combat his influence? It is also striking that Rabbi Yohanan had one Galilean student, Hanina ben Dosa, and this is a figure that has sometimes been compared with Jesus. On that see further Møller, *Vermes Quest*, especially ch. 9.

19. Boyarin, "Women's Bodies," 88; Ilan, *Jewish Women*, 136–41.

a finger of blame and culpability at those authorities, in his act of tracing his finger through the dust.

Ironically, one of the motivations for eliminating the ritual may have been what we might consider a feminist one. There is a significant double standard that favors husbands over against wives inherent in the law pertaining to the ritual.[20] Jealous husbands may subject their wives to this. A jealous wife isn't even recognized as having a legitimate complaint, since having a wife and also concubines and/or additional wives was perfectly permissible.[21] Other evidence suggests that a reason for ending the ritual was a slightly different concern, namely that too many people were actually getting away with adultery as a result of it! Whatever the motivation, there is an important lesson that Jesus likely took away from considering this case that was closely tied to the cessation of the practice of the ritual of the bitter waters. When one eliminates one particular expression of discrimination without addressing the wider problem of its underlying causes, the kind and degree of harm shifts elsewhere. In most cases women were undoubtedly better off as a result of the elimination of this practice. In the case brought before Jesus, however, it was clear that the patriarchal outlook that first conceived of the ritual was still a factor as much as ever. Removal of this release valve for the jealousy of suspicious husbands would benefit some women, but could cost others their lives. I am not suggesting that Jesus desired a reinstatement of a ritual that humiliated women. Rather, I am suggesting that he protested the elimination of an option that provided a suspicious husband with an alternative to accusing the wife of a crime that brought with it a sentence of death. Moreover, according to the rabbis, a woman could refuse to undergo the ritual, and that led to divorce and the wife's family compensating the husband, but the woman's life was spared.[22] The *sotah* ritual, like the story in

---

20. See the controversial treatment of what the woman might have done next in Coffey, *Hidden Women*, 75. On Jesus's more egalitarian view of marriage see Boer, *Mary Magdalene*, 33. Even if one adopts the classic understanding of the story as about a woman who had indeed committed adultery, readers can still envisage Jesus recognizing the unfairness of patriarchal norms, in which a man unhappy in marriage could find another woman, but a woman was denied the same option.

21. Ellens, "Numbers," 79.

22. Greenfield, "Theater of Deviance," 115–16. Swidler, *Jesus Was a Feminist*, 57 notes Jesus's radically egalitarian view on divorce. Could this incident or one like it have inspired Jesus's view of the matter, as it brought home the unfairness of the way things were?

John 8, provides a way of avoiding a death sentence, even though it may leave the woman unvindicated and the truth of the matter unresolved.

There may have been more to Jesus's action of tracing his finger through the dust than just a protest against the discontinuation of the *sotah* ritual without offering an alternative. Jesus may have been taking time to think about the case before him. I have sometimes also imagined (not entirely seriously) that Jesus might be outlining the connections between individual suspects and pieces of evidence on the ground, much as detectives pin those details on a bulletin board in television crime dramas, highlighting in the process where there are missing pieces. By way of a more serious suggestion, however, prophets have always been those who see ordinary things and experience God speaking to them through or in conjunction with those things. Amos saw a basket of fruit (8:2), Jeremiah saw an almond tree and a tilted pot (1:11,13), and each saw more in those everyday things than anyone else did. They felt that God was speaking to them. Jesus may have found the star-like mosaic of the temple floor spoke to him in that moment, perhaps resonating with Scripture as well. The descendants of Abraham will be like the stars (Gen 15:5; 22:17; 26:4; Exod 32:13; Deut 1:10; 10:22).[23] This woman, and her unborn child, are children of Abraham, no less worthy of life than the many other mothers and children in Scripture who may have deserved death but were spared and are now the ancestors of the nation in his time.[24] The righteous shall shine like stars, Dan 12:3 says. This woman is righteous, yet pregnant and not by her husband or fiancé. How can that be? Perhaps it was taking time to think while contemplating the mosaic upon the temple floor which led him to the insight that the girl might be an innocent victim of rape whom he must work to ensure is spared.[25] But

23. Perhaps he also thought of Deut 28:62, which warned of the reduction of the population through exile and punishment for disobedience, in conjunction with 4:19 and 17:3 which speak of the sin of the people in worshiping the stars (among other things). He may also have thought of 2 Kgs 21:3–5 or 2 Chr 33:3–5, in which altars to the stars are built in the temple courts, desecrating the holy place, and recognized that the proceedings currently taking place were likewise every bit as inappropriate there. Another text that may have come to mind is Job 25:5–6, which is not necessarily wrong just because of Bildad's inappropriate application of it to Job. In Mark 13:25, it may once again be the star-like mosaic floor in the temple that inspires Jesus to speak of the casting down of the stars in conjunction with the temple's destruction.

24. It would be fun to imagine Jesus sharing his thoughts on this with his disciples, and this directly inspiring the inclusion of Tamar and Bathsheba in the genealogy in Matthew's Gospel!

25. Some writers envisage Jesus thinking in this context of his mother and what

how to best do that? Did they deliberately set him a puzzle from which they withheld pieces, hoping to expose his lack of insight if he deduced wrongly about what had happened? If so, how might he evade their trap and still help the woman?

Jesus's approach is yet another example of how he avoids pitfalls cunningly. Moreover, this woman's case may have taught him that deducing her or anyone's precise guilt mattered less than compassion. The fact that we as readers find ourselves missing crucial pieces of information may be a reflection of the characters in the story withholding information. I suggested early on that this story might belong in the category of the "whodunnit?" It then proceeds to frustrate us by not providing a reveal of who did what. But perhaps that is part of the point of the story. We have an instinctive desire to solve, to conclude, to judge. A key element in Jesus's teaching is that we often need to refrain from judgment. I am sure this woman either helped him learn this lesson or reinforced its importance.[26] For us as readers, the mosaic floor that we failed to notice as a piece of the puzzle of this story comes with nice symbolism. A mosaic is pieces fit together. Whether or not Jesus thought of the aptness of putting together the few pieces of the puzzle he had been given while tracing the pieces of the temple floor mosaic, we as readers can and should.

---

might have happened to her if Joseph had not married her after she was found to be pregnant. It is unlikely that Jesus heard such stories, and indeed the virginal conception and accusations of illegitimacy seem to represent polemical sparring between religious viewpoints in a later time. However, if Jane Schaberg and others are correct who think that Mary may have been raped and become pregnant as a result, then the scenario we are exploring here might have resonated with Jesus as a result—*if* Mary ever shared with him what had happened, which again seems unlikely even if this is what happened. Most women find it hard to talk about such experiences with anyone, never mind with their own children, and perhaps least of all with a child conceived as a result of the rape. However, children sometimes overhear conversations their parents never intend them to.

26. Bailey, *Jesus Through Middle Eastern Eyes*, 234 suggests that Jesus was showing his knowledge of rabbinic interpretation of the Sabbath law, writing in the dust being permissible because it left no lasting mark. Did he need to show his literacy? Expose his opponents' lack of awareness of his education and/or expose shortcomings in their own? Any writing of words would have gone over the heads of many present, but may nonetheless have conveyed his education and his ability to comment on a legal matter.

Conclusion: Case Closed?

The scribes set a trap for Jesus. Jesus saw they were focusing on that, and on the trap the husband and father felt they were in because they were unable to find a resolution they could agree on within the constraints of the Law. They were largely ignoring, or at least relegating to lesser importance, the trap that the woman was caught in.[27] While they tried to trap Jesus, he was simultaneously working to free her from hers. Yet even though Jesus does get the woman free, the story doesn't end the way we expect a mystery to. Perhaps that is for a good reason and makes an important point. Perhaps the key to understanding the story is to take seriously the fact that Jesus simply didn't know for certain what the precise circumstances were. Jesus may also have recognized that the girl was too traumatized for there to be any value in questioning her now. The way Jesus behaves throughout the story indicates a concern to protect the girl. That theme is taken up and expanded in one later adaptation of the story. According to Lesley Hazleton, there is a tradition in the Arab world that Jesus shielded the woman with his body and said whoever is without sin should cast the first stone *at him*.[28]

On the other hand, his words to her ("go, sin no longer") leave the question of her guilt or molestation unresolved, and perhaps place the blame on her.[29] This seems rather cruel, given how much rape victims are prone to blame themselves for what happened to them. Yet Jesus could not have resolved on the spot something that we today know may require years of counseling for a victim to accept. Moreover, we need to consider the question of the woman's culpability not only in relation to our own laws and moral sense, but also those of her ancient context. According to the Law, what constituted transgression? One thing alone is said to determine whether the girl is held to be blameworthy, and it is mentioned in precisely the law that is at the heart of this woman's case (Deut 22:22–27). It is heartbreaking to think that what mattered in terms of the girl's guilt or innocence is whether she cried out for help. The Law gives the woman the benefit of the doubt if the rape occurred in a remote location where it is possible she did cry out and no one heard her. We today understand the

---

27. On the way the accusers use the woman as merely a means to an end see Moloney, *Woman First Among the Faithful*, 25.

28. Lesley Hazleton, *First Muslim*, 55.

29. We cannot explore here why some scribes add "from now on" before "no longer sin." On this element see Winter, *WomanWord*.

paralyzing fear that can prevent a victim from screaming. It is appropriate to reflect on the huge gulf between ancient morals and laws and those of our own time. Against the background of that time, however, "go and sin no more" may mean "in the future, cry out." The way the matter ended on this occasion would hopefully make other relatives and neighbors feel obligated to respond in support if she did so. "Whichever of you is without sin" could specifically denote the sin on trial—they knew the molester and tolerated him. Not only he but all of them were guilty and could not stone her. [30] Perhaps Jesus's words can be seen as empowering her to resist should abuse continue, and, by forcing the community to recognize its own guilt, he had primed them to support her if she cried out for help. Even so, Susanna had cried out, exactly as the Law demanded, exactly as norms required, and yet had been falsely accused and not believed even so. Would it be different for this young woman? One could only hope. The command to "go sin no longer" might also be an encouragement to take advantage of the opportunity provided by this outcome of the "trial" (such as it was). Her fiancé would have no legitimate reason not to accept her as his wife. If things worked out, she might be able to leave her abusive home through that means—one of the only means by which a woman could do so in this ancient society. There is of course another option open to us as interpreters aware the story is a later addition to the Gospel of John. The phrase "go, sin no longer" is lifted directly from an earlier story in chapter 5. Perhaps the person who added the story borrowed that and other phrases from the existing Gospel in an effort to make their new addition fit. From a historical perspective, we could then set the phrase aside and not attribute it to Jesus as part of what was

---

30. Their departure may perhaps be telling. According to the Law, false accusers should suffer the fate that would have befallen the one they accused had their perjury not been exposed. Was one motivation for them to leave a desire to avoid repercussions for themselves, and not merely a decision that they could not execute the girl? See further Clanton, "(Re)dating," 129–30. Some were of the view that this penalty was inflicted only if the accused actually suffered the fate in question, while others considered the fact that they came close to suffering it to be sufficient. Not knowing whether everyone would refrain from stoning the woman, nor what opinion they held on this legal matter, those most directly aware of the falsity of the charge or at least the weakness of the case against the woman may have left as soon as they sensed that the truth might be uncovered, before they might be exposed and suffer the same fate she did. Sergio (*Jesus and Woman*, 52) suggests that the legal experts were aware that they were sinning precisely in letting the man escape punishment when adulterers were supposed to be executed together. See also Wahlberg, *Jesus According to a Woman*, 19–26.

remembered about this incident. It would be a plausible move to make, but it feels too much like an attempt to avoid having Jesus be a man of his time in ways that disturb us. That is why we have proceeded under the assumption that those words are part and parcel of the story and need to be made sense of within the framework of the interpretation we have been offering. The truth is that even if we could omit those words, we would still find ourselves deeply troubled by the way things are left. We feel that Jesus, or someone at any rate, ought to have done more for the young woman at the center of it.

What more could Jesus have done in the circumstances? Is the omission of the story from the Gospels perhaps an indication that the earliest disciples were aware of Jesus's own ambivalence about this incident, about how he had handled it and/or about the outcome? In that situation, the best one could realistically hope for was repentance from the male relative committing the abuse or "rescue" through marriage. There was nothing like a Child Protection Agency. Jesus did what he could, but he himself may have felt it wasn't enough. Even if we try to soften the apparent harshness and blame in Jesus's parting words to her, interpreting them more along the lines of how the protagonist in a series might say a last "stay out of trouble, kid" before the episode ends and the supporting character vanishes from the show, the rest of their story left untold, we still feel uneasy.

Rereading this familiar story again, now as part of an investigation of what Jesus learned from women, I feel ashamed, being suddenly made aware that I had not truly seen and heard the woman at the center of this story before now. Not really. All the pieces of the puzzle I have assembled in this chapter were there in the evidence available. They are insufficient to solve the case, but they are more than adequate to bring the woman into clearer focus than we do. We allow the camera angle of the ancient director, as it were, to lead our eyes to the male protagonists. The woman is brought before us, probably naked, and even so we fail to see her—and not because we, like Jesus, keep our eyes on the ground in the interest of modesty and respect. Jesus stoops down and remains quiet, and even so we pepper him with questions like the woman's accusers, and yet never call for her testimony, never piece it together from the few details provided in the story and in relevant sources of cultural and historical information. I wish Jesus could have done more for this woman, but he did better by her than I ever have as a reader of her story. He subtly yet clearly made room for us to hear her. We, like the ancient court that was deciding her fate, have refused to listen, focusing our attention instead where the male accusers direct it.[31] In an era when there is long-overdue public discussion of our collective failure as a society to listen to and believe women, I see in this story a glimpse of Jesus doing just that. From the perspective of our own time and culture that is actively seeking to address these issues, we see what Jesus said and did and wish he could have said and done more. Deep down, however, we know that what is really being exposed in this story is the impossibility of a satisfactory resolution to such cases without changes to society and to law. No matter what Jesus might have said or done on that occasion, he could not have made the situation for the woman going forward safer or fairer. That would take a collective effort. The way Jesus handles the situation provides a necessary first step. He makes room for her voice to be heard, even if it requires clearing all the other men from the scene that had been speaking. He prevents her condemnation and execution. Those are important positive contributions. But the case and thus the story calls for a collective effort that does more. Like so many of Jesus's parables, the lack of a satisfactory ending represents a call for us to decide how the story continues. Its open-endedness is an invitation to become part of the story and determine where it goes from here. Perhaps the male teller of this story grasped more of Jesus's style of teaching, and his understanding of the realities confronting women in society, than I initially gave him credit for.

To sum up, in saying "go and sin no more," Jesus was accepting the Law's verdict even though he had secured her release. We may view him as also doing more than that. He was empowering her to try to prevent this happening again, to cry out against a relative who she hopefully now saw was using her but unwilling to defend her and prevent her death by confessing his own sin, his own crime in raping her. Would the community come to her rescue, and would they believe her? Would they recognize that what happened on a future occasion, if the male relative was not too frightened now to do it again, was what had happened on this one? There was no way to predict that. The story is as open-ended as many of Jesus's parables, and that is fitting, because Jesus cannot safeguard the girl's future no matter how he might decide the case. That will take the entire community. The fact that I resist leaving the matter there exposes a bias in myself. While some will find this entire project troubling because

---

31. See further Knust, "Can An Adulteress Save Jesus?" 405–7.

it approaches Jesus as someone who learns rather than as one who is all-knowing, I must recognize that even when it comes to Jesus learning I have an instinctive desire for Jesus to be a perfect learner. I am troubled that he might not have listened to and learned from the situation of this young woman in important ways.

We mentioned at the beginning that this story seems not to have originally been part of the Gospel of John. However it ended up here, it is not as poor a fit to its current setting as has sometimes been thought. The remainder of John 8 focuses on being children of Abraham or illegitimate children whose father is the devil. There are multiple resonances with the story about the woman. The rabbinic tractate *Sotah* which is focused on this ritual connects the use of dust in it with Abraham and the divine promise of offspring to him. Significant attention is also paid by the rabbis to the presence of the divine name in the oath that is written and used in the ritual.[32] In John 8, Jesus utters "I am" in a manner that is thought to indicate that he himself bears the divine name which the Gospel later explicitly says has been bestowed upon him.[33] The rabbis also make a connection with the mention of dust in Genesis 3. John's discussion of being children of the devil may recall the interpretation of Genesis in which Eve was thought to have conceived Cain, the first murderer, with the serpent/devil rather than with Adam.[34] The accusation that Jesus's opponents are children of the devil is connected with their seeking to kill him. Whether the story about the woman accused of adultery was added later or an original part of the Gospel of John, it is possible to draw connections with its literary context once it ends up there, and that may have been intentional, irrespective of when it happened and what the precise process was that led to its placement there.

If we ask why we are not told explicitly that the accusation was false if indeed it was, the question of genre as well as the aptitude of the storyteller may be factors. There are many variations on the detective story genre. In some, the reader or viewer is expected to solve the case alongside the detective, and that is part of the fun. In the famous example of the television series *Columbo*, the viewer was shown the crime at the start of the episode and knew who was responsible. The fun was in watching how Columbo would figure it out. The very early detective stories

---

32. Grushcow, *Writing*, 64, 84–90, 101–2.
33. McGrath, *John's Apologetic Christology*, 65–68, 104–7.
34. Byron, Cain and Abel, 15–17; Cousland, "Adam and Evel".

in Daniel are of this type. In some stories, the revelation of "whodunit" seems to come out of left field near the end and leaves the reader/viewer unsatisfied. In the case of this story, the accusers intentionally withhold information, and the way they depart leaves no opportunity to get the truth out of them. At the conclusion of the story no specific revelations of guilt have been offered and no crime has been solved. It may be because those who heard it found this story of an unresolved case unsatisfactory, or because the lack of a full cohort of clues led many hearers to misunderstand it, that early Christians opted to omit the story, regardless whether that was done in the process of composition or of copying the Gospel of John. For its creator or the person who wrote it down in this form, perhaps it was Jesus's wisdom in escaping a trap set for him that was felt to be most important. He didn't even need to ask questions or conduct an investigation as Daniel had in order to find a solution. In a sense, he couldn't have done so in the same way. If Jesus had heard the story of Susanna and the elders, so too had his adversaries. They would have rehearsed their story in case Jesus tried the same tactic Daniel had of questioning the witnesses separately. He would have to find another way, and he did. Yet however clever that solution to the problem was, some may nonetheless have wondered whether the story was effective in conveying that Jesus was wiser than Daniel. It is also worth noting that in Susanna it is a couple of elders who try to seduce her and then falsely accuse her. Were readers expected to think of that when John said, using the same Greek word, that the crowd dispersed *beginning with the elders*?

Perhaps one reason why so many important details are not provided to the reader is because the story is based on a historical event. If things unfolded in the manner described, key information would never have been provided to Jesus. Perhaps the storyteller has resisted the temptation to take on the role of omniscient narrator and provide additional information that would need to be creatively fabricated to serve this purpose. Sometimes one must choose between making a story as compelling or effective as possible, and sticking as closely to the limited evidence available regarding what actually unfolded. Whether that is a factor or not, every reader of the story has probably felt, however satisfied they may ultimately have been with its ending, that far too many questions are left unanswered for us to be entirely content. Perhaps that was the intended lesson all along, and we have for the most part missed it. The key to embracing Jesus's teaching not to judge is not only becoming aware of our own sin instead of focusing on that of others. We must also recognize that, when we are called on to judge, more often than not we do not have all the information that is necessary to make a fair judgment. Puzzle pieces are always missing from a human perspective. That is why God alone should be left to judge. If that is the point then the story works incredibly well. Was the woman in fact guilty? Were her accusers lying? We don't know, and neither did Jesus. He said that the one who was without sin should cast the first stone. Our biggest sin, at the root of so many others, is the arrogance of thinking we have the God's-eye perspective needed to make a judgment. But we cannot see it all. We cannot cross-examine anyone in this story. We'll never know precisely what letters or patterns Jesus traced on the mosaic floor of the temple. That, dear Watson, is the point of the story. Is it a point that Jesus had already grasped prior to this event? Or was it his encounter with this woman that helped him learn it, influencing in the process some of his most famous teaching about both judgment and humility?

In the end, the reason we aren't given enough information to solve the mystery is that Jesus wasn't given enough information to do so either. That's why he came up with a solution to the situation that didn't depend on him doing so. This is helpful to reflect on, since "if you have ever sinned you cannot judge" would mean that no crimes could ever be punished until such time as an all-knowing God holds people accountable. Interpreters ancient and modern have had problems with that implication, and rightly so. Jesus's statement is a way of justifying bringing a case to a conclusion without the truth becoming known and with no conviction. It doesn't preclude drawing a conclusion when the evidence is sufficient to allow us to. It merely acknowledges that not all cases can be solved in the manner we might ideally like. In recognizing that the case brought before him was such a case, and coming up with a solution that both escaped the trap set for him and addressed the situation of the accused woman without needing to have more evidence, Jesus demonstrated wisdom. As a man in a patriarchal society, he could simply have condemned her, regardless of whether she was in fact guilty, and the matter would have been considered resolved. We know that this frequently happened and continues to happen today. Jesus does not choose that option which some might have viewed as easier and simpler. He saw the need to do better because he paid attention to the way women were treated and how they viewed things, including but not limited to the one who had been dragged before him on that day.

Perhaps it is incorrect to say that Jesus didn't solve the case. He seems to have deduced and exposed the salient point, that everyone connected with the woman's story was guilty. Perhaps the reason we have struggled to make sense of the story is not that we had too few clues, but too many. True, the accusers withheld evidence that might have allowed specific names to be implicated. This very fact, however, makes the culpability of all clear. Some played an active role in what transpired, some conspired through their silence. As Hercules Poirot is made to say in the 1974 film version of Agatha Christie's famous *Murder on the Orient Express*, there are too many clues, because (spoiler alert) everyone was involved. There as here, no criminal is identified. There unlike here, however, it is at least possible from one perspective to say justice was done.

Before we say goodbye to this woman and her story, let me bring back the narrator from the beginning of the chapter to have the last word.[35]

> . . . It was perhaps two decades later when I came across some followers of that rabbi—the one from my story. I had no idea there was still a movement around him, and I was surprised to hear the things they were saying about him. I listened patiently, waiting until there was an opportunity to ask questions. I spoke up and asked the man who was speaking whether he'd heard the story about the girl they wanted to stone in the temple. He said that he had, and many others connected with the group also nodded to indicate that they knew the story I was referring to. I told them I had been there that day, and asked if the rabbi had ever talked about the event. I asked if he ever indicated that he wondered or cared what had happened to the girl after that. The men looked at each other, hesitating. At that point a woman spoke up and said, "our Lord thought about her all the time. He said that he only came to see how much of an impact that experience had on him when, later on, he spent more time hanging out with prostitutes." At that, there was something of an uproar from some men in the crowd who were astonished and appalled by this information that they clearly had not been privy to before. But the woman who was speaking didn't let them distract her. She had her gaze firmly on me. "Jesus said it was only after he heard the stories of more women, women who had been in homes where they had been

---

35. I especially wish to thank Revs. Joy and John Amick for insights and suggestions that helped shape the approach taken in this chapter.

raped and abused, that he really grasped what that girl's situation must have been like for her, and what kind of future he might have sent her back to. He couldn't have taken her away from that situation, and he knew it. But his encounter with her was one of the key things that prompted him to formulate a vision of God's kingdom in which there is no longer marriage, and no need any longer for all the different laws, rules, and statuses for men and women that are connected with marriage. She never knew it, but she helped him see that the future God has in store for his people must be something better, something more perfect than these current institutions and ways of being in this world will allow. To eliminate sin and bring about a world of peace and love you couldn't just change one law or address one situation. The transformation had to be deeper, a new creation. He hoped that one day he would meet her again to tell her she had helped him realize this, but of course he had so little time left at that point and never did. Most of all, I think he wanted to know whether she was alright, and listen to her in a way he couldn't on that day."

I thanked the woman and another question was immediately forthcoming from the crowd. It was a man who wanted to know more about this connection of their teacher with prostitutes and sinners. I faded back into the crowd and went on my way. I didn't tell them that the girl we had been talking about was me, and that even now I cannot speak about what I went through when just a child without talking about it as though it were happening to someone else . . .

Mary Magdalene
What Jesus Learned about the Power
of Naming and Keeping Demons at Bay

They say that unclean spirits are the spirits of the giants, the offspring of those sons of God of old, the angels who lusted after human women and took them as their wives. Today's unclean spirits take after their fathers, pursuing women who are not yet married, and in particular those who are soon to be married. Having been betrothed to be married so late in my life, it is no surprise that several unclean spirits took a particular interest in me, that they pursued me with particular ferociousness.

I understand why few women have sympathy with my story when I tell it. Although I remained unmarried for so long, during that time I had privileges that most other women did not. My father surely wished he had a son, as all fathers do. But I never felt it. He not only mentored me in his successful business of dyeing fabrics, but he arranged for my education in much the same way that he would have if I had been a son. I did not know at the time that his friends (and even more so, his enemies) called him a fool for doing so. Indeed, at the time I did not know how unusual I was, learning to read and to count with the assistance of a wax tablet. I knew even as a child that my father was treated with great respect. I knew that it was my responsibility to thread ornamental beads onto the wool threads, even before I grasped that it was my tiny child's hands that made me particularly suited to this task, and well before I understood how much it cost my father if I dropped and shattered a bead. I knew from childhood that my father's recipes for making and mixing dyes, to produce shades of blue, gold, and pink that were richer and more vibrant than those of his competitors, were secrets that I must not divulge even to family friends who tried to offer me sweet dates in exchange for the information. But when my father suddenly became ill, and he bequeathed his business and his property to me, his daughter, by then I was old enough to hear and understand the criticisms that his friends and enemies alike directed at him. Despite the attempts of some very distant relatives to lay claim to it all, I have managed to hang on to my inheritance and keep my father's legacy alive.

If my father had lived longer, I am sure he would have arranged a good marriage for me. My mother died when I was young and I had no brothers, and so the responsibility was my father's alone by the time I was of marriageable age. No one should blame him for delaying as long as he did. So many would-be suitors were clearly unsuitable, merely seeking to elevate themselves and grasp at my father's business. Others were suitable as far as their family backgrounds were concerned, but my father still judged them to be more interested in profit than in me. He understood (in ways that I did not appreciate at the time as a teenager who envied her friends' marriages) that granting my hand to someone whose interest was only in his business would hurt not only me but also his business and ultimately his reputation. Still, as his health suddenly took a turn for the worse and he found himself unable to move and speak, he was unable to manage either the business or my marriage prospects. No one should fault him. And I hope they will not fault me for having dismissed all interest in marriage as I sought to step into my father's place, to manage his business and secure his legacy.

Our family's business had been passed down from generation to generation, from father to eldest son. Jacob of Magdala's fine fabrics, named for each eldest son who passed the name and the business to their successor. I vaguely remember when the name referred first and foremost to my grandfather, and that some still spoke to him, this man who seemed ancient to me, as though he were himself still merely the son running his father's business. Then it was my father's turn. He had the misfortune to have only one child, a daughter, who could not step into the role of the next Jacob of Magdala, maker of fine fabrics. But I could continue the work nevertheless, and keep his name alive through his business. If ever I had a son, I could name him Jacob and the legacy could continue, although the prospect of that occurring now seemed increasingly slim. Property, wealth, business—all these things normally pass from fathers to sons. As a daughter, despite the educational opportunities and apprenticeship that I had been afforded, I could not keep this legacy afloat without the utmost dedication. I had no choice but to set aside any thought of marriage and children while I focused on managing the business, without my father there to guide me with his wisdom. I knew deep down that if the family legacy were not to end with me, I would need to have a son, a male heir. But there was no time for such thoughts when my father first became ill. And as years and then decades passed, the possibility that I would ever marry became increasingly remote.

I fell into a routine shaped by these realities. And so I scarcely noticed when one of our longtime customers, Hananiah, began stopping by the workshop even when he had no order to place or to pick up. At first, when I did begin to notice, I found it an inconvenient distraction from my responsibilities. But soon I found it pleasant to have an opportunity to talk about something other than colors, patterns, and quantities of merchandise. I realized that Hani (as his friends called him) could make me laugh in a manner than I had not allowed myself to for years. In a society in which men jostle for honor, as one of the few women who owned a business, I had to wrap myself in an air of seriousness and respectability, even more than I needed to wear a garment crafted by my best workers whenever I was in public, one that showcased our skill and the finery that resulted from it. I was perceived to be somber, unreadable, even unwomanly. Men dictate the terms of social interaction appropriate for someone like me, and yet have the nerve to comment and complain that I followed it! But as I said, Hani broke through the barriers and airs with which I had surrounded myself, not in a forceful way, but in a manner that was charming and genuinely endearing. As a longstanding client who purchased our fabrics, turned them into fine garments, and shipped them by land and sea, he had no particular need of my wealth or my inheritance. If my father had been alive, he would have been delighted to finally have a suitor for me about whom he need not be suspicious. Even so, Hananiah knew that I had lived long in my unmarried state, and that it would be awkward for me to now contemplate marriage at my age, well into my forties. He took his *time and did not rush into things, nor did he rush me. Hani was a good fifteen years my junior, and so there would undoubtedly be comments about that. But his family's status and wealth made him a more than suitable match by any standard.*

But at the beginning, I was not thinking about how suitable it was that a maker of exquisite dyed fabric should be wed to one of the most skilled tailors and shipping merchants in the region. I was thinking about how at long last I was laughing and smiling again as I had not in a long time.

Hani waited far longer to ask for my hand than he might have if I had been a teenager. His awkward shyness simply made him all the more endearing to me. And when he finally proposed that we should wed, it was only then that it struck me that I had no one to consult—no father or mother who was still alive, no elder brother—but was free to make the decision myself. Again, I know that few women will sympathize with the pang of grief that I felt as I thought of my father's illness and death before he could arrange a match for me as I am sure he had wanted to, or as I thought of my mother who died before I was old enough even to fix a clear memory of her. Few will feel any twinge of sorrow for an only child and orphan like me, who survived not by begging on the street but by continuing her father's successful business. I was privileged as few women are to decide my own destiny, my own future, and I want you to know that, for all the sadness I felt as I thought of those who would have wished to participate in that moment but did not have the opportunity, I fully understood the unique autonomy that was mine. I also understood fully that to receive a marriage proposal in the fourth decade of one's life was not just a rarity, but perhaps even a miracle.

I told Hani yes.

My answer wasn't immediate, however. At first I called him a fool. I pointed out that, at my age, I was unlikely to have children, and it made no sense for the two of us to be the ones to unite our family businesses, only to have it then end up in the hands of one of his brothers and their children. I asked him why he wanted to be mocked by villagers for choosing to marry an old woman like me, when any of the younger ones would have been lucky to have him, and he luckier to have them than me. Hani, like me, had lost his father, but his mother still lived. He might be free to decide whom to marry as eldest male of the household, but surely his mother must object to what he was proposing? Hani told me that his mother respected and admired me, and was fully supportive, something she eventually told me herself, although it took some time for me to believe it even when I heard it from her own lips. Whatever my protestations might be, Hani always had an answer. What ultimately persuaded me was not the content of his answers, though, so much as the mere fact that he offered them, and did so with conviction and certainty.

When I did finally say yes we did not waste much time beginning preparations for our wedding. It was around then that I started to notice a dryness in my throat and eyes, a slight scratchiness or roughness as I was breathing, and an occasional pounding in my ears. Sometimes when these all came at once, my head began to ache and throb. I had the financial wherewithal to seek assistance, the best available in our region, and that was when I was told that unclean spirits regularly harass women, especially those who have recently been betrothed. I was offered "cures" that did nothing to help me. I inhaled the fumes of foul-smelling concoctions that exorcists claimed would drive away the malevolent forces that plagued me, and I buried a bowl an exorcist inscribed with an incantation underneath the threshold of my home. Still I did not feel as I used to. Then the outbursts began. I was no longer consulting exorcists and doctors at that stage, having done so for months and having felt worse rather than better. But I heard people talking, as sometimes my fits of anger or unexpected tears erupted while I was in a public place, and try as I might, I failed to keep them under control. Those who knew that not only my harsh words and mouth were part of this, but that my eyes, ears, and nose were also affected, sometimes whispered with astonishment that someone of such status could suffer at the hands of seven demons, as they counted the orifices in my head that either experienced discomfort, or erupted forth with tears or harsh words they could not explain when I had previously been a tower of calm. Some thought perhaps I deserved my ailments to counterbalance my many blessings. Some suspected that jealous people had cursed me, using black magic to will demons my way. I sought to be upright and prayed for God's help. When the demons were preparing to afflict me most severely, I sometimes saw flashes of light, which I know were angels surrounding me, fighting for me, even if they could not ultimately protect me from harm.

I did not expect to be affected by my anticipated change in status as much as I was. I expected the change in others even less. Even though we were not yet married, there were some who began referring to me as "Hananiah's Mary" where previously I had been "Jacob's Mary" to them. Others who previously spoke to me with the greatest respect would focus on Hani and have their conversation with him now, even though we were not yet married, even though the matter pertained to my business which was still under my purview and authority. It was my father's business, and now my own. Why would they speak to Hananiah and not to me? He would be my husband, and I have the utmost respect for him, but he has never dyed wool and has never woven fabric. That they were treating us as a typical married couple when we were still engaged, even though he was so much younger than I and had a great but still very different sort of business experience, caused me some distress. Was I now to suddenly be expected to pretend I was a naïve young bride, marrying a man twice my age as per custom and deferring to him, rather than a capable independent woman marrying one many years my junior?

I remember the pains so vividly that afflicted me then. I would still suffer from them now, were it not for my good fortune to have welcomed Jesus from Nazareth into my home.

Jesus had among his students a distant cousin of mine, now living in Capernaum. When they sent word that they would pass through Magdala, I said what I was expected to, that they would be welcome in my home. It was my home, and I extended my invitation to my cousin and his teacher to come and refresh themselves. When I informed Hani of the invitation, he accepted it without comment. Soon it was clear, however, that he was annoyed that I had not consulted him. Even so we were both bound to extend hospitality to visitors, all the more so if a promise of welcome has been made. As we planned for their arrival, I found the unclean spirits becoming increasingly active. As Hani gave orders to my employees and made arrangements without consulting me, it was as though a rage from somewhere beyond me were taking over. I kept it under control as long as I could, but on the day that these guests were scheduled to arrive, it boiled over like a pot left unattended—even though I was aware of it and had sought with all the strength I could muster to prevent it from bursting forth and overflowing. I am strong, but those unclean spirits at times were stronger than I.

We were also at the same time preparing for our wedding day. More and more of the arrangements ceased to be in my hands, and the throbbing pain in my head became more frequent. I would tell my trusted servants to make arrangements, and then busy myself with matters related to my business, only to find that the servants had received contradictory instructions from my betrothed or his family and had followed them instead. I was not spared this pain on any day of the week, and no longer did a week pass without suffering. The agony was especially intense on Fridays as I prepared to go to Sabbath worship. It would interfere with my prayers.

The throbbing of my temples on the day I met Jesus was unbearable. I was arguing with my betrothed on that day. I cannot now recall about what. The words that flowed forth from me were full of rage, and I had a sense both that they reflected my frustration, and that they were not my own but came from somewhere beyond me, some malevolent force that was taking hold of me. I was exploding, gesticulating, complaining, when suddenly we were in my house, and there was this man who was a stranger to me at the time, the man that I would soon come to know as Jesus of Nazareth. He was relaxed and making himself at home, surrounded by more of his entourage than I could count with a glance. He stood as I entered and approached me.

"Mary Magdalene?" he asked as he approached me. "I have heard so much about you. Thank you for welcoming me into your home." He spoke to me in a way that did far more than merely recognize me as head of household. At our first meeting, he bestowed on me a nickname that was remarkable—and it stuck, as I'm sure you know. I had no idea what Hani was thinking or even doing at that moment. What took over my thoughts was that I had a guest, and suddenly I was the hostess again, the woman who ran the household, whose authority was recognized. Later I would hear his disciples tell the story of how Jesus's very presence caused unclean spirits to flee from me. But I remember aspects of the day that they never mention. Jesus had heard my fiancée and I arguing even before reaching the house. He had been told that I was a woman in my forties, betrothed now to a younger man. He had appreciated what the experience of this change in my status would mean for me. And he had greeted me, not as Mary daughter of Jacob, not as Mary wife of Hananiah, but as Mary the Magdalene, Mary of Magdala. He recognized that he

was in my home, and that I was the hostess, and he treated me with the same respect that was due to a man under the circumstances. I would later discover that mischievous nicknames and wordplay are something he is famous for, telling me subtly that I am still a tower of strength as I had been before, my own person of authority and worth.

There was certainly a divine power at work in and through him. He knew the power of words and used them more effectively than anyone else I ever met. But ultimately it was his teaching about community, his empathy, and conversations with him and others of his followers that created a situation in which not just healing but a permanent cure of my condition could take place. People like me, whose situation he seemed to understand intuitively. I knew that I must not have been the first woman whose awkward status in our society he found himself able to empathize with, into whose life he had brought healing. But in my case, he did not just recognize my authority in my home, or my seniority in relation to my soon-to-be husband. He had been told of my leadership role in managing the business that had once been my father's but which was now mine. He must have seen in me at least the potential that he saw in the inner circle he had already gathered around himself. He did not dismiss one of them to make room for me, but neither did he dismiss me or relegate me to a secondary status in relation to them. He just said, towards the end of his time in my home, what I later learned he had said to many before me. "Follow me." I did just that. As happy as Hani had made me, I realized that the new society that Jesus envisaged and that he was seeking to build brought me much greater joy. I called off our betrothal, even though it hurt my reputation and led to my being called every insult you can imagine. The words still hurt, but far less than the pains in my head which even now did not return.

Some speak of Jesus's power as being such that a mere word from him sends demons fleeing, never to return. There is certainly truth in that. I knew it from the moment he first said my name, a sound that would echo in my dreams and in my waking moments for years to come. The respect that was implicit in the way he referred to me as "Mary Magdalene." The understanding, the valuing that was there even as soon as I heard just my name in the way that he uttered it: "Mary . . . " Yet his initial words to me were not the secret of his power to bring long-term healing. Jesus himself spoke of how frequent it was for a demon to be driven out, only for it to come back with its friends to make the person's condition worse than it had been before. I had experienced that myself before I met Jesus. I had sought the help of other healers and exorcists, and sometimes experienced some initial relief as a result. But my symptoms always returned, and the relapse always added new ones to my torment. Flashes of light, nausea, and other sufferings associated themselves with the intense pain in my head that I had experienced a few times even earlier in my life, but which in recent years had become a weekly occurrence.

Then I met Jesus.

Later, when Jesus spoke of seven demons returning to an individual after an exorcism, he would glance in my direction and give me a knowing smile, since it was my story that he was sharing, what he had learned from my experience of being cured. Jesus spoke of the need to replace the presence of the demonic with the Spirit of God. That meant being part of a healing community, one in which the frustrations caused by the injustices, inequities, and power games of our society are brought crumbling down within our group, as a testimony to those around us of how different life can be. Every time someone calls me "Mary Magdalene," it reminds me of that first encounter. It encourages me and soothes my soul. Some do so out of deep respect for the master, some merely follow his lead without thinking about it, and some utter the words in an ironic tone. It doesn't make a difference. When I hear them, the voice of Jesus echoes in them no matter what, and I rejoice that I am free.

It is sad and distressing that things so basic as listening, empathizing, and communicating with respect towards women can be so rare that these actions and their effect come to be viewed as nothing short of miraculous. But that is the beauty of the kingdom that Jesus proclaimed: a kingdom that embraces all people and all things, so that within it the mundane seems miraculous, and the miraculous seems mundane . . .

Jesus ♥ *Mary*

If your only prior familiarity with Mary Magdalene is through certain streams of popular culture, then you may have a ready-made answer to the question of what Jesus learned from Mary: "How to be a good husband." The idea that Jesus and Mary Magdalene were married, in love, or whatever else can be found in places like *Jesus Christ Superstar* or Dan Brown's novel *The Da Vinci Code*. But is there any historical basis for that idea? The question of whether Jesus was married to *anyone*, let alone Mary Magdalene, is impossible to answer definitively from the evidence in the New Testament.[1] Really, I'm not just conspiring to cover up the truth! The earliest sources do not mention Jesus having been married or unmarried. The question that confronts historians is what to make of the silence. Should we assume Jesus was typical and thus most likely married? Or should we assume that if a wife isn't mentioned there probably wasn't one? Most modern readers will probably naturally incline towards the second option. But there is a problem with that. If we read the Gospels, we would probably assume that Peter and other apostles were also unmarried, were it not for the passing reference to his mother-in-law, which clearly implies that Peter was married (Mark 1:29–31). Paul confirms this through a brief reference in one of his letters (1 Cor 9:5). Women were often left unmentioned in ancient texts where today we would expect them to be mentioned. Our modern expectations are often a poor guide when it comes to ancient literature. If we were to simply go with the most likely scenario all around, we might decide that Jesus was likely a widower by the time he started his public ministry. Most men married before age 30. Many women died young, often in childbirth. If we go with what is statistically probable, that might be the best option, and explain why Jesus appears to have no wife. This chapter, however, is not about Jesus learning heartache and loss from the death of a wife he may not have had, or learning other things from her before she died. This is one of those instances when engaging in plausible speculation would likely distract from the subject at hand.

None of this directly impacts what we might wish to say here about Mary Magdalene. Whether Jesus was a bachelor or a widow when he started his public ministry, neither would prevent him from marrying Mary. But we would do well to ask why it is that we are inclined to care so much about Jesus's marital status one way or the other, and what motivates our desire to draw a particular conclusion. The truth is that

---

1. Sometimes the argument is made that Jesus's special calling would have precluded his marrying (so, e.g., Hebblethwaite, *Six New Gospels*, 44n38). However, most men and women had their marriages arranged by their parents. We would therefore have to imagine Jesus in his early teens insisting that his parent(s) not arrange a marriage for him. While possible, there is simply no evidence for this being what happened.

neither a married Jesus nor an unmarried one is inherently liberating or oppressive towards women. Some claim Jesus was married to Mary but view her value mostly or entirely in terms of her serving as the receptacle—the holy grail—for Jesus's offspring. Others view them as having engaged in something more like an egalitarian partnership so that her post-resurrection role as "apostle to the apostles" was not a striking innovation but a natural progression.[2] Some claim Jesus was unmarried because they believe that having a wife could only distract from and interfere with one's commitment to the kingdom of God. Others prefer Jesus to be unmarried because marriage in that era imposed patriarchy on women while remaining unmarried provided a relative degree of autonomy. Any reconstruction of Jesus's relationship to Mary Magdalene may serve a feminist or anti-feminist agenda. Perhaps the big question is whether anyone can hope to be impartial enough as to let the evidence drive their conclusion, without being swayed by hopes, values, and ideological commitments that we impose on our interpretations of ancient texts even when we try to avoid doing so.

I'd like to suggest that what some might view as our "sauciest" and most scandalous extracanonical source regarding this matter may have significant light to shed on the question.[3] I'm referring to the Gospel of Philip, an ancient text that says that Jesus loved Mary more than the other apostles and that he used to kiss her frequently. Where did he kiss her, you might ask? Well, the author of the Gospel of Philip apparently tried to tell us. Yet there is damage to the manuscript (in technical terms a lacuna) at precisely that point. Was the damage intentional? Was it the result of so much interest that the manuscript deteriorated there? It is hard to say. It is easy to fill in the blank with whatever seems most appropriate, inappropriate, audacious, lewd, or prudish. Lips? Cheek? Hand? Knee? Although this text has no claim to be an early enough source for historians to rely on, it may nevertheless provide an accurate reflection of how some in later centuries understood the relationship between Jesus and Mary Magdalene. He kissed her frequently somewhere. Do we need to know more?

---

2. On Mary as apostle in Hippolytus and other early church authors see Boer, *Mary Magdalene Cover-Up*, 108–14; also 170 on Gregory of Antioch.

3. For those who may be wondering about it, the so-called Gospel of Jesus's Wife is pretty much universally agreed to be a modern forgery. See Sabar, *Veritas*, and the various contributions on this topic in Burke, *Fakes, Forgeries, and Fictions*.

As it happens, a little reflection on what this text says as a whole, rather than just at this one spot, tells us a great deal. Think about it. If Jesus and Mary Magdalene were husband and wife, it would be very odd for the author to have written that he loved her more than other disciples and kissed her frequently. Of course he did! And if they were not married, then if he kissed her as though they were might indeed be worth mentioning, but would seem to require a different sort of mention than this, with at least a little more detail and explanation. There is, however, another option that is typically neglected, one that allows us to make perfect sense of this text. But it requires us to let go of a number of assumptions, prevailing cultural images, and pull ourselves free of the unconscious as well as conscious influence of the many movies and books that propose conspiracies, cover-ups, and in a few cases scandalous sex rituals. Instead we can provide a scenario that is much more mundane, one that will never make the tabloids, and alas will prevent this book from selling anything like the number of copies that it might have if we had opted for a reconstruction that is more sensational.

In most art and most fiction, as well as in most historians' reconstructions, Mary Magdalene is a woman who is about the same age as Jesus or younger. Does that have any firm basis in the textual sources from the first few centuries? Not that I can detect. And so, if we once again look to the cultural context for guidance as to what is probable and makes sense, whom might a rabbi love more than his male disciples without doing so in a manner that requires extensive explanation or invites scandalous speculation? Whom might a rabbi kiss so frequently that it was worth mentioning, but not in the same way that kissing a spouse or an unmarried woman on the lips might be mentioned and require explanation? If Mary Magdalene was a couple of decades older than Jesus, so that her natural relationship to him was more like adopted aunt than suspected lover within the mores of the time, that would fit what the Gospel of Philip says quite perfectly.[4] That text also says that this third Mary in Jesus's life, alongside his mother and sister of the same name, was his "companion." The Greek word used shares the root of the word usually translated "fellowship." It is rather like the word "partner" in English, which can denote a romantic relationship, a shared business endeavor, and any number of other relationships. As with the English, so with the Greek, context matters a great deal, and that includes both literary and

4. Moltmann-Wendell, *Women Around Jesus*, 69 is one of the few scholars to entertain the possibility that Mary might have been significantly Jesus's senior.

cultural context. The mentions of Mary and Jesus do not clearly indicate that the word is being used in a romantic sense. Many assume that to be the case nonetheless.

So why is the possibility that Mary was more like an adopted aunt and patron rather than a love interest not mentioned in most other treatments of this topic? Because of a tendency to sexualize the relationship in a way that poorly fits the historical and cultural context, and which also deprives Mary of the opportunity to be a senior, more experienced individual who supports, teaches, and commands a certain respect from Jesus and his younger male disciples. The history of art and film, as we have alluded to, has reinforced our image that Mary was a young woman. But she is listed as one of the women who supported Jesus financially (Luke 8).[5] Among people Jesus's age at that time and in that part of the world, only someone from a truly wealthy family who had an allowance, or someone whose parents had died and from whom they had inherited substantial wealth, would be in a position to do this if they were relatively young. Otherwise, we should imagine someone who is older, and who is thus more likely to have received their inheritance, or to have developed a thriving business that provided them with income.[6] People whose parents were living, whether men or women, would not have independent means of this sort. In this situation, would a tender kiss on the forehead or cheek, bestowed on someone whose status was akin to an adoptive aunt or kind elder, be more appropriate to imagine? If the text depicts Jesus showing respect, honor, and admiration for a noteworthy woman who was his elder, the pieces fall into place from our canonical and extracanonical sources. But they do so in a way that will require substantial revision to our mental images.

Before concluding this section, I want to emphasize that Mary being older than Jesus does not in itself rule out the possibility that they were married or romantically involved. I wove that possibility into the fictional elaboration of Mary's story that begins this chapter, yet with a different younger man as the love interest. It would be unfortunate to

---

5. Cooper, *Band of Angels*, 55 mentions that "genuinely independent women—the heads of households and business owners—played a critical role in the early Christian communities" (see also 67). Perroni and Simonelli, *Mary of Magdala*, 39 on the other hand consider it mere conjecture to assume that Mary was part of the wealthy class simply because she is mentioned before and alongside Joanna.

6. On daughters inheriting when there were no sons to do so see Ilan, *Jewish Women*, 50–52; Bauckham, *Gospel Women*, 122.

try to eliminate misogyny towards Mary only to replace it with ageism. The main reason for not envisaging Jesus and Mary as husband and wife is that the way they relate and interact in the texts that mention them, while not excluding altogether the possibility of marriage or a desire to be married, contain nothing specific that would encourage us to understand their relationship in those terms. Nonetheless, as we will explore further below, the status change that Mary would have experienced in this cultural context if she became betrothed to be married late in life may have contributed to the condition from which the Gospels tell us that she suffered.

Mary and the City of Magdala

In Jesus's time women were distinguished from one another through association with their father, spouse, or children, rather than the place they were from as men were.[7] There are several instances in the New Testament in which we have a woman who is simply said to be "of" a particular man, without it being specified whether that meant "daughter of" or "wife of." This convention conveyed that a woman's identity was defined by their relationship to an authoritative male. It would be helpful to know more about how Mary got her nickname Magdalene, presumably meaning "from Magdala." There are so many instances in the New Testament of Jesus bestowing nicknames on disciples, and the nickname is so unusual for that time period, that the odds seem to favor it being a nickname Jesus gave her rather than one already attached to Mary before

---

7. Welborn, *De-Coding Mary Magdalene*, 18; Seim, *Double Message*, 35–36; Perroni and Simonelli, *Mary of Magdala*, 24; Taschl-Erber, "Mary of Magdala," 432–33. As will become clear in what follows, we are assuming the consensus view that "Magdalene" indicates that Mary was from the city of Magdala. Other suggestions have included that it meant "hairdresser" or that it denotes her metaphorically as a "tower" much as Peter is called a "rock." See further Camry-Hoggatt, "Images," 20; Boer, *Mary Magdalene Cover-Up*, 12; Hebblethwaite, *Six New Gospels*, 116n4; Sebastiani, *Tra/Sfigurazione*, 41, 52; Schrader, "Mary of Bethany," 388–89. Taschl-Erber, "Mary of Magdala," 432 notes that the epithet "Magdalene" (as with other similar nicknames such as "Nazarene" and "of Tarsus") only served to distinguish an individual when they traveled elsewhere. As a businesswoman connected with a trade who will have traveled for that purpose, and with a family whose goods were sold far and wide, the place name being associated with the family and its business would have made sense, and that is the scenario we have explored in the fictional account with which we began the chapter. It is obviously not the only possible scenario whereby the moniker could have come to be applied to Mary.

they met. The nicknames that Jesus chose tended to be quite distinctive. If Jesus called one of his key followers "Rocky" (that's the equivalent of Peter in English), then he might have called another "the Tower," which is what the name of the ancient city of Migdal meant.[8] It could have been a pun as well as indicating where she was from. Her nickname, however, is closer to that of Jesus, being called "Nazarene" because he was from Nazareth. The two nicknames parallel one another in an interesting way, making Mary's more like Jesus's own and less like those he typically gave to his followers.[9]

The name also highlights a difference between Jesus and Mary, and something that stands out about her background. Magdala was one of the major cities in the region, and while its importance at this time may not have equaled that of Sepphoris or Tiberias, it was still much more akin to those urban centers than to the towns and villages Jesus is said to have spent most of his time in. It is noteworthy that we are never told Jesus visited any of the largest and most important cities in Galilee, and that he likewise does not seem to have attracted followers from there, at least not ones who are explicitly labeled as such. Except, that is, for Mary Magdalene, who stands out in this regard. Did he meet her in her native city or somewhere else? Even today, urban and rural populations, and populations of different social statuses, do not typically just happen to cross paths. We may not be able to pinpoint the precise circumstances, but we can certainly explore a plausible scenario, and list others. Doing so helps us understand Jesus, Mary, and their world better.

Did Jesus actually visit Magdala? The only possible direct evidence for Jesus having been in its vicinity is in Mark 8:10 and Matt 15:39. In these two Gospels Jesus is said to have visited a place called Magadan or the region of Dalmanutha. Neither of these names is known from other ancient sources, leading many modern scholars (as well as some ancient scribes) to think that Magdala may have been in mind.[10] Esther de Boer suggests that we can be confident that Jesus visited Magdala even apart from those two verses, if archaeologists and historians are correct

---

8. Taylor, "Missing Magdala," 222.

9. The Talmud understands the Aramaic word behind the moniker to mean "hairdresser." Cf. Sebastiani, *Tra/Sfigurazione*, 52.

10. See DeLuca and Lena, "Magdala/Taricheae," 289. Some manuscripts of Matthew in fact read "Magdala" at this point. In Mark the reference is instead to the region of "Dalmanutha" which may be a corruption of Migdal Nunya, "The Tower of the Fish" (so for instance Ricci, *Mary Magdalene*, 131).

to identify the location of Magdala as that of modern day Mejdel. Boer writes, "If Magdala in fact lay on the site of Mejdel, then Jesus *must* have been there. The city was on the road from Nazareth, the small village where Jesus grew up (around twenty miles from Magdala) to Capernaum, where he later went to live."[11]

Migdal is the Hebrew form of the name which means "tower," while Magdala is the Aramaic form. There were in fact many places known as the "such-and-such tower." It isn't always clear whether we are dealing with one place or two in some of our ancient sources. Rabbinic sources mention a "Tower of the Dyers" and that may in fact be the same location as the Magdala from which Mary came, the city being associated with (at least) two major industries, fish-salting and dyeing fabric. In the short fictional exploration of what Mary's story may have been like, we opted to associate her with the dyeing industry rather than fishing, not for any particular reason, although given the predominance of people involved in the fishing trade among the circle of Jesus's followers it seems appropriate to envisage people in other lines of work and other industries when opportunities allow. We will note at least one possible connection between a saying attributed to Jesus and dyeing, but there are also sayings related to fishing as well.

Places were often known by more than one name. In addition to "The Tower of the Fish" and "The Tower of the Dyers," the city was also called "(Place/Tower) of the Fish-Salters" (Taricheae), and by this name the location is mentioned by several famous authors from around the Roman world. The city was world-famous for the quality of its products, and that would have made it a multicultural metropolitan hub.[12] There were several major cities in Galilee in Jesus's time. If anyone imagines that Jesus came from a region that was isolated from the possibility of contact with Roman culture, they are mistaken. Yet Jesus seems not to have visited those cities, or at least the Gospel authors never provide evidence that he did. Even Sepphoris, which was near his hometown, does not get a mention, although we have reason to conclude that he likely spent time there nonetheless. Archaeology reveals Magdala to have had even more Greco-Roman influence on its architecture and other elements of daily life. In this instance too, the evidence concerning whether Jesus ever

---

11. Boer, *Mary Magdalene*, 22.

12. Boer, *Mary Magdalene*, 24–25; Ricci, *Mary Magdalene*, 130–31; DeAngelo, "Reconstructing," 122.

went there is ambiguous at best.[13] Historians have often wondered what to make of Jesus's apparent avoidance of cities and preference for villages and smaller towns. Rarely, however, have they sought help from Mary Magdalene in finding an answer to this question.

It is possible that Mary met Jesus somewhere other than her home city. Indeed, people tended to be known by their place of origin once they were living or spending time regularly in other places. Nevertheless, if we ask what might have brought Jesus to Magdala, one possible answer is *religion*.[14] In archaeological work on the site believed to be that of ancient Magdala, a number of fascinating and distinctive objects have been unearthed that inform us about religious aspects of life in the city in the time of Jesus. The synagogue there included ornate mosaics, and a stone was also found there that is engraved on its sides with ornamentation that included pillars, archways, and a menorah, suggesting that its aim was to call to mind the temple in Jerusalem.[15] We don't know for certain what the stone was used for, but its form and decoration are distinctive. Not far from the synagogue in Magdala, immersion pools have been discovered which also have features that were not typical: they drew water from an underground source.[16] Most Jews who practiced immersion would have found the nearby lake more than adequate, and so one wonders what motivated the construction of these structures. Perhaps they were connected with followers of John the Baptist, or members of a movement related to or similar to his. Some believed it necessary that immersion be in running water. "Living water" would be the way of saying this in Aramaic.[17] Might the presence of a significant number of followers of John the Baptist have attracted Jesus to Magdala, whether because Jesus already knew them, or

---

13. On the architecture in Magdala, which made it more like Tiberias than Sepphoris, see Root, *First Century Galilee*, 171; Shivti'el, *Cliff Shelters*, 30-32.

14. DeAngelo, "Reconstructing," 122 points out the geographic likelihood of Jesus visiting there early in his activity, as well as the tendency for people to be known by a place of origin precisely because they have relocated to elsewhere.

15. Ristine, *Mary Magdalene*; Ristine, "Magdala Stone"; Ryan, *Role of the Synagogue*, 70-71.

16. Zapata-Meza, "Los Mikva'ot de Magdala," 63-64. See also however DeLuca, "Magdala," 306-7, who offers a different perspective on the findings.

17. The Mandaeans are one group that reflects this kind of emphasis. Mereyey/Miriai in Mandaean sources is unlikely to be Mary Magdalene, or Mary the mother of Jesus for that matter, since the Mandaean figure is not allied with the Jesus movement, while conversely we have no evidence that the Marys connected with Jesus forsook it for a baptist group that rejected his messianic status.

because they represented a natural audience for his message which built upon John's and yet moved things in a different direction? We cannot say for certain. But there is enough evidence for Magdala having been culturally and religiously distinctive that it makes sense to think of Mary in those terms as well. If Jesus went there because of a religious community that he was already connected with, Mary from Magdala brought with her into Jesus's circle some distinctive perspectives that grew up and flourished in that location. When people from new backgrounds enter a movement, they do not leave it unchanged, even if their joining it represents a conversion. If Mary's religious background was distinctive, it would have offered something to the movement around Jesus. It is striking that, in extracanonical texts, we encounter evidence of tensions between Mary and Jesus's other disciples. It is entirely possible that those tensions were not something that emerged for the first time after the crucifixion, as part of a struggle over who would lead the community and what gender they should be.[18] There may have also been different perspectives on the appropriate direction to pursue or about particular practices. The close connection between Jesus and Mary suggests that the perspective that she brought was not only welcomed by him as part of its inclusive diversity, but highly valued. The singling of her out as "Magdalene Mary" may have been akin to dubbing someone "Big Apple Barbara" when they were the only New Yorker in a group, and thus the only one to bring the perspective from that influential urban center. The analogy is limited, however, because the distinctive flavor that Mary added to the group may well have been spiritual and not merely the representation of urban culture, not that the latter was something insignificant.

Mary contributed more than one thing to Jesus and his movement that stood out in that context. Esther de Boer writes,

> She had grown up in a place where Jewish and Hellenistic culture lived side by side. She had also grown up with people from different countries and of different religions who came to Magdala with their trade. That could have made her receptive to Jesus' emphasis on people's dispositions, on their inner life and the way in which they really acted, rather than external differences. And this could have made her receptive to the conviction that God has mercy on all without distinction, because God is a God of the whole creation: the God of human beings is also the

---

18. On this see further Brock, *Mary Magdalene*.

God of nature, which particularly around Magdala proved to be so abundant and rich.[19]

Exploring this in connection with the focus of the present study leads us to ask the following questions: Did Mary help Jesus learn these things, or was she merely receptive to the message he already proclaimed because of where she was from? Jesus was surprised by the faith of gentiles. Did people like Mary, used to living at the intersection of Jewish and non-Jewish life, help him process these experiences and find an authentic Jewish response that could welcome and embrace it, and incorporate it into the framework of his Jewish messianic vision?

Ultimately we know less about Magdala than we would like, just as we know less about Mary than we would like. Its connection with the fishing industry would have put Mary just a few steps removed from Jesus once he became closely associated with people involved in fishing along the northern shore of the lake.[20] Although there is much that is uncertain, we are not engaging in idle speculation. By drawing on a combination of specific information about individual women who interacted with Jesus, and more general information, we may dare to hope with some confidence that the things we propose are true *of Jesus and some women he knew*, even if we cannot always be certain which individual woman played a specific role. The mention of financial support from women is important evidence and provides one example related to the point we are making here. Did Mary help Jesus work out an economic model to sustain his activity? Was it rather Joanna? Was it both of them or someone else entirely? We do not know, but we can guess based on the clear role of women in supporting the movement, and the mention of certain names among those supporters, that particular individuals played an important role, while others may have participated after this way of doing things had already been developed.[21]

---

19. Boer, *Mary Magdalene*, 41, 119.

20. Schaberg, *Resurrection*, 312, cites rabbinic sources saying that Magdala is the place where the daughters of Job are buried. There are far more numerous interesting possible connections with Magdala than we can explore in this context.

21. It is often surmised that Mary and Joanna may have been friends independently of their connection with Jesus. That is certainly plausible. While not of the same status as far as we can tell, they were nonetheless well positioned to meet and form a bond among the influential people and families in the networks of power and trade around the Sea of Galilee. There is more that one might speculate, but much of it would go too far beyond the evidence for us to pursue it here. Mary was the most common and popular name in this era. While we cannot talk about specific motivations

Jesus made some radical (if not entirely unprecedented) moves related to gender. However, it is important to remember that, as Michael Haag writes,

> [T]he real radical was not Jesus. The radicals were the women. Jesus may have been unusual and inclusive in his outlook, but there was no question of having women in his movement unless—against almost all the laws and customs of Jewish society in Palestine—these women could live independently of family ties. The women in Jesus' entourage were not performing the conventional female roles of cooking meals and washing clothes, or if they were Luke does not say so, but what he does say is that neither Jesus nor any of his followers, women or men, were engaged in economically productive work. Just as the men have given up their employment to follow Jesus, Mary Magdalene and the other women exercised their independence and used their financial means to make the mission possible.[22]

Jesus may have been radical in his inclusiveness, but the brunt of any social cost for the contravention of norms would have been borne more by the women than others. As Jesus listened to their experiences of the impact of their connection with him, he learned much. On the other hand, Luise Schottroff writes,

> Wealthy, truly independent, upper-class women were common in all regions of the Roman Empire. In spite of differences in their legal situation, their social reality was fairly uniform; and in spite of some legal limitations, the factual situation of these women was one of nearly unrestricted freedom. In this period women everywhere owned wealth, administered it independently, and bought assets as businesswomen, even when married.[23]

---

of Mary's parents for giving her that name, we can note the significance of a context in which there was appreciation of Mariamne the Hasmonean princess, perhaps over against Herod or even in response to Herod killing her, that may be one reason for the surge in popularity of the name in this era. Would being named Mary have impacted her friendship with Joanna, who was associated with the family of Herod? Would the two women being brought together have been comparable to having a zealot and a tax collector among the male disciples? Did Jesus learn about navigating reconciliation between opposing views through these women before he applied it to men, if they were involved very early on?

22. Haag, *Quest*, 44.

23. Schottroff, *Let The Oppressed Go Free*, 80–81. See too Seim, *Double Message*, 65–66, 77–86.

We must beware of two pitfalls: imagining ancient people as precisely like us, and generalizing as though their experience was uniform regardless of culture, social status, location, and other factors. One real possibility is that urban women felt freer to travel and engage in commerce independently than rural women did, reflecting differences of lifestyle as well as of values. Jesus's teaching often sits at the intersection of those two worlds, offering pairs of sayings that include and acknowledge women as equal participants in the kingdom of God, yet within the framework of traditional social and family roles.[24] He also tells stories set in and with characters from both urban and rural contexts. Mary and other women who traveled with Jesus may in some instances have been the first independent urban women to visit this or that village, although in most cases the constant interplay between city/town and countryside would have provided opportunities for prior encounters or at least observations. The lives and expectations of women in patriarchal societies are not uniform, and even in modern societies that strive for gender equality this remains the case to a greater or lesser extent. Jesus's inclusive vision was of a kingdom that welcomed, included, and transformed not only some but all. Jesus clearly listened to and learned from both urban and rural women, probably throughout his life and not simply as an adult. However, having a close and profound friendship with an urban woman of independent means like Mary provided opportunities to learn, and in particular to wrestle with the disparate discriminatory impacts of societal values in different locations and for different people.

Just as Jesus's contact with theater and fishing are reflected in imagery he used, Mary seems also to have contributed something to Jesus's repertoire of symbols and analogies. She lived in a center of the fish-salting enterprise. Salt was crucial for preserving food even more than enhancing taste. A fish sauce known as garam was especially popular as a flavor-enhancer. In some parts of the world today similar kinds of sauces continue to play this role. Salt had unique properties and crucially important uses for ancient people, living in a world without refrigeration. What would happen, Jesus asked, if salt suddenly lost its distinctive properties (Mark 9:50)? There would be nothing else to "salt" the now unsalty salt with. Indeed, the use of the word salt as a verb as well as a noun is an indication of this. Salting is literally as well as linguistically inseparable from salt. When something isn't salted enough either to preserve it or make it

---

24. On this see especially Parks, *Gender and Rhetoric*, 4–5, 153–54.

taste good, the solution is to add salt. If salt ceases to be salty, what do you do then? Rather than debate what Jesus meant by this riddle, here we can focus on Mary, and perhaps friends of hers that she introduced to Jesus, as the source of Jesus's imagery, and in turn one of the audiences that Jesus's metaphor was intended for. Salt was a commodity that at times was literally worth its weight in gold. What would happen if the precious suddenly became worthless? What could restore its worth? Salt was extremely valuable, and yet a commodity that rural people would have found more familiar and relatable than gold and pearls. Mary probably helped Jesus come up with and develop this striking image.

If we look beyond the New Testament canon, another text immediately offers itself as possibly reflecting Mary's influence. The Gospel of Philip includes the following:

> God is a dyer. As the good dyes, which are called "true," dissolve with the things dyed in them, so it is with those whom God has dyed. Since his dyes are immortal, they become immortal by means of his colors. Now God dips what he dips in water.

And then again slightly later it says:

> The Lord went into the dye works of Levi. He took seventy-two different colors and threw them into the vat. He took them out all white. And he said, "Even so has the Son of Man come as a dyer."

This latter instance of the use of dyeing in the Gospel of Philip comes immediately before the mention of Mary Magdalene where it refers to him kissing her frequently, which we discussed earlier. The appearance of imagery drawn from the realm of dyeing, describing Jesus as having contact with and even visiting a location where this trade was practiced, is all the more striking when it comes in the context of a work that emphasizes Mary Magdalene's relationship to Jesus.[25] Nowadays, most kinds of products are produced and sold just about everywhere. In the ancient world this was not the case. Particular places were connected with specialized trades and products. This increases the likelihood that the Gospel of Philip or the tradition behind it envisages Jesus visiting Magdala in the company of Mary. This isn't to claim that what the Gospel of Philip describes is historical either in detail or in broad outlines. It does seem,

---

25. The terminology used for dyeing in Aramaic referred to dipping/soaking and was thus the same word that denoted baptism, adding another layer of resonance to this imagery. Cf. DeLuca and Lena, "Magdala/Taricheae," 287–89.

however, that certain associations were remembered at the very least, their ripples leaving an impression even on this later literary work.[26]

Jesus is reported to have spoken of himself as one who is greater than Jonah, and to have referred to his generation being offered the "sign of Jonah." While Matthew's Gospel turns that into a prediction of the resurrection (12:40), a comparison with the other Gospels shows that originally Jesus referred to no sign being given, and then again to no sign being given other than Jonah's, which originally meant the same thing. Jonah performed no miracle for the Ninevites, according to the story told about him in the Bible. The people of Nineveh responded to his warning of destruction nonetheless. Jesus's point seems to have been that his contemporaries should respond to his call simply on the merits of the message, without requiring confirmation from miraculous signs. That is in keeping with an emphasis in the Jewish Scriptures (Deut 13:1–5) that even amazing signs do not justify heeding a call to worship other gods. The reverse is thus also presumably true, i.e., that a call to worship God alone and to do so correctly and uprightly should be heeded even if no sign accompanies it.

There may be more to what Jesus was saying than that, and it may have a connection to Mary Magdalene. These stories about a demand for a sign and Jesus's response are situated by Mark and Matthew in the very region Mary was from. Jesus may have felt his words were directly relevant to that context for a number of reasons. One is the popularity of Jonah there. Jonah is the one prophet in the Hebrew Bible clearly from and connected with Galilee. Gath-Hepher (Jonah's hometown) was not far from Nazareth, while a unique mosaic depicting the story of Jonah has been found in a synagogue in Huqoq, which is not far from Magdala. While that mosaic is from centuries after Mary's time, it indicates the popularity of the stories about Jonah in the region. Jonah becomes one of the most popular focuses of early Christian art. It may be that these regional connections were in Jesus's mind when he responded to the demand for a sign by refusing to grant one, except perhaps (according to Matthew and Luke) the sign of Jonah. Is this indicative of Jesus's sense that Mary's healing ought to have been a sufficient testimony to the city? John 7:52 depicts the Jewish leaders as ironically forgetting about Jonah, and being dismissive of Jesus, the prophet from Galilee, as a result. Jonah was famous for having been so zealous for his own people that he tried to

---

26. See also Taylor, *What Did Jesus Look Like?* on the wearing of dyed fabric clothing.

avoid going to proclaim the message to others. When he did go, however, his message is heeded. Jesus, on the other hand, had become increasingly inclusive, and people in his native Galilee did not respond positively. It is not surprising that we find echoes of Jonah in Jesus's words.

There are other places where we might see a contrast being drawn between Jesus and Jonah already in the New Testament, in addition to his own words. For example, the story of the crossing of the sea appears to depict Jesus as the anti-Jonah: he is taken into the boat and the storm stops, where Jonah being thrown into the sea had the same effect. Taken together the evidence suggests that, when Jesus spoke about Jonah in precisely the area Mary was from, he did so purposefully. We see this most clearly when Jesus goes on to offer one of his characteristic gender-paired sayings, referring to the Queen of the South coming to hear Solomon's wisdom, and the people of Nineveh repenting at Jonah's preaching (Luke 11:29–32; Matt 12:38–42). The version in Matthew is situated in between an accusation related to Jesus's exorcistic activity, and a further discussion that focuses on the plight of someone briefly liberated from a demon only to have seven more join it when it returns. We cannot help but think of Mary Magdalene in connection with that, and we should probably see her influence on him in that saying. Focusing on Nineveh and the Queen of Sheba together might have suited an audience in any affluent city like Magdala, but the reference to a woman traveling to learn from a teacher of wisdom, contrasted with Jesus's hearers in that location, makes it seem likely that Jesus is drawing their attention to Mary Magdalene, reminding them of her example and what they should know and accept from and through her.[27] Since as far as we know Jesus himself had not been active there, he is rebuking them for not responding to and learning from this woman who had traveled elsewhere to hear him, and presumably returned with news about him, only to be ignored or scoffed at.

Confusing Mary with Other Women

There is a long history of readers confusing Mary with other women in the Gospels. Perhaps the most notorious example is the identification of her as the unnamed "sinful woman" mentioned in the Luke 7:36–50. That

27. Parks, *Gender*, 80, 85, 89–90. We cannot explore in detail how we might understand Mark 7–8 and parallels differently if Mary is actually present when Jesus visits the region of Magdala. This is envisaged but not fleshed out much in Hebblethwaite, *Six New Gospels*, 134–35.

story is one that we have already discussed in another chapter in connection with Mary of Bethany, who is yet another distinct individual with whom Mary Magdalene is sometimes identified. The identification of Mary Magdalene with the woman in Luke historically went even further, identifying her as a prostitute, something that is not even hinted at in the Gospel. As Margaret Hebblethwaite writes, "The tradition that Mary was a prostitute is among the most extraordinary and implausible inventions ever woven out of gospel texts."[28] That idea emerges only from the twisted minds of male readers who hear that a woman is "sinful" and immediately think of sex. As Mary Thompson wryly puts it, "It is also interesting to remember that Peter says to Jesus, 'Depart from me for I am a sinful man' (Luke 5:9). Who concludes that Peter was a prostitute?"[29]

If Mary were the same woman who features in Luke 7, there are other sins that ought to come to mind given what we know about her. For instance, Martha Driscoll envisages Mary losing her parents when she was young and resorting to cutthroat and at times dishonest business practices in order to keep her father's small shop running and fend for herself.[30] Since we have no reason to identify Mary with the repentant woman in Luke, the short fiction that began this chapter did not pursue that scenario. But if one is inclined to make the identification, then they should still not assume that the sins she had a reputation for were sexual in nature.[31] Widows and orphans were the most vulnerable people in ancient Mediterranean societies. When we meet Mary in the New Testament, she is an independent woman not known by association with either parents or spouse. She apparently has sufficient means not only to care for herself, but also to take on the role of benefactor and supporter of Jesus's activity. The vulnerable often have to make difficult choices and become hardened by their circumstances, and there would be nothing implausible about an orphaned or widowed woman becoming quite ruthless in her business practices in order to survive in a patriarchal

28. Hebblethwaite, *Six New Gospels*, 119n16. Pope Gregory seems to have been the one who started this tradition (Haas, *Quest*, 232–38; Thompson, *Mary of Magdala*, 5).

29. Thompson, *Mary of Magdala*, 15. See also Moorehead, *Healed*, 27. Moltmann-Wendel, *Women Around Jesus*, 67, asks pointedly, "What would our tradition look like if it had made Peter a converted pimp?"

30. Driscoll, *Reading Between The Lines*, 70–71.

31. Adam, *Magdalene Mystique*, 53. The fact that the woman was still alive, when crimes such as adultery were punishable by death, should perhaps exclude many if not indeed all of the sins that the woman is presumed by preachers and other interpreters to have committed.

system that made life even more difficult for her. However, in order to avoid lending credence to an association between two completely distinct Gospel characters that simply has no basis whatsoever in the evidence, it seemed best not to weave this possibility into our fleshing out of Mary's story. As Kate Moorehead observes, "By cloaking Mary Magdalene in sex and shame, we have effectively silenced her."[32] We are making every effort to avoid doing that here.

Seven Demons

For some, the reason for associating Mary with the "sinful woman" in Luke is because of her demons. However, unlike in our time in which demons are largely ignored except in horror films and Pentecostal churches, in the first century demons were not associated with people being evil, or at least not any more than illness in general was. Some people certainly thought that those who suffered for whatever reason were being punished for their sinfulness, with demons as the causative factor to which illnesses were attributed.[33] That is a very different concept than what most people hold in the present day when it comes to illness and/or demons. As we see in the story in John 9, some were as likely to blame the sinfulness of parents for suffering as the individual themselves. Amy Welborn puts the matter succinctly when she writes, "nowhere in the New Testament is the condition of possession synonymous with sinfulness."[34] Elizabeth Watson writes, "Seven demons are not to be equated with seven deadly sins. The woman with a bent back had a demon, but there is no suggestion she

---

32. Moorehead, *Healed*, 23. See also Ashcroft, *Spirited Women*, 21: "Linked with Mary Magdalene and the sinful woman who anointed Jesus, Maria was conflated into a symbol, not of a woman's strength, understanding, and courage, but of women's fleshly weakness, shame, and unending penitence . . . The 'sinful woman'—the prostitute who anoints Jesus—was not driven to prostitution by rebelliousness or carnality (as were her customers) but by desperate poverty. This woman could not have been the same as the woman who owned, with her sister, a house in Bethany. If this mistake was not intentional, it was highly motivated by a subconscious need to disgrace the women followers of Jesus."

33. See for instance Moorehead, *Healed*, 48–49, where she quotes Hippolytus's words about exorcism as part of baptism, as evidence that "The presence of unclean spirits was considered part and parcel of the human condition prior to baptism." See too Atwood, *Mary Magdalene*, 32.

34. Welborn, *De-Coding Mary Magdalene*, 20 (see also 52). See too Ricci, *Mary Magdalene*, 132–35.

was immoral. And the Syrophoenician woman's daughter had a demon, but hardly seems like a sinner."[35] Note as well that physical ailments are attributed to demons, and not only what we would categorize as psychological ones.[36] Having seven demons meant multiple symptoms or very severe ones, but not necessarily multiple personalities or other things people today associate with "demon possession."

Demons afflicting someone could also be viewed as the result of their having been cursed, of someone deliberately seeking to bring misfortune on another person through what we might call black magic. Many people appealed to angels for protection and assistance, and some sought to harness the power of similar but malevolent forces to direct harm at others. We know of this from texts from the ancient world, but also from incantation bowls and amulets that were used in the hope that they might offer protection. Being afflicted by demons might indicate that someone else wished you ill, rather than that you deserved to suffer. In some ancient magical texts, the seven celestial spheres (representing the sun, moon, and five visible planets that were thought to orbit the Earth) were viewed as malevolent forces. It is unclear whether that cosmological significance of the number seven was the reason for referring to Mary as having had seven demons go out from her. Another possibility is that it reflects the seven openings on the head, which can all be sources of discomfort in the case of certain ailments.[37] Whichever was the case, the main point to remember is that victims of demonic affliction were not generally held to be blameworthy. Where today those who think about demons at all tend to think of them getting inside people who dabble in the black arts, ancients thought of them primarily as afflicting the innocent, sometimes but not always at the behest of those who practice magic arts seeking to cause harm to others.

It is worth noting that all the women listed in Luke 8 were cured of demon-illnesses. All of them supported Jesus's work financially. Two of them could be mentioned and immediately recognized with no reference to a male, whether father or husband, while the status of a third

---

35. Watson, *Wisdom's Daughters*, 116.

36. Ghosn, *Encounters*, 42 considers Mary's afflictions to most likely have been physical ailments.

37. Boer (*Mary Magdalene Beyond the Myth*, 50) mentions a possible connection with the idea of the soul having eight parts, with a footnote to the idea of seven malevolent forces corresponding to the seven planets holding human beings under their sway.

is confirmed by the mention of who her husband was. It seems justified to conclude that all of these were women of status. All of them are likely to have experienced frustrations that come with relative privilege and freedom in a patriarchal society that remained largely stratified in ways that made it difficult to be a woman, and challenging in particular ways to be an exception to prevailing rules and norms.[38] In a study of the phenomenon of "evil spirit disease" in the present day, Yoram Bilu writes, "A possession episode is usually precipitated in an emotionally loaded context of intrafamily or interneighbor dispute. A short phase of complete immobility subsequent to an abrupt loss of consciousness is followed by a bulk of disorganized and uncontrollable agitated behaviors that rapidly escalate. An afflicted woman may be indiscriminately violent, verbally and physically."[39] That study also mentions the vulnerability of newly-married women to such illness across a variety of cultures, probably due to the status curtailment and deprivation they experience.[40] It is interesting that we find this reflected in the ancient story of Tobit in the Apocrypha, which is important reading for anyone interested in ancient Jewish views of demons and exorcism.

The relevance of such anthropological studies of demon illness for a discussion of Mary Magdalene is clear, and we have sought to incorporate these insights into our telling of a small part of Mary's story. Somewhat ironically, two diametrically opposed situations cause frustration to older women in a patriarchal society. On the one hand, women who remain unmarried longer than is the cultural norm can be plagued by self-doubt as well as societal suspicion of their unworthiness. People are prone to assume that potential suitors must have found something displeasing in her and to speculate what it might be. On the other hand, women who become betrothed and/or marry suddenly find their status transformed in ways that can be disconcerting even to a young bride marrying an older and more experienced man, as was the cultural norm, but will be all the more so for a mature woman. Put both of these situations together and severe distress resulting in symptoms of illness were likely to follow. To go from having more independence than most of one's female peers, to playing second fiddle to a man younger than oneself, would cause

---

38. Taschl-Erber, "Mary of Magdala," 440 views Mary as having been transformed into a wealthy patron of status in later tradition, considering this incompatible with her demon-possessed state.

39. Bilu, "Moroccan Demon," 26.

40. Bilu, "Moroccan Demon," 34.

significant stress. Across a wide array of societies and time periods, the frustrations of women in patriarchal societies have expressed themselves in the form of what Bilu calls "evil spirit disease," which he considers to be a form of female protest.[41] Carla Ricci has proposed that it was pent up psychological frustration that manifested in this way for Mary.[42]

Exorcisms performed on women who were experiencing this were often felt to be necessary, and repeatedly so, since the underlying causes were not being addressed. Mary probably had this sort of experience before meeting Jesus, in connection with whom she experienced permanent recovery. This tells us that through her contact with him, underlying family and societal factors of her malady were addressed in some way. He did not completely change society as a whole, but his teaching did influence families as well as creating an alternative community of support. If Jesus's contact with Mary and the other women mentioned in Luke took place early in his activity, then they presumably helped him to discover the connection between long-term recovery from illness and changes in how people in general and women in particular were treated and supported. Others would have seen this as Jesus permanently healing a woman whom multiple exorcists (perhaps seven) had previously tried to "tame" without success. His approach to women and his teaching provided the crucial context for the effectiveness of his spoken exorcistic words. At some point, we can say with confidence, Jesus learned to understand important aspects of the experience of women in his time and place and how those differed from his own. The evidence points to Mary having been one of those from whom he did so. No healer can work effectively without learning about and from those they seek to heal. In order to heal Mary and others like her, Jesus had to learn things that men then as now did not always understand about the way women suffer in patriarchal settings, whether through the combination of circumstance and social structure, or as a result of harm directly inflicted by men. Long-term cure was not brought about by restoring the status quo of male dominance, but by creating a new community that addressed in

---

41. Bilu, "Moroccan Demon," 35. Maisch, *Mary Magdalene*, 3–5 discusses her illness as psychosomatic in connection with her socioeconomic status. Hebblethwaite, *Six New Gospels*, 119–20 depicts the condition Mary suffered from as manic depression. See also Davies, *Spirit Possession*, 116–21.

42. Ricci, *Mary Magdalene*, 136–37.

some way the hierarchies and power stratifications that were among the underlying causes.[43]

Passive Exorcism?

The way Luke refers to Mary's experience of liberation is striking. He does not say that Jesus drove seven demons out of her, but that "seven demons had gone out" from her. The use of a passive verb deserves attention. In ancient Judaism it was common to avoid referring to God by speaking in precisely this indirect manner. If Jesus had meant in his beatitudes "blessed are you who mourn, for I will comfort you," that's what he would have said. But to express a different idea, he said "blessed are you who mourn, for you shall be comforted (by God)." The same might be true here. In the fictionalized exploration of Mary's story with which we started the story, we sought to explore what that might indicate, such as a spontaneous experience based on encounter with Jesus rather than a formal exorcism involving the usual ritual procedures. In this we have sought to do justice to the specific wording used, and at the same time the overall impression that Jesus was nonetheless the one who had healed her. One possibility is that seven demons, seven illnesses or symptoms, had gone out from her repeatedly but had always returned, until Jesus ultimately drove them out. But another possibility is that it was not a direct attempt to cast out the demons, but a combination of Jesus's presence, attitude, words, the community he created, and the values he brought to the family environments of those who became part of that community that led to her full recovery. Witnessing this may have helped Jesus to learn how powerful this combination could be, that he could offer something more than what other exorcists did. This is summed up nicely in terms of the connection the Gospels make between Jesus's more powerful exorcisms and offer of ongoing wellness, and the arrival of the kingdom of God with the new way of life that entailed for those who chose to embrace and enter it.

---

43. On the difference between healing and curing in the socioeconomic context of Jesus's activity see further Yamaguchi, *Mary and Martha*, 70–71. On the importance of community in long-term healing of psychological illness see Moorehead, *Healed*, 67–69; Bernabé Ubieta, "Mary Magdalene and the Seven Demons" (= "Siete Demonios" in Gomez-Acebo, *Maria Magdalena*, 51). Chilton, *Mary*, 4–8, 13, regards Mary (as well as Jesus) as being of low status. On Jesus's social status see McGrath, "Was Jesus Illegitimate?"

Ancient sources indicate to us that exorcism was an art, a set of practices that people learned. With any learned practices, there is also an experience of improving in the practice, of learning more as one hones one's skill. We suggested in an earlier chapter that Jesus might have learned some of his healing techniques from women in his own family, who were often the keepers and key practitioners of folk medicine. Whether exorcism was among the things he learned from relatives we cannot hope to say. He may also have learned from John the Baptist, whether initially or developing further skills he had begun cultivating at home. Once again, we do not know. But we can know that Jesus learned the art of exorcism, because we know that exorcism as a practice existed, because Jesus's actions are not unlike those we read about in other ancient stories about exorcism, and because Jesus compares and relates his own exorcistic activity to this broader practice.[44] In this chapter, we are exploring the likelihood that, in freeing the women who were among his earliest followers from ailments believed to have been caused by demons, Jesus practiced his craft but also learned more about practicing it effectively in the process. He would have learned about the framework that made ongoing wellness possible, rather than mere temporary alleviation of symptoms. Mary's experience was likely crucial in that development.

Carmen Bernabé Ubieta notes a connection between what we're told about Mary and Luke 11:24-26, which describes demons being driven out from a person only to return with "friends," so that the individual suffers even more than previously. Luke's reference to seven demons having left Mary may indicate that there had been prior attempts to liberate her that were unsuccessful or only offered temporary relief.[45] Each earlier attempt at healing her ailment may have led to additional symptoms, without the original ones going away.[46] It is interesting to observe how Jesus describes

---

44. See further Witmer, *Jesus, the Galilean Exorcist*, 51-55; also Matt 12:27 // Luke 11:19.

45. Bernabé Ubieta, "Mary Magdalene," 219. See also Getty-Sullivan, *Women*, 184; Boer, *Mary Magdalene Cover-Up*, 23. This has a parallel in Matt 12:45 and thus stems from Q.

46. Revelation's seven spirits may also allude to this saying of Jesus and/or show the impact of Jesus's words and exorcistic practice. Just as there were typically seven malevolent celestial forces in the worldview of that time, it was common to believe that there were seven principle angels. By identifying the spirits of the churches with those seven figures, the author of Revelation depicts communities from which malevolent celestial forces have been or are being driven out not to leave a vacuum, but by the presence of benevolent celestial presences. John's vision owes something to Jesus's

an exorcist as cleaning a home, making an analogy to what was typically an activity that women were responsible for in that cultural context. Unless something new replaces what had been there before, the unclean spirits will return and find the equivalent of a welcome mat.[47] If Mary's home had been less than ideally prepared when he first visited it, and was tidier on the second visit when he returned with still more of his entourage in tow, Jesus's saying may have been directly inspired by the memory of his first and second meetings with Mary. A person who is healed in the way that Mary is said to have been may have new strength that allows them to bring order to their environment exterior to themselves in ways that parallel and reflect the inner transformation they have undergone.

Ultimately the Gospels attribute the effectiveness of Jesus's exorcisms and those of his followers to God's action through the Spirit. Jesus speaks of himself as one who casts out demons, and he authorizes his followers to do the same. His sense of the extent of the authority that he had been given may well have come through seeing the way power was evidenced even when he did not deliberately perform rituals or act directly. We saw this in the case of the woman with chronic hemorrhaging: the woman experienced healing, but it wasn't as a result of a deliberate action to heal on the part of Jesus. Luke's description of Mary's experience may hint at something similar in her case as well. In the Gospels we see Jesus exorcize and heal using methods widely practiced in his time. Yet we also see him healing with a word, or through mere contact. If there is a development in his practice, and his perception of what it implied about his power and authority and the dawning of the kingdom, Luke may provide a clue about Mary's role in that development.

One more thing may be worth mentioning. I've long felt puzzled by Jesus's reply to the opponents who accused him of casting out demons by harnessing demonic power. He asks them, "If Satan casts out Satan, how can his kingdom stand?" (Matt 12:24-27 = Luke 11:15-19). This seems to assume that the kingdom of Satan would indeed stand—otherwise it doesn't really work as a counterargument. Perhaps at some moment

---

vision that may owe something to what he learned from Mary.

47. Although we do not have time to explore it here, the work known as 1 Enoch helps us understand the belief in this time that unclean spirits were the spirits of the Nephilim who lost their bodies in the flood and now seek to occupy new bodies. Certain details in that text suggest it was written in Upper Galilee, and that it may have emerged from a worldview shared by Jesus and Mary, and/or been known to them and have influenced their thinking. See further Brand, *Evil*, esp. 149-217.

Jesus experienced a turning point, one that eventually led him to see his activity as bringing about the downfall of Satan's kingdom as opposed to merely winning minor skirmishes in a battle that would be ongoing. Jesus spoke of seeing Satan fall like lightning from heaven after his disciples returned from carrying out successful exorcistic activities of their own. His confidence in commissioning them to accomplish this reflected a confidence he had already gained in the authority given to him, and that is reflected in his belief that he could not merely drive out demons only to have them return later to afflict their victim again, but offer ongoing wellness by replacing their presence with that of the more powerful Spirit of God. It seems inherently plausible that Mary's major recovery from demonic affliction as narrated by Luke helped Jesus learn that his exorcistic ability would surpass that of others, which in turn provided a different framework for his understanding of himself and his role in the dawning of the kingdom of God.[48] Her effectiveness performing exorcisms herself may have clinched the matter for him.

Throughout this chapter, I have talked a lot about status and stress, gender roles and healing. I am aware that some readers may feel that I am ignoring the fact that the Gospels say that demons left Mary—not stresses or microbes, but demons. I have not been ignoring it but leaving it until now. Experiences of demons are documented across a wide array of cultures, although we have drawn in this chapter on cases from cultural contexts closely related to those that shaped the Gospels. The symptoms experienced are closely associated with particular circumstances and the psychological coping mechanisms people use in response to them. The Gospels do not, on the other hand, mention viruses, bacteria, the immune system, psychology, or any of the things that those of us familiar with modern medicine must. There are two main options open to interpreters in view of the evidence. One is that we are simply talking about the same thing ancient people were but using different language. Not that our language is always consistently different. We still talk about someone's demons as a metaphor, and we personify illnesses even when the medical cause is a non-sentient microorganism or our own genetic code. In most cases we are aware that we are using this language metaphorically

---

48. While the story of Jesus expelling a "legion" of demons involves a greater display of exorcistic power in terms of the sheer number expelled, that story appears to have begun as political satire. One wonders whether it was later interpreted literally in an attempt to make Mary's story seem less impressive in contrast with one involving a man.

where ancient people might have understood it literally. There is, however, another alternative for those who feel obligated to accept the reality of personal supernatural agents. There is no denying that experiences of the demonic correlate closely to life situations. Perhaps those events in human life, and/or the way we ourselves and those around us respond to them, open us up to malevolent forces. Either way, the symptoms experienced as illness and psychosis are triggered and exacerbated by social realities. Demonic entities and activities, whether literal or metaphorical, are factors but not the underlying cause per se. Even when we think of the use of spells and black magic, the effort to summon demons to attack another person, the cause is human hatred, with real or imagined demons coming into the situation because our hatred summons the demonic. Thus, in focusing on underlying causes here, we are not ignoring the fact that some people still believe demons are literal personal spirit beings. We are merely focusing on the underlying causes that Jesus in the Gospels, as well as modern studies, indicate are at the root of these phenomena.

Moorehead is right to say, "We could not remove the thread of exorcisms from the synoptic gospels without tearing the fabric of the narratives themselves."[49] Nonetheless, as Ida Fröhlich writes, "Ancient Near Eastern cultures attributed illnesses, anxiety and psychological disorders, afflictions, epidemics, and all kinds of natural evil to the work of demons. However, spirits and demons were believed to mediate not only in physical plagues, illnesses and dysfunctions of the body and soul. Negative emotions and troubles in human relationships were similarly attributed to demonic agents."[50] Modern readers cannot avoid pondering the meaning of the language used in the New Testament in its original context and our simultaneous inability, in light of advances in knowledge of medicine and psychology, to adopt precisely the same view of illness in our time as ancient people did.

Mary as Disciple and Teacher

Bernabé Ubieta and Boer both note that the only way the *reminder* about Jesus's teaching given to the women in Luke 24:6–8 makes narrative sense

---

49. Moorehead, *Healed*, 36. See also 38–39 on the breadth of reference of the term "demon," covering a range of behaviors and ailments.

50. Fröhlich, "'For He Loves Her ...'" 33.

is if the author and readers alike assumed that the women were present and learned along with Jesus's core group of male disciples.[51] It would be very easy to miss the significance of this, but we must not do so. While the appearance of Mary in the Gospels primarily at the cross and tomb leaves those traditions largely outside the scope of this book, this text is directly relevant, providing an important indication about Mary's activity in the group around Jesus during his public activity and not only later. In teaching his inner circle of disciples, Jesus was training them, preparing them to be sent out as his emissaries and representatives, extensions of his own mission. Matt 10:7 and Luke 10:9 make clear that part of the role of the twelve and the seventy or seventy-two whom Jesus sent out in pairs was to proclaim his message as well as heal and carry out exorcisms. These were the activities Jesus himself was known for. Disciples learned what he taught and how he healed and then did likewise. There is nothing in Luke that suggests the larger group of emissaries consisted only of men, and even when the twelve were sent out in pairs, they may have traveled paired with their wives rather than with each other. Although there is awkwardness to the way Paul expressed himself in 1 Cor 9:5, his reference to the other apostles being accompanied by a "sister-wife" suggests that such a pairing was the norm, and that he in lacking a spouse who collaborated with him in his endeavors was the exception. Where individuals were sent out who were unmarried, they may have traveled with someone else who was likewise unmarried.

Extracanonical texts go much further in emphasizing Mary's role as a student, teacher, and authority in the early church, one whose status was challenged by some male leaders. Much of what those sources say only make sense if there was a tradition emphasizing Mary's teaching activity, as well as another that sought to downplay and counter her authority.[52] The contents of these works are not historical accounts of Mary and what she taught, but they reflect the impact of that historical reality nonetheless. These works also appeal to male authorities from the Christian movement, and even when the teaching they attribute to them is fabricated, the false attribution of the material only makes sense if the individuals in question were widely known to have been teachers with authority. Watson writes, "Her prominence in the Jesus movement

51. Bernabé Ubieta, *Maria Magdalena*, 117, 124 and Boer, *Mary Magdalene*, 37.
52. Boer, *Mary Magdalene Cover Up*, 184–94. Elsewhere Boer writes, "John is the only evangelist who makes Mary speak" (*Mary Magdalene Beyond the Myth*, 56). Of course, Boer is referring here only to the canonical Gospels.

probably bothered many men and made them want to put her down."[53] That Mary only taught others after Easter seems unlikely. Those figures that we know were involved in teaching in the earliest days of the church are precisely those who were involved in Jesus's activity in that capacity before his death. Above all else a disciple was an apprentice. Jesus sent those who studied with him to teach and perform exorcisms. Mary would have participated in these activities. And in the process of preparing, just like any teacher worth his salt (an expression particularly apt to this discussion), Jesus would have learned from as well as taught his students, including Mary. Mention should also be made of Paul's greeting to someone named Mary in Rom 16:6. She was presumably a leader in the community of some description, given the context as well as whom Paul singles out to greet in his letters. We have no reason to think that the Mary Paul mentions was Mary Magdalene.[54] Even if this was not the same person, however, she is worth mentioning if only to raise the question: If one Mary could be a leader in a Christian community, why not another?

Given the existence of a Gospel of Mary and other such works, we need to address the idea that groups of Gnostics (or whatever one may prefer to call them) preserved secret teaching from Mary. This seems no more likely than that these works preserved secret teaching of Thomas or other male apostles. Perhaps they do on occasion, but for the most part they seem interested in latching on to a known authority figure in order to bolster the authority of what goes into the text. That is an important observation in this context. These works do seem to have preserved something that reflects genuine historical information: the memory of Mary as a leader and authority figure like the male apostles. They get the authority of the teaching of the male apostles right. Why (apart from chauvinism) would we suspect that their similar information about Mary was completely inaccurate? Even if we do not treat such sources as reliable records of Mary's teaching on the whole, there are nevertheless places where extracanonical sources may preserve sayings that reflect historical information. For example, in calling Mary "Magdalene" Jesus addressed her in a manner usually reserved for men. This could have been understood as "making her male," and we find a saying about precisely that in Gospel of Thomas 114. There Peter asks Jesus to send Mary away since

---

53. Watson, *Wisdom's Daughters*, 117. See also 139–41 on the challenges of writing Mary of Bethany's story.

54. Boer, *Mary Magdalene*, 62–63.

females are not worthy. Jesus says that he will make her male and a living spirit.[55] This saying often troubles those who judge it to be historical, as well as those who are simply fond of the Gospel of Thomas for its spiritual teachings. It certainly reflects ancient patriarchal biases. The saying probably refers to women participating fully in the radical asceticism of early Christian community, and also in courageous acts that were felt to be masculine in character, including not only teaching but declarations before accusing authorities and even martyrdom.[56] Even if framed within ancient patriarchal assumptions that characterize strength as masculine and masculinity as superior, Jesus recognizes Mary's capacity for greatness in this saying. It is problematic, to be sure, to measure the success of women exclusively in terms dictated by men and male values. Yet for many men in patriarchal settings, recognizing that women can and do achieve those things may be a first step away from chauvinism, even if more is required to reach a genuine egalitarian outlook.

The tendency to put Mary and her alone in a special category that supposedly accounts for a unique connection between her and Jesus is problematic. That three of the male apostles appear to have been closer to Jesus than the others does not typically lead interpreters to deduce anything other than that those three (Peter, James, and John) were particularly good students, or were particularly good at accomplishing the things Jesus called upon them to do, or simply managed to form a deeper bond of friendship with their teacher. We should do the same in the case of Mary. If she was noteworthy as a disciple, why do so many find it difficult to believe that it was simply because of her aptitude for learning, her insightful questions in response to what Jesus said, her effectiveness as a speaker and an exorcist?[57] If she was noteworthy, why do so many

---

55. Some have seen hints of conflict between communities behind this. See however Pardee, "Gnostic Magdalene," 70–73.

56. Henery, "Early Christian Sex Change"; Barker, "Perception of Women"; also Amy-Jill Levine's 2002 Chautauqua Institution lecture "Mary Magdalene" available on their website: https://online.chq.org/ci/sessions/2449/view.

57. Pardee, "Gnostic Magdalene," observes that in *Dialogue of the Savior*, "The Savior consistently praises Mary for her questions and contributions . . . Mary is more than simply a passive recipient of knowledge . . . she too offers clarity and instruction— she makes clear, even reveals, the words of the Savior" (57). Similarly of *Pistis Sophia* Pardee writes, "Mary is depicted as an exemplary dialogue partner full of understanding and purely spiritual. She is a fruitful recipient of knowledge, but also a revealer in her own right. Her questions and interpretations do not merely serve as a pretext for the Savior to speak; they contain significant gnostic insights themselves" (60).

prefer to say that it was because of a romantic connection than that it was because she was a good teacher?[58] We know why, once we think about the matter. But we may not even notice we are doing this unless it is called to our attention.

Conclusion: What Jesus Learned from Mary of Magdala

Among the key things to take away from this chapter is the extent to which Mary convinced Jesus that women can be leaders. He may have seen examples of this already. However, we still get the impression that Mary stood out because of her abilities. Even those who believe something in principle learn more and allow it to shape their worldview more when they see it lived out in practice in an exceptional manner. Mary also helped Jesus learn about and reflect on the difference between healing and cure, and what led to the latter as opposed to merely accomplishing temporary relief.[59] If we fixate on the departure of demons from Mary we miss the more well-rounded depiction of her in our ancient sources. That detail is merely indicating that she was seriously afflicted by multiple illnesses or ailments and experienced transformative healing. It is treated as denigrating her by later readers who wished to curtail her influence, whereas in actual fact it highlights her experience of Jesus and of God that sets the stage for her role as supporter, disciple, and proclaimer of the good news about Jesus and as a major influence on him as well as on others on his behalf.

In many respects, this chapter was the most difficult to write. So much has been written about Mary Magdalene, and there are so many views and assumptions, that there is no way to address every alternative readers may have encountered. My biggest concern is that readers will be so used to sensationalized portrayals that my depiction of her will seem, in a word, boring by comparison. However, in the end I realized that the sensationalism always centers around Mary in a typical role that ancient men would have considered suited to a woman—whether prostitute or

---

58. Mary's authority and leadership among the female disciples, and the disciples in general, is compatible with our suggestion that she may have been older than most of Jesus's disciples, and was accorded the respect that was felt to be due to elders. However, age and status in and of themselves do not explain Mary's leadership role. Joanna was almost certainly of a more elite social status than Mary yet does not appear nearly as prominently in the tradition.

59. See Yamaguchi, *Mary and Martha*, 70–71.

spouse and mother of Jesus's child.[60] Yet the most ancient sources that seek to downplay her authority do not focus on either of these options. She is not turned into a prostitute until centuries later, nor is the matter of her authority—whether accepted or challenged—focused on her being Jesus's wife or lover. Something far more controversial than that is at the center of the discussion, namely the idea that Mary could have been one of Jesus's closest friends. In this chapter I have sought to restore Mary to her rightful place as an ancient woman whose significance for us is her friendship with Jesus, which entails her influence on him as well as the reverse. She may seem ordinary compared to the headline-making portrayals, but the most important friends of influential people often seem that way to those hungry for sensational gossip or scandal. As far as we know from our earliest sources, the reason she was important for Jesus was the friendship that developed at the intersection of their personalities and life experiences. That was enough for Jesus, and hopefully will be enough for you. If you hoped for something more sensational, there are plenty of other places that you can find it. My hope is that this portrait of Mary as simply a woman with whom Jesus clicked, someone from whom he learned as well as whom he taught (rather than thinking of her as important to him because he wanted her to be a receptacle for his bloodline or anything else along those lines) may help readers not only to appreciate Mary more fully, but also Jesus as a genuine first-century human being as well.

Some readers may be surprised that we have managed to pinpoint so few specific things that Jesus learned from the woman whose name is most closely associated in many people's minds with his adult life. It should not be surprising. If we are asked what we learned from others, it is in the case of our closest friends, and those we've known the longest, that we may find ourselves struggling to be specific. When we have learned much from someone, and been shaped by our friendship with them over many years, we have been impacted in more ways that we ever realize. Hopefully for all the unanswered questions that remain, we have helped bring into focus important evidence regarding what set Mary apart among the women in the early Jesus movement. She was not simply a wealthy member of the elite who could provide financial support, nor a potential or actual romantic partner, but a student and at the same time a friend. It is the ability to see and appreciate women beyond the scope of

60. Schaberg, *Resurrection*, 102. Fisk, "Stood Weeping," focuses mostly on the resurrection accounts but also covers many of the novelizations about Mary and Jesus.

assigned cultural and societal roles that is one of the crucial lessons men need to learn if they are going to work to dismantle patriarchy.

Joanna

What Jesus Learned by Having a Friend in High Places

When Herod killed my husband, I thought sure my days were numbered as well. I deserved to die more than he did. I was the one who had attracted him to that rabbi who was preaching the arrival of the kingdom of God, challenging the immorality that sustained the luxury of the wealthy and powerful, and calling the entire people to change our ways.

I'm referring at this point, of course, to John the baptizer.

My husband Chuza was a Nabataean, a distant cousin of the tetrarch on that side of his family. It was only the fact that I have relatives who are Roman citizens that saved my life, leading to my exile from Judea, the place I had grown up, rather than my execution.

If I were a man, you would know my story already. I am still surprised that some think of me mainly in connection with my husband Chuza, as though someone of my status were not a well-suited match for a distant cousin of a royal family. I have no interest in boasting of my own status or that of my family. But if anyone could boast, I could. I was involved in Jesus's endeavors before they were public. We go way back, having been introduced when John was still active, when we were both supporting his efforts each in our own way. I provided more of the financial support than anyone else, by far, and perhaps more than all the men in his entourage did. I say this not to claim some special worthiness for having done what John and subsequently Jesus taught us to do. I say it because if I had been a man you'd already know about it. Jesus also taught us to stand up for those who are downtrodden, and I will continue to use my influence to address the way women are treated, even in the ongoing movement of Jesus's own followers. Yet I fear that all my efforts will be forgotten, and that I'll get at most a passing reference when the story of Jesus is told.

My family's influence goes back generations. Our ancestors lived in the vicinity of Jericho for as long as Israel has been in the land. If you know the city, it is a place where Jews, Idumaeans, Nabataeans, and others lived side by side. But our family was one of the first to forge an alliance with the Nabataeans, to recognize that they had amazing skills they had cultivated living in Arabia such as tentmaking and other forms of leatherworking which, if we could learn them, or even simply trade with them or become their business partners, it could give us a financial advantage.

As it turned out, it made us rich.

When the Syrian king whose name I won't mention outlawed the Jewish law, some of our family members whose positions put them at risk fled to the farthest reaches of his empire, especially to Asia Minor, where that policy wasn't a concern. Ironically, we who were persecuted for being Jews and observing our ancestral customs in our homeland could become citizens there. God turned the schemes of the oppressor back upon him and worked to the advantage of his people. What the tyrant meant for evil, God worked for our good. Even after he died and the crisis of those times ended, some of us stayed in Cilicia and elsewhere in the Diaspora, maintaining the economic and family ties with our ancestral home that we would depend on if we were to survive there. In the end, that proved to lead to more prosperity, as characteristics of the distinctive tents of the Nabataeans became features of the theater curtains and backdrops one could find in Asia. Before long, they were highly sought after elsewhere in the Greek and Roman worlds as well. Our family's wealth flowed along the trade routes from Arabia to Cilicia and back. Jericho is the gateway from the land of Israel to Edom and Arabia, and so you might say our family became a trade route unto itself. This allowed us to support many projects, including building synagogues, and facilitating reform and protest movements like that of the Pharisees, of John, and of Jesus. John had quite a reach among the Nabataeans as well as very diverse scattered pockets of Israelites *of every sort who live in Transjordan, preserving ancestral traditions in a variety of forms.*

My family has relatives in every major city between Jericho and Tarsus, and there has always been a lot of temporary movement. The more devout of our diaspora cousins often sent their children to study in Jerusalem or elsewhere in the land of Israel. Some of them became rabbis, and when they did so, they might get involved in the ruling councils, or return to the diaspora and find work in local synagogues. Our women married well, and that smoothed the way for trade every bit as much as the involvement of a few of our male family members in politics and education. As for me, I was given in marriage to form a strategic alliance with the Herods. He was a mixture of Jewish, Idumaean, and Nabataean ancestry and his family thus spread across a wide stretch of territory and language. Someone like me, who could understand Nabataean well while also having a strong Jewish identity was a perfect match to get our family more directly connected to the royal court, even if only via a distant cousin. A few of my relatives, and one cousin in particular, was adamantly opposed to my marriage, saying that it represented a compromise and a dilution of our heritage, a betrayal of our family's commitment to Judaism. When I went through with it, he turned into something of a zealot. The persecution by the Syrian king in earlier times had already radicalized some of us. Many others were like dry brush, seemingly harmless until a certain spark set them ablaze.

I played the role of that spark more than once, as it turned out.

At first I thought it was ironic that our Diaspora relatives were the most narrow and uncompromising. But when you think about it, when you don't have the benefit of a connection to land and strength in numbers, there's nothing to hold onto except identity and tradition. Even so, I eventually came to recognize how fragile our hold on the covenant with God is even in the land of Israel. John was right that the nation needed to repent, and not merely rely on a connection to God based on who our ancestors were. It was being able to look within Herod's household that helped me see this clearly. Herod could seem quite devout on the surface. No idols. No pork. But also no respect for human life, and no concern for the poor that went beyond a bit of charity while we all continued to live in opulent luxury. Chuza and I were part of that lifestyle of excess until we heard John's message and found we could not ignore his words about living in luxury and waste while others had nothing. We believed him when he said that wasn't what God wanted for his people. We thought that the change in us might win over others within the palace, leading to genuine change at that level.

But then John made an enemy of Herod.

You know the story of what happened. It is only recently that I have begun to be able to think and talk about it without being unable to sleep for days afterwards. I was at the dinner, and I suffered from nightmares for years afterwards. As one of John's sympathizers, afterwards I beseeched the king to allow John's body to be given to his disciples for burial. He gave the decapitated corpse to others of John's disciples . . . and sent me John's severed head. I asked Chuza to come away with me then, to leave there, but he refused.

Chuza and I were lucky to have escaped with our lives once Herod decided to eliminate John. Having sympathizers in Herod's own family might lead other members of John's movement to hope that they could continue, that they might be able to use us as a route to access political power, whether wresting control from the Herods, or merely seeking information that would allow them to evade the king's efforts to apprehend them should it ever come to that. But the followers of John had dispersed, and it didn't seem that the anger of the tetrarch was going to persist. Herod spared Chuza's life and mine and let the matter drop . . . for the time being.

Eventually Chuza and I ended up in Tiberias in Galilee, Herod's new city being in need of someone to manage Herod's property holdings in the region, and a good stopping point on our family's trade route. It made perfect sense for him to send us there. If Herod could be unforgiving, he could also be magnanimous, especially when his own interests stood to benefit.

Then Jesus reappeared, saying that the work John had begun would continue, and that he had a vision for taking things in a new direction.

As I think I mentioned already, we had actually met previously when he was part of John's entourage. I regret that I did not get to know him better then. I do recall from our gatherings with John that he was already an exceptional storyteller. He had us laughing, crying, and most importantly, he challenged us in ways that got past our instinctive defenses and made us take a long hard look at our own beliefs and actions. I still recall pointing out to him that the characters in his stories being mostly men—as so typically in the stories men told—made it hard for women to see ourselves in them as easily as men did. I could tell from the look on his face that he felt disappointed in himself immediately. It was a week or so later, when he finished telling one of his typical short tales, and we who were listening assumed he was done, that he surprised us by launching immediately into another story. It was just as good, and made the same point, but the central character was a woman! I clapped my hands with delight, and many others among John's female followers gave vocal expression of their appreciation. It makes such a difference to know as women that we are being heard, and that we are noticed and being spoken to directly and explicitly by men.

I've encountered people who think the Herods kill their opponents because they don't take the Scriptures seriously. The opposite is in fact the case. They know that one day God might bring a better kingdom. They also believe that in the absence of the miraculous appearance of God's kingdom it is the time of rulers like themselves. They believe that God would have prevented Herod the Great from building the best version of the temple anyone had ever seen, grander than Solomon's, if God did not approve of his kingship. Whether there was something better in the future, or this was itself the fulfillment of the promises and hopes of Israel, only God could say. Meanwhile, if someone tried to take up arms or plot, that wasn't God at work but self-interest. Nothing wrong with that in and of itself, as far as the Herods were concerned. It had got them where they were. But it meant you were part of the present age, and there was no need for kings or tetrarchs to defer to someone else like themselves if they were capable of holding on to the reins of power. I shared this view of things with Jesus when he told me that he was of the line of David, and that he thought perhaps he might be the one to bring to fruition what John had begun, to fulfill what John had predicted. I told him that if God wanted him to rule over Israel, it would take a miracle. And so he should wait for God to act, while humbly preparing himself and the nation for God to do so. He asked me if I thought the Herods would leave him alone if he approached the kingdom of God that way, humbly and patiently. I bluntly told him no—that would take a miracle too. We had both been deeply traumatized by what happened to John. He had attacked Herod Antipas directly, and so there was no surprise that it happened. A ruler's marriage is connected with their heirs and their dynasty, and if you criticize that you may as well be predicting that their dynasty will be replaced by another. John had also challenged the temple, which wasn't just a matter of attacking priestly authority and their monopoly on forgiveness, but a symbol of the legitimacy of the rule of the Herods as well, who had invested so much in renovating and expanding it. Jesus could easily steer clear of the former topic, but if he continued proclaiming John's message about the latter, he would still be in trouble.

When Herod's opposition to Jesus grew, he remembered everything that had angered him about John. He became increasingly short-tempered with my husband Chuza even though he was at best a sympathizer. I was the one who was active as a supporter of both teachers. Chuza told me he would have to divorce me if Herod demanded that he do so. I told him I would not begrudge him even if he decided to do so sooner. He would be taking steps to preserve his own life, and I cared for him enough to want him to do so. In the end, Herod never gave him the chance. Once when Herod was in Tiberias, Chuza went as usual to report on finances and property, and never returned. Servants of friends in the court brought me word from the palace that my husband was dead. Apparently in the same breath Herod had denied he had anything to do with Chuza's death, and indicated that the same fate awaited Jesus.

When word reached me I was with Jesus and others of our group. Jesus got angry and called Herod a fox, and dared to taunt him, telling the servants something he knew would get back to the palace: he would be heading to Jerusalem, out of Herod's territory. But the Romans had been hearing more and more about him, and so it turned out not to be safer. I would undoubtedly have been killed or banished myself had I not been away from home, moving around with Jesus and his sizable band of followers at the time when Herod had Chuza murdered. But fleeing is not that different from being banished and exiled. I was forced to leave my children behind with relatives in Arabia, and I feared for them constantly. When Jesus spoke of forsaking family, men listening assumed he had them in mind, their traveling with him for extended periods before returning home to see their families. But I know Jesus was thinking more of people like me, who couldn't know if we would see our children again. Who knew they would not see their spouse again. Not in this life, at any rate. When they killed Jesus, that was the last time I showed my face in Jerusalem before leaving for Asia. His death was just as brutal as John's, and in some ways more horrific, because of how humiliating and painful, how long and drawn out, crucifixion is. And this time, unlike with John, I saw the whole thing with my own eyes. But having been healed by Jesus of the nightmares and headaches that plagued me after John was killed, I wasn't going to be anywhere else but there in those moments, honoring him, standing with him in his moment of agony even if others forsook him.

I obviously didn't expect to see Jesus again. I expected I might dream of him, of his torment and suffering, even as I had dreamt of John. I wondered who would now console and heal me if the headaches returned as I suffered and grieved his loss. We had all comforted each other when we lost John. Who would comfort and guide us now? Instead of having nightmares about his death, Jesus really and truly came to me in a dream and not only consoled and comforted me but commissioned me. Even as he had sought out John's followers after John was killed and said that things were far from over, he appeared to me and echoed those words I had heard him say before, as we had sought out John's scattered followers and regrouped. He also said I would represent him in a distant land, and that even the one who had most vehemently stood against me from my own family would become a tool in his hand so that the kingdom of God spread even among the gentiles.

As I began that work in the Diaspora and connected more closely with my relatives there, I had occasion to travel to Rome on business. That was where I first met my distant cousin Andronicus. He had moved to Rome years earlier. I learned that once while he was in Jericho he had heard and responded to Jesus! Finding a relative who shared my beliefs in that distant place seemed like a miracle. We corresponded and eventually married. We hope to travel together to proclaim the kingdom even further.

I enjoy ending my story, when I tell it, with a fitting illustration of God's justice. Jesus's talk of the kingdom stirred up in Herod the desire for a title greater than tetrarch. He asked the emperor to grant him the title of king, thinking his position would be more secure against others who spoke of a kingdom if he himself bore the title. Instead, Caligula exiled him to Gaul . . .

Joanna and Junia: One Woman or Two?

I will confess that I did not originally anticipate including a chapter about Joanna in this book. That isn't because she isn't intriguing for a wide variety of reasons. It was merely because so little is said about her when she is mentioned in the Gospel of Luke (8:3; 24:10), I feared that I would have to speculate far too much on the basis of far too little evidence. I will also confess that when I first encountered a mention of the possibility that Joanna and Junia (to whom Paul sends greetings in Rom 16:7) might be the same person, I was extremely skeptical, or rather dismissive. True, it was a common practice for Jews who moved regularly between Aramaic and Greek or Latin linguistic environments to have two names, and where possible, to use a Greek or Latin name that is similar to their Jewish one. But that practice wasn't enough of a reason to identify these two figures. I was also cognizant of the tendency of interpreters of the Gospels to identify women as the same individual with very little basis, with results that should trouble us. The identification of Mary Magdalene with Mary of Bethany and as the "sinful woman" who wiped Jesus's feet with her hair had at least two negative consequences: it has not only served as a way to denigrate and demean Mary Magdalene as an authority figure in early Christianity, but it also reduces the number of strong female disciples visible in the stories. Thus I was not merely initially skeptical of the suggestion that Joanna and Junia might be the same person. I felt that I had good reason to try to avoid pursuing this.

Yet I have considered so many unconventional possibilities in this book, and been so surprised and impressed by what I have found, that my curiosity got the better of me and I thought I had better pull at the threads and see where they lead, and whether they make for a natural connection. What I discovered excited me as much as any discovery I made in the writing of this book. When we take what we know about Joanna and Junia separately and begin filling in the historical details connected with what our sources explicitly tell us, the two dovetail together in a way that is unlikely to be a coincidence. We start connecting the dots and a pattern, a picture, naturally emerges. If this identification means that we have one female leader where we otherwise believed we have two, the way that we can flesh out the details of her story is increased to such an extent that I hope it more than makes up for anything that is felt to be lost. Instead of two female leaders about whom we know next to nothing, we will find ourselves with one extremely influential leader whose role stretches from the time of Jesus's public ministry through the spread of the gospel into the wider Roman world. When we consider all the evidence, the significance that we find Joanna/Junia to have had is greater than most interpreters recognize either as having when they assume them to be separate individuals.[1]

Prominent among the Apostles

That Paul had relatives who were themselves apostles, or even if they were simply "of note in the eyes of the apostles" as some prefer to translate it, and that these individuals were in Christ before Paul, constrains the possible time frame and makes it very likely that one or more relatives of Paul's were present at events described in the Gospels.[2] Richard Bauckham writes, "It has always seemed remarkable that Paul could call two apostles of whom we never hear anywhere else in early Christian literature 'prominent among the apostles' (Rom 16:7). Perhaps we do in fact hear of at least one of these in Luke's Gospel, where she is already prominent among the women followers of Jesus."[3] Indeed, the fact that Luke mentions Joanna as playing a leading role in close connection with the Twelve is as close a fit to the description of Junia as "prominent among the apostles" and "in Christ before me" as we could hope to find in the Gospels. It would make sense for at least one female leader from the early period, who knew Jesus personally, to get mentioned somewhere in Paul's letters, just as some male apostles do.[4] That Luke's Gospel, which is

---

1. See further Cohick, *Women in the World*, 314–18; Bauckham, *Gospel Women*, ch. 5; Lunceford, *Biblical Women*, 111–13. Mathew, *Women in the Greetings*, 101 judges the identification of Joanna and Junia as the same person to be very speculative. Clark, "Exploring the True Identity," tries to make Joanna the daughter of Theophilus ben Ananus the high priest, whom she also identifies as the one to whom Luke-Acts is dedicated. But we have no evidence that that high priest was a Christian, and making Paul's relative Junia a Levite rather than a Benjamite also creates problems. See also Creamer et al., "Theophilus."

2. See Cohick, *Women in the World*, 216 for the case that the phrase means that Junia and Andronicus were themselves apostles, and not merely held in esteem by others who were apostles. See also Ellis, "Coworkers."

3. Bauckham, *Gospel Women*, 184. Ben Witherington also explores the identification of Joanna and Junia in his novel *Priscilla* (see esp. 97–101).

4. Note that Paul greets a "Mary" in Rom 16:6 in close proximity to his greeting to Andronicus and Junia. We will refrain from speculating here about whether this Mary might be the same individual as any other Mary mentioned in the New Testament. Mary was such a common Jewish name in this period that we cannot presume any

connected with Paul, is the only one to mention Joanna is also intriguing evidence.[5]

If we consider Joanna in relation to the developing church and the influence she might have had on it as an apostle, we must make reference to Manaen, mentioned in Acts 13:1 as a friend of Herod the Tetrarch. We know almost nothing else about him. However, the very fact that we have another member of the Christian movement connected with Herod's household raises the question of how his involvement relates to someone from that same circle who was associated with it even earlier. An earlier individual named Manaen was an Essene and was associated with an earlier generation of the Herod family. Whether the two were related is impossible to say. The name is presumably the Greek version of the Jewish name Menachen or some variation thereof, which isn't a particularly common name.[6] In connection with him, the threads we've already begun to follow and found to intertwine link up once again. Acts mentions Manaen alongside Saul, as well as a Lucius of Cyrene, while Paul mentions a Lucius who was his kinsman. There may well be family connections (blood relationships, but also a broader network of long-standing multigenerational connections) running through the group mentioned in Acts. Even apart from that, however, it would seem very likely that one who was connected with Herod's household and prominent among the apostles would have had an influence on Manaen coming to believe in Jesus.

Of the Tribe of Benjamin

Paul emphasizes in Phil 3:5 that he was of the tribe of Benjamin. That is yet another thread that seems to connect naturally with the identification of Joanna as Junia, Paul's relative. The tribe of Benjamin was historically

---

two individuals with this name are the same individual without additional evidence.

5. Haag, *Quest*, 73 mentions Luke's indication that an apostle was one who witnessed everything beginning with Jesus's baptism, which Joanna might have, and which Junia would have to have if Paul understood apostleship in the same way (although whether Paul too saw or at least was aware of these things at the time of Jesus's baptism is unclear).

6. Menachem is a more common form, and even it is relatively rare. See further Bauckham, *Gospel Woman*, 138. Bayler, *Manaen*, 122-24, 137-38, depicts Joanna and Manaen as knowing one another, but also makes Manaen not Jewish, which is unlikely given his name. For a different fictional reconstruction see Rourke, *Two Women*.

located in the region around the cities of Jerusalem and Jericho. The latter city had a significant Idumaean population.[7] It was a natural place, perhaps the only one, for a prominent Jewish woman to end up with Nabataean and Idumaean connections. The region served as a gateway between the territories on the two sides of the Jordan, as well as between two major thoroughfares for trade, the King's Highway and the Via Maris.[8]

That Paul means "relatives" in the literal sense when talking about Junia and Andronicus is clear from the fact that Paul greets others who were fellow Jews in Romans 16, and so part of the same people as himself, yet he does not single them out as "relatives." Clearly Paul is greeting people whom he can call "brothers and sisters" in the sense that all Christians were, and among those a subset are Jews and so his "brothers and sisters" in that ethno-religious sense. Yet even among that subgroup he singles some out as "relatives." No other meaning is more likely, in light of this, than that Paul means these are his relatives in the literal biological sense, people with known family ties.[9]

Some other pieces of this family puzzle suddenly fall into place when Joanna's part of the story is brought into the picture. In connection with her we learn of the family's connections with Transjordan/Arabia, the region inhabited by the Nabataeans. It has been a longstanding puzzle why Paul's initial response to his turnaround from opponent to supporter of the Jesus movement was to go to Arabia. Did he go to see relatives, perhaps even to see Joanna herself, who might well have initially fled there from Herod before eventually making her way to Rome? It would make a great deal of sense if one of the first things Paul did, right after he experienced his turnaround, was to connect with family in Jericho and Transjordan who were Christians, especially if their involvement had been one of his major motivations for opposing the movement. Starting by making amends with family, then returning to Damascus, before going to see the apostles in Jerusalem, would be an appropriate course of action. Damascus may also have under Nabataean rule during this period, and it may have something to do with his connections to family who were

---

7. Cross, *Canaanite Myth*, 339. Mark 3:8 mentions Idumaeans among those that flocked to see and hear Jesus.

8. Josephus records (*Ant.* 15.3.3) that Herod had his brother-in-law Aristobolus III murdered under guise of an accident in baths in Jericho. It was thus also a place of political intrigue involving the major players in this era.

9. Contra Mathew, *Women in the Greetings*, 106.

Nabataean as well as Jewish Christians that led him to single out Damascus as where he would focus his opposition to the Christian movement. Perhaps he knew that allegiance to Jesus was spreading among his family and he had relatives in Damascus.

The fact that a representative of Aretas, the Nabataean ruler, at one point sought to apprehend Paul when he was in Damascus is also far from self-explanatory, until we bring his (admittedly distant) connection to the household of Herod into the picture. William Barker envisages Chuza being torn between his loyalty as a Nabataean and his loyalty to Herod as events unfolded and it became clear that Aretas, Herod's father-in-law, would retaliate for his treatment of his daughter Phasaelis.[10] For all we know, Chuza's allegiance being suspect and that of Joanna along with him may have resulted in his death and her flight, even apart from their connection with John and/or Jesus. Then again, given that Herod's divorce of Aretas's daughter to marry Herodias was a focus of John's criticism of Herod according to the Gospels, we needn't choose between the two motives. When there are so many possible reasons for Herod to have eliminated Chuza, we may evaluate the scenario we envisage regarding Joanna being widowed and leaving for Rome to be highly plausible, if not indeed quite probable, even if we remain uncertain about a number of details. With this another piece of the Paul puzzle falls into place, and along with it another part of the wider picture encompassing Joanna and Jesus as well.

Apart from his movement while persecuting Christians and immediately after repenting of doing so, there is more that we can say about Paul that fills in the story of Joanna and her relation to Jesus. Paul is said in Acts to have been a "tentmaker" (using a Greek word we need to say more about). His trade (however translated) involved working with leather.[11]

---

10. Barker, *Women and the Liberator*, 102.

11. If we work under the assumption that leatherworking (whether for tents, theatrical sets, both, or neither) was a family trade, this too tells us something about the family. Paul is depicted as practicing the profession in Acts. Leather was widely used and not prone to carry ritual impurity. Even tanners who turned animal skins into leather, and who were therefore in constant contact with animal carcasses, did not acquire impurity thereby so long as the animals were kosher ones that were slaughtered rather than having died or been killed by another animal. There was thus no inherent incompatibility between the strict Pharisaic view of purity that sought to infuse daily life with the sacredness of the temple and these professions. The reference to Simon having his revelation about accepting gentiles while staying at the home of a tanner (Acts 9:43) just after Paul becomes a believer is worth further consideration. Would the tanner have been someone that Paul also knew, given his profession? See further

The Nabataeans are justly famous for Petra and that construction out of stone, but during most of their history they left behind far less in the way of monuments and archaeological remains that tourists can visit. That's because they lived in tents. It was a characteristic of their way of life. At one point the Nabataeans do start having houses built, but not a single Nabataean house has been found from the period prior to that, confirming what texts about them also inform us: they dwelt in tents. They would have become particularly skilled tentmakers as a result, and even if they transitioned to a different way of life, they would have retained leatherworking and similar abilities as among their chief skills.

It is surely not a coincidence that Paul is associated with this trade. Many sources point out that Cilicia where Tarsus was located was known for (even giving its name to) what we might call "sackcloth," in Latin *cilicium*. Paul's place of upbringing was known for that type of material, while nomadic peoples of the Levant and Arabia use that type of fabric for tents even today.[12] There is nothing that connects Cilicia with tents or tentmaking per se. The connection that many authors have made seems to be based on Paul, not a result of independent knowledge of the region his family was located. However, when we connect Paul's place of upbringing and his Benjamite heritage, then a natural connection with this profession emerges.[13] Prisca and Aquila in Corinth are also said to share Paul's trade as "tentmakers," and in Romans 16 we find them in Rome when Junia and Andronicus, Paul's relatives, are also there. The gospel message and those who bore it traveled along networks of family and trade. Paul's greetings as well as stories about him indicate how the two intersect, with the lines and contours of the network becoming clearer when Joanna/Junia is part of the picture.

Although I've used the longstanding translation of Paul's profession as "tentmaker," the Greek term translated that way in the New Testament is only found very rarely in Greek literature from close to the time of the New Testament. There it refers not to the making of tents, but to the making of sets for theatrical performances—scene-making rather than tent-making. If Paul worked in this trade, and if it was a family trade, then this would connect with Jesus's interest in theater and use of metaphors derived from there which we discussed earlier in this book. Even

---

Oliver, "Simon Peter Meets Simon the Tanner."

12. Layne, *Home and Homeland*, 56.
13. See Augé, "Nabataean Age" on Tarsus as on a trade route connected to Nabataea.

apart from this question of how to translate the profession that Acts ascribes to Paul, there is a certain likelihood that a woman of elite status, connected to the family of Herod, would enjoy theatrical performances and/or have occasion to participate in the audience and even to sponsor performances in a household setting for a smaller audience. Joanna may well have invited Jesus and his entourage to such events, and it is also possible that Jesus and his followers were among those who told stories and offered a "performance" that would have entertained and at the same time challenged such individuals. It can be difficult for modern people to imagine Jesus and his "troupe" as traveling performers. If they were indeed hired and then sponsored to tell stories that dared to present a challenging message to those who were the source of their livelihood, that is definitely to their credit. The practices of traveling troupes of performers may have provided Jesus with a model for his itinerant activity, which seems to have maintained a base of operations in Capernaum and on occasion elsewhere, and from there relied on hospitality in local areas where he and his group provided at the very least storytelling and healing, with sponsorship from wealthy patrons covering what local hospitality could not provide.[14]

It is not only in Romans that we hear about relatives of Paul. According to Acts 23:12–16, Paul's nephew was in a position to hear about plotting against him. This access to meetings of powerful and influential people, even when plotting secretly, tells us something about the family.[15] Paul's sister's family in Jerusalem probably were not Christians. The

14. On Jesus and theater see also the chapter on what he learned from his grandmother. It is intriguing to consider that Anna and Joanna might have known one another via patronage of theater before any other connections emerged. For those who are not persuaded that Jesus and John the Baptist were cousins, a detail found only in Luke's Gospel and nowhere else, it could be that Jesus's time with him came about as a result of Joanna supporting John and recommending this to Jesus's grandmother! If John and Jesus were indeed related, then the direction of influence and recommendation might have run the other way, since John would presumably be Anna's sister's son if he and Jesus were first cousins. Here too there are scenarios that it may be useful to explore further imaginatively to see where they lead, beyond what we have been able to incorporate into this chapter.

15. The placement of Paul in what had been Herod's palace (praetorium) in Caesarea in this story is also perhaps indicative of a family connection. Not because he was being treated like royalty. Not at all, although neither was he being treated like a common criminal. Being distantly related to the former household manager of Herod Antipas, who was probably in some equally distant way related to the family of Herod, made Paul and Agrippa II (to quote a famous line from *Spaceballs*) "absolutely nothing." But if Luke and many of his readers knew more about Paul's family than he

nephew may not have sympathized with his uncle but merely saved his life out of family loyalty. That he was in a position to overhear the plot against his uncle suggests that the rest of the family was not thought to be aligned with Paul, otherwise they would have taken more precautions. Their presence at gatherings of leading figures was clearly not unexpected or suspicious. Kin loyalty kicked in at this moment when loyalty to the wider group and its rulers was presumed to be what they would focus on. This too suggests something about Paul's family. Their sense of Jewish identity was passed along to Paul and Joanna, but that doesn't imply that most of them had any interest whatsoever either in Paul's newfound obsession with ritual purity or Joanna's involvement with apocalyptic/messianic leaders.[16]

It has long struck readers of the Gospels that Jesus seems to avoid the major cities of Galilee during his public activity recorded in the Gospels. There is a striking contrast with Paul's mission, which focused exclusively on cities. But perhaps the contrast is more apparent than real. Mary and Joanna were both connected with the cities of Galilee. Perhaps Jesus felt they had already had the good news proclaimed to them and had rejected it? Or perhaps his supporters there advised him that the strong Herodian presence meant it was safer to keep himself away from

---

explicitly tells us, it might have been his intention to subtly convey that Paul had more right to be living there than Felix the representative of Roman power. Paul at least had a family connection to those who built the palace and previously ruled in it. Felix did not have even that. Herod Agrippa, in Acts 26:28, may have been alluding to how long it took Paul to become a Christian, when he asks if he would persuade him so quickly. He may have known something of his story even before this encounter. Also, you may have noticed that all this implies that Antipas's enemies were not automatically those of Agrippa II. If one looks at their family history, it is easy to see why this should be so. Herodias plotted jealously against Agrippa I, and so the fact that Chuza had been executed and Junia exiled by Antipas and Herodias might have inclined Agrippa II and those connected with him to listen favorably to Paul and his nephew, once they found out who these individuals were.

16. Note as well that Paul calls Andronicus and Junia his "fellow-prisoners" or "fellow captives of war" as well as his relatives. See further Bauckham, *Gospel Women*, 170–72. We could, if space permitted, include a section (if perhaps not a full chapter) on what Jesus learned from Herodias, although the things he learned from her were not positive in the same way as others considered in this book. For instance, when we consider Jesus's deliberate determination not to make himself king, he may have been influenced by the example of Herod Agrippa who, prompted to do so by Herodias, sought the title of king from Caesar, and as a result had even his title of tetrarch taken away from him. He may also have seen that sometimes someone other than the one sitting on the throne has great power through influence.

the cities? Alternatively, did the women he knew from Tiberias and Magdala, Joanna and Mary, hear about what Jesus was doing in someplace like Capernaum and travel the short distance from there to where he was?[17] Either way, city connections and family connections play a role in the stories of both Jesus and Paul, perhaps most of all at the points where we now see the two stories to intersect even before Paul's turnaround.

What Do We Know About Joanna's Husband(s)?

Joanna is identified in Luke 8 through her connection with Chuza, her husband. Chuza is said to play a role in Herod's household that is perhaps best translated as "estate manager." While we would love to have more information about him and precisely what his role entailed, the little we know is sufficient for us to be certain that Joanna and her husband were important, powerful, influential individuals.[18] Chuza is a Nabataean name, i.e., a name that associates him with the non-Jewish part of Herod's own family background.[19] Chuza was likely high born, and came to court during Herod's first marriage. He probably converted in marrying Joanna but may not have adhered to Jewish beliefs and practices, at least not rigidly.[20]

The family of Herod moved in two worlds, yet most readers of the New Testament only know about their role in a predominantly Jewish setting, in places like Judea and Galilee. Unless we know the part of the story that stretches further southward and eastward from there we are missing a significant part of the whole picture. Herod the Great's mother was a Nabataean.[21] Herod Antipas's first wife, Phasaelis, was also Nabataean. He divorced her to marry Herodias.[22] And so there already you can see how the part of the story of the dynasty of Herod that you may already be familiar with intersects with a larger story the details of which you may not have heard. While this book cannot provide a detailed account of the

17. Spencer, *Salty Wives*, 113. Mary and Joanna appear to be associated with one another in Luke. Do we have indication here of an earlier phase of Jesus's activity, unrecorded in the Gospels, during which Jesus visited or intersected with people from the cities that are striking for their absence from the Gospels?

18. See further Bauckham, *Gospel Women*, 136–37.

19. Bauckham, *Gospel Women*, 150–57.

20. Haag, *Quest*, 69–70; Bauckham, *Gospel Women*, 158–61.

21. Bauckham, *Gospel Women*, 157.

22. Haag, *Quest*, 69.

story of the Herods, if you take the time to learn more information about that powerful family, you will be better poised to situate Joanna's story in its historical and cultural context.

An intriguing possibility is that Chuza could be the royal official who appears in John 4.[23] There is nothing to suggest that he was, nor anything to definitively exclude the possibility. However, we have nothing at all to indicate that they ever lived in Capernaum, and so in my judgment the identification seems forced. If they were the same person, that might have marked a turning point for Chuza. His wife had been healed by Jesus and so he at least tolerated her support for his work. But having their son healed may have won him over. More likely this was a different individual, but even then it would certainly be someone that Joanna and Chuza knew. A royal official in Capernaum would be known to the tetrarch's estate manager living in Tiberias. One way or another, the healing would have become known to Chuza and made an impression, assuming of course he was still alive at this point.

It is possible that Joanna's marriage to Chuza made an impression on her cousin Saul, of a negative sort. Did his relative marrying a Nabataean influence Saul's zeal to protect his nation's purity? And on the other hand, did Joanna and her marriage challenge Jesus's assumptions about intermarriage, gentiles, and/or the Herods? It is useful to think of Joanna in intersectional terms. Like the Herods, she occupied multiple worlds and identities simultaneously. One could be advantaged by status and disadvantaged by gender, or vice versa. One can be less disadvantaged than other women thanks to status or wealth, and yet also have some restrictions imposed that a poor woman might never need to worry about. It is possible to be privileged by status yet despised because of family associations.[24] Helen Bond and Joan Taylor note that the building of Tiberias with money extracted from the populace of Galilee through taxes would have made for resentment of the city and the Herodian elite who

---

23. So McCook, *Women Friends*, 159; Farrar, *Life of Christ*, 1:230-32; Cohick, *Women in the World*, 310. Bock discusses this possibility briefly in his commentary. Bauckham, *Gospel Women*, 137-38 views this as at most a possibility but not likely in view of the terminology and geographical location.

24. Mackall, *Kindred Sisters*, 117 notes that Joanna may have been made to feel less than welcome in the movement precisely because of her status. Fuchs, *We Were There*, 61 mentions her possibly having to bear the brunt of Jewish hatred for Herod and his household. On the sentiment of dislike and resentment ordinary people would have felt towards members of Herod's household see Seim, *Double Message*, 36; Bauckham, *Gospel Women*, 120, 150. For a different view see Cohick, *Women*, 314.

lived there.[25] One can be accepted by one's fellow people yet also viewed negatively because of having married someone from a different ethnic and religious background, and feel the pain of hearing disparaging things said about one's spouse's people. It is only when people form community across multiple differences, share their stories, and listen to how others envy and/or pity one another reciprocally, that intersectional realities come into focus. It was only through the presence of women like Joanna in his movement that this would become clear to Jesus.

She also gave him the chance to see his impact on someone relatively wealthy. Richard Bauckham writes, "her following of Jesus was also a conversion to the poor. She may have seen her financial contribution to Jesus' ministry as putting to rights some of the economic wrongs in which she had been involved as Chuza's wife."[26] Mary Ellen Ashcroft writes,

> Scholars figure that Joanna would have been the most sophisticated and educated of the women (or perhaps of all Jesus' followers). Living in Herod's household, she would have been fluent in Greek and Aramaic and used to the sophistication of court life—the fancy parties, political intrigues, and celebrities.
>
> The court that Joanna abandoned to follow Jesus was known to be decadent. It is unclear whether Joanna was present when Herodias's daughter danced, and Herod was so "moved" by her dancing that he delivered John the Baptist's head on a platter. But the immorality and debauchery of that household would have been her normal milieu before she met Jesus.[27]

Ashcroft also adds that her bilingual capability would have allowed her to move between Aramaic and Hellenistic communities. "With her political savvy, she would have anticipated some of the conflicts within the early community."[28] Elizabeth Watson observes that Joanna was likely better educated than any other female disciple of Jesus.[29] We would add that she was probably better educated than most of his male disciples, too.

Joanna is connected with John the Baptist's head in later tradition, giving it a proper burial when it was separated from John's body and the rest of his corpse was sent to others of John's disciples. It is even possible

25. *Secret History,* season 16 episode 9, "Jesus' Female Disciples: The New Evidence."
26. Bauckham, *Gospel Women,* 150.
27. *Spirited Women,* 38.
28. *Spirited Women,* 38.
29. Watson, *Wisdom's Daughters,* 20.

that Joanna may have been at the dinner described in the Gospels, at which the request for the head of John the Baptist was made.[30] All this has led us to consider the possibility that Joanna may have been at least a sympathizer of John's, and perhaps even a supporter of him as she would later be of Jesus.[31] Tal Ilan draws attention to the experience Herod the Great had of a plot against him by Pheroras in which his wife had been involved, and the wife's connection with and support for the Pharisees.[32] Lucy Fuchs compares Joanna to modern women of means whose husbands are often away and who get involved in supporting charities.[33] Joanna being a supporter of Pharisees, John, and/or Jesus at various points might have made Herod Antipas think of his father's experience, and worried him. That Joanna might have supported the Pharisees is a possibility that should not surprise us.[34] There were certainly Pharisees that were adamantly opposed to both John and Jesus. Not all were, however, and especially when we consider the fact that Joanna had a famous relative who was a Pharisee, her supporting them as well seems likely.[35] On the other hand, as her views changed, it is possible that she shifted her financial support from the Pharisees to John and then Jesus. If she did so, that would have angered further Saul and made him hostile to the Jesus movement from the outset. At one point in Luke (13:31), Jesus is warned by Pharisees that Herod was pursuing him. It is unsurprising that the warning did not come directly from a contact in the household of Herod. We would expect someone in the palace to convey the information through a third party. For all we know, Chuza may have been alive

30. Haag, *Quest*, 30–31. Schottroff, *Let the Oppressed Go Free*, 81 says that powerful women in this era "use their marriage and their husbands for expanding their areas of influence, and they do not flinch at the sight of a chopped-off head of someone who was in their way." Joanna may or may not have been more sensitive generally to executions, but in the scenario we have depicted she was an admirer of John's and would have been bothered by his execution for that reason, perhaps rethinking her own actions, and/or complicity in the brutal actions of others, when seeking power and influence in the past.

31. Note as well that Luke places the question of Jesus's relationship to John, his anointing by a woman, and the mention of his female patrons in close succession (Luke 7–8). Bieberstein, *Verschwiegeneliingerinnen*, 27.

32. Ilan, *Integrating Women*, 24; followed by Bauckham, *Gospel Women*, 161; Spencer, *Salty Wives*, 123.

33. Fuchs, *We Were There*, 61.

34. Haag, *Quest*, 51.

35. Recall how Saul's teacher Gamaliel was more tolerant of the Jesus movement than his student.

at that stage and sent word through the Pharisees. If Joanna was a patron of Pharisees, it would nicely connect these details. She herself may have notified Pharisees who in turn warned Jesus, or as we depict here, they may have come to warn their patroness that she as well as the rabbi she associated with were in danger.[36] Whichever of these was the case, we can say that Jesus learned from and through Joanna not only about the role women can play as patrons of religious movements, but also how useful it can be to have a patron who is well connected to the political arena, especially if one is engaging in activities that are liable to draw undesired attention from such authorities.

It might seem natural to assume that the Latin name Junia was probably not one she adopted while in Galilee or elsewhere in Herod's territory, but only after moving to Rome or elsewhere in the Latin-speaking world. However, even in the New Testament we encounter references to individuals with Latin nicknames living in Judea, including most famously (as well as most relevantly for our current topic) Junia's own relative Saul who also went by the Latin name Paulus.[37] Others include John Mark and Joseph Justus (Acts 1:23).[38] Be that as it may, if anyone might have adopted a Latin name in this part of the world, it was a member of Herod's household.[39] As Bauckham writes, "one of the few circles in which one could find Palestinian Jews bearing Latin names was . . . the Herodian aristocracy of Tiberias."[40]

Was Andronicus another name that Chuza went by, or did Joanna marry again? We have opted for the latter option as more likely for a number of reasons, but we cannot be certain.[41] The name Andronicus is

---

36. Ilan, *Integrating Women* 31–37, discusses the attraction of wealthy women in particular to Pharisaism. Cp. Barker, *Women and the Liberator*, 106.

37. Paul was not from an area where Latin was spoken and yet had a Latin cognomen, just like his relative Junia. This is equally true whether one considers him in relation to his birthplace Tarsus or in relation to Jerusalem.

38. See further Williams, "Alternative Names"; Benjamin, "Study of Latin Words," 9–10.

39. Bauckham, *Gospel Women*, 181–86. See also Epp, *Junia*, 94n23; Pederson, *Lost Apostle*, 239n29.

40. Bauckham, *Gospel Women*, 186. Bauckham finds it impossible to choose between the two options in favor of Junia having already adopted the name in Palestine or having adopted it after relocating to Rome.

41. Amy Peeler suggests that Andronicus was a common slave name, which might imply that Saul's relative ended up in Rome against his will, later being freed. If the name were only popular in that social group, it would seem to be unlikely that Chuza would adopt it. The name is more widely popular, however.

a classical Greek name and quite widespread. At least two of Antiochus IV's emissaries bore this name, but so did the Egyptian Jewish scholar of the 2nd century BCE, Andronicus ben Meshullam. Some connect the presence of Saul's family in Tarsus with the granting of citizenship by Antiochus IV to those who settled there after he annexed it. That potentially answers the question of how a Jewish family of the tribe of Benjamin ended up in Tarsus, with branches that have Roman citizenship, and also with at least one person or family from Tarsus returning to Judea. Nevertheless, given that Antiochus IV conquered Cilicia where Tarsus is located and encouraged people from elsewhere in his territory to settle there, the popularity of the name Andronicus among Antiochus IV's emissaries and its belonging to a relative of Paul is probably not a coincidence. Perhaps this suggests that Andronicus was a cousin of both Saul and Junia who himself had a connection with Tarsus.

Whether Andronicus and Junia were married deserves to be asked. Paul's reference to them sounds like he is referring to a married couple, but also that he is referring to individuals who are his kinfolk. Both could easily be true, since marriage between cousins was common. Perhaps Andronicus had lived in Judea or a neighboring region for a time and heard about Jesus there. He may have relocated to Rome in conjunction with a mission by Peter, fleeing persecution, or for business purposes, among other possibilities. As a relative of Saul's and a follower of Jesus, his presence in a community was liable to attract persecution in their direction, and so he may have been motivated by that fact to leave for Rome, and have connected with Junia there. It is possible that they are relatives who are both unmarried or widowed who share a home but are not married to one another, or even that Paul simply greets them because they are both cousins who were Christians before he was and so it seemed natural to mention them together. According to one significantly later tradition, Andronicus and Junia were among the seventy or seventy-two that Jesus sent out. While we should not make too much of that (everyone famous in the early Christian movement seems to be identified as part of that group at some point in church history), it isn't at all impossible that they may both have lived in Galilee at the same time and been connected with the Jesus movement there, been separated by circumstances, only to meet again in Rome. It is also possible that Chuza may have died and Junia remarried far earlier than my retelling envisages. There is so much we would like to know that we do not. What we can say is that, as Heidi Parales and Michael Haag both note, it is unlikely that Chuza, while still in Herod's household, had his wife traveling with Jesus during the time Herod took a concerned interest in him.[42] Haag thus suggests that, if Junia was Joanna and we find her married in a later time to a different man named Andronicus, "Chuza might have been dead, or he might have divorced Joanna."[43]

Support, Service, and Sponsorship

Joanna is mentioned as part of a group of women who served and supported Jesus's mission. There has been significant debate about what that implies.[44] Richard Bauckham writes,

> Luke is not telling his readers that the women cooked the meals, washed the dishes, and mended the clothes. Perhaps they did (though cf. Luke 9:13; 22:8; John 4:8), but it is not what Luke says ... Thus the true male counterpart to the women's "service," as described in Luke 8:3, is not preaching or leadership but the abandonment of home and family by the twelve (Luke 5:11; 18:28–29) ... Both the men and the women among Jesus' disciples behave in a significantly countercultural way with regard to material resources. But the differing positions of men and women in the society from which they come mean that, perhaps rather surprisingly but entirely intelligibly, it is the women, rather than the men, who have disposable financial resources from which to supply the economic needs of the itinerant group.[45]

Elisabeth Moltmann-Wendel writes of "Joanna, the minister's wife, who had left her husband, King Herod's Minister of Finance, and despite her

---

42. Haag, *Quest*, 51, 70 and Parales, *Hidden Voices*, 39.

43. Haag, *Quest*, 51. If Junia married Andronicus and they both collaborated with Paul, it is unlikely that she simply left her husband, as Ashcroft suggests (*Spirited Women*, 38). Ashcroft offers a somewhat more plausible scenario when she imagines the scene in more detail, as Joanna reflects on the response of the rich young man to Jesus, and tells Chuza they cannot stay where they are and asks him to leave with her. He becomes angry and eventually asks *her* to leave (48–49). However, for all we know, when Joanna appears in the Gospel of Luke she may have already been a widow, and yet still known as the wife of Chuza (Ricci, *Mary Magdalene*, 154; Bauckham, *Gospel Women*, 117, 134–35, 186; Spencer, *Salty Wives*, 110). There is a tradition that Andronicus and Junia brought the Gospel to Pannonia, roughly where the northern part of Serbia is today.

44. See the helpful discussion in Spencer, *Salty Wives*.

45. Bauckham, *Gospel Women*, 114–15.

high status remained with Jesus, the enemy of the state, until his death and then Easter. The early church is unthinkable for Luke without the active, influential and well-to-do women around Jesus."[46]

That at least some of that group of women were involved in supporting Jesus financially seems clear. Did they also subsidize if not directly participate in some of the more practical activities that were considered a woman's role in that culture? Kate Moorehead writes, "Seldom do we consider who fed Jesus." She likens Mary, Joanna, and others to the behind the scenes "tech crew" of Jesus's ministry.[47] Elisabeth Tetlow takes the statement differently. She writes, "Luke characteristically qualified every mention of women by a reference to some negative aspect of their character . . . This is a literary device used throughout the Gospel of Luke to present women as both weak and sinful. Luke also describes the role of the women as providing for Jesus and the Twelve materially. This is likewise a Lukan device, found in a number of passages, to restrict the ministry of women to one of providing financial aid, omitting any reference to women exercising a ministry of proclamation. This passage is found only in the gospel of Luke."[48] Was Luke elevating the women by referring to them "serving" in much the same ways that male disciples also did, or relegating them to typical gender roles by omitting their activity of learning and teaching? These are questions we cannot fully settle in this context. Either way, however, we can recognize Joanna as a leader in a group that, in one form or another, did things that were counter-cultural, even if they also did things that were culturally expected. No one is counter-cultural all the time.

Luke 22:25–27 must surely be influenced by Joanna, and probably others like her. Wealthy women becoming patrons of religious movements was not uncommon. Such women actually joining the movement on the other hand seems to be without parallel.[49] Joanna may not merely "exemplify" what Jesus's teaching looked like when literally put into practice. She may have been its prototype and inspiration. When Jesus made reference to gentile kings considering themselves benefactors while lording it over their subjects, and to himself as serving, he cannot but have thought of Joanna, a woman connected with a royal household,

---

46. Moltmann-Wendel, *Women Around Jesus*, 23. On Chuza as Minister of Finance see also Haag, *Quest*, 51; Parales, *Hidden Voices*, 39; Hansen, *John the Baptizer*, 282.

47. Moorehead, *Healed*, 65–66.

48. Tetlow, *Women and Ministry*, 103.

49. See further Bauckham, *Gospel Women*, 162–65.

who became a benefactor without lording it over the one she supported, and who became actively involved in service in whatever form. Joanna was not only a financial supporter of Jesus. She was also a source of inspiration.

Often it is assumed that women are protected and have less to lose in an honor-shame society than men do, whose every interaction is a sparring match of point-scoring for esteem and relative status. But women were also extremely vulnerable. If wealth and status often shielded women from the worst effects of that, this was not true in Herod's household, in which neither gender nor bonds of blood or marriage made one safe. As Mackall observes, "Joanna probably even risked her life to join the ministry of Jesus."[50] The call to count the cost impacted both men and women, even if at times in different ways in that social setting, just as it did for rich and poor, and those of high or low status. When Jesus referred to the need to weigh the cost before following him, Joanna probably came to mind before anyone else and inspired his understanding of that point, since having more than most of his followers, she had more to lose, and in all likelihood did indeed lose more.

Joanna, Jesus, and Paul

It is difficult not to allow oneself to be totally distracted from the focus of this book by the implication of our study of Joanna that Saul of Tarsus was at most one degree of separation from the historical Jesus. While we must resist the temptation to turn all of our attention to that interesting topic, filling in the implications of this for our understanding of Paul will also enrich our ability to say more about Joanna and Jesus. If we had letters from and knew about the life of famous relatives of other women to whom chapters in this book are dedicated, we'd be able to know more about them and it would ultimately enhance our understanding of what Jesus learned from them. And so, without allowing Paul to become a focus in his own right, adding him into the picture in the background to the connection between Jesus and Joanna allows us to say more about Joanna and about Jesus, which is the point here.

There have been discussions throughout history of whether Paul had met Jesus during the time of his public activity. We are no more able to answer that question in light of this study than anyone before. But in

50. Mackall, *Kindred Sisters*, 116.

light of the considerations in this chapter, we can feel confident that Paul was aware of the Jesus movement, and that his opposition to it was not unconnected to the involvement of his relatives. Even in our time, people who might otherwise merely express disapproval about a religious group they see on the news may become active opponents if their relatives join it. Even if we must leave the implications for our understanding of Paul to one side for the most part, there is a significant extent to which envisaging Paul on the sidelines to the story of Jesus and Joanna genuinely illuminates the question at the heart of our study here. If Joanna was a supporter of Jesus while her relative Saul (connected as a disciple/student to influential figures among the Pharisees) was a detractor, we may appropriately consider this an influence on Jesus's teaching about families being divided on account of him. His followers experienced this, even as we must assume that Jesus himself did. While there is a tendency to group his mother and brothers together, it is more likely that James who came to lead the church in Jerusalem had been a supporter throughout, and likewise his mother, while others may have been opposed to or at least unsure what to make of his activities and public statements. The experience of a very early supporter like Joanna facing challenges from both her blood relatives and perhaps also her husband and his family (not to mention Herod) would have been influential on Jesus's thinking as he developed his own self-understanding.

Paul speaks of having been zealous for the ancestral traditions, and when he came to believe that Jesus was the anointed one of the line of David, he quickly understood it to include a welcome for non-Jews. It is not far-fetched to imagine Paul having been indignant about his relative Joanna's marriage to a Nabataean, and to have opposed a movement that welcomed her without challenging her on this point.[51] Indeed, if Paul had understood the movement that viewed Jesus as the Messiah to be too lax about such matters, his reversal would have immediately conveyed to him that he was wrong about this just as he was about Jesus. In a sense, Joanna becomes the bridge between the good news that Jesus proclaimed, focused on Israel, and Paul's broadening of the audience

---

51. Jews in Paul's time may have viewed Nabataeans as descendants of Ishmael and thus as distant kin, although not heirs to the promise. This is a complex question, and no matter how one views the matter Paul may still have been zealous about Jewish/Israelite identity in a narrower sense. It is intriguing to consider that his family connections to Ishmael might have played a role in his formulation of his argument about Isaac and Ishmael in Galatians.

to include non-Jews. Just as Samaritans responding to Jesus opened up the question of non-Jewish Israelites becoming part of the movement, a follower of Jesus who was of the tribe of Benjamin being married to a Nabataean, who was thus at best an Ishmaelite, a descendant of Abraham but not of Isaac and Jacob/Israel, opened the door for a still broader inclusivity, one that pushed at the boundaries of the Mosaic covenant even if it could still be encompassed within the realm of the descendants of Abraham. When Paul formulated his case for including gentiles in the children of God in terms of descent from Abraham (Gal 3–4; Rom 4 as well as Rom 11:1) he may have had his own family in mind. Indeed, his emphasis on his Benjamite identity may hint that he recognized his own outsider status in relation to Judah and Judaism. Benjamin had famously aligned itself with Judah in the great schism with the northern tribes. But the retention of a Benjamite identity and the bestowal of the name Saul, the king of Israel from the tribe of Benjamin who was replaced by David of the tribe of Judah, suggests something in Paul's background and heritage that preserved a sense of belonging to something larger. Joanna's involvement with a movement that sought to embody that "something larger," and her marriage that went beyond the bounds of Israel, offended Paul in the identity he sought within Judaism. His reversal to accept the messiahship of the one who had accepted and been accepted by Joanna was the catalyst for everything else he came to realize. While this isn't something that Jesus learned from Joanna during his lifetime, Jesus's interaction with Joanna indicates that he learned some of these important points from and through her, as well as laying the groundwork for future followers to learn still more and take things even further in the direction of greater inclusivity. That is one of the beautiful things about studying what Jesus learned from women. It shows us not only a Jesus who learned, and who learned from women, but a Jesus who did not object to others learning still further things beyond what he himself taught them. "Whoever is not against us is for us" (Mark 9:40). This aspect of what Jesus taught and exemplified to his disciples influences the trajectory that Christianity follows, both initially and down to the present day, even if it doesn't always or consistently characterize the followers of Jesus ancient or modern.

When we think about it, it becomes obvious how ridiculous it is to imagine that Saul first heard about the movement that would later be called Christianity around the time of Stephen's martyrdom. The only people I have encountered who seem adamant about this are fringe internet voices eager to deny that there even was a historical Jesus, despite what historians conclude about the matter. Even without the connection to a relative who was part of the Jesus movement before him, it would be unimaginable that Paul suddenly hears information about Jesus for the first time after he becomes a follower, or right in the moment he gets more actively involved in persecuting the movement. Knowing that he had relatives who preceded him makes it all the more so.

Including and Addressing Women Directly

Sara Parks has shown that Jesus was distinctive in telling stories that feature gender pairings, in other words, a story with a male central character being coupled with one with a female central character.[52] There is obviously no way of knowing whether Joanna was someone who talked with Jesus about this. What seems clear is that Jesus must have listened to women, heard their perspective on how stories that focused exclusively on male experience failed to speak to them or connect with them as powerfully as stories about women could. This is undoubtedly an example of something that Jesus learned from women. We don't know who he learned it from, and it was likely from more than one person. But it may have taken a woman who had married into a culture which some evidence suggests was more egalitarian, and who as a woman of status also may have had greater freedom as well as experience of speaking her mind, to come right out and say this to him.[53]

Conclusion

As I mentioned at the start of this chapter, there are several reasons why I initially resisted the idea that Joanna and Junia might be the same person. One was a desire not to reduce the number of women who played an important role in the early Christian movement. Another that I did not mention there is my experience of fictional franchises (you may be able to guess which one in particular I have in mind) in which attention is turned in prequels and fanfiction to the backstories of main characters. Often when this is done, it turns out that many of them intersected and

---

52. Parks, *Gender in the Rhetoric of Jesus*, 2.

53. On women among the Nabataeans, especially during this time period, see Alzoubi et al., "Woman in the Nabataean Society."

knew each other previously, even though there was no hint of this in the earliest stories we were told about them, and even though the characters were spread across an entire galaxy. The odds against their having all been previously connected in this way are quite literally astronomical, but you should never tell me the odds. (Okay, yes, I'm talking about Star Wars.) In an ancient village or town, on the other hand, people were inevitably connected, and even in a very large ancient city, the likelihood of people knowing one another was much higher than in most urban settings in our time. The population of Jerusalem in Jesus's time was in the tens of thousands, not the millions one associates with modern cities. People also relied on family and other social connections when they traveled, rather than checking into a hotel as we might do today. This required awareness and maintenance of relationships over long distances. And so what seem like improbable connections between people from our perspective would have been typical and expected in the first century. By resisting the possibility that many characters in the Gospels and other New Testament literature might have known one another previously or been related, I was imposing my own time and its assumptions on a very different world.

Ultimately the question of whether Joanna and Junia were the same person, while it affords us ways of fleshing out Joanna's story and reconstructing her personality, does not change the answer to the question of whether Jesus learned from her, and if so what. She was an influential person who experienced the cost of siding with Jesus. Jesus got to see precisely how much influential people were in a position to contribute to his ministry. And he got to see precisely how much it could cost them. Joanna is the first person of that sort of social status that we learn became part of Jesus's movement. When Jesus later told others they would need to count the cost of following him, that their families would be divided, he undoubtedly had the pioneering experiences of Joanna and others like her particularly in mind.

There is no one else that we are told Jesus knew or had within his movement that connected him to Herod's household in this way. We can be certain he learned things from Joanna that he could not learn from anyone else he knew. Consider what we know about her as we draw together the many points in her biography that we have explored in this chapter. Connected with the household of Herod. Married to a Nabataean. Connected to John the Baptist and subsequently to Jesus. Sponsor of the activity of Jesus. Related to Paul. Able to relocate to Rome. Joanna/

Junia was clearly one of the most influential figures in the Jesus movement and related strands of Judaism, and yet like so many women in an ancient patriarchal context, most of the things we would like to and ought to know about her are obscured from our view.

Those who undertake genealogical research know the importance searching laterally from our own lineage can have. One may hit a dead end in the records, but later be able to find a sibling or cousin that allows progress to continue. In other cases, the addition of other family members may simply add detail to our understanding of the family as a whole of which our ancestral lineage was a part. Adding Joanna not only adds to our understanding of Paul the Apostle, and vice versa, but both then enrich our understanding of Jesus and his impact as well as their impact on him. Those who do family history research also know the challenges involved in finding information about—and often even simply finding—female ancestors. By definition each of us has as many female as male ancestors, and yet family names of males have historically been preserved while those of their wives have been obliterated. Joanna is a similar case, inasmuch as we are informed about her in relation to her husband Chuza and then in relation to Andronicus and Paul. Yet we have seen her come into focus here as someone deserving of attention in her own right. The little we know about her not only enriches our understanding of the historical Jesus, but more specifically of what he learned from this influential woman who, in a different time and place, we would expect to be able to learn far more about.

Conclusion

What Jesus Learned from Women

Hopefully it has become clear over the course of this book's exploration of what Jesus learned from women that this in no way denigrates him, unless one views him as not having been an actual human being. In many respects, we have seen that Jesus's attention to his female contemporaries' life experiences and stories makes him quite remarkable for his time. It is of course true that it would have been better had this not been the case—in other words, if listening to and learning from women were not the exception but the rule. In our era in which discussions of feminism and toxic masculinity are to the fore, with Christian denominations often a battleground between radically divergent viewpoints all of which appeal to Jesus in support of their stance, the relevance of a book on this subject is hopefully clear. But we should not simply leave it to others to explore those further ramifications for subjects ranging from Christology to church leadership. Even if briefly, it seems appropriate to conclude this book with a few reflections on what we have learned from what Jesus learned from women, and where we might go from here.

When it comes to Christology, it is definitely worth reiterating the point we have already made, namely that we must choose between a Jesus who learned as other human beings do, and a Jesus who was not in fact genuinely human. There is no way to be human and bypass all the ways that others mentor and influence us. For some Christologies (i.e. theological views of the person of Jesus), this will require changes, whether minor adjustments or radical revisions. But the view of Jesus as a genuine person who learned is embedded in our earliest Christian writings about him, and so it is fully compatible with a view of Jesus as theologically important. One avenue that merits further exploration is Paul's language of Jesus as the second Adam. This idea was popular in the early church (Irenaeus in particular made it central to his thinking), but is less of a focus today (unless one counts using Paul's language about Adam and Christ as a prooftext in dubious ways in relation to the biological sciences). Paul's view, in a nutshell, is not that Jesus was something other than human, but that he "did the human being thing" the way we all ideally could and should. This way of characterizing Jesus might be judged a theological framework that Paul and then others brought to Jesus and imposed upon him. But in light of our study, we should perhaps ask whether this way of viewing Jesus might not have been influenced by the impression Jesus made, and not merely imposed on him as a theological dogma. In rabbinic tradition, Adam is sometimes viewed as having been originally created as both male and female. Jesus being more balanced with respect to gender may have led to his depiction as second Adam, as ideal human being, rather than the latter simply being a template imposed on him.

It is nevertheless clear from our study that Jesus was not an abstract idealized human being but a *man* in a patriarchal context. If our study shows him to have been more open to learning from women than some of his contemporaries, it does not provide a basis for claiming that he was more open than anyone else, much less than that he was not a gendered human being like others but say perfectly on the balance point between male and female. Rather, the evidence shows him as a figure that we might be able to speak of not as idealized human being but as nonetheless an ideal man, a figure whose masculine identity in a patriarchal context did not keep him from being willing to transgress assigned gender norms and challenge accepted conventions in the interest of a profound concern for justice. That may not make Jesus the unique figure that some theological systems are compelled to make him out to be. But it makes him a figure whose human existence we can take as a pattern and seek to emulate, as Paul in his letters encourages us to do.[1]

What the Historical Jesus Learned from Women

As we indicated from the outset, an effort to listen to voices that have not been fully allowed to be heard in our extant sources, and ask about their

1. On Jesus as intersex see Kateusz, "Jesus Woman."

influence on Jesus, must involve a significant amount of creative filling in of gaps. We have sought to do so throughout this volume both at the literary level, in ways that do justice to what we are told in stories about Jesus, as well as at the historical level, exploring what the real events might have been like that lay behind and gave rise to those stories. As we look back on these individual efforts to present interpretations that are plausible, and (when the evidence has allowed us to do so) historical reconstructions that are indeed probable, a pattern emerges that should lead us to draw some broader conclusions that relate to the theme of this book and the quest for the historical Jesus. In order to see a Jesus who learned, whose thinking and teaching developed in response to transformative encounters with women (as well as with men), it was not necessary to force the material into a predetermined framework. We simply had to look for this Jesus, and he emerged readily from the stories and came into view. That this is so is important, since none of the Gospels shows any indication of having been seeking to convey this. From the perspective of the historian, when sources record elements consistently despite these not having been emphases of their authors, that suggests such things were already part of the tradition the authors were drawing on. That brings us closer to their source, with increasing likelihood of historicity. One criterion that historical scholars have often applied is the criterion of multiple attestation. In other words, when major themes or specific stories appear in independent testimonies, and in different kinds of material, those are more likely to be historical, for the simple and perhaps obvious reason that this perception of Jesus must have been early, widespread, and already largely taken for granted. That Jesus learned from women fits this criterion, as do some of the specific things that he learned from women. This adds an intriguing possibility of adding a new principle to historians' criteria of evidence. If the sources suggest a pattern of openness to learning, whether from specific individuals, categories of people, or in general, it may perhaps offer support not only for the historicity of this learning process, but also of the things so learned. This is especially true in the case of Jesus (and other figures) some of whose disciples wished to emphasize that he knows all things (see, e.g., John 16:30). This is a theme that cuts against the grain of what some Gospel authors were interested in emphasizing, and yet it emerges as soon as we look for it.

That it emerges so readily from these texts, and yet has not been systematically studied, should give us reason to pause and reflect. The quest for the historical Jesus has been going on for centuries. There is only one explanation for the fact that this aspect of Jesus's life has been given so little attention. Scholars have not asked these questions in any systematic and sustained way, if they have done so at all. We have looked for Jesus, but we have not looked for a Jesus who learned from women. This is certainly a reason for collective embarrassment, shame, and repentance on the part of the academic community. Explanations for this neglect readily present themselves. Academic study was largely carried out by men until relatively recently, and the sources being studied were written by men who did not draw attention to these aspects of Jesus's life. The view of Jesus as divine and thus above the need to learn also impacted scholarship, even among those who did not share an allegiance to the historic creeds of Christendom. But these are explanations and not *excuses*. In offering this study, I confess my own failure to pay attention to these questions and the relevant details in the Gospels until recently. What I have discovered now that I have done so has been genuinely exciting, and I hope that readers will find themselves motivated to continue this line of investigation, thinking about Jesus as one who learned as well as taught, and paying attention to those women he learned from and what they taught him.

In calling for collective repentance and a new direction on the part of the academy, I must recognize that there have been exceptions, and that for the most part they have been women themselves. To offer but one example, Esther de Boer writes, "There are also stories from which it emerges that Jesus knows the world of women's experience from the inside and takes it seriously."[2] Sometimes female scholars have repeated interpretations and followed the directions of previous male-dominated scholarship. Even more often, male scholars have failed to listen to and learn from female colleagues who noticed and understood aspects of stories that they did not. As I worked on this book, no special effort was needed in order to ensure that women were well-represented in the bibliography. Indeed, I think I can say that this book would have been the same in essence if the only works consulted had been those of female authors. To be sure, there are countless ways in which those female academics have drawn and built upon what male as well as female scholars wrote in the past. My point here is simply to highlight a case in which it seems appropriate for academics who study Jesus to ask *what would Jesus do?* One answer that must now be added to the many other possible

---

2. Boer, *Mary Magdalene*, 36.

answers to that question is that he would learn from women. Go and do thou likewise. Reading both male and female scholars as they wrote about the stories in the Gospels that have been our focus in this book, it was often glaringly obvious where male scholars of the past had failed to follow Jesus's example in this regard, and this was very clearly to the detriment of their understanding of the Gospels and of Jesus.

Also worthy of further exploration is the question of what male role models Jesus had and how they may have helped him understand himself as a male in a way that fostered his openness to listening to women and valuing their perspectives. It was not only from women, we may presume, that Jesus learned to learn from women. This is important not only for a well-rounded historical portrait and understanding of Jesus, but also as an oft-neglected other side of the coin of feminist and gender studies endeavors in the present day. The ongoing influence and dominance of patriarchy can be seen in the fact that so often discussions of women's equality and gender are simply assumed to be discussions about, by, and for women, with men and maleness treated as a default that doesn't call for study in the same way. (The same point needs to be made about the relative neglect of the study of whiteness as an ethnic identity, showing the persistence of the treatment of that as the unquestioned norm and default category over against which ethnic identities are judged by their difference.)

Ultimately this book intersects with multiple research interests of mine, multiple identities, and multiple contexts. It relates to what I do as an academic researcher and writer, as a classroom educator at a university, in my Sunday school class, and in my home. It is impacted by my own experience of communities, relationships, my own gender identity, and countless other things. It embodies my interest in the Gospels as literature and as history, with the division between those interests blurring in ways that I wish to argue are profoundly appropriate. I hope that this book can be considered an attempt to exemplify what a contemporary approach to historical reconstruction might look like if it takes seriously the critique of the older way of doing things, that tried to treat individual sayings and stories on their own, to cut away all layers of theological and other kinds of interpretation to get a historical core. The stories surveyed in this book never give us "just the facts." Some may not give us the facts at all, and yet may still be ripples of the historical impact of Jesus, and the impact the women he knew had upon him.

"And What More Shall I Say?"

After surveying a number of examples of faith, Hebrews 11 offers a very succinct list of others that time prevented the author from elaborating on. Given how much more we said about each individual in this book than the author of the letter to the Hebrews did, in this brief overview of still other women in the life of Jesus we can do more than merely list them, even if we cannot devote full chapters to them.

We would love to be able to tell the stories of Jesus's sisters. So little is said about them. His brothers are named, while his sisters are not. And yet just as it was safe to assume that Jesus learned from his mother and his grandmother, his sisters were absolutely among his teachers. We could easily envisage some concrete stories and scenarios simply by drawing on what, in rare instances, ancient authors have said about sisters. Peter's mother-in-law also deserves attention. Jesus's healing of her may have been one of his first. She is also the first woman we are told is healed by Jesus and who responds by meeting the needs of Jesus and his followers in some way. Peter's wife and the wives of his other disciples would also be fascinating to hear more about in terms of their impact on Jesus. They'd be fascinating to hear more about, period. And what might Jesus have learned from brief encounters, such as the woman who exclaimed from the crowd, "Blessed the womb that bore you and the breasts at which you nursed!" (Luke 11:27)?

The woman who is described as "bent" is another one we wish we could say more about than we will here (Luke 13:10–17). Women often suffered malnutrition due to giving their children food at their own expense, and this took a toll on them physically, sometimes in the form of medical conditions that are plausible candidates for what this woman was suffering from.[3] Ana Hernandez and Turid Seim both note a connection between Luke's reference to the woman as a "daughter of Abraham" and 4 Macc 15:28 and 18:20 (see also 14:20 and 17:6).[4] There the woman so designated is a heroic mother who suffers because her sons are martyred. While we can only guess the sacrifices of the woman Jesus referred to in this way, he was choosing a phrase that probably already had connotations of heroism for the Jewish people and faith. Yet we should not assume that the bent woman also had experienced martyrdom of her sons.

---

3. See Driscoll, *Reading Between The Lines*, 62–67 who explores the difficult life of a woman with a humpback from childhood.

4. Hernandez, "Las mujerescomoportadoras," 106; Seim, *Double Message*, 43–57.

On the contrary, he may be indicating through the phrase that sacrifices made by mothers that are less appreciated in a patriarchal culture, being thought of as less masculine, are equally heroic. If Jesus had healed a male war veteran of a battle injury on the Sabbath, there might still have been disapproval, but it would not have been voiced. Not in the same way, at any rate. They wouldn't have dared complain about this act on behalf of a hero appreciated by the community. The language Jesus used said that she was a valiant hero wounded in battle as well, the struggle to raise another generation of Abraham's descendants.[5] Jesus had not only learned from women about the different ways men and women were treated, but also the unfair differences in how the contributions of men and women to society were valued or undervalued.

Megan Mckenna draws attention to the way that the woman's situation was blamed on a demon.[6] This could easily have been a way for the community to shift blame from the quite literally backbreaking work the woman had to do because of her socioeconomic place in the community. Paul, saying that people in churches must bear one another's burdens, ultimately derived that emphasis from Jesus. Jesus learned it from women like this one. It was prohibited to carry a burden on the Sabbath. Yet this woman was forced to carry a burden that Satan imposed on her every day without rest. It could be argued that the synagogue leader who objected to Jesus alleviating her of this burden was, in essence, in favor of her being forced to continue to carry her burden on the Sabbath. He was making the Sabbath itself a burden, when it was supposed to be a time of relief from work and for laying down one's burdens. Seeing and learning from her situation undoubtedly helped Jesus formulate his view that the Sabbath was made for human beings rather than vice versa. When she is healed, she is said to be *freed*, the only instance in which the word is used of healing in the New Testament.[7] In how many instances do we lack the context in the life of Jesus that would indicate where particular

---

5. Watson, *Wisdom's Daughters* 73–81, tells the story powerfully across multiple generations, since rheumatoid arthritis tends to run in families. Her telling even features singing in the synagogue in response to the woman's healing! She also notes (80) Jesus calling the woman to come to him in the men's section. "He must have realized that 'separate but equal' space in the synagogue is oppressive to women" (81). Luke says Jesus was teaching, however, and so we would presume him to be at the front. Moreover, Brooten disputes the existence of a separate gallery for women in this period based on the archaeological record (*Women Leaders*, 103–38).

6. Mckenna, *Not Counting Women and Children*, 52–53.

7. Barker, *Women and the Liberator*, 71.

experiences, including but not limited to interactions with women, contributed to Jesus's formulation of his teaching in the memorable form we hear it? If the author of the Gospel had made a different choice, giving us Luke 14:5 in that context but not 13:15 in its context, we would never have known this woman's impact on Jesus. Even so, we wish we knew more.

We didn't feel we had enough to explore this woman's story for an entire chapter, but it deserved to be told somewhere. There are still others about whom we wish we had more information to allow us to connect the dots. Some identify Salome as the wife of Zebedee, which would mean that John and James's mother sometimes traveled with the group.[8] We have no stories from or about prostitutes, at least none explicitly identified as such. Yet there is a longstanding impression Jesus was to be found in the company of "prostitutes and tax collectors." Perhaps "whores" was just an insulting label others placed on the women who surrounded Jesus, precisely because they spent time with and even traveled with him in ways that some felt was inappropriate? But he may have listened to the stories of actual sex workers and discovered that they were victims of economic hardship rather than wanton and lascivious seekers of sexual pleasure, deserving of kindness and not contempt. Economic realities in an ancient patriarchal context forced women to resort to sex work who would not have chosen this path without such constraints. Men were their customers, the male-dominated society often forced women into that profession, and at the same time men denigrated those women for what they did. Even listening to women who were not prostitutes (despite the way their stories have sometimes been told by male interpreters) could have prepared Jesus to see the situation of prostitutes more clearly, as people who were the victims many times over of the male-dominated society they lived in, and who were blamed in ways that added insult to injury (often in a literal as well as the figurative sense of that phrase). To this list should also be added the women who appear in Jewish Scriptures and storytelling from whom Jesus learned. We have seen this on occasion

---

8. See further Driscoll, *Reading Between the Lines*, 43–47; Moltmann-Wendel, *Women Around Jesus*, 120–27. Coffey, *Hidden Women*, 103–8 explores Salome's perspective and the motivation for her famous request to Jesus on behalf of her sons. In the *Secret History* season 16 episode 9 documentary "Jesus' Female Disciples: The New Evidence," Helen Bond and Joan Taylor highlight the chapel dedicated to Salome, together with the possibility that Jesus sent out apostles "two by two" in male-female pairs, since someone of one gender baptizing or anointing the other for healing would be deemed inappropriate.

in the chapters of this book, but there can be little doubt that Jesus also learned from other stories than those we considered there. Putting all these influences on Jesus through living contact, observation, and story together we can say, as Bonnie Ring puts it, "Some of these women are the only figures in the Gospels to change the mind of Jesus. Though resistant at first, he becomes receptive to opinions that differ from his own."[9] Jesus was indebted to them, and that means everyone who is indebted to Jesus owes them a debt of gratitude as well.

We borrowed a phrase from the letter to the Hebrews as we began this section. But unlike the list almost entirely of *men* whose faith that author highlights, here we do not end by saying that there are too many to name, too many to mention. Instead, it seems more appropriate to emphasize here at the end of this study that there are too many women in the life of Jesus who are not named even though they are mentioned, and too many again who must have been present and yet who were never mentioned at all. Hebrews 11 illustrates the challenge our sources confront us with. Seriously, can you believe that it mentions Barak but not Deborah and Jael? Women were ignored, neglected, and marginalized in the ancient world in countless ways, including but not at all limited to whom and what male authors chose to write about or not write about. Women were omitted even when it would have been perfectly natural and should have been obvious to include them, even if an author was not interested in inclusion and representation. This continues today, in a variety of ways that sometimes are very similar to what one sees in antiquity, while at others look very different.

It is appropriate to feel anger about this, not only from the perspective of feminist concerns, but also from that of a historian. The silencing of women and the exclusion of their stories from what was written is the equivalent of the burning of the library of Alexandria. Valuable historical knowledge has been lost that we will never recover, which we'll never get the slightest hint or gist of. In light of my exploration in this book, I genuinely believe that Jesus was angry about this in his time. We see him angry on a number of occasions, including several involving how women were treated. In his teaching and his example, we also learn about how he approached anger and taught his disciples to manage theirs. Did women help Jesus learn that it is not only OK, but appropriate, to be angry at times, especially as a response to injustice? Did they help him discover

---

9. Ring, *Women Who Knew Jesus*, 234.

positive ways to channel such anger rather than either stifling it or acting violently and destructively, being much more experienced in doing so? Notice who some of the other key nonviolent but not passive activists for justice and social change have been. Mohandas Gandhi and Martin Luther King Jr. were both victims of oppression and yet at the same time had opportunities for education that most others alongside them did not have. The women in Jesus's life collectively had similar situations. Jesus clearly learned enough from them to feel angry about what they were subjected to. He may well also have learned from the ways they found to challenge and push back at the status quo without simply lashing out or becoming bitter. It is of course telling that our minds so readily turn to Martin Luther King Jr. as an example, sometimes neglecting to note the influence of Mary Louise Smith, Claudette Colvin, and Rosa Parks on him.

As I worked on this book, I was struck time and time again by how frequently I read interpretations of the stories of women who met Jesus that are filled with details that are historically, culturally, and/or practically implausible. Some of that is due to a failure to try to narrate their stories, at least partly due to a methodological divide between historical reconstruction and narration. The paucity of detail in the sources is also often a barrier, or an excuse, that has led to them not receiving the attention they deserve. As I explored them, I found the stories of these women to come alive and suggest all sorts of historical and narrative possibilities far beyond what was directly related to the central theme of this book. There is far more that could be and deserves to be written about them than has been, or than I have been able to here. As Sara Parks puts it, we miss a lot even about the male-focused and male-dominated stories in ancient sources, and about this literature as a whole, when we neglect female-focused questions and approaches.[10]

In pondering how to conclude this study, it struck me forcefully that Jesus continued to learn things from women right up to the end. The earliest Gospels say that only women remain with Jesus even through his crucifixion.[11] Jesus learned one last thing from women right before he died, as he gazed upon their faithful presence there in the crowd. He learned that his recognition of their leadership abilities and confidence in them had not at all been misplaced. It is my hope that through this book, more of Jesus's followers today will learn this as well.

10. Parks, *Gender*, 8, 151–52.
11. Swidler, *Jesus Was a Feminist*, 79.

Bibliography

Adam, Betty Conrad. *The Magdalene Mystique: Living the Spirituality of Mary Today*. Harrisburg: Morehouse, 2006.

Aernie, Jeffrey W. *Narrative Discipleship: Portraits of Women in the Gospel of Mark*. Eugene, OR: Pickwick, 2018.

Agosto, Efrain. *Servant Leadership: Jesus and Paul*. St. Louis: Chalice, 2005.

Aitken, Ellen B. "At the Well of Living Water: Jacob Traditions in John 4." In *The Interpretation of Scripture in Early Judaism and Christianity: Studies in Language and Tradition*, edited by Craig A. Evans, 342–52. London: Bloomsbury, 2000.

Aletti, Jean-Noël. "Analyse narrative de Mc 7,24–30. Difficultés et propositions." *Biblica* 93 (2012) 357–76.

Alonso, Pablo. *The Woman Who Changed Jesus: Crossing Boundaries in Mk 7,24–30*. Leuven: Peeters, 2011.

Alzoubi, Mahdi, et al. "Woman in the Nabataean Society." *Mediterranean Archaeology and Archaeometry* 13 (2013) 153–60.

Andrade, Nathanael J. *Syrian Identity in the Greco-Roman World*. Cambridge: Cambridge University Press, 2013.

Arcari, Luca, "Which Messiah for Women? Jewish Messianisms and Early Christologies from the Perspective of Gender." In *Gospels: Narrative and History*, edited by Mercedes Navarro Puerto et al., 97–120. Atlanta: Society of Biblical Literature, 2005.

Arias, Juan. *La Magdalena: El último tabú del cristianismo*. Buenos Aires: Aguilar, 2005.

Arnal, William E. "Gendered Couplets in Q and Legal Formulations: From the Rhetoric to Social History." *JBL* 116 (1997) 75–94.

Ashcroft, Mary Ellen. *Spirited Women Encountering the First Women Believers*. Minneapolis: Augsburg Fortress, 2000.

Ashley, Edith. "Women in Luke's Gospel." MA thesis, University of Sydney, March 2000. https://ses.library.usyd.edu.au/handle/2123/804.

Asikainen, Susanna. "Women out of Place: The Women Who Challenged Jesus." *Neotestamentica* 52 (2018) 179–93.

Athans, Mary Christine. *In Quest of the Jewish Mary: The Mother of Jesus in History, Theology, and Spirituality*. Maryknoll, NY: Orbis, 2013.

Atwood, Richard. *Mary Magdalene in the New Testament Gospels and Early Tradition*. Bern: Peter Lang, 1993.

Augé, Christian. "The Nabataean Age (4th century BC–1st century AD)." In *Atlas of Jordan: History, Territories and Society*, edited by Myriam Ababsa, 142–50. Beirut: Presses de l'Institut Français du Proche-Orient, 2013.

Aviam, Mordechai. "The Decorated Stone from the Synagogue at Migdal: A Holistic Interpretation and a Glimpse into the Life of Galilean Jews at the Time of Jesus." *NovT* 55 (2013) 205–20.

Badet, R. P. *Jésus et les femmes dans l'Évangile.* Paris: Delhomme et Briguet, 1895.

Bailey, Kenneth E. *Jesus Through Middle Eastern Eyes: Cultural Studies in the Gospels.* Downers Grove, IL: Intervarsity, 2008.

Bain, Katherine. *Women's Socioeconomic Status and Religious Leadership in Asia Minor in the First Two Centuries C.E.* Minneapolis: Fortress, 2014.

Baker, Cynthia M. *Rebuilding the House of Israel: Architectures of Gender in Jewish Antiquity.* Stanford: Stanford University Press, 2002.

Balstrup, Sarah K. "Interpreting the Lost Gospel of Mary: Feminist Reconstructions and Myth Making." *Literature and Aesthetics* 25 (2015) 7–22.

Bar-Ilan, Meir. *Some Jewish Women in Antiquity.* Atlanta: Scholars, 2020.

Barker, Katherine Helen. "The Perception of Women in Late Antiquity and the Impact It Had on Female Asceticism." MA thesis, University of Wales, Trinity St. David, 2014.

Barker, William P. *Women and the Liberator.* Old Tappan: Fleming H. Revell, 1972.

Barreau, Jean-Claude. *Les Mémoires de Jésus.* Paris: Jean-Claude Lattès, 1978.

Bashaw, Jennifer Garcia. "'When Jesus Saw Her . . .': A Hermeneutical Response to #MeToo and #ChurchToo." *Review and Expositor* 117 (2020) 288–97.

Batey, Richard A. *Jesus and the Forgotten City: New Light on Sepphoris and the Urban World of Jesus.* Grand Rapids: Baker, 1991.

Batten, Alicia. "More Queries for Q: Women and Christian Origins." *BTB* 24 (1994) 44–51.

Bauckham, Richard. *Gospel Women: Studies of the Named Women in the Gospels.* Grand Rapids: Eerdmans, 2002.

———, ed. *Magdala of Galilee: A Jewish City in the Hellenistic and Roman Period.* Waco, TX: Baylor, 2018.

Bauks, Michaela, et al., eds. *Gender and Social Norms in Ancient Israel, Early Judaism and Early Christianity: Texts and Material Culture.* Gottingen: Vandenhoeck & Ruprecht, 2019.

Bayler, Robbie Munn. *Manaen: Prophet to the King.* Mustang, OK: Tate, 2009.

Baynes, Leslie. "The Parables of Enoch and Luke's Parable of the Rich Man and Lazarus." In *Enoch and the Synoptic Gospels: Reminiscences, Allusions, Intertextuality,* edited by Loren T. Stuckenbruck and Gabriele Boccaccini, 129–51. Atlanta: Scholars, 2016.

Bazzell, Pascal D. "A Marginal Asian Reading of Mark 7:24–30. An Interfaith Filipino Homeless Community's Encounter with the Syrophoenician Woman." In *Pathways for Interreligious Dialogue in the Twenty-First Century,* edited by Vladimir Latinovic et al., 231–43. London: Palgrave Macmillan, 2016.

Beattie, Tina. "Discipleship of Love: Mary of Bethany and the Ministry of Women." *The Month* (May 1997) 171–75.

Beattie, Tina. *The Last Supper according to Martha and Mary.* New York: Crossroad, 2001.

Beavis, Mary Ann L. "The Deification of Mary Magdalene." *Feminist Theology* 21 (2013) 145–54.

———. *The Lost Coin: Parables of Women, Work, and Wisdom.* Sheffield: Sheffield Academic Press, 2002.

———. "Mary of Bethany and the Hermeneutics of Remembrance." *CBQ* 75 (2013) 739–55.
———. "Reconsidering Mary of Bethany." *CBQ* 74 (2012) 281–97.
———. "Who is Mary Magdalene?" In *Women in the Bible*, 23–29. Waco, TX: The Center for Christian Ethics at Baylor University, 2013.
Beavis, Mary Ann, and Ally Kateusz, eds. *Rediscovering the Marys: Maria, Mariamne, Miriam.* London: Bloomsbury T. & T. Clark, 2010.
Beirne, Margaret. *Women and Men in the Fourth Gospel: A Genuine Discipleship of Equals.* JSNTSup 242. Sheffield Academic Press, 2003.
Ben-Eliyahu, Eyal. *Identity and Territory: Jewish Perceptions of Space in Antiquity.* Oakland: University of California Press, 2019.
Benjamin, Esther Laverne. "A Study of Latin Words in the Greek New Testament." MA thesis, Butler University, 1949. https://digitalcommons.butler.edu/grtheses/427.
Bennett, Judith M. *History Matters: Patriarchy and the Challenge of Feminism.* Philadelphia: University of Pennsylvania Press, 2010.
Berkowitz, Beth A. *Execution and Invention: Death Penalty Discourse in Early Rabbinic and Christian Cultures.* Oxford: Oxford University Press, 2006.
Bernabé Ubieta, Carmen. *Con ellas tras Jesús. Mujeres modelos de identidad Cristiana.* Estella: Verbo Divino, 2011.
———. *María Magdalena. Tradiciones en el Cristianismo Primitivo.* Estella: Verbo Divino, 1994.
———. "Mary Magdalene and the Seven Demons in Social-scientific Perspective." In *Transformative Encounters: Jesus and Women Re-viewed*, edited by Ingrid Rosa Kitzberger, 203–23. Leiden: E. J. Brill, 2000.
———. "Relevancia de la memoria de María Magdalena como testigo y apóstol." *Cuestiones Teológicas* 41 (2014) 279–306.
———. *Qué se sabe de . . . María Magdalena.* Estella: Verbo Divino, 2020.
Betsworth, Sharon. *The Reign of God is Such as These: A Socio-Literary Analysis of Daughters in the Gospel of Mark.* London: T. & T. Clark, 2010.
Bieberstein, Sabine. *Verschwiegene Jüngerinnen-vergessene Zeuginnen. Gebrochene Konzepte im Lukasevangelium.* Freiburg: Vandenhoeck & Ruprecht, 1998.
Bilu, Yoram. "The Moroccan Demon in Israel: The Case of 'Evil Spirit Disease.'" *Ethos* 8 (1980) 24–39.
Binz, Stephen J. *Women of the Gospels.* Grand Rapids: Brazos, 2011.
Bird, Jennifer Grace, *Permission Granted: Take the Bible Into Your Own Hands.* Louisville: Wesminster John Knox, 2015.
Black, David Alan, and Jacob N. Cerone, eds. *The Pericope of the Adulteress in Contemporary Research.* London: Bloomsbury, 2016.
Blacker, Jean, et al. *Wace, The Hagiographical Works: The Conception Nostre Dame and the Lives of St Margaret and St Nicholas.* Leiden: E. J. Brill, 2013.
Bloch, René. "Part of the Scene: Jewish Theater in Antiquity." *Journal of Ancient Judaism* 8 (2017) 150–69.
Bloomer, W. Martin, ed. *A Companion to Ancient Education.* Hoboken, NJ: John Wiley & Sons, 2015.
Blue, Debbie. *Consider the Women. A Provocative Guide to Three Matriarchs of the Bible.* Grand Rapids: Eerdmans, 2019.
Blundell, Sue. *Women in Ancient Greece.* Cambridge, MA: Harvard University Press, 1995.

Bock, Darrell L., and James H. Charlesworth, eds. *The Parables of Enoch: A Paradigm Shift*. London: Bloomsbury T. & T. Clark, 2013.

Boer, Esther A. de. *Gospel of Mary: Beyond a Gnostic and a Biblical Mary Magdalene*. London: T. & T. Clark, 2004.

———. *Mary Magdalene: Behind the Myth*. Harrisburg: Trinity Press International, 1997.

———. *The Mary Magdalene Cover-up: The Sources Behind the Myth*. London: T. & T. Clark, 2007.

Bonanate, Mariapia. *Il Vangelo secondo una donna. Ieri e oggi*. Milano: Paoline, 2008.

Bond, Helen K. *The First Biography of Jesus: Genre and Meaning in Mark's Gospel*. Grand Rapids: Eerdmans, 2020.

———. "What Can We Know about the Roman Centurion?" *Bible Odyssey*. https://www.bibleodyssey.org:443/en/places/related-articles/roman-centurion.

Bourgeault, Cynthia. *The Meaning of Mary Magdalene: Discovering the Woman at the Heart of Christianity*. Boston: Shambala, 2010.

Bourgel, Jonathan. "John 4: 4–42: Defining A Modus Vivendi Between Jews And The Samaritans." *JTS* 69 (2018) 39–65.

———. "The Samaritans during the Hasmonean Period: The Affirmation of a Discrete Identity?" *Religions* 10 (2019). https://www.mdpi.com/2077-1444/10/11/628.

Boyarin, Daniel. "Women's Bodies and the Rise of the Rabbis: The Case of Sotah." In *Jews and Gender: The Challenge to Hierarchy*, edited by Jonathan Frankel, 88–100. Oxford: Oxford University Press, 2000.

Brand, Miryam T. *Evil Within and Without: The Source of Sin and Its Nature as Portrayed in Second Temple Literature*. Göttingen: Vandenhoeck and Ruprecht, 2013.

Brant, Jo-Ann A. *John*. Paideia Commentaries on the New Testament. Grand Rapids: Baker Academic, 2011.

Brock, Ann Graham. *Mary Magdalene, the First Apostle: The Struggle for Authority*. Cambridge, MA: Harvard University Press, 2003.

Brooten, Bernadette. "Early Christian Women and their Cultural Context: Issues of Method in Historical Reconstruction." In *Feminist Perspectives on Biblical Scholarship*, edited by Adela Yarbro Collins, 66–91. Chico: Scholars, 1985.

———. "Jewish Women's History in the Roman Period: A Task for Christian Theology." *HTR* 79 (1986) 22–30.

———. *Women Leaders in the Ancient Synagogue*. Chico: Scholars, 1982.

Brooten, Bernadette, and Norbert Greinacher, eds. *Frauen in der Mannerkirche*. München: Kaiser / Mainz: Grünewald, 1982.

Brown, Raymond E., et al., eds. *Mary in the New Testament*. New York: Paulist, 1978.

Brutscheck, Jutta. *Die Marta-Maria Erzählung: eine redaktionskritische Untersuchung zu Lk 10:38–42*. BBB 64. Frankfurt: Hanstein, 1986.

Buby, Bertrand. *Mary of Galilee. Volume I: Mary in the New Testament*. New York: Alba, 1994.

Burgess, Ruth. *Bare Feet and Buttercups: Resources for Ordinary Time—Trinity Sunday to the Feast of the Transfiguration*. Glasgow: Wild Goose, 2008.

Burke, Tony, ed. *Fakes, Forgeries, and Fictions: Writing Ancient and Modern Christian Apocrypha: Proceedings from the 2015 York Christian Apocrypha Symposium*. Eugene, OR: Cascade, 2017.

Burkill, T. A. "The Historical Development of the Story of the Syrophoenician Woman (Mark VII: 24–31)." *NovT* 9 (1967) 161–77.

Bursi, Adam Collins. "Holy Spit and Magic Spells: Religion, Magic And The Body In Late Ancient Judaism, Christianity, And Islam." PhD diss., Cornell University, 2015. https://ecommons.cornell.edu/handle/1813/40591.

Byron, John. *Cain and Abel in Text and Tradition: Jewish and Christian Interpretations of the First Sibling Rivalry*. Leiden: E. J. Brill, 2011.

Cadwaller, Alan H. "When a Woman is a Dog: Ancient and Modern Ethology Meet the Syrophoenician Women." *Bible and Critical Theory* 1 (2005) 35.1–35.17.

Calduch-Benages, Nuria, ed. *Donne dei Vangeli*. Milano: Vita e Pensiero, 2018.

———. *El perfume del Evangelio: Jesús se encuentra con las mujeres*. Estella: Verbo Divino, 2011.

Calvert-Koyzis, Nancy, and Heather E. Weir, eds. *Strangely Familiar: Protofeminist Interpretations of Patriarchal Biblical Texts*. Atlanta: Society of Biblical Literature, 2009.

Cameron, Averil, and AmelieKuhrt. *Images of Women in Antiquity*. Detroit: Wayne State University Press, 1993.

Camery-Hogatt, Jerry. "Images of Mary Magdalene in Christian Tradition: A Case of Prostituted Identity." *Priscilla Papers* 18 (2004) 19–24.

Cangh, Jean-Marie Van. "La femme dans l'Évangile de Luc. Comparaison des passages narratifs propres à Luc avec la situation de la femme dans le judaïsme." *RTL* 24 (1993) 297–324.

Carey, Holly J. "Jesus and the Syrophoenician Woman: A Case Study in Inclusiveness." *Leaven* 19 (2001), Article 8. http://digitalcommons.pepperdine.edu/leaven/vol19/iss1/8.

Carlisle, Thomas John. *Beginning with Mary: Women of the Gospels in Portrait*. Grand Rapids: Eerdmans, 1986.

Carman, Amy Smith. "Ave Maria: Old Testament Allusions in the Magnificat." *Priscilla Papers* 31 (2017) 14–18.

Caron, Gérald, et al. *Women Also Journeyed with Him: Feminist Perspectives on the Bible*. Collegeville, MN: Liturgical, 2000.

Case, Shirley Jackson. "Jesus and Sepphoris." *JBL* 45 (1926) 14–22.

Catchpole, David. *The Quest for Q*. London: Bloomsbury, 2015.

Ceragioli, Ferruccio. *Sette donne del Vangelo: Una introduzione alla preghiera*. Torino: Effata' Editrice, 2005.

Chalet, Jennifer. "The Characterization of the Magdalene in the Gospels according to John, Thomas, Philip and Mary." MA thesis, Concordia University, 2012.

Chancey, Mark. "The Cultural Milieu of Ancient Sepphoris." *NTS* 47 (2001) 127–45.

Charlesworth, James H., ed. *Jesus and Archaeology*. Grand Rapids: Eerdmans, 2006.

———. *Jesus and Temple: Textual and Archaeological Explorations*. Minneapolis: Fortress, 2014.

Chilton, Bruce. *Mary Magdalene: A Biography*. New York: Image, 2005.

Chinen, Mark A. "Crumbs from the Table: The Syrophoenician Woman and International Law." *Journal of Law and Religion* 27 (2012) 1–57.

Chrétien, Jean-Louis, et al. *Marthe et Marie*. Paris: Desclée de Brouwer, 2002.

Clanton, Dan W. "(Re)dating the Story of Susanna: A Proposal." *JSJ* 34 (2003) 121–40.

Clark, Constantinia A. "Exploring the True Identity of Junia: Prominent among the Apostles." *Journal of Early Christian History* 8 (2018) 96–106.

Clark, Elizabeth A. "Early Christian Women: Sources and Interpretation." In *That Gentle Strength: Historical Perspectives on Women in Christianity*, edited by Lynda L. Coon et al., 19–35. Charlottesville: University of Virginia Press, 1990.

———. *History, Theory, Text: Historians and the Linguistic Turn*. Cambridge, MA: Harvard University Press, 2004.

———. "The Lady Vanishes: Dilemmas of a Feminist Historian after the 'Linguistic Turn.'" *Church History* 67 (1998) 1–31.

———. "Women, Gender, and the Study of Christian History." *Church History* 70 (2001) 395–426.

Clement, Ann Mary. "Women Disciples." *Focus* 17 (1997) 255–60.

Clements, E. Anne. *Mothers on the Margin? The Significance of the Women in Matthew's Genealogy*. Eugene, OR: Pickwick, 2014.

Coffey, Kathy. *Hidden Women of the Gospels*. New York: Crossroad, 1996.

Cohen, Shaye J. D., ed. *The Jewish Family in Antiquity*. Atlanta: Scholars, 1993.

Cohick, Lynn. *Women in the World of the Earliest Christians: Illuminating Ancient Ways of Life*. Grand Rapids: Baker Academic, 2009.

Connor, Alice. *Fierce: Women of the Bible and their Stories of Violence, Mercy, Bravery, Wisdom, Sex, and Salvation*. Minneapolis: Fortress, 2017.

Conway, Colleen M. *Behold the Man: Jesus and Greco-Roman Masculinity*. Oxford: Oxford University Press, 2008.

———. *Men and Women in the Fourth Gospel: Gender and Johannine Characterization*. Atlanta: SBL, 1999.

Cooper, Jeannette M. *Woman to Woman: Conversations With Mary*. Notre Dame: Ave Maria, 1988.

Cooper, Kate. *Band of Angels: The Forgotten World of Early Christian Women*. New York: Overlook, 2013.

Copăcianu, Emanuel. *Maria Magdalena*. Galați: Partener, 2016.

Corley, Kathleen E. *Women and the Historical Jesus: Feminist Myths of Christian Origins*. Santa Rosa: Polebridge, 2002.

Cornelius, Elma M. "Patriarchy and the New Testament." *Acta Patristica et Byzantina* 13 (2002) 50–65.

Cousland, J. R. C. "Adam and Evel: Did Satan Sleep with Eve in the Greek and Latin Lives of Adam and Eve?" *JTS* 71 (2020) 134–57.

Coutts, Laurence. *Jesus' Encounters with Women*. Melbourne: MaddingCrowd, 2008.

Creamer, Jennifer M., et al. "Who is Theophilus? Discovering the Original Reader of Luke-Acts." *Skriflig* 48 (2014) 1–7. http://www.scielo.org.za/scielo.php?script=sci_arttext&pid=S2305-08532014000100009.

Cross, Frank Moore. *Canaanite Myth and Hebrew Epic: Essays in the History of the Religion of Israel*. Cambridge, MA: Harvard University Press, 1973.

Crowder, Stephanie Buckhanon. *When Momma Speaks: The Bible and Motherhood from a Womanist Perspective*. Louisville: Westminster John Knox, 2016.

———. "When Mommy Goes to Work: A Contemporary Analysis of the Canaanite Mother." In *Matthew*, edited by Nicole Wilkinson Duran and James P. Grimshaw, 81–92. Texts @ Contexts Series. Minneapolis: Augsburg Fortress, 2013.

Croy, N. Clayton. "Translating for Jesus: Philip and Andrew in John 12:20–22." *Neotestamentica* 49 (2015) 145–74.

Cunneen, Sally. *In Search of Mary: The Woman and the Symbol*. New York: Random, 1996.

D'Angelo, Mary Rose. "Reconstructing 'Real Women' in Gospel Literature: The Case of Mary Magdalene." In *Women and Christian Origins*, edited by Ross Shepard Kraemer and Mary Rose D'Angelo, 105-28. Oxford: Oxford University Press, 1999.

Dark, Ken. *Roman-Period and Byzantine Nazareth and Its Hinterland*. New York: Routledge, 2020.

Davies, Stevan L. *Spirit Possession and the Origins of Christianity*. Dublin: Bardic, 2014.

DeVries, LaMoine F., *Cities of the Biblical World: An Introduction to the Archaeology, Geography, and History of Biblical Sites*. Peabody, MA: Hendrickson, 1997.

DeConick, April D. *Holy Misogyny: Why the Sex and Gender Conflicts in the Early Church Still Matter*. New York: Continuum, 2011.

———. "The Memorial Mary Meets the Historical Mary: The Many Faces of the Magdalene in Ancient Christianity." In *The Tomb of Jesus and His Family? Exploring Ancient Jewish Tombs Near Jerusalem's Walls*, edited by James H. Charlesworth, 267-90. Grand Rapids: Eerdmans, 2013.

Deen, Edith. *All of the Women of the Bible*. New York: Harper and Row, 1955.

DeLuca, Stefano with Anna Lena. "Magdala/Taricheae." In *Galilee in the Late Second Temple and Mishnaic Periods, Volume 2: The Archaeological Record from Cities, Towns, and Villages*, edited by David A. Fiensy and James Riley Strange, 280-342. Minneapolis: Fortress, 2015.

Dermience, Alice. "La péricope de la Cananéenne (Mt 15,21-28): rédaction et théologie." *Ephemerides Theologicae Lovanienses* 58 (1982) 25-49.

Destro, Adriana. *The Law of Jealousy: Anthropology of Sotah*. Atlanta: Scholars, 1989.

Dewey, Joanna. *The Oral Ethos of the Early Church: Speaking, Writing, and the Gospel of Mark*. Eugene, OR: Cascade, 2013.

Dicken, Frank. *Herod as a Composite Character in Luke-Acts*. Tübingen: Mohr-Siebeck, 2014.

Dillon, Sheila, and Sharon L. James, eds. *A Companion to Women in the Ancient World*. Malden: Wiley Blackwell, 2012.

Donnelly, Doris K., ed. *Mary, Woman of Nazareth: Biblical and Theological Perspectives*. New York: Paulist, 1990.

Dreyer, Yolanda. "Jesus and the Full Personhood of Women: Through the Lens of a Hermeneutics of Affect." *Journal of Early Christian History* 8 (2018) 57-73.

Driscoll, Martha E. *Reading Between The Lines: The Hidden Wisdom of Women in the Gospels*. Liguori, MO: Liguori, 2006.

Dube, Musa W. *Postcolonial Feminist Interpretation of the Bible*. St. Louis: Chalice, 2000.

———. "Reading for Decolonization (John 4:1-42)." *Semeia* 75 (1996) 37-59.

Duckworth, Penelope. *Mary: The Imagination of Her Heart*. Cambridge: Cowley, 2004.

Duncan, Carrie. "Inscribing Authority Female Title Bearers in Jewish Inscriptions." *Religions* 3 (2012) 37-49. https://www.mdpi.com/2077-1444/3/1/37/htm.

Dunning, Benjamin H., ed. *The Oxford Handbook of New Testament, Gender, and Sexuality*. Oxford: Oxford University Press, 2019.

Duran, Nicole Wilkinson, and James P. Grimshaw, eds. *Matthew*. Texts @ Contexts Series. Minneapolis: Augsburg Fortress, 2013.

Easterling, Pat, and Edith Hall, eds. *Greek and Roman Actors: Aspects of an Ancient Profession*. Cambridge: Cambridge University Press, 2002.

Ebeling, Jennie R. *Women's Lives in Biblical Times*. London: T. & T. Clark, 2010.

Eck, Ernest van. *The Parables of Jesus the Galilean: Stories of a Social Prophet*. Eugene, OR: Cascade, 2016.

Eckhardt, Ashley. "Participating in Public: Female Patronage and Economic Prominence at Hellenistic Priene." MA thesis, Washington University in St. Louis, 2012. https://openscholarship.wustl.edu/etd/735.

Edrey, Meir. "The Dog Burials at Achaemenid Ashkelon Revisited." *Tel Aviv* 35 (2013) 267–82.

Egasse, Corinne. *Le lavement des pieds: Recherche sur une pratique négligée*. Geneva: Labor et Fides, 2015.

Ehrman, Bart D. *Peter, Paul, and Mary Magdalene: The Followers of Jesus in History and Legend*. Oxford: Oxford University Press, 2006.

Eisen, Ute E. *Women Officeholders in Early Christianity: Epigraphical and Literary Studies*. Collegeville, MN: Liturgical, 2000.

Eisenhart, George H. *Mary of Magdala*. Reading: I.M. Beaver, 1919.

Eklund, Rebekah. *Jesus Wept: The Significance of Jesus' Laments in the New Testament*. LNTS 515. London: Bloomsbury T. & T. Clark, 2015.

Ekwunife, Ezenwa Fabian. "The Hermeneutics of Women Disciples in Mark's Gospel: An Igbo Contextual Reconstruction." STL thesis, Boston College, 2018. http://hdl.handle.net/2345/bc-ir:108068.

Elkins, Kathleen Gallagher. *Mary, Mother of Martyrs*. Indianapolis: Dog Ear, 2018.

Ellens, Deborah L. "Numbers 5.11–31: Valuing Male Suspicion." In *God's Word for Our World: Biblical Studies in Honor of Simon John De Vries*, edited by J. Harold Ellens et al., 59–68. London: T. & T. Clark, 2004.

Ellis, E. Earle. "Coworkers, Paul and His." In *Dictionary of Paul and His Letters*, edited by Gerald F. Hawthorne and Ralph P. Martin, 183–89. Downers Grove, IL: IVP Academic, 1993.

Epp, Eldon Jay. *Junia: The First Woman Apostle*. Minneapolis: Augsburg Fortress Press, 2005.

Ernst, Allie. *Martha from the Margins: The Authority of Martha in Early Christian Tradition*. Leiden: E. J. Brill, 2009.

Esler, Philip F., and Ronald A. Piper. *Lazarus, Mary and Martha: Social-Scientific Approaches to the Gospel of John*. Minneapolis: Fortress, 2006.

Evans, Craig A. *Jesus and His World: The Archaeological Evidence*. Louisville: Westminster John Knox, 2012.

Evans, Rachel Held. *Inspired: Slaying Giants, Walking on Water, and Loving the Bible Again*. Nashville: Nelson, 2018.

———. *A Year of Biblical Womanhood*. Nashville: Thomas Nelson, 2012.

Faxon, Alicia Craig. *Women and Jesus*. Philadelphia: United Church Press, 1973.

Fiensy, David, and Ralph Hawkins, eds. *The Galilean Economy in the Time of Jesus*. Early Christianity and Its Literature 11. Atlanta: SBL, 2013.

Fiensy, David A., and James Riley Strange, eds. *Galilee in the Late Second Temple and Mishnaic Periods, Volume 1: Life, Culture, and Society*. Minneapolis: Fortress, 2014.

Fiorenza, Elisabeth Schüssler. *Jesus: Miriam's Child, Sophia's Prophet: Critical Issues in Feminist Christology*. London: Bloomsbury T. & T. Clark, 2015.

Fisk, Anna. "Stood Weeping Outside the Tomb: Dis(re)membering Mary Magdalene." In *The Bible and Feminism: Remapping the Field*, edited by Yvonne Sherwood, 150–69. Oxford: Oxford University Press, 2017.

Fleddermann, Harry T. *Q: A Reconstruction and Commentary*. Leuven: Peeters, 2005.

Focant, Camille. *TheGospel according to Mark: A Commentary*. Eugene, OR: Pickwick, 2012.
Folda, Jaroslav. "The Church of Saint Anne." *Biblical Archaeologist* 54 (1991) 88–96.
Foskett, Mary F. "Mary, the Mother of Jesus." In *The Oxford Handbook of New Testament, Gender, and Sexuality*, edited by Benjamin H. Dunning, 449–68. Oxford: Oxford University Press, 2019.
———. *A Virgin Conceived: Mary and Classical Representations of Virginity*. Bloomington: Indiana University Press, 2002.
Foster, Paul. "Educating Jesus: The Search for a Plausible Context." *JSHJ* 4 (2006) 7–33.
Fredriksen, Paula. "Did Jesus Oppose the Purity Laws?" *Bible Review* 11:3 (1995) 19–25, 42–47.
Fritz, Maureen. "The New Teaching Paradigm Guidelines for Teaching." *Journal of Religious Education* 56 (2008) 50–57.
Fröhlich, Ida. "'For He Loves Her . . . ' The Figure of the Demon in the Book of Tobit." *The Arabist* 37 (2016) 25–35.
Frymer-Kensky, Tikva. "The Strange Case of the Suspected 'Sotah' (Numbers 5:11–31)." *VT* 34 (1984) 11–26.
Fuchs, Ilan. "Women's Testimony in Jewish Law: A Historical Survey." *HUCA* 82–83 (2012) 119–59.
Fuchs, Lucy. *We Were There: Women in the New Testament*. New York: Alba, 1993.
Gaden, Janet, and John Gaden. "Women and Discipleship in the New Testament." *The Way* 26 (1986) 113–23.
Garrison, Webb. *Women in the Life of Jesus*. Indianapolis: Bobbs-Merrill, 1962.
Gaventa, Beverly Roberts. *Mary: Glimpses of the Mother of Jesus*. Columbia: University of South Carolina Press, 1995.
Gaventa, Beverly Roberts, and Cynthia L. Rigby, eds. *Blessed One: Protestant Perspectives on Mary*. Louisville: Westminster John Knox, 2002.
Gench, Frances Taylor. *Back to the Well: Women's Encounters with Jesus in the Gospels*. Louisville: Westminster John Knox, 2004.
George, Margaret. *Mary, Called Magdalene*. New York: Berkley, 2003.
Getty-Sullivan, Mary Ann. *Women in the New Testament*. Collegeville, MN: Liturgical, 2001.
Ghosn, Margaret. *Encounters between Jesus and Women: Models of Discipleship*. Northcote: Morning Star, 2017.
Giles, Kevin. *What the Bible Actually Teaches on Women*. Eugene, OR: Cascade, 2018.
Glancy, Jennifer. "Jesus, the Syrophoenician Woman, and Other First Century Bodies." *Biblical Interpretation* 18 (2010) 342–63.
Gómez-Acebo, Isabel, ed. *María Magdalena. De apóstol a prostituta y amante*. Bilbao: Desclée de Brouwer, 2007.
Good, Deirdre, ed. *Mariam, the Magdalen, and the Mother*. Bloomington: Indiana University Press, 2005.
Goodacre, Mark. "Scripturalization in Mark's Crucifixion Narrative." In *The Trial and Death of Jesus: Essays on the Passion Narrative in Mark*, edited by Geert van Oyen and Tom Shepherd, 33–47. Leuven: Peeters, 2006.
Gormley, Beatrice. *Poisoned Honey. A Story of Mary Magdalene*. New York: Alfred A. Knopf, 2010.

Gosbell, Louise A. *"The Poor, the Crippled, the Blind, and the Lame": Physical and Sensory Disability in the Gospels of the New Testament*. WUNT2, 469. Tübingen: Mohr Siebeck, 2018.

Grassi, Joseph A. *The Hidden Heroes of the Gospels: Female Counterparts of Jesus*. Collegeville, MN: Liturgical, 1989.

Grassi, Joseph A., and Carolyn, *Mary Magdalene and the Women in Jesus' Life*. Kansas City: Sheed & Ward, 1986.

Greenfield, Shivi. "The Theater of Deviance and the Normative Boundaries of Society: Lessons from the Rabbinic Interpretations to the Biblical Law of Sotah." *Journal of Law and Religion* 28 (2012–2013) 105–42.

Gruber, Peter. "A Pregnant Interpretation of the PericopeAdulterae in John 8." https://www.academia.edu/27446233/A_Pregnant_Interpretation_of_the_Pericope_Adulterae_in_John_8.

Grushcow, Lisa. *Writing the Wayward Wife: Rabbinic Interpretations of Sotah*. Leiden: E. J. Brill, 2006.

Guijarro, Inmaculada Eibe. "La Cananea, Modelo de Mujer Creyente para la Comunidad (Mt 15,21–28)." In *Con ellas tras Jesús. Mujeres modelos de identidad Cristiana*, edited by Carmen Bernabé Ubieta, 23–75. Estella: Verbo Divino, 2011.

Guijarro, Santiago. "Magdala: un enclave galileo del comercio entre Roma y Oriente." *Estudio Agustiniano* 54 (2019) 519–46.

Guijarro, Santiago, and Ana Rodríguez. "The 'Messianic' Anointing of Jesus (Mark 14:3–9)." *BTB* 41 (2011) 132–43.

Gupta, Nijay. "Teach Us, Mary: The Authority of Women Teachers in the Church in Light of the Magnificat (Luke 1:46–55)." *Priscilla Papers* 29 (2015) 11–14.

Haag, Michael. *The Quest For Mary Magdalene: History and Legend*. London: Profile, 2016.

Haber, Susan, *They Shall Purify Themselves: Essays on Purity in Early Judaism*. Edited by Adele Reinhartz. Atlanta: Society of Biblical Literature, 2008.

Haberman, Bonna Devora. "The Suspected Adulteress: A Study of Textual Embodiment." *Prooftexts* 20 (2000) 12–42.

Hachlili, Rachel. "The Zodiac in Ancient Jewish Synagogal Art: A Review." *JSQ* 9 (2002) 219–58.

Hakola, Raimo. *Identity Matters: John, the Jews and Jewishness*. Leiden: E. J. Brill, 2005.

Hanrahan, Mary. "The Syrophoenician Woman Tells Her Story to Her Friend Rebecca." *Spirituality* 8 (2002) 295–96.

Hansen, Brooks. *John the Baptizer: A Novel*. New York: W. W. Norton, 2009.

Hanson, Mary Stromer. *The New Perspective on Mary and Martha*. Eugene, OR: Wipf & Stock, 2013.

Hardman, Sarah. "'My Soul Rejoices': Empowerment, Prophecy, and Luke's Gospel." *Mutuality* 26 (2019) 13–15. https://www.cbeinternational.org/resources/article/mutuality/my-soul-rejoices-empowerment-prophecy-and-luke%E2%80%99s-gospel.

Harmer, Elizabeth C. "'One Woman with Many Faces': Imaginings of Mary Magdalen in Medieval and Contemporary Texts." MA thesis, McMasters, 2005. https://macsphere.mcmaster.ca/bitstream/11375/9566/1/fulltext.pdf.

Hartman, Tracy. *Letting the Other Speak: Proclaiming the Stories of Biblical Women*. Lanham: Lexington, 2012.

Harnish, James A. *Women of the Bible. Converge Bible Studies*. Nashville: Abingdon, 2013.
Harsh, Charles Clark. *Jesus Christ the Emancipator of Women*. Chicago: Woman's Temperance Association, 1887.
Hart, Lawrence. "The Canaanite Woman: Meeting Jesus As Sage and Lord: Matthew 15:21–28 & Mark 7:24–30." *Expository Times* 122 (2010) 20–25.
Harvey, Susan Ashbrook. "On Mary's Voice: Gendered Words in Syriac Marian Tradition." In *The Cultural Turn in Late Ancient Studies: Gender, Asceticism, and Historiography*, edited by Dale B. Martin and Patricia Cox Miller, 63–86. Durham: Duke University Press, 2005.
Haskins, Susan. *Mary Magdalen: Truth and Myth*. London: Pimlico, 2005.
Hastings, Adrian. *Prophet and Witness in Jerusalem: A Study in the Teaching of Saint Luke*. Baltimore: Helicon, 1958.
Haubert, Katherine M. *Women as Leaders: Accepting the Challenge of Scripture*. Monrovia: MARC, 1993.
Haughton, Rosemary. *The Re-Creation of Eve*. Springfield, IL: Templegate, 1985.
Hazleton, Lesley. *Mary: A Flesh-and-Blood Biography of the Virgin Mother*. London: Bloomsbury, 2004.
Hearon, Holly E. *The Mary Magdalene Tradition: Witness and Counter-witness in Early Christian Communities*. Collegeville, MN: Liturgical, 2004.
Hebblethwaite, Margaret. *Six New Gospels: New Testament Women Tell Their Stories*. Boston: Cowley, 1994.
Heine, Susanne. "Eine Person von Rang und Namen: Historische Konturen der Magdalenerin." In *Jesu Rede von Gott und ihre Nachgeschichte im frühen Christentum: Beiträge zur Verkündigung Jesu und zum Kerygma der Kirche*, Dietrich-Alex Kochet al., 179–94. Geburtstag. Gütersloh: Mohn, 1989.
Hendricks, Obery Mack. *Living Water: A Novel*. San Francisco: HarperCollins, 2003.
Henery, Jennifer Lynne. "Early Christian Sex Change. The Ascetical Context of 'Being Made Male' in Early Christianity." PhD diss., Marquette University, 2011. http://epublications.marquette.edu/dissertations_mu/154.
Hentschel, Anni. *Diakonia im Neuen Testament Studien zur Semantik unter besonderer Berücksichtigung der Rolle von Frauen*. WUNT 2, 226. Tübingen: Mohr Siebeck, 2007.
Hernández, Ana Unzurrunzaga. "Las mujeres comoportadoras y creadoras de memoria de los orígenes (Lc 24,1–11)." In *Con ellas tras Jesús. Mujeres modelos de identidad Cristiana*, edited by Carmen Bernabé Ubieta, 77–118. Estella: Verbo Divino, 2011.
Hesemann, Michael. "Mary Magdalene in History, Tradition and Legend." *El Pensador* 5 (2013) 21–31.
Heyse, Paul. *Mary of Magdala: An Historical and Romantic Drama in Five Acts*. New York: Macmillan, 1903.
Hezser, Cathering. *Jewish Slavery in Antiquity*. Oxford: Oxford University Press, 2005.
Hicks, Jane E. "Moral Agency at the Borders: Rereading the Story of the Syrophoenician Woman." *Word and World* 23 (2003) 76–84.
Hollies, Linda H. *Jesus and Those Bodacious Women*. Cleveland: Pilgrim, 2007.
Hooker, Morna. *The Gospel According to St. Mark*. London: Continuum, 2001.
Hooper, Richard J. *The Crucifixion of Mary Magdalene: The Historical Tradition of the First Apostle and the Ancient Church's Campaign to Suppress it*. Sedona: Sanctuary, 2005.

Houlden, J. L., ed. *Jesus: The Complete Guide*. London: Continuum, 2003.
Hureaux, Roland. *Jésus et Marie-Madeleine*. Paris: Tempus/Perrin, 2005.
Hylen, Susan. *Women in the New Testament World*. Oxford: Oxford University Press, 2019.
Ilan, Tal. "In the Footsteps of Jesus: Jewish Women in a Jewish Movement." In *Transformative Encounters: Jesus and Women Re-Viewed*, edited by Ingrid Rosa Kitzberg, 115–36. Leiden: E. J. Brill, 1999.
———. *Integrating Women into Second Temple History*. Tübingen: Mohr-Siebeck, 1999.
———. *Jewish Women in Greco-Roman Palestine. An Inquiry Into Image and Status*. Tübingen: Mohr-Siebeck, 1995.
———. *Massekhet Hullin: Text, Translation, and Commentary*. Tübingen: Mohr Siebeck, 2017.
———. "Post-Biblical and Rabbinic Women." In *Jewish Women: A Comprehensive Historical Encyclopedia*. Jewish Women's Archive, 2006. https://jwa.org/encyclopedia/article/post-biblical-and-rabbinic-women.
Irons, Kendra Weddle, and Melanie Springer Mock. *If Eve Only Knew: Freeing Yourself from Biblical Womanhood and Becoming All God Means You To Be*. St. Louis: Chalice, 2015.
Izquierdo, Antonio. *La Donna nel Vangelo di San Marco*. Vatican City: Libreria Editrice Vaticana, 2008.
Jackson, Glenna Sue. "Enemies of Israel: Ruth and the Canaanite Woman." *HTS* 59 (2003) 779–92.
———. *"Have Mercy on Me": The Story of the Canaanite Woman in Matthew 15:21–28*. JSNTSup 228. Sheffield: Sheffield Academic Press, 2002.
Janes, Regina. "Why the Daughter of Herodias Must Dance (Mark 6.14–29)." *JSNT* 28 (2006) 443–67.
Jarrell, Robin. *Fallen Angels and Fallen Women: The Mother of the Son of Man*. Eugene, OR: Wipf and Stock, 2013.
Janssen, Claudia. "Verachtet und ausgegrenzt? Menstruation und jüdisches Frauenleben (Mk 5,25–34)." In *Antijudaismus im Neuen Testament? Grundlagen für die Arbeit mit biblischen Texten*, edited by Dagmar Henze et al., 98–106. Gütersloh: Chr. Kaiser/Gütersloher Verlagshaus, 1997.
Jensen, Morten Hørning. *Herod Antipas in Galilee: The Literary and Archaeological Sources on the Reign of Herod Antipas and its Socio-Economic Impact on Galilee*. Tübingen: Mohr Siebeck, 2010.
———. "Rural Galilee and Rapid Changes: An Investigation of the Socio-Economic Dynamics and Developments in Roman Galilee." *Biblica* 93 (2012) 43–67.
Johnson, Elizabeth A. *Truly Our Sister: A Theology of Mary in the Communion of Saints*. New York: Continuum, 2003.
Kalas, J. Ellsworth. *Strong Was Her Faith: Women of the New Testament*. Nashville: Abingdon, 2007.
Kassel, Maria. *Das Evangelium, eine Talenteschmiede? Tiefenpsychologische Revision eines verinnerlichten christlichen Kapitalismus*. Münster: LIT, 2001.
Kateusz, Ally. "The Jesus Woman and the Jesus Women." Westar Institute Seminar Papers (Spring 2019). https://westarinstitute.org/wp-content/uploads/2019/03/S2019-Kateusz-Jesus-Woman.pdf.
———. *Mary and Early Christian Women: Hidden Leadership*. Cham: Palgrave Macmillan, 2019.

———. "The Samaritan Woman at the Well: Two Texts and Two Traditions in Art." Lecture Slides. https://www.academia.edu/40451425/The_Samaritan_Woman_at_the_Well_Two_Texts_and_Two_Traditions_in_Art?email_work_card=title.

Keith, Chris. *The Pericope Adulterae, the Gospel of John, and the Literacy of Jesus.* Leiden: E. J. Brill, 2009.

———. "Recent and Previous Research on the Pericope Adulterae (John 7.53–8.11)." *Currents in Biblical Research* 6 (2008) 377–404.

Kelly, Elizabeth M. *Jesus Approaches: What Contemporary Women Can Learn about Healing, Freedom and Joy from the Women of the New Testament.* Chicago: Loyola, 2017.

Kern, Paul Bentley. *Ancient Siege Warfare.* Bloomington: Indiana University Press, 1999.

Kgatle, Mookgo S. "Crossing Boundaries: Social-scientific Reading of the Faith of a Canaanite Woman (Mt 15:21–28)." *Stellenbosch Theological Journal* 4 (2018) 595–613.

Kidd, Sue Monk. *The Book of Longings.* New York: Viking, 2020.

Kienzle, Beverly Mayne, and Pamela J. Walkers, eds. *Women Preachers and Prophets through Two Millennia of Christianity.* Berkeley: University of California Press, 1998.

Kim, Joy H. "Female Patronage of Public Space in Roman Cities." Senior thesis, Trinity College, Hartford, CT (2017). http://digitalrepository.trincoll.edu/theses/653.

King, Karen L. *The Gospel of Mary of Magdala: Jesus and the First Woman Apostle.* Salem, OR: Polebridge, 2003.

Kinukawa, Hisako. "De-colonizing Ourselves as Readers: The Story of the Syro-Phoenician Woman as a Text." In *Distant Voices Drawing Near: Essays in Honor of Antoinette Clark Wire,* edited by Holly E. Hearon, 131–44. Collegeville, MN: Michael Glazier, 2004.

———. *Women and Jesus in Mark: a Japanese Feminist Perspective.* Maryknoll, NY: Orbis, 1994.

Kirk-Duggan, Cheryl A. "Proud Mary: Contextual Constructions of a Divine Diva." In *Blessed One: Protestant Perspectives on Mary,* edited by Beverly Roberts Gaventa and Cynthia L. Rigby, 71–84. Louisville: Westminster John Knox, 2002.

Kitzberger, Ingrid Rosa. *Interfigural Readings of the Gospel of John.* Atlanta: SBL, 2019.

Klancher, Nancy. *The Taming of the Canaanite Woman Constructions of Christian Identity in the Afterlife of Matthew 15:21–28.* Göttingen: De Gruyter, 2013.

Kloha, Jeffrey. "Elizabeth's Magnificat (Luke 1:46)." In *Texts and Traditions: Essays in Honour of J. Keith Elliott,* edited by Peter Doble and Jeffrey Kloha, 200–219. Leiden: E. J. Brill, 2014.

Koltun-Fromm, Naomi. *Hermeneutics of Holiness Ancient Jewish and Christian Notions of Sexuality and Religious Community.* Oxford: Oxford University Press, 2010.

Knight, Jennifer Lassley. "Herodias, Salomé, and John the Baptist's Beheading: A Case Study of the Topos of the Heretical Woman." *International Social Science Review* 93 (2017) 1–15.

Knust, Jennifer. "Can an Adulteress Save Jesus? the Pericope Adulterae, Feminist Interpretation, and the Limits of Narrative Agency." In *The Bible and Feminism: Remapping the Field,* edited by Yvonne Sherwood, 402–31. Oxford: Oxford University Press, 2017.

———. "Too Hot to Handle: The Story of the Woman Taken in Adultery in Late Antique Exegesis, Liturgy and Art." In *From the Margins 2: Women of the New Testament and Their Afterlives,* edited by Christine E. Joynes and Christopher C. Rowland, 143–63. Sheffield: Sheffield Phoenix Press, 2009.

———. *Unprotected Texts: The Bible's Surprising Contradictions About Sex and Desire.* New York: HarperOne, 2011.

Knust, Jennifer, and Tommy Wasserman. "Earth Accuses Earth: Tracing What Jesus Wrote on the Ground." *HRT* 103:4 (2010) 407–46.

———. *To Cast the First Stone: The Transmission of a Gospel Story.* Princeton: Princeton University Press, 2019.

Korpman, Matthew J. *Saying No to God: How to Read the Bible Radically and Faithfully.* Orange: Quoir, 2019.

Kowalczyk, Andrzej. *The Origin of the Gospel according to Mark.* Peplin: Wydawnictwo Bernardinum, 2016.

Kraemer, Ross Shepard. "Implicating Herodias and Her Daughter in the Death of John the Baptizer: A (Christian) Theological Strategy?" *JBL* 125 (2006) 321–49.

———. *Women's Religions in the Greco-Roman World: A Sourcebook.* Oxford: Oxford University Press, 2004.

Kraemer, Ross Shepard, and Mary Rose D'Angelo. *Women and Christian Origins.* Oxford: Oxford University Press, 1999.

Kreitzer, Larry J., and Deborah W. Rooke, eds. *Ciphers in the Sand: Interpretations of The Woman Taken in Adultery (John 7.53–8.11).* Sheffield: Sheffield Academic Press, 2000.

Kuen, Alfred. *La femme dans l'Église.* Saint-Legier: Emmaus, 1994.

Küng, Hans. *Women in Christianity.* London: Continuum, 2001.

Lahr, Jane. *Searching for Mary Magdalene: A Journey through Art and Literature.* New York: Welcome, 2006.

Landrivon, Sylvaine. *Marie de Magdala «apôtre»? Vers une réintroduction du rôle des femmes dans l'Eglise.* Paris: Cerf, 2017.

———. *Marie-Madeleine: La fin de la nuit.* Paris: Cerf, 2017.

Lapp, Eric C. *Sepphoris II: The Clay Lamps from Ancient Sepphoris: Light Use and Regional Interactions.* Winona Lake, IN: Eisenbrauns, 2016.

Lawrence, Louise J. *Sense and Stigma In The Gospels: Depictions Of Sensory-Disabled Characters.* Oxford: Oxford University Press, 2013.

Layne, Linda L. *Home and Homeland: The Dialogics of Tribal and National Identities in Jordan.* Princeton: Princeton University Press, 2019.

Lee, Dorothy A. "The Faith of the Canaanite Woman (Mt. 15.21–28): Narrative, Theology, Ministry." *Journal of Anglican Studies* 13 (2015) 12–29.

———. "Presence or Absence? The Question of Women Disciples at the Last Supper." *Pacifica* 6 (1993) 1–20.

LeMarquand, Grant. "The Canaanite Conquest of Jesus (Mt 15:21–28)." In *Essays in Honour of Frederik Wisse: Scholar, Churchman, Mentor,* edited by William Kappeler, 237–47. ARC 33. Montreal: McGill University Press, 2005.

Lester, Meera. *The Everything Mary Magdalene Book: The Life And Legacy of Jesus' Most Misunderstood Disciple.* Avon: Adams Media, 2006.

Levine, Amy-Jill, "Discharging Responsibility: Matthean Jesus, Biblical Law, and Hemorrhaging Woman." In *Feminist Companion to Matthew,* edited by Amy-Jill Levine, 70–87. London: Continuum, 2001.

———. *The Misunderstood Jew: The Church and the Scandal of the Jewish Jesus*. New York: HarperSanFrancisco, 2006.

———. "'This Poor Widow . . .' (Mark 12:43): From Donation to Diatribe." In *A most reliable witness: essays in honor of Ross Shepard Kraemer*, edited by Susan Ashbrook Harvey, Nathaniel DesRosiers, Shira L. Lander, Jacqueline Z. Pastis, and Daniel Ullucci, 183–193. Providence: Brown Judaic Studies, 2015.

———. *Short Stories by Jesus: The Enigmatic Parables of a Controversial Rabbi*. New York: HarperOne, 2014.

———. *"Women Like This": New Perspectives on Jewish Women In the Greco-Roman World*. Atlanta: Scholars, 1991.

Levine, Amy-Jill, and Ben Witherington, III. *The Gospel of Luke*. Cambridge: Cambridge University Press, 2018.

Levine, Étan. *Marital Relations in Ancient Judaism*. Wiesbaden: Harrassowitz, 2009.

Lin, Yii-Jan. "Junia: An Apostle before Paul." *JBL* 139 (2020) 191–209.

Liu, Rebekah. "A Dog under the Table at the Messianic Banquet: A Study of Mark 7:24–30." *Andrews University Seminary Studies* 48 (2010) 251–55.

Lofts, Norah. *How Far to Bethlehem?* Garden City: Doubleday, 1965.

Lopes, Mercedes. "Martha's Role in the Johannine Community." *VOICES* 39 "Feminist Theology Reaching New Borders" (2016) 91–103.

López, Elisa Estévez. *El poder de una mujer creyente: Cuerpo, identidad y discipulado en Mc 5,24b-34. Un estudio desde las ciencias sociales*. Estella: Verbo Divino, 2003.

Love, Stuart L. *Jesus and Marginal Women: The Gospel of Matthew in Social-Scientific Perspective*. Cambridge: James Clarke, 2009.

Luff, Rosemary Margaret. *The Impact of Jesus in First-Century Palestine: Textual and Archaeological Evidence for Long-standing Discontent*. Cambridge: Cambridge University Press, 2019.

Lunceford, Joe E. *Biblical Women—Submissive?* Eugene, OR: Wipf & Stock, 2009.

Lupieri, Edmondo, ed. *Mary Magdalene from the New Testament to the New Age and Beyond*. Leiden: E. J. Brill, 2019.

———. *Una sposa per Gesù. Maria Maddalena tra antichità e postmoderno*. Roma: Carocci, 2017.

Lutzer, Erwin, and Rebecca Lutzer. *Jesus: Lover of a Woman's Soul*. Carol Stream: Tyndale, 2006.

Lyons-Pardue, Kara J. "A Syrophoenician Becomes a Canaanite: Jesus Exegetes the Canaanite Woman in Matthew." *Journal of Theological Interpretation* 13 (2019) 235–50.

Mackall, Dandi Daley. *Kindred Sisters: New Testament Women Speak to Us Today*. Minneapolis: Fortress, 1996.

Magness, Jodi. *The Archaeology of the Holy Land: From the Destruction of Solomon's Temple to the Muslim Conquest*. Cambridge: Cambridge University Press, 2012.

———. "Heaven on Earth: Helios and the Zodiac Cycle in Ancient Palestinian Synagogues." *Dumbarton Oaks Papers* 59 (2005) 1–52.

Maisch, Ingrid. *Mary Magdalene: The Image of a Woman Through the Centuries*. Collegeville, MN: Liturgical, 1998.

Malone, Mary T. *Women and Christianity. Volume I: The First Thousand Years*. Maryknoll, NY: Orbis, 2000.

Malvern, Marjorie M. *Venus in Sackcloth: The Magdalen's Origins and Metamorphoses*. Carbondale, IL: Southern Illinois University Press, 1975.

Marano, Lou. "Sepphoris: Secret of the Prince of Peace?" *United Press International* April 10, 2002. https://www.upi.com/Archives/2002/04/10/Sepphoris-Secret-of-the-Prince-of-Peace/7131018411200/.

Marjanen, Antti. *The Woman Jesus Loved: Mary Magdalene in the Nag Hammadi Library and Related Documents*. Leiden: E. J. Brill, 1996.

Marquis, Christine Luckritz. "The Life of Mary Magdalene: A New Translation and Introduction." In *New Testament Apocrypha: More Noncanonical Scriptures Volume 2*, edited by Tony Burke, 223–38. Grand Rapids: Eerdmans, 2020.

Marshall, Jonathan. *Jesus, Patrons, and Benefactors: Roman Palestine and the Gospel of Luke*. Tübingen: Mohr-Siebeck, 2009.

Maseno, Loreen, and Elia Shabani Mligo. *Women within Religions: Patriarchy, Feminism, and the Role of Women in Selected World Religions*. Eugene, OR: Wipf & Stock, 2020.

Massey, Lesly F. *Women and the New Testament: An Analysis of Scripture in Light of New Testament Era Culture*. Jefferson: McFarland, 1989.

Mathew, Bincy. *The Johannine Footwashing as the Sign of Perfect Love: An Exegetical Study of John 13:1–20*. Tübingen: Mohr Siebeck, 2018.

Mathew, Susan. *Women in the Greetings of Romans 16.1–16: A Study of Mutuality and Women's Ministry in the Letter to the Romans*. London: Bloomsbury, 2013.

Mathewes-Green, Frederica. *Mary as the Early Christians Knew Her. The Mother of Jesus in Three Ancient Texts*. Brewster: Paraclete, 2013.

Mbuvi, Andrew. "Jesus and His Mother: An Analysis of Their Public Relationship as a Paradigm for African Women (Widows) Who Must Circumvent Traditional Authority in Order to Thrive in Society." In *Mother Goose, Mother Jones, Mommie Dearest: Biblical Mothers and Their Children*, edited by Cheryl A. Kirk-Duggan and Tina Pippin, 129–39. Atlanta: SBL, 2009.

McClure, Laura K. *Women in Classical Antiquity: From Birth to Death*. Medford: Wiley Blackwell, 2020.

McCook, Henry C. *The Women Friends of Jesus*. London: Hodder & Stoughton, 1888.

McGrath, James F. *John's Apologetic Christology: Legitimation and Development in Johannine Christology*. Cambridge: Cambridge University Press, 2001.

———. "Obedient Unto Death: Philippians 2:8, Gethsemane, and the Historical Jesus." *JSHJ* 14 (2017) 223–40.

———. "Was Jesus Illegitimate? The Evidence of His Social Interactions." *JSHJ* 5 (2007) 81–100.

McHugh, John. *The Mother of Jesus in the New Testament*. London: Darton, Longman, and Todd, 1975.

McKenna, Megan. *Leave Her Alone*. Maryknoll, NY: Orbis, 2000.

———. *Mary: Shadow of Grace*. Maryknoll, NY: Orbis, 1995.

———. *Not Counting Women and Children: Neglected Stories from the Bible*. Maryknoll, NY: Orbis, 1994.

McKnight, Scot. *The Real Mary: Why Evangelical Christians Can Embrace the Mother of Jesus*. Brewster: Paraclete, 2007.

McVey, Kathleen E. "Ephrem the Syrian: a theologian of the presence of God." In *Orthodox and Wesleyan Spirituality*, edited by S. T. Kimbrough, 241–63. Crestwood: St. Vladimir's Seminary Press, 2002.

Meacham, Tirzah. "Legal-Religious Status of the Suspected Adulteress (Sotah)." *Jewish Women: A Comprehensive Historical Encyclopedia*. February 27, 2009. Jewish

Women's Archive. https://jwa.org/encyclopedia/article/legal-religious-status-of-suspected-adulteress-sotah.
———. "Legal-Religious Status of the Virgin." *Jewish Women: A Comprehensive Historical Encyclopedia*. February 27, 2009. Jewish Women's Archive. https://jwa.org/encyclopedia/article/legal-religious-status-of-virgin.
Mendonça, José Tolentino. *Jesus and the Woman: Revealing God's Mercy*. Mahwah: Paulist, 2015.
Meyers, Eric M., and Mark A. Chancey. *Alexander to Constantine, Volume III: Archaeology of the Land of the Bible*. New Haven, CT: Yale University Press, 2012.
Meyers, Eric M., et al. *Sepphoris*. Winona Lake, IN: Eisenbrauns, 1992.
Meyers, Rachel. "Reconsidering Opportunities for Female Benefactors in the Roman Empire: Julia Antonia Eurydice and the Gerontikon at Nysa." *L'Antiquité Classique* 81 (2012) 145–59.
Miller, Geoffrey David. "Attitudes towards Dogs in Ancient Israel: A Reassessment." *JSOT* 32 (2008) 487–500.
Miller, Stuart S. *Studies in the History and Traditions of Sepphoris*. Leiden: E. J. Brill, 1984.
Miller, Susan E. *Women in Mark's Gospel*. JSNTSup 259. London: T. & T. Clark Continuum, 2004.
Mitchell, Colleen C. *Who Does He Say That You Are? Women Transformed by Christ in the Gospels*. Cincinnati: Servant, 2016.
Mohri, Erika. *Maria Magdalena: Frauenbilder in Evangelientexten des 1. Bis 3. Jahrhunderts*. Marburg: N. G. Elwert, 2000.
Møller, Hilde Brekke. *The Vermes Quest: The Significance of Geza Vermes for Jesus Research*. London: Bloomsbury, 2017.
Moloney, Francis J. *The Gospel of Mark: A Commentary*. Grand Rapids: Baker, 2002.
———. *Mary: Woman and Mother*. Collegeville, MN: Liturgical, 1998.
———. *Woman: First Among the Faithful*. Notre Dame: Ave Maria, 1986.
Moltmann-Wendel, Elisabeth. *The Women Around Jesus*. Crossroads, 1990.
Monica, Madeleine Della. *L'Aimée de Jésus Marie la Magdaléenne*. Paris: Godefroy de Bouillon, 1998.
Monnickendam, Yifat. *Jewish Law and Early Christian Identity: Betrothal, Marriage, and Infidelity in the Writings of Ephrem the Syrian*. Cambridge: Cambridge University Press, 2020.
Moorehead, Kate. *Healed: How Mary Magdalene was Made Well*. New York: Church Publishing, 2018.
Moss, Candida R. "The Man with the Flow of Power: Porous Bodies in Mark 5:25–34." *JBL* 129 (2010) 507–19.
Muir, Elizabeth Gillan. *A Women's History of the Christian Church: Two Thousand Years of Female Leadership*. Toronto: University of Toronto Press, 2019.
Mullany, Katherine Frances. *Miriam of Magdala: A Study*. New York: Magdala, 1906.
Munro, Winsome. "Women Disciples: Light from Secret Mark." *Journal of Feminist Studies in Religion* 8 (1992) 47–64.
———. "Women Disciples in Mark?" *CBQ* 44 (1982) 225–41.
Myers, Alicia D. *Blessed among Women? Mothers and Motherhood in the New Testament*. Oxford: Oxford University Press, 2017.
———. "Gender, Rhetoric and Recognition: Characterizing Jesus and (Re)defining Masculinity in the Gospel of John." *JSNT* 38 (2015) 191–218.

Nagy, Rebecca Martin. *Sepphoris in Galilee: Crosscurrents of Culture*. Winona Lake, IN: Eisenbrauns, 1996.

Nanos, Mark D. "Paul's Reversal of Jews Calling Gentiles 'Dogs' (Philippians 3:2): 1600 Years of an Ideological Tale Wagging an Exegetical Dog?" *Biblical Interpretation* 17 (2009) 448–82.

Navarra Puerto, et al., eds. *Gospels: Narrative and History*. Atlanta: SBL, Atlanta, 2015.

Nelavala, Surekha. "Jesus Asks the Samaritan Woman for a Drink: A Dalit Feminist Reading of John 4." *Lectio Difficilior* 1 (2007). http://www.lectio.unibe.ch/07_1/surekha_nelavala_jesus_asks_the_samaritan_woman.htm.

———. "Smart Syrophoenician Woman: A Dalit Feminist Reading of Mark 7:24–31." *ExpT* 118 (2006) 64–69.

Newsom, Carol A., and Sharon H. Ringe, eds. *Women's Bible Commentary*. Louisville: Westminster John Knox, 1998.

Neyrey, Jerome H. "What's Wrong With This Picture? John 4, Cultural Stereotypes of Women, and Public and Private Space." *BTB* 24 (1994) 77–91.

Nickelsburg, George W. E. "Enoch, Levi, and Peter: Recipients of Revelation in Upper Galilee." *JBL* 100 (1981) 575–600.

Nicolaides, Angelo. "Mary Magdalene and Orthodoxy: Apostle, Heroine or Feminist?" *Pharos Journal of Theology* 99 (2018). https://www.pharosjot.com/uploads/7/1/6/3/7163688/article_13_vol_99_2018_nicolaides_unisa.pdf.

Nonnus of Nisibis. *Commentary on the Gospel of Saint John*. Translated by Robert W. Thomson. Atlanta: SBL, 2014.

Nordsieck, Reinhard. *Maria Magdalena, Die Frau an Jesu Seite*. Münster: LIT, 2014.

Nyce, Dorothy Yoder. *Jesus' Clear Call to Justice*. Peace and Justice Series. Scottdale: Herald, 1990.

Nyirimana, Rose Mukansengimana. "The Peace-making Mother: John 2:1–12 in Context of Rwandan Post Genocide Women." *Scriptura* 112 (2013) 1–16.

O'Day, Gail R. "Surprised by Faith: Jesus and the Canaanite Woman." In *Feminist Companion to Matthew*, edited by Amy-Jill Levine, 114–25. London: Continuum, 2001.

O'Day, Gail R., and Susan E. Hylen. *John*. Westminster Bible Companion. Louisville: Westminster John Knox, 2006.

Oliver, Isaac W. "Simon Peter Meets Simon the Tanner: The Ritual Insignificance of Tanning in Ancient Judaism." *NTS* 59 (2013) 50–60.

Osiek, Carolyn. "Diakonos and prostatis: Women's patronage in Early Christianity." *HTS Teologiese Studies/Theological Studies* 61 (2005) 347–70.

———. "Jesus and Cultural Values: Family Life as an Example." *HTS Teologiese Studies/Theological Studies* 53 (1997) 800–814.

Oyen, Geert van, ed. *Reading the Gospel of Mark in the Twenty-First Century: Method and Meaning*. ETL 301. Leuven: Peeters, 2019.

Pape, Dorothy. *God and Women: A Fresh Look at What the New Testament Says About Women*. London: Mowbray, 1976.

Paquette, Sylvie. *Les femmes disciples dans l'évangile de Luc: Critique de la redaction*. PhD diss., Université de Montréal, 2008.

Parales, Heidi Bright. *Hidden Voices: Biblical Women and Our Christian Heritage*. Macon, GA: Smyth &Helwys, 1998.

Pardee, Cambry G. "The Gnostic Magdalene: Mary as Disciple and Revealer." In *Mary Magdalene from the New Testament to the New Age and Beyond*, edited by Edmondo Lupieri, 50–78. Leiden: E. J. Brill, 2019.

Park, M. Sydney. "Inerrancy and Blood: Women and Christology in Leviticus 12 and 15, and Mark 4:21–43." *Presbyterion* 45 (2019) 83–95.

Parker, Angela N. "'And the word became ... gossip?' Unhinging the Samaritan woman in the Age of #MeToo." *Review and Expositor* 117 (2020) 259–71.

Parker, Holt N. "Women Doctors in Greece, Rome, and the Byzantine Empire." In *Women Healers and Physicians: Climbing a Long Hill*, edited by Lilian R. Furst, 131–50. Lexington: University of Kentucky Press, 1997.

Parkin, Tim. "The Roman Life Course and the Family." In *A Companion to Families in the Greek and Roman Worlds*, edited by Beryl Rawson, 276–90. Malden: Wiley-Blackwell, 2011.

Parks, Sara. "'The Brooten Phenomenon': Moving Women from the Margins in Second-Temple and New Testament Scholarship." *The Bible and Critical Theory* 15 (2019) 46–64. https://www.bibleandcriticaltheory.com/issues/vol15-no1-2019/vol-15-no-1-2019-the-brooten-phenomenon-moving-women-from-the-margins-in-second-temple-and-new-testament-scholarship/.

———. *Gender in the Rhetoric of Jesus: Women in Q*. Lanham: Lexington/Fortress, 2019.

———. "Historical-Critical Ministry? The Biblical Studies Classroom as Restorative Secular Space." *New Blackfriars* 100 (2018) 229–44.

Patterson, Stephen J. *The Forgotten Creed: Christianity's Original Struggle Against Bigotry, Slavery, and Sexism*. Oxford: Oxford University Press, 2018.

Pederson, Rena. *The Lost Apostle: Searching for the Truth About Junia*. San Francisco: Wiley, 2006.

Peeler, Amy. "Junia/Joanna: Herald of the Good News." In *Vindicating the Vixens: Revisiting Sexualized, Vilified, and Marginalized Women of the Bible*, edited by Sandra Glahn, 273–85. Grand Rapids: Kregel Academic, 2017.

Peirano, Ana María Casarotti. "Una mujer que silenció a los discípulos." *Anais do Congresso Internacional da Faculdades EST* 1 (2012) 987–1001.

Pennacchietti, Fabrizio A. "Dirsi 'ipocrita' in greco, ebraico e arabo." In *James Joyce: Whence, Whither and How. Studies in Honour of Carla Vaglio—Studi in onore di Carla Vaglio*, edited by Giuseppina Cortese et al., 257–67. Alessandria: Edizioni Dell'Orso, 2015.

Perkinson, Jim. "A Canaanitic Word in the Logos of Christ: Or the Difference the Syro-Phoenician Makes to Jesus." *Semeia* 75 (1996) 61–84.

Perroni, Marinella. *Le Donne di Galilea: Presenze Femminili nella Prima Comunità Cristiana*. Bologna: Dehoniane, 2015.

Perroni, Marinella. and Cristina Simonelli. *Mary of Magdala: Revisiting the Sources*. New York: Paulist, 2019.

Perot, Michelle, ed. *Writing Women's History*. Oxford: Blackwell, 1992.

Petersen, Silke. *Maria aus Magdala: Die Jüngerin, die Jesus liebte*. Leipzig: Evangelische Verlagsanstalt, 2011.

Pillay, Miranda. "Luke 7:36–50: See This Woman? Toward a Theology of Gender Equality in the Context of HIV and AIDS." *Scriptura* 89 (2005) 441–55.

Plaskow, Judith. "Christian Feminism and Anti-Judaism." *CrossCurrents* 28 (1978) 306–9.

---. "Feminist Anti-Judaism and the Christian God." *JFSR* 7 (1991) 99–108.
Ponessa, Joseph, and Laurie Watson Manhardt. *Come and See: The Gospel of John.* Steubenville: Emmaus Road, 2004.
Price, Eugenia. *The Unique World of Women.* Grand Rapids: Zondervan, 1969.
Quaglia, Rocco. *Le «Piccole» Donne dei Vangeli.* Milano: Paoline, 2014.
Rajak, Tessa. "Paideia in the Fourth Book of Maccabees." In *Jewish Education from Antiquity to the Middle Ages: Studies in Honour of Philip S. Alexander,* edited by George J. Brooke and Renate Smithuis, 63–84. Leiden: E. J. Brill, 2017.
Ransom, Caroline L. *Studies in Ancient Furniture: Couches and Beds of the Greeks, Etruscans and Romans.* Chicago: University of Chicago Press, 1905.
Reed, Jonathan L. *Archaeology and the Galilean Jesus: A Re-examination of the Evidence.* Harrisburg: Trinity Press International, 2000.
Reeder, Caryn A., *Gendering War and Peace in the Gospel of Luke.* Cambridge: Cambridge University Press, 2019.
Reid, Barbara E. *Choosing the Better Part? Women in the Gospel of Luke.* Collegeville, MN: Liturgical, 1996.
Reilly, Frank. "Jane Schaberg, Raymond E. Brown, and the Problem of the Illegitimacy of Jesus." *Journal of Feminist Studies in Religion* 21 (2005) 57–80.
Riberi, Paolo. *Maria Maddalena e le Altre: Le Figure Femminili Dimenticate degli Gnostici.* Torino: L'Eta del Acquario, 2015.
Ricci, Carla. *Mary Magdalene and Many Others: Women who Followed Jesus.* Minneapolis: Fortress, 1994.
Ricci, Nino. *Testament.* Boston: Houghton Mifflin Harcourt, 2003.
Richlin, Amy. *Slave Theater in the Roman Republic: Plautus and Popular Comedy.* Cambridge: Cambridge University Press, 2017.
Riesner, Rainer. "The Nazareth of Jesus." In *The Earliest Perceptions of Jesus in Context: Essays in Honor of John Nolland,* edited by Aaron White et al., 1–19. LNTS, 566. London: Bloomsbury T. & T. Clark, 2018.
Ring, Bonnie. *Women Who Knew Jesus.* Bloomington: Author House, 2015.
Ringe, Sharon H. "A Gentile Woman's Story." In *Feminist Interpretation of the Bible,* edited by Letty M. Russell, 65–72. Louisville: Westminster John Knox, 1985.
Ristine, Jennifer. "The Magdala Stone: The Jerusalem Temple Embodied." *Bible History Daily* (January 19, 2019). https://www.biblicalarchaeology.org/daily/ancient-cultures/ancient-israel/the-magdala-stone/.
---. *Mary Magdalene: Insights from Ancient Magdala.* Magdala: Magdalena Institute, 2018.
Rivers, Francine. *Unafraid.* Wheaton, IL: Tyndale, 2001.
Rhodes, David. "Jesus and the Syrophoenician Woman in Mark: A Narrative Critical Study." *JAAR* 62 (1994) 343–75.
Robbins, Vernon K., and Jonathan M. Potter, eds. *Jesus and Mary Reimagined in Early Christian Literature.* Atlanta: SBL, 2015.
Roberson, Harriette Gunn. *Mary of Magdala: A Tale of the First Century.* Chicago: Saalfield, 1909.
Roberts, Margaret Joyce. "Speaking Out: An Analysis of the Markan Characterization of the Greek Syrophoenician Woman." MA thesis, University of British Colombia, 1999.
Roberts, Michèle. *The Secret Gospel of Mary Magdalene.* New York: Pegasus, 1984.

Rodríguez Moreno, Mery Betty. "Un gesto de mujer como inspiración del lavatorio de los pies de Jesus." In *Con ellas tras Jesús. Mujeres modelos de identidad Cristiana*, edited by Carmen Bernabé Ubieta, 165-98. Estella: Verbo Divino, 2011.

Rodríguez Moreno, et al. "Discípulos que no son discípulos. Mujeres como paradigma del laicado Lucas 8,1-3." *Franciscanum* 19:167 (2017) 277-318.

Root, Bradley W. *First Century Galilee: A Fresh Examination of the Sources*. Tübingen: Mohr-Siebeck, 2014.

Rosen-Zvi, Ishay. *The Mishnaic Sotah Ritual: Temple, Gender and Midrash*. Leiden: E. J. Brill, 2012.

Rourke, Mary. *Two Women of Galilee*. New York: MIRA, 2006.

Rowlands, Jonathan. "Difficult Texts: 'A dog at the table' in Matthew 15.21-28." *Theology* 122 (2019) 285-88.

Ruether, Rosemary Radford, ed. *Religion and Sexism: Images of Women in the Jewish and Christian Traditions*. New York: Simon and Schuster, 1974.

Ruffing, Janet K. "Martha and Mary: Integrating or Disintegrating Images for Action and Contemplation." *The MAST Journal* 12 (2002) 16-23.

Rüggemeier, Jan. *Poetik der markinischen Christologie: eine kognitiv-narratologische Exegese*. Tübingen: Mohr-Siebeck, 2017.

Ruiz, Jean-Pierre. *Readings from the Edges: The Bible and People on the Move*. Maryknoll, NY: Orbis, 2011.

Rukundwa, Lazare S., and Andries G. van Aarde. "Revisiting Justice in the First Four Beatitudes in Matthew (5:3-6) and the Story of the Canaanite Woman (Mt 15:21-28): a Postcolonial Reading."*HTS* 61 (2005) 927-51.

Ruschmann, Susanne. *Maria von Magdala im Johannesevangelium. Jüngerin—Zeugin—Lebensbotin*. Münster: Aschendorff, 2002.

Rushing, Sandra M. *The Magdalene Legacy: Exploring the Wounded Icon of Sexuality*. Westport: Bergin and Garvey, 1994.

Ruttenberg, Danya, ed. *The Passionate Torah: Sex and Judaism*. New York: New York University Press, 2009.

Ryan, Jordan J. *The Role of the Synagogue in the Aims of Jesus*. Minneapolis: Fortress, 2017.

Sabar, Ariel. *Veritas: A Harvard Professor, a Con Man, and the Gospel of Jesus' Wife*. New York: Doubleday, 2020.

Sankamo, Juho. *Jesus and the Gentiles*. Turku, Finland: Åbo Akademi University Press, 2012.

Sawicki, Marianne. "Archaeology as Space Technology: Digging for Gender and Class in Holy Land." *Method and Theory in the Study of Religion* 6 (1994) 319-48.

———. *Crossing Galilee: Architectures of Contact in the Occupied Land of Jesus*. London: Continuum, 2000.

Sawyer, Dorothy F. *Women and Religion in the First Christian Centuries*. London: Routledge, 1996.

Schaberg, Jane. "How Mary Magdalene Became a Whore." *Bible Review* 8 (1992) 30-37, 51-52.

———. *The Illegitimacy of Jesus: A Feminist Theological Interpretation of the Infancy Narratives*. San Francisco: Harper & Row, 1987.

———. *The Resurrection of Mary Magdalene: Legends, Apocrypha, and the Christian Testament*. New York: Continuum, 2004.

Schenk, Christine. *Crispina and Her Sisters: Women and Authority in Early Christianity.* Minneapolis: Fortress, 2017.
Schiffman, Lawrence. "Matthew 9:20-22: 'And Behold, a Woman Who Had Suffered from a Hemorrhage'—The Bleeding Woman in Matthew, Mark, and Luke: Perspectives from Qumran and Rabbinic Literature." In *The Gospels in First-Century Judaea: Proceedings of the Inaugural Conference of Nyack College's Graduate Program in Ancient Judaism and Christian Origins, August 29th, 2013,* edited by R. Steven Notley and Jeffrey P. García, 5-19. Leiden: E. J. Brill, 2016.
Schneider, Matthew. "Writing in the Dust: Irony and Lynch-Law in the Gospel of John." *Anthropoetics* 3 (1997; Special Issue on Religion). http://anthropoetics.ucla.edu/ap0301/dust/.
Schnusenberg, Christine C. *The Relationship Between the Church and the Theatre.* Lanham: University Press of America, 1988.
Schottroff, Luise. "'Behold, These Are My Sisters' (Matt 12:49): Female Disciples of Jesus the Messiah in the Major Cities of the Roman Empire." In *Gospels: Narrative and History,* edited by Mercedes Navarro Puerto and Marinella Perroni, 53-68. Atlanta: SBL, 2015.
———. *Lydia's Impatient Sisters.* Louisville: Westminster John Knox, 1995.
Schrader, Elizabeth. "Was Martha of Bethany added to the Fourth Gospel in the second century?" *HTR* 110 (2017) 360-92.
Schüssler Fiorenza, Elisabeth. *But She Said: Feminist Practices of Biblical Interpretation.* Boston, Beacon, 1992.
———, ed. *Feminist Biblical Studies in the Twentieth Century: Scholarship and Movement.* Atlanta: Society of Biblical Literature, 2014.
———. *In Memory of Her: A Feminist Theological Reconstruction of Christian Origins.* New York: Crossroads, 1995.
Schuster, Angela M. H. "Ancient Sepphoris." *Archaeology* 50 (1997) 64-67.
Schwartz, Joshua. "Dogs in Jewish Society in the Second Temple Period and in the Time of the Mishnah and Talmud." *JJS* 55 (2004) 246-77.
Scott, Joan Wallach. *Gender and the Politics of History.* New York: Columbia University Press, 1999.
Sebastiani, Lilia. *Svolte: Donne negli Snodi del Cammino di Gesù.* Assisi: Cittadella Editrice, 2008.
———. *Tra/Sfigurazione: Il Personaggio Evangelico di Maria di Magdala e il Mito della Peccatrice Redenta nella Tradizione Occidentale.* Brescia: Queriniana, 1992.
Seibert-Cuadra, Ute. "La mujeren los evangelios sinópticos." *Revista de Interpretación Bíblica Latinoamericana* 15 (1993) 87-106.
Seim, Turid Karlsen. *The Double Message: Patterns of Gender in Luke and Acts.* London: T. & T. Clark/Continuum, 1994.
Selvidge, Marla J. *Woman, Cult, and Miracle Recital: A Redactional Critical Investigation on Mark 5: 24-34.* Lewisburg: Bucknell University Press, 1990.
Septién, Pía. *Women of the New Testament: Their Lives, Our Hope.* Liguori: Liguori, 2012.
Sergio, Lisa. *Jesus and Woman: An Exciting Discovery of What He Offered Her.* McLean: EPM, 1975.
Setzer, Claudia. "Mark 7:28: 'Even the Dogs Under the Table Eat the Children's Crumbs'—Women, Food, and Learning." In *The Gospels in First-Century Judaea: Proceedings of the Inaugural Conference of Nyack College's Graduate Program in*

Ancient Judaism and Christian Origins, August 29th, 2013, edited by R. Steven Notley and Jeffrey P. García, 97–106. Leiden: E. J. Brill, 2016.

———. "Three Odd Couples: Women and Men in Mark and John." In *Mariam, the Magdalen, and the Mother*, edited by Deirdre Good, 75–92. Bloomington: Indiana University Press, 2005.

Sheingorn, Pamela. "'The Wise Mother': The Image of St. Anne Teaching the Virgin Mary." *Gesta* 32 (1993) 69–80.

Shivti'el, Yinon. *Cliff Shelters and Hiding Complexes: The Jewish Defense Methods in Galilee During the Roman Period: The Speleological and Archaeological Evidence*. Göttingen: Vandenhoeck & Ruprecht, 2019.

Shoemaker, Stephen J. *Mary in Early Christian Faith and Devotion*. New Haven, CT: Yale University Press, 2016.

———. "Rethinking the 'Gnostic Mary': Mary of Nazareth and Mary of Magdala in Early Christian Tradition." *Journal of Early Christian Studies* 9 (2001) 555–95.

Sim, Ronnie. "The Samaritan Woman in John 4." *Journal of Translation* 11 (2015) 1–34.

Slaughter, Carolyn. *Magdalene*. New York: M. Evans and Company, 1978.

Sly, Dorothy. *Philo's Perception of Women*. Brown Judaic Studies 209. Atlanta: Scholars, 1990.

Smith, Anne Marie. "The Ashkelon Dog Cemetery Conundrum." *Journal for Semitics* 24:1 (2015) 93–108.

Smith, Dennis E., et al. *New Testament Women. The Storyteller's Companion to the Bible v13*. Etobicoke: United Church, 1999.

Smith, Mitzi J. *Womanist Sass and Talk Back: Social (In)Justice, Intersectionality, and Biblical Interpretation*. Eugene, OR: Cascade, 2018.

Snyder, Frankie, et al. "What the Temple Mount Floor Looked Like." *Biblical Archaeology Review* (2016) 56–59.

Snyder, Glenn E. "Paul Beyond the Jew/Gentile Dichotomy: A Perspective from Benjamin." *Expositions* 9 (2015) 125–37.

Sölle, Dorothee, and Joe H. Kirchberger. *Great Women of the Bible In Art and Literature*. Minneapolis: Fortress, 2001.

Sölle, Dorothee, and Luise Schottroff, *Jesus of Nazareth*. Louisville: Westminster John Knox, 2002.

Spaeth, Barbette Stanley, ed. *The Cambridge Companion to Ancient Mediterranean Religions*. Cambridge: Cambridge University Press, 2013.

Spedalieri, Francesco. *Maria nella Scritura e nella Tradizione della Chiesa Primitiva*. Messina: La Sicilia, 1961.

Spencer, F. Scott. *Dancing Girls, Loose Ladies, and Women of the Cloth: The Women in Jesus' Life*. New York: Continuum, 2004.

———. *Salty Wives, Spirited Mothers, and Savvy Widows: Capable Women of Purpose and Persistence in Luke's Gospel*. Grand Rapids: Eerdmans, 2012.

———. "A Woman's Touch: Manual and Emotional Dynamics of Female Characters in Luke's Gospel." In *Characters and Characterization in Luke-Acts*, edited by Frank Dicken and Julia Snyder, 73–94. LNTS 548. London: Bloomsbury T. & T. Clark, 2016.

Speyr, Adrienne von. *Three Women and the Lord*. San Francisco: Ignatius, 1996.

Stager, Lawrence E. "Why Were Hundreds of Dogs Buried at Ashkelon?" *BAR* 17 (1991) 26–42.

Stagg, Frank, and Evelyn Stagg. *Woman in the World of Jesus*. Philadelphia: Westminster, 1978.

Stanford, Thomas J. F. *Luke's People: The Men and Women Who Met Jesus and the Apostles*. Eugene, OR: Wipf & Stock, 2014.

Stegemann, Wolfgang, eds. *The Social Setting of Jesus and the Gospels*. Minneapolis: Fortress, 2002.

Stewart, Roberta. "Slave Labor in Plautus." In *A Companion to Plautus*, edited by Dorota Dutsch and George Fredric Frank, 361–77. Hoboken: John Wiley and Sons, 2020.

Storkey, Elaine. *Women in a Patriarchal World: Twenty-five Empowering Stories from the Bible*. London: SPCK, 2020.

Stowe, Harriet Beecher. *Woman in Sacred History: A Series of Sketches Drawn from Scriptural, Historical, and Legendary Sources*. New York: John B. Alden, 1888.

Strange, James F. "Recent Discoveries at Sepphoris and Their Relevance for Biblical Research." *Neotestamentica* 34 (2000) 125–41.

Strange, James F., et al., eds., *Excavations at Sepphoris. Volume 1: University of South Florida Probes in the Citadel and Villa*. Leiden: E. J. Brill, 2006.

Strickland, Danielle, and Vicky Beeching, *The Liberating Truth: How Jesus Empowers Women*. Oxford: Monarch, 2011.

Swidler, Leonard. *Biblical Affirmations of Woman*. Louisville: Westminster John Knox, 1979.

Szesnat, Holger. "What Did the ΣΚΗΝΟΠΟΙΟΣ Paul Produce?" *Neotestamentica* 27 (1993) 391–402.

Tambasco, Anthony J. *What Are They Saying About Mary?* New York: Paulist, 1984.

Tamez, Elsa. *Jesus and Courageous Women*. New York: Women's Division, General Board of Global Ministries, United Methodist Church, 2001.

———. *Las Mujeres en el movimiento de Jesús el Cristo*. Quito: CLAI, 2004.

Taschl-Erber, Andrea. "Mary of Magdala: First Apostle?" In *Gospels: Narrative and History*, edited by Mercedes Navarra Puerto et al., 431–54. Society of Biblical Literature, Atlanta, 2015.

Taylor, Joan E. "Missing Magdala and the Name of Mary 'Magdalene.'" *PEQ* 146 (2014) 205–23.

———. *What Did Jesus Look Like?* London: Bloomsbury T. & T. Clark, 2018.

Taylor, Marion Ann, and Heather E. Weir, eds. *Women in the Story of Jesus The Gospels through the Eyes of Nineteenth-Century Female Biblical Interpreters*. Grand Rapids: Eerdmans, 2016.

Tervahauta, Ulla, et al., eds. *Women and Knowledge in Early Christianity*. VCSup 144. Leiden: E. J. Brill, 2017.

Tetlow, Elisabeth M. *Women and Ministry in the New Testament*. New York: Paulist, 1980.

Thompson, Mary R. *Mary of Magdala: What The Da Vinci Code Misses*. Mahwah: Paulist, 2006.

Thorley, John. "Junia, a Woman Apostle." *NovT* 38 (1996) 18–29.

Thurston, Bonnie. *Women in the New Testament: Questions and Commentary*. New York: Crossroads, 1998.

Tigay, Jeffrey H. "Examination of the Accused Bride in 4Q159: Forensic Medicine at Qumran." *Journal of the Ancient Near Eastern Society of Columbia University* 22 (1993) 129–34. https://www.sas.upenn.edu/~jtigay/4q159.pdf.

Torjesen, Karen Jo. *When Women Were Priests: Women's Leadership in the Early Church and the Scandal of Their Subordination in the Rise of Christianity.* HarperSanFrancisco, 1995.

Towers, Susanna Clare. "An analysis of Philo's Exegesis of the Sotah Ritual." *Women in Judaism* 11 (2014). https://wjudaism.library.utoronto.ca/index.php/wjudaism/article/view/21735.

Trenchard, Warren C. *Ben Sira's View of Women: A Literary Analysis.* Chico: Scholars, 2020.

Trimble-Familetti, Paula. *Prostitutes, Virgins and Mothers Questioning Teachings About Biblical Women.* Chicago: Personhood, 2014.

Tucker, Ruth A., and Walter Liefeld. *Daughters of the Church: Women and Ministry from New Testament Times to the Present.* Grand Rapids: Academie/Zondervan, 1987.

Turnage, Marc. "The Linguistic Ethos of the Galilee in the First Century C.E." In *Jesus as the Women Knew Him*, by H. G. Tunnicliff, 110–81. Strand: Ivor Nicholson and Watson, 1934.

Tyson, Joseph B. "Jesus and Herod Antipas." *JBL* 79 (1960) 239–46.

Unnik, W. C. van. "A Note on the Dance of Jesus in the 'Acts of John.'" *VC* 18 (1964) 1–5.

Valcárcel, Dorothy. *The Women Who Met Jesus: New Testament Stories of Lives Transformed by the Savior.* Grand Rapids: Revell, 2009.

Valerio, Adriana. *Donne e Bibbia. Storia ed esegesi.* Bologna, Dehoniane, 2006.

———. *Maria di Nazaret: Storia, traditioni, dogmi.* Bologna: il Mulino, 2017.

Vasko, Elisabeth T. *Beyond Apathy: A Theology for Bystanders.* Minneapolis: Fortress, 2015.

Velasco, Carmiña Navia. "Mary of Nazareth Revisited." *The Many Faces of Mary. Concilium* 4 (2008) 19–26.

Viola, Frank, and Mary DeMuth. *The Day I Met Jesus: The Revealing Diaries of Five Women from the Gospels.* Grand Rapids: Baker, 2015.

Vuong, Lily C. *The Protevangelium of James.* Eugene, OR: Cascade, 2019.

Wahlberg, Rachel Conrad. *Jesus according to a Woman.* New York: Paulist, 1986.

Wainwright, Elaine M. *Towards a Feminist Critical Reading of the Gospel according to Matthew.* BZW 60. Berlin: Walter de Gruyter, 1991.

———. *Women Healing/Healing Women: The Genderization of Healing in Early Christianity.* London: Equinox, 2006.

Wapnish, Paula, and Brian Hesse. "Pampered Pooches or Plain Pariahs? The Ashkelon Dog Burials." *The Biblical Archaeologist* 56 (1993) 55–80.

Ward, Seth. "Sepphoris in Sacred Geography." In *Galilee Through the Centuries: Confluence of Cultures*, edited by Eric M. Meyers, 391–406. Winona Lake, IN: Eisenbrauns.

Warner, Marina. *Alone of All Her Sex: The Myth and the Cult of the Virgin Mary.* Oxford: Oxford University Press, 1976.

Wassen, Cecilia, "Jesus and the Hemorrhaging Woman in Mark 5:24–34: Insights from Purity Laws from Qumran." In *Scripture in Transition: Essays on Septuagint, Hebrew Bible, and Dead Sea Scrolls in Honour of Raija Sollamo*, edited by Anssi Voitila and Jutta Jokiranta, 641–660. Leiden: E. J. Brill, 2008.

———. *Women in the Damascus Document.* Atlanta: SBL, 2005.

Wasserfall, Rahel R., ed. *Women and Water: Menstruation in Jewish Life and Law.* Hanover: Brandeis University Press, 1999.

Waterman, Leroy. *Preliminary Report of the University of Michigan Excavations at Sepphoris, Palestine, in 1931.* Ann Arbor: University of Michigan Press, 1937.

Watson, Alan. "Jesus and the Adulteress." *Biblica* 80 (1999) 100–108.

Watson, Elizabeth G. *Wisdom's Daughters: Stories of Women Around Jesus.* Cleveland: Pilgrim, 1997.

Watterson, Meggan. *Mary Magdalene Revealed: The First Apostle, Her Feminist Gospel and the Christianity We Haven't Tried Yet.* Carlsbad: Hay House, 2019.

Waxman, Chaim I. "The Jewish Father: Past and Present." National Jewish Family Center, American Jewish Committee, January 1984. Reprinted in *A Mensch Among Men: Explorations in Jewish Masculinity*, edited by H. Brod, 59–73. Freedom: Crossing Press, 1988.

Webb, Ruth. *Demons and Dancers: Performance in Late Antiquity.* Cambridge, MA: Harvard University Press, 2008.

Weiler, Lucía. "Jesús y la samaritana." *Revista de Interpretación Bíblica Latinoamericana* 15 (1993) 123–30.

Weir, Heather E., and Marion Ann Taylor, eds. *The Gospels through the Eyes of Nineteenth-Century Female Biblical Interpreters.* Grand Rapids: Eerdmans, 2016.

Weiss, Zeev. "Josephus and Archaeology on the Cities of the Galilee." In *Making History: Josephus and Historical Method*, edited by Zuleika Rodgers, 385–414. JSJSup 110. Leiden: E. J. Brill, 2007.

———. "Sepphoris: The City and Its Hinterland in Roman Times." In *Judaea/Palaestina and Arabia: Cities and Hinterlands in Roman and Byzantine Times*, edited by Achim Lichtenberger et al., 95–107. Heidelberg: Propylaeum, 2019.

———. "Theatres, Hippodromes, Amphitheatres, and Performances." In *The Oxford Handbook of Jewish Daily Life in Roman Palestine*, edited by Catherine Hezser, 623–40. Oxford: Oxford University Press, 2010.

Welborn, Amy. *De-Coding Mary Magdalene: Truth, Legend, and Lies.* Huntington: Our Sunday Visitor, 2006.

Wilcock, Penelope. *Equality is Biblical: Lifting the Curse of Eve.* London: SPCK, 2020.

Wilcox, Felicia. *What Did Jesus Do All Day?: Discovering the Teen Jesus.* New York: Morehouse, 2013.

Williams, Margaret H. "The Use of Alternative Names by Diaspora Jews in Graeco-Roman Antiquity." *JSJ* 38 (2007) 307–27.

Wilson, Brittany E. *Unmanly Men: Refigurations of Masculinity in Luke-Acts.* Oxford: Oxford University Press, 2015.

Winter, Miriam Therese. *Gospel According to Mary: A New Testament for Women.* New York: Crossroad, 1994.

———. *WomanWord: A Feminist Lectionary and Psalter: Women of the New Testament.* New York: Crossroad, 1990.

Wire, Antoinette. "Ancient Miracle Stories and Women's Social World." *Forum* 2 (1986) 77–84.

Witherington, Ben. *Priscilla: The Life of an Early Christian.* Downers Grove, IL: IVP Academic, 2019.

———. *Women and the Genesis of Christianity.* Cambridge: Cambridge University Press, 1990.

Witmer, Amanda. *Jesus, the Galilean Exorcist: His Exorcisms in Social and Political Context.* London: Bloomsbury T. & T. Clark, 2014.

Wolf, Joan. *Daughter of Jerusalem.* Brentwood: Worthy, 2013.

Wood, Beulah. *The People Paul Admired: The House Church Leaders of the New Testament*. Eugene, OR: Wipf & Stock, 2011.
Wray, T. J. *Good Girls, Bad Girls of the New Testament: Their Enduring Lessons*. Lanham: Rowman & Littlefield, 2016.
Wrembek, Christoph. *Die so genannte Magdalenerin: Maria Magdalena—die namenlose Sünderin und die Schwester der Marta und des Lazarus*. Leipzig: Benno, 2008.
Wright, Addison G. "The Widow's Mites: Praise or Lament?—A Matter of Context." *CBQ* 44 (1982) 256–65.
Wyant, Jennifer S. *Beyond Mary or Martha: Reclaiming Ancient Models of Discipleship*. Atlanta: SBL, 2019.
———. "Giving Martha Back Her House: Analyzing the Textual Variant in Luke 10:38b." *TC* 24 (2019). http://jbtc.org/v24/TC-2019-Wyant.pdf.
Yamaguchi, Satoko. *Mary and Martha: Women in the World of Jesus*. Maryknoll, NY: Orbis, 2002.
———. "Rethinking the Life of Mary, the Mother of Jesus." *Journal of Early Christian History* 8 (2018) 74–95.
Zapata-Meza, Marcela. "Los Mikva'ot de Magdala. Un encuentro con lo sacro." *El Pensador* 5 (2013) 58–66.
Zamfir, Korinna. *Men and Women in the Household of God: A Contextual Approach to Roles and Ministries in the Pastoral Epistles*. Göttingen: Vandenhoeck & Ruprecht, 2013.
Zangenberg, Jürgen, et al., eds., *Religion, Ethnicity, and Identity in Ancient Galilee: A Region in Transition*. Tübingen: Mohr-Siebeck, 2007.
Zangenberg, Jürgen K., and Jens Schröter, eds. *Bauern, Fischer und Propheten: Galiläa zur Zeit Jesu*. Darmstadt: Zabern, 2012.
Zeichmann, Christopher B. "Rethinking the Gay Centurion: Sexual Exceptionalism, National Exceptionalism in Readings of Matt. 8:5–13//Luke 7:1–10." *Bible and Critical Theory* 11 (2015) 35–54.
Zetterholm, Karin Hedner. "'Jewish Teachings for Gentiles in the Pseudo-Clementine Homilies: A Jewish Reception of Ideas in Paul and Acts Shaped by a Jewish Milieu?'" *Journal of the Jesus Movement in Its Jewish Setting* 6 (2019) 68–87.
Zlotnick, Helena. *Dinah's Daughters: Gender and Judaism from the Hebrew Bible to Late Antiquity*. Philadelphia: University of Pennsylvania, 2002.
Zwiep, Arie. *Jairus's Daughter and the Haemorrhaging Woman: Tradition and Interpretation of an Early Christian Miracle Story*. Tübingen: Mohr-Siebeck, 2019.

www.ingramcontent.com/pod-product-compliance
Lightning Source LLC
Chambersburg PA
CBHW021649230426
43668CB00008B/564